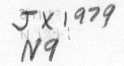
INTERNATIONAL

REGIONALISM

READINGS

Joseph S. Nye, Jr.
Harvard University

Little, Brown and Company · Boston

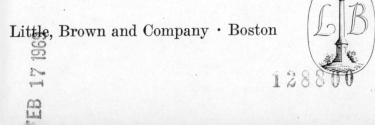

Contents

Introduction

The number of international regional arrangements is increasing. Of twenty-three regional groupings listed in a recent text, only one—the inter-American system—existed before World War II. By a recent account 92 countries are members of one or more of the nine regional organizations with mutual security commitments.[1] If United Nations regional commissions and regional development banks were added to the table on p. xii, few countries would not be included in that list of members of regional arrangements.

Regionalism has recently been called "a halfway house between the nation-state and a world not ready to become one," "the next big step forward in international cooperation," "the most hopeful event in Asia today," and "the only hope of achieving the viability that is essential [in Africa]." Even General de Gaulle has said that "it is in keeping with the conditions of our times to create entities more vast than each of the European states.[2] The United States, long a supporter of European regional integration and the "switchboard for most of the regional and joint efforts in the free world" in the early 1950's,[3] has publicly committed itself to support of a Latin American Common Market and has revamped its aid program for Africa to emphasize regional cooperation. In the view of one

[1] Donald C. Blaisdell, *International Organization* (New York, 1966), p. 209; Philip Jacob and Alexine Atherton, *The Dynamics of International Organization* (Homewood, Ill., 1965), pp. 115-116 (Commonwealth excluded).

[2] Sir Oliver Franks, quoted in Francis O. Wilcox, "Regionalism and the United Nations," *International Organization*, XIX (Summer 1965), p. 811; *Christian Science Monitor*, March 25, 1965; *TIME*, February 3, 1967; *New York Times*, January 12, 1966; Press Conference of President de Gaulle, September 9, 1965.

[3] Norman J. Padelford, "Regional Organization and the United Nations," *International Organization*, VIII (May 1954), p. 206.

authority, "regionalism can without exaggeration be termed a cornerstone of American foreign policy."[4]

Textbooks on international politics, international organization and American foreign policy, however, have not kept pace with our changing world. Too often the issues have been discussed in the general terms of regionalism vs. globalism in the security field, terms of the bureaucratic and political debate during World War II and the immediate post-war period. Thus, the new variety of important questions that regionalism poses for policy and for theory about the changing nature of the international system has been ignored.

The articles in this book have been selected from recent works by scholars of both international relations and regional studies. Some articles emphasize theoretical analysis and others are descriptive. The guiding principle has been to illustrate the variety of new problems and issues that regionalism involves, rather than to provide a description of every regional arrangement. Since it is impossible to include all good articles on regionalism, priority has been given to those which have not been reprinted in other anthologies. Other interesting works are listed in the suggestions for further reading at the end of each section.

Unfortunately, "region" is an ambiguous term in common usage. Many hours were wasted at the 1945 United Nations Conference in San Francisco trying to define it precisely. Textbooks reflect this confusion. Some authors use the term so broadly that it includes all international behavior or organization that is less than global regardless of geographical content. In this sense, the widely dispersed British Commonwealth or Afro-Asian voting blocs at the United Nations are "regional."

More frequently some geographical component is included in the definition of "region" and this helps to narrow the concept. The spectrum of limited-membership international groupings ranges from those with a great degree of geographical contiguity such as the European Economic Community (EEC), through those quasi-regional groupings such as the North Atlantic Treaty Organization (NATO), to those with virtually no geographical component such as the British Commonwealth. There are no "absolute" or "naturally determined" regions. Relevant geographical boundaries vary with different purposes; for example, a relevant region for security may not be one for economic integration. Indeed this is one of the factors that has

[4] Ruth C. Lawson, *International Regional Organizations: Constitutional Foundations* (New York, 1962), p. vi.

hindered the various efforts to give NATO a non-military aspect. Core areas can be determined and various boundaries delineated by analysis of mutual transactions, effective organization and interdependence of political decision-making.[5] From this point of view, an international region can be defined broadly as a limited number of states linked by a geographical relationship and by a degree of mutual interdependence. Which of the large number of potential regions become relevant in international politics depends on political decisions. International regionalism in the descriptive sense is the formation of interstate associations or groupings on the basis of regions; and in the doctrinal sense, the advocacy of such formations.

Advocacy of international regionalism was rare in the period between W.W. I and W.W. II when the doctrine (if not the practice) of collective security was dominant. Regionalism, which seemed to indicate limitations of international commitments, looked suspicious to those who believed that peace is indivisible and that aggression anywhere on the globe should be met by a coalition of all the non-aggressors. By the 1940's however, an increasing number of influential people were advocating "escape from a theoretical and ineffective universalism into practical and workable regionalism."[6]

The debate between advocates of regionalism and those of "pure" collective security was never satisfactorily settled, and therefore the ambiguity in policy was written into the United Nations Charter as Inis Claude describes in the first article below. In practice, however, the rise of the Cold War and the loss of confidence in the United Nations as a collective security system led to the formation of "selective security" regional defense pacts, and to a reversal of American policy—a reversal that meant no effective subordination of regional arrangements to the global organization.

By the 1960's a number of important changes in international politics—the easing of the intensity of the Cold War, the independence of scores of poor states that had been part of colonial empires, the successful initiation of the European integration experience—gave rise to a new range of questions about regionalism that now makes the collective security and military defense focus of the writings in the early 1950's (and their afterglow in the textbooks) seem at best quaint and at worst misleading. The growing success of European regionalism led scholars in the late 1950's to what Ernst

[5] See Bruce Russett, *International Regions and the International System* (Chicago, 1967).

[6] E. H. Carr, *Nationalism and After* (London, 1945), p. 45.

Haas called "the new challenge of regionalism, . . . the potentialities of the field for insights into the process of community formation at the international level."[7] Similarly the vast increase in the number of poor and insecure states has stimulated scholarly interest in the 1960's in the problems of relating the European experience to other parts of the world and of overcoming the economic problems of small but sovereign states in the less developed areas.

* * * * * *

Nearly all the articles in the book consider some aspect of regionalism and world order. The article by Robert Gregg in Part IV on the regional economic commissions discusses a frequently neglected aspect of the relationship of the United Nations to regionalism. The first article in Part I, by Inis Claude, concentrates on the traditional debate between regionalism and collective security. The second article, by John Pinder, considers two of the broader claims and implications of the European experience for world order. One implication concerns inter-regional relations. Is it likely that we are seeing the creation of important new inter-unit relations?[8] How closed are regional systems? Do they harden divisions? The other is the claim of a beneficial "demonstration effect" that the European experience has on the rest of the world. If the European states are pioneering new "relations between men and states,"[9] how likely is it that these relations can be models for the planned economies? And if the European Community is not a new model, is its "demonstration effect" a beneficial one? Pinder's article advocates caution in answering such questions, but deliberately advocates limited optimism as a guide for policy.

The third article, by David Mitrany, presents a dissenting view about the beneficient value of European regionalism for world order. Although the European experience might have a beneficial effect if it were limited to modest functional service agencies such as Euratom or the European Coal and Steel Community (ECSC), Mitrany fears that the expansive aspirations and broad tasks of the Eurocrats are leading not to new forms of transcending the sovereign nation-state, but merely to a larger sovereign state in Europe. The fact that such

[7] Ernst B. Haas, ''The Challenge of Regionalism,'' *International Organization*, XII (Autumn 1958), p. 441.

[8] See Amitai Etzioni, ''European Unification and Perspectives on Sovereignty,'' *Daedalus*, 92 (Summer 1963), p. 515.

[9] The term used by Jean Monnet, ''A Ferment of Change,'' *Journal of Common Market Studies*, I, 3, p. 211.

a state would be "federal" does not satisfy him, for he argues that federations are conservative political systems representing delicate balances of internal power and, therefore, they tend to be "closed" toward the outside world. The "demonstration effect" of European integration for the rest of the world may not encourage new forms transcending the nation-state system, but rather may encourage similar "hardened" larger sovereignties with no guarantee of peaceful relations among them. Mitrany prefers as an ordering principle the concept of functionalism: a variety of international organizations designed to fulfill specific technical and functional needs, cutting across national boundaries and thus creating a web of interdependence that gradually makes state sovereignty irrelevant or at least diminishes its potential for conflict. While regionalism need not conflict with functionalism (indeed, some would argue that it provides the most fertile ground for it), Mitrany fears the kind of regionalism that tempts people beyond pure functionalism to federation and thus away from global ties. For Mitrany, the faith of the Eurocrats who have used functionalism as a means toward the goal of a federal Europe is reminiscent of the simple faith of Mazzini, the 19th-century Italian patriot, who believed that the creation of national states would lead to peace.

Despite the outcome of the traditional debate referred to in Claude's article, a number of problems remain in the security field—the focus of Part II. Longstanding advocates of regional security arrangements claim that they are more efficient in conciliating local disputes; and that they can relieve the burden on the global organization by "making peace divisible," thus preventing local solvable issues from becoming tangled into insolvable global issues.[10] President Julius Nyerere of Tanzania has said, "certain regional and ideological associations have an advantage over the U.N. As a means of preventing or settling disputes, talking is more productive, and certainly easier, the greater the general feeling of sympathy and friendship among the participants. . . ."[11] But this *a priori* case is less impressive when we look at the peacekeeping record of regional organizations presented in the article by Linda B. Miller. It is interesting to contrast the record of the Organization of American States (OAS) with that of the Organization of African Unity (OAU) in peacekeeping. In several cases, particularly in Central America, the

---

[10] See Anwar Hussain Syed, *Walter Lippmann's Philosophy of International Politics* (Philadelphia, 1963), p. 196.

[11] *Dag Hammarskjoeld Memorial Lecture* (Dar es Salaam, 1964), p. 6.

OAS has been successful. A major reason for this success, however, has been the dominant role and leadership of the United States within the organization. The price of effectiveness has been related to a traditional great power sphere of influence as described by Gordon Connell-Smith in the article below.

Two other interesting questions remain in the field of regionalism and security. One question is the extent to which a military regional pact such as NATO, which, in light of the nature of warfare in the nuclear age, developed an organizational structure far surpassing any alliance system in the past, can be an effective contributor to the "new challenge of community building." The article by Henry Kissinger indicates that positive contributions to collective defense and elaborate structures notwithstanding, many of the problems of traditional alliances among sovereign states persist in NATO. The other question is the extent to which regional groupings that are ostensibly directed toward economic or welfare objectives, such as those described by Bernard Gordon in the article on Southeast Asia, are used by national governments to jockey for political alliances in a way more advantageous to security concerns than to welfare concerns.

Part III is devoted to the most important case of regionalism in the world today—the European Community of the Six. The importance of the European experience is twofold. One aspect is the possibility that it represents a new relationship between men and states— the exceptional case of sovereignty overcome—which can serve as a model for the rest of the world.[12] The prospects for a new kind of technocratic politics and regional government in the post-ideological age are imaginatively elaborated in the article by Ernst Haas and submitted to skeptical analysis in the article by Stanley Hoffmann.

The other important aspect of the European experience is less its importance as a new model than its effect in creating a web of interests and procedures which has created a security community or "island of peace" in an area notorious for its conflicts. Leon Lindberg's article illustrates the way in which old power politics and new technocratic politics coexist and interact in a subtle way to create a new system that is *sui generis*. Finally, Lawrence Scheinman's analysis of the failure of Euratom to live up to the great hope held for it in 1957 by devoted Europeans raises questions about the effectiveness of the specific functional model, which Mitrany prefers to the

[12] See Lord Gladwyn, "World Order and the Nation-State—A Regional Approach," *Daedalus*, 95 (Spring 1966), p. 703.

wider ranging EEC, as a means of tying the new kind of web around the nation-state and "emptying it of its former string."[13]

Part IV deals with the problems raised by the existence of some 90 less developed countries with populations under 15 million (including 60 with populations under five million).[14] When multiplied by per capita incomes of a few hundred dollars per year, these population figures mean markets roughly the size of a small European city, thus limiting the available economies of scale and the range of efficient industrial production. Moreover, each small state must support the burden of the full panoply of services that goes with sovereign status. Small wonder that many people recommend regional arrangements that would make "the underpinning of world order at subsidiary levels much more stable."[15] But can the European experience be a "formula to redress economic imbalances in a world of haves and have-nots, a world of vast industrial giants and of mini-states?"[16] Are the less developed countries caught in a tragic dilemma because their political processes are very different from those that underlie the European regional integration? Rather than giving up part of their sovereignty, most less developed states are striving for more sovereignty in the sense of political control, while at the same time they would like to escape some of its economic limitations. Thus one of the crucial problems about economic regionalism and small less developed countries is to discover the political dynamics of regional integration and to discover if external factors can help to overcome the missing elements.

The article by Miguel Wionczek presents the economist's case for regional economic integration in less developed areas as well as the political problems it involves with special reference to the Latin American Free Trade Association. E. Kanovsky's description of the persistent problems that have prevented the Arab Common Market from being much more than a scrap of paper is a good illustration of why there are more aspirations than achievements of regional economic unity among less developed countries. The articles by the editor present the contrasting experience of two cases of the highest degree of regional economic integration among sovereign less developed states—the East African and Central American common

---

[13] The term used by Stanley Hoffmann in his article below.

[14] Sidney Dell, *A Latin American Common Market* (London, 1966), p. v.

[15] Barbara Ward, *Nationalism and Ideology* (New York, 1966), p. 107.

[16] Leonard Tennyson, Director of the European Community Information Service, quoted in *The Boston Globe*, April 14, 1967.

markets—and try to explain their internal political dynamics and the extent to which external factors can help to overcome the deficiencies The role of one such external factor, the United Nations regional commissions, is assessed in the article by Robert Gregg.

Regionalism runs the risk of becoming the latest international fad as new statesmen seek to escape from isolation, respond to the instant brotherhood of regional summit meetings, and deal with the serious political and economic weaknesses of their states. Increasingly, editorial writers and government officials concerned with American foreign policy seem eager to jump on the bandwagon. New groupings constantly appear—most of them ephemeral. Many existing groupings fail to live up to expectations held by their supporters. There is a danger that over-advocacy of regionalism may lead to a reaction against it, and students of international relations will be faced with another fruitless debate of regionalism vs. globalism. The debate will be fruitless because it will pose the issues in abstract terms which elicit either doctrinaire or trivial ("yes regionalism, but within a global framework") answers. It is important that the analyst preserve an open, yet skeptical attitude toward regionalism and that he try to formulate explicit propositions about its role and limits in local peacekeeping, economic development, and community building. These propositions should be tested by more studies of specific cases such as those presented here rather than by reference to the United Nations Charter, statements of faith, or *a priori* claims for abstract principles of world order.

MAJOR NON-MILITARY REGIONAL GROUPINGS

GROUPING	MEMBERSHIP
EUROPE	
Benelux	Belgium, Netherlands, Luxembourg
Council of Europe	17 European states
European Communities (EEC, ECSC, EURATOM)	France, Germany, Italy, Belgium, Netherlands, Luxembourg
European Free Trade Association	Britain, Sweden, Norway, Denmark, Austria, Switzerland, Portugal
Council for Mutual Economic Assistance	Soviet Union, Poland, East Germany, Czechoslovakia, Bulgaria, Hungary, Rumania
Nordic Council	Norway, Sweden, Denmark, Finland, Iceland

ASIA

Asian and Pacific Council (ASPAC)	Japan, South Korea, Taiwan, South Vietnam, Australia, New Zealand, Philippines, Thailand, Malaysia
Association for Southeast Asia (ASA)	Thailand, Malaysia, Philippines
Mekong Basin Committee	Thailand, Cambodia, Laos, South Vietnam
Regional Cooperation for Development (RCD)	Pakistan, Iran, Turkey

AFRICA AND MIDDLE EAST

Arab League	Algeria, Iraq, Jordan, Kuwait, Lebanon, Libya, Morocco, Saudi Arabia, Sudan, Syria, Tunisia, United Arab Republic, Yemen
Organization of African Unity (OAU)	38 independent African states (excluding South Africa and Rhodesia)
Conseil de l'Entente	Ivory Coast, Niger, Dahomey, Upper Volta, Togo
East African Common Services Organization (EACSO)	Kenya, Uganda, Tanzania
Organisation Commune Africaine et Malgache (OCAM)	12 former French colonies plus Congo (Kinshasa) and Rwanda
Union Douaniere et Economique de l'Afrique Centrale (UDEAC)	Cameroun, Gabon, Central African Republic, Chad, Congo (Brazzaville)

WESTERN HEMISPHERE

Organization of American States (OAS)	United States, Trinidad and Tobago and the 20 Latin American states (The *government* of Cuba is expelled)
Central American Common Market (CACM)	Guatemala, El Salvador, Honduras, Nicaragua, Costa Rica
Latin American Free Trade Association (LAFTA)	The 10 Latin states of South America plus Mexico

Note: This somewhat arbitrary list is merely illustrative. It does not include United Nations regional groupings (except the Mekong Committee); the African, Asian, and Inter-American Development Banks; a number of limited technical groupings in Africa and the Caribbean; the Organization for Economic Cooperation and Development which is quasi-regional because of Japanese membership. It does include the quasi-regional OCAM.

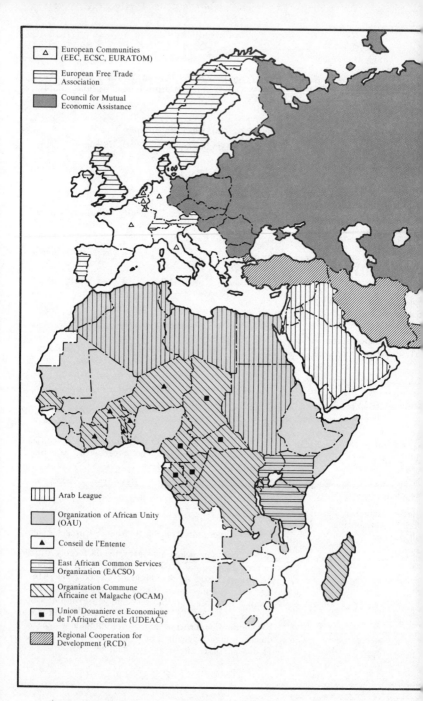

European Communities
(EEC, ECSC, EURATOM)

European Free Trade
Association

Council for Mutual
Economic Assistance

Arab League

Organization of African Unity
(OAU)

Conseil de l'Entente

East African Common Services
Organization (EACSO)

Organization Commune
Africaine et Malgache (OCAM)

Union Douaniere et Economique
de l'Afrique Centrale (UDEAC)

Regional Cooperation for
Development (RCD)

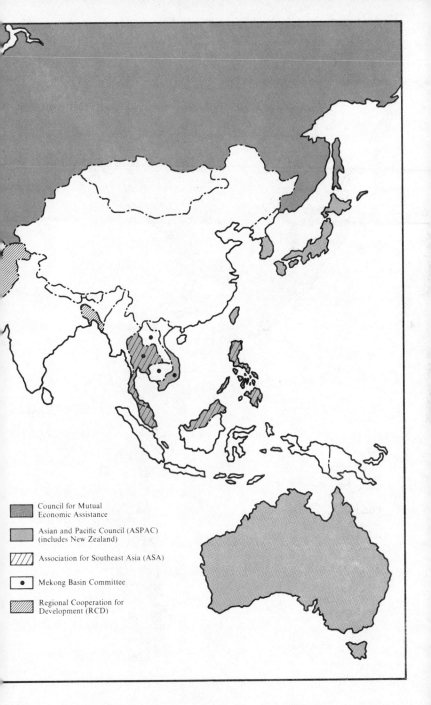

Council for Mutual
Economic Assistance

Asian and Pacific Council (ASPAC)
(includes New Zealand)

Association for Southeast Asia (ASA)

Mekong Basin Committee

Regional Cooperation for
Development (RCD)

Organization of American States (OAS)

Latin American Free Trade
Association (LAFTA)

Central American
Common Market (CACM)

PART ONE

REGIONALISM AND WORLD ORDER

Inis L. Claude, Jr.

The OAS, the UN and the United States

REGIONALISM IN THE UN CHARTER

Theoretical debate as to the superiority of the regional or the universal approach to international organization for the handling of political and security problems is a rather sterile exercise, for experience suggests that statesmen need not, and do not, choose one of these approaches to the exclusion of the other. In its original design, and even more in its actual development, the post-World War II system of international organization has combined regional elements with the basic universalism of the United Nations. It might be argued that the real question is not which approach to adopt, but which to emphasize; in these terms, the international decision in 1945 was clearly to assign predominance to general international organization. In practice, however, even this question proves rather too abstract. The decision of the San Francisco Conference to make the United Nations the primary agency in the sphere of international politics provided no precise indication of the contemplated division of competence and responsibility between it and regional agencies, much less a firm basis for predicting the nature of the relationships that would emerge in the dynamic interplay of the United Nations and regional organizations during the next two decades. In the final analysis, the problem of the relationship between general and regional international institutions involves a set of specific questions

Reprinted from *International Conciliation*, No. 547 (March 1964), with the permission of the author and the Carnegie Endowment for International Peace.

posed by developing political circumstances, rather than a single issue of principle that can be settled in the abstract.

This study represents an attempt to develop an understanding of the evolving relationship between the Organization of American States and the United Nations in the political and security sphere. While the OAS is merely one of many regional agencies on the contemporary scene, it stands out as the only one that has been significantly involved in formal controversies concerning the interpretation and application of the provisions of the United Nations Charter bearing upon the role of such agencies in relation to the world organization.[1] Making due allowance for the unique features of the OAS case, we may hope that an examination of the interplay between that organization and the United Nations in the political-security realm will contribute to an understanding of the general political process whereby the working relationships of universal and regional bodies are determined and progressively altered.

Moreover, the preponderance of the United States in the OAS and the prominence of the region embraced by that agency in foreign and defense policy concerns of the United States indicate that the relationship between the OAS and the United Nations is something more than a test case in the admixture of regionalism and universalism. It is an issue of prime importance in United States foreign policy, and the very considerable influence of the United States upon the shaping of the OAS-United Nations relationship has been exercised less for the purpose of promoting an ideal pattern of international institutional arrangements than for the achievement of more immediate national policy objectives. Hence, this study should provide some insight into the particular aspects of international political rivalry which affect the evolution of regional-global organizational patterns. It is at once a study of international organization and of United States foreign policy, and, in the nature of the case, it cannot successfully deal with the former topic without dealing with the latter.

In the initial phase of wartime thought regarding the international political structure that should be erected after World War II, the regional theme assumed great prominence. Winston Churchill placed particular emphasis upon the potential role of regional councils as vehicles for the leadership of the great powers and appeared to assign distinctly secondary importance to a world organization.

---

[1] The most relevant provisions of the United Nations Charter are to be found in Articles 33 and 51-54. For texts of these articles, see the Appendix.

President Franklin D. Roosevelt had not clearly committed himself to a scheme of postwar organization, but, perhaps under the influence of Sumner Welles, he tended to agree with the Churchillian conception. Secretary of State Cordell Hull waged a vigorous battle against this view, arguing that dominant regionalism might recreate a competitive balance-of-power system conducive to war, and that emphasis upon regional organization might provide "a haven for the isolationists, who could advocate all-out United States cooperation in a Western Hemisphere council on condition that we did not participate in a European or Pacific council."[2] Hull insisted that a general international organization should have supreme responsibility for political and security questions, and that regional agencies should function as subordinate and supplementary bodies. In the course of 1943, Hull's arguments prevailed. The official planning mechanism in the United States adopted the proposition that postwar organization should rest upon a universal rather than a regional basis, and Hull succeeded in incorporating this principle in the Moscow Declaration, signed on 30 October 1943 on behalf of the governments of China, the Soviet Union, the United Kingdom, and the United States. This agreement provided the essential impetus for the process that resulted in the creation of the United Nations.[3]

Thenceforward, United States officials adhered to the general position that regional arrangements were, unavoidable in some instances and might serve as useful supplements to the global institution, but that it was vitally important to ensure their subordination and control by the projected United Nations.[4]

The attitude toward regionalism that had crystallized within the United States government found expression in the Dumbarton Oaks Proposals, formulated in the autumn of 1944 by the same powers that had produced the Moscow Declaration.[5] This preliminary version of the Charter provided that the existence of regional bodies for dealing with peace and security matters should not be precluded, if their arrangements and activities were consistent with the purposes and

[2] *The Memoirs of Cordell Hull* (New York: Macmillan, 1948), II, p. 1645.

[3] The material in this paragraph was drawn largely from ibid., pp. 1639-48.

[4] See Ruth B. Russell, and Jeannette E. Muther, *A History of the United Nations Charter* (Washington: The Brookings Institution, 1958), pp. 121, 255, 398-99. For provisions relating to regional agencies in various drafts developed within the United States planning mechanism, see *Postwar Foreign Policy Preparation 1939-1945*, U.S. Dept. of State Pub. 3580 (Washington: GPO, 1949), pp. 482, 531, 586-87, 596, 600.

[5] [Deleted by editor.]

principles of the general organization. This rather negative and conditional endorsement was followed by more positive provisions: the Security Council should encourage such agencies to promote the peaceful settlement of disputes among their members and should, in appropriate cases, utilize them for enforcement action under its authority. Finally, the draft reverted to the negative tone in stipulating that regional enforcement action should not be taken without authorization by the Security Council, and that the Council should be kept fully informed of activities undertaken or contemplated by regional bodies in the peace and security sphere. In summary, the authors of the Dumbarton Oaks draft conceded that regional agencies might be useful, but considered that they might be dangerous if not effectively subordinated to the Security Council.

This triumph of universalist ideology was short-lived. "Regionalism Resurgent" was emblazoned on the banner hoisted at the Inter-American Conference on Problems of War and Peace in Mexico City, which culminated in the signing of the Act of Chapultepec on 3 March 1945. At this gathering, representatives of the Latin American states expressed their misgivings about the universalist bias of the Dumbarton Oaks Proposals, affirmed the value of the Inter-American system, proclaimed the intent to refurbish and strengthen that system, and insisted that the constitution of the new world organization should leave the way open for the functioning of a politically active and largely autonomous Inter-American agency. The United States, in signing the Act of Chapultepec, virtually acknowledged its responsibility for helping to secure the alteration of the Dumbarton Oaks draft in a pro-regionalist direction, and accepted the necessity of collaborating to some degree with its Latin neighbors in their projected campaign to make the United Nations Charter safe for regionalism.

The battle over the role of regional agencies which had been foreshadowed at Mexico City took place as scheduled at San Francisco, centering in Committee 4 of Commission III of the Conference.[6] Senator Arthur H. Vandenberg dealt with the regional problem for the United States. He pressed the cause of the Latin Americans in negotiations with other delegations and within the United States delegation; at one point he warned his United States colleagues who were resisting a proregionalist move "that if this

---

[6] *Documents of the United Nations Conference on International Organization, San Francisco, 1945*, Vol. XII (London and New York: UN Information Organizations, 1945). This collection is hereinafter cited as UNCIO.

question is not specifically cleared up in the Charter, I shall expect to see a Reservation on the subject in the Senate and . . . I shall support it.''[7] The major task at San Francisco was to achieve a compromise between those spokesmen for the United States who stressed the primacy of the world organization and those who shared the Latin American concern for regional autonomy. Once this was accomplished, the United States succeeded in having its formula incorporated in the Charter.

The crucial issue related to the anxiety aroused by the Dumbarton Oaks clause prohibiting enforcement action under regional auspices without the authorization of the Security Council: the apprehension that regional response to aggression might be paralyzed by this requirement, particularly in view of the fact that the veto formula dictated by the great powers would enable any permanent member of the Security Council to prevent the authorization of regional action. The interests of various groups of states converged on the point that the requirement of Security Council approval of enforcement action, which was to be incorporated in Article 53 of the Charter, should be liberalized. The European great powers were accommodated by a provision, inserted in Article 53, which emancipated their anti-Axis mutual assistance pacts from this requirement for an indefinite period. In turn, the advocates of the autonomy of the Inter-American system were satisfied by the introduction into the Charter of Article 51, acknowledging a right of collective as well as individual self-defense, in the exercise of which a group of states might respond to armed attack, report their action to the Security Council, and continue it until and unless the Council should itself undertake to deal with the situation. This provision, applicable only in cases involving armed attack, reversed the significance of negativism in the Security Council; an unfriendly veto could not be used to block regional action, but a friendly veto could be used to prevent Security Council interference in regional action. While Article 51 was couched in terms of general applicability, it was proclaimed by Latin American delegates and acknowledged by others as a prescription designed primarily to remove the regional organs of the Western Hemisphere, existing and projected, from the sphere of Security Council control in the most critical cases. The Latin Americans were not particularly concerned to fight for regionalism in general; indeed, some of them proposed that the Charter should

[7] *The Private Papers of Senator Vandenberg*, ed. Arthur H. Vandenberg, Jr. (Boston: Houghton Mifflin, 1952), p. 189.

single out the Inter-American system as an approved regional arrangement enjoying a high degree of autonomy.[8]

The United States delegation was distinctly unhappy at the prospect of the emancipation of all and sundry regional groups under the terms of Article 51. Those members of the delegation who had posed difficulties for Senator Vandenberg in his development of the formula had not been so much opposed to autonomy for the Inter-American system as worried about the generalization of regional autonomy. The Senator himself regarded with considerable distaste the necessity of generalizing the privileges of Article 51. He had toyed with the idea of attempting to secure an explicit exception from the rule of Article 53 in favor of the Western Hemispheric organization, and he tried hard but vainly to develop a formula which would have the effect of legitimizing autonomous operations by that agency without giving equally free rein to other regional groups whose activities, he feared, would be detrimental to world order.[9] In later years, the United States has found unexpected uses for Article 51, but it supported the inclusion of that provision in the Charter in spite of, not because of, the fact that the article weakened the control of the Security Council over collective self-defense arrangements other than those contemplated in the Act of Chapultepec.

In addition to the urge to secure the emancipation of their regional system from the requirement of Security Council authorization for enforcement action, the Latin American states expressed a strong demand for recognition of the primary jurisdiction of Inter-American organs in promoting peaceful settlement of intraregional disputes. Considering the attitude toward external intervention in the affairs of the Western Hemisphere which had long been associated with the Monroe Doctrine, it is surprising that United States plans for a world organization had not dealt with this point. But the influence of the universalist viewpoint had been so dominant that regional contributions to peaceful settlement had received no special emphasis.

There was no reversal of policy in the endorsement by the United States of the Dumbarton Oaks Proposals, which provided that the Security Council should encourage settlement of local disputes through regional machinery, but in no sense conceded to regional agencies a peculiar status with regard to the handling of disputes among their members. Indeed, regional methods were not even

[8] See UNCIO, Vol. XII, pp. 771, 773, 779.
[9] *The Private Papers of Senator Vandenberg*, op. cit., pp. 187-92.

mentioned in the list of alternative approaches to peaceful settlement in Chapter VIII, Section A, of the Proposals, which disputants were adjured to explore before resorting to the Security Council.

At San Francisco, several Latin American delegations urged the adoption of provisions that would have assigned the function of promoting the peaceful settlement of intraregional disputes to regional organizations, permitting the Security Council to intrude only if the regional body handling a given case should so request, or if a dispute should threaten to spread beyond the boundaries of a single region.[10] As a result of this pressure, Committee III(4) recommended, and the Plenary Conference approved, the incorporation in the Charter of the stipulation that members of regional organizations should attempt to settle their local disputes at the regional level before referring them to the Security Council (Article 52[2]), and the addition of resort to regional agencies to the list of recommended methods of peaceful settlement which states should explore before turning to the Security Council (Article 33[1]). Thus, the Charter went significantly beyond the Dumbarton Oaks Proposals in stressing the role of regional bodies as agencies of the first resort for dealing with disputes among their own members. Behind the generality of these provisions lay the particular intent of acknowledging the primacy of Inter-American institutions in matters pertaining to the Western Hemisphere.

This Latin American victory was neither complete nor clear-cut. Under Article 33, resort to regional mechanisms of peaceful settlement was treated as only one of several options for disputants in their preliminary efforts to find a solution for their difficulties. Article 52(2) was stronger, in that it appeared to oblige members of regional agencies to exhaust the pacificatory resources of those bodies before turning to the United Nations, but this provision was qualified and perhaps confused by the addition of Article 52(4), stipulating that the Article did not impair the application of Articles 34 and 35, which recognized the competence of the Security Council to investigate disputes or situations to determine whether they might endanger international peace and security, and authorized states to bring such cases to the attention of the Council or the General Assembly. Moreover, under Article 36, the Security Council was authorized, at any stage of a dispute, to recommend methods of peaceful settlement. Considering this entire complex of provisions, one can conclude that

[10] See Doc. 269, UNCIO, Vol. XII, pp. 764-84.

the framers of the Charter intended to assign to regional agencies a primary role in the solution of local problems, while retaining the principle that the Security Council should have over-arching responsibility and unrestricted competence to intervene in any case at any time.

At the meeting of Committee III(4), which approved the package of proposals designed to meet the pro-regionalist demands of the Latin Americans, a Peruvian spokesman articulated his concern that the changes did not clearly preclude the Security Council from asserting jurisdiction over intraregional disputes at any stage; he was disappointed that the exclusiveness of regional responsibility for dealing initially with local disputes had not been recognized and safeguarded.[11] The president of the Committee, speaking for Colombia, offered reassurance. He saw no problem of double jurisdiction but believed that the newly adopted provisions established the rule that the Security Council must leave initial efforts at peaceful settlement of local disputes to regional agencies; the Council might investigate to determine whether such disputes threatened international peace, but it could not intrude upon the regional settlement process unless and until the latter had failed. His government believed that the revised formula constituted "a statute for regional arrangements, entirely satisfactory to the American nations, which are linked together by an almost perfect system of peace and security."[12]

The Peruvian comment was more accurate than the Colombian but it is perhaps fortunate that the latter was convincing to the Latin American bloc, since this permitted the issue to be closed. An ambiguous compromise had been reached, allowing champions of regionalism to assert that they had won a clear victory for the autonomy and primacy of regional agencies, and universalists to congratulate themselves that the supremacy of the Security Council in matters affecting peace and security had not been impaired.

Spokesmen for the United States tended to insist that complete success had been achieved in reconciling the competing viewpoints concerning the relationship of the United Nations and regional organizations. Senator Vandenberg declared:

We have found a sound and practical formula for putting regional organizations into effective gear with the global institution. . . . We have

[11] UNCIO, Vol. XII, p. 685.
[12] Ibid., p. 687.

infinitely strengthened the world Organization by . . . enlisting, within its over-all supervision, the dynamic resources of these regional affinities. [In supporting the Pan-American regional system] we are no less faithful to the world ideal and to the dominant supremacy of the United Nations in the maintenance of peace and security.[13]

Secretary of State Edward R. Stettinius, Jr., interpreted the provisions introduced into the Charter at San Francisco pertaining to peaceful settlement as simply a formula to "make more clear that regional agencies will be looked to as an important way of settling local disputes by peaceful means."[14] In similar vein, he reported to the President that the changes made at the Conference had indicated that the procedures of regional systems would be utilized to the fullest possible extent, but had maintained the basic principle of the ultimate authority of the world organization.[15] In analyzing the Charter for the Senate Committee on Foreign Relations, Stettinius commented that it "encourages the use of regional arrangements and agencies in the peaceful adjustment of local disputes."[16]

Leo Pasvolsky, Special Assistant to the Secretary of State for International Organization and Security Affairs, interpreted the Charter as providing that regional agencies "should be used to their utmost" in facilitating settlement of local disputes.[17] John Foster Dulles, who had served as an adviser to the United States Delegation at San Francisco, presented this summary of the Charter's impact upon the position of regional organizations:

Without the Security Council and the new world organization we could have had in this hemisphere a regional organization which was wholly autonomous and which could act on its own initiative to maintain peace in this hemisphere without reference or regard whatsoever to any world organization. As it results from the Charter at San Francisco, the world security organization is given the first opportunity to maintain peace everywhere, using presumably regional organizations which it is invited to do but not absolutely compelled to do.

If, however, the Security Council fails to maintain peace and despite the

---

[13] UNCIO, Vol. XI, p. 52-53.

[14] See his statement for the press, 15 May 1945, No. 25, reproduced in *Hearings Before the Committee on Foreign Relations, U.S. Senate, 79th Cong., First Sess., on The Charter of the United Nations* (Washington: GPO, 1945), p. 306. Hereinafter cited as *Charter Hearings.*

[15] See *Report to the President on the Results of the San Francisco Conference by the Chairman of the United States Delegation, the Secretary of State,* U.S. Dept. of State Pub. 2349, Conf. Series 71 (Washington: GPO, 1945), pp. 101-08.

[16] *Charter Hearings,* p. 210.

[17] Ibid., p. 302.

existence of the Security Council there is an armed outbreak, then the regional organization moves in without regard to the Security Council.[18]

None of these statements by leading participants in the work of the United States Delegation supported the view that the Charter had assigned to regional agencies, and denied to the Security Council, the task of initiating efforts at peaceful settlement of local disputes. All of them emphasized the basic value of the supremacy of the United Nations, and reflected the view that the virtue of the compromise worked out at San Francisco lay in the fact that it had accommodated the demands of regionalists and provided for the utilization of the potential contributions of regional agencies without sacrificing that fundamental value. The United States, which had started with a universalist premise, was happy with the result of the negotiations at the Conference.

The basic Latin American urge, on the other hand, had been to establish the autonomy of the Inter-American system — and, so far as necessary, that of other regional arrangements. In contrast to the United States, most Latin American states had hoped to deprive the Security Council of competence to deal with local disputes until regional agencies had completed efforts to achieve a solution and, in espousing the interpretation stated by the Colombian representative, they purported to believe that this had been accomplished. This belief was incompatible with the understanding of the United States as to what had been decided at San Francisco concerning the role of regional agencies in the quest for solution of disputes among their members.

To provide for the utilization of regional bodies in promoting peaceful settlement of local disputes is one thing, but to establish the exclusive jurisdiction of regional bodies over such cases in their initial stages is quite another. It appears that the United States was correct in the view that the framers of the Charter should be understood as having attempted the former, not the latter. This interpretation rests ultimately upon the implications of Article 52(4). As Stettinius put it, this paragraph "insure[d] the paramount authority of the Council and its right to concern itself if necessary with disputes of this [intraregional] character."[19] It reserved the right of the Security Council to deal with any dispute — local or not — whenever it should decide that its primary responsibility for the maintenance of international peace and security so required. For

---

[18] Ibid., p. 650.
[19] *Report to the President* . . . , op. cit., p. 105.

better or for worse, this attribution of fundamental responsibility to the Security Council was the keystone of the Charter.

In summary, the San Francisco Conference retained the broad principle of universalism as the fundamental basis for the new system of international organization, while making significant concessions to the demands of champions of regional organization. With regard to the issue of enforcement action, the Conference produced the ambiguous combination of Articles 51 and 53. This ambiguity favored regional autonomy; the emancipation of regional agencies from meaningful Security Council control over their responses to armed attack tended to reduce United Nations supremacy in this vital area of activity to a doctrinal fiction. With regard to the issue of jurisdiction over disputes at the pacific settlement stage, the Conference produced the ambiguous combination of Article 52(2) and Article 52(4), with Articles 34 and 35 linked to the latter. This ambiguity, in contrast to the one noted above, favored United Nations supremacy; despite the stipulation that regional efforts should have priority, the clauses safeguarding the discretion of the Security Council as to how it should exercise its world-wide authority and responsibility tended to reduce regional agencies to subordinate bodies whose role might be determined by the Council.

Given this pair of ambiguities — each pushing in a different direction — it is difficult to sustain the view that a "clear" delineation of the relationships between the general and regional organizations was written into the Charter. It was "clear" only that the United Nations and regional agencies would coexist, and the political controversy concerning their proper relationships was likely in the actual operation of the system. The United States hoped that the provisions of the Charter would "mesh into the system of international security established on a universal basis such existing or future regional instrumentalities as might serve to further its objectives without detracting from its authority and effectiveness," and, more concretely, that the projected organs of the Inter-American system would constitute "an integral and valuable element of an effective collective security system on a world-wide basis . . . without establishing a precedent which might engender rivalry between regional groups at the expense of world security."[20] These official comments reflected the continuing bias of the United States toward the principle of universalism in matters of peace and security.

[20] *Ibid.*, pp. 101, 108.

THE REGIONALIST CHALLENGE
TO UN SUPREMACY

Many close observers of the actual performance and development of the postwar system of international organization have pointed out that the Charter scheme for relating regional agencies to the United Nations has been drastically altered. Regionalism has come back into its own, producing agencies that have figured more prominently in world affairs and functioned more independently of the United Nations than was foreshadowed in the Charter. Edgar S. Furniss Jr., expressed the view that ''In the name of regional arrangements the United Nations has been placed in a position of inferiority, so that now the links between the regional arrangements and the world organization exist at the practical pleasure of the former.''[21]

Concerning contemporary regional organizations in general, one can say that they have been more active in the security sphere and less active in the field of peaceful settlement than the framers of the Charter appeared to expect or intend. The principle laid down in Article 53, that regional agencies should not take enforcement action without the authorization of the Security Council, has been overshadowed by the exceptions stipulated in that Article and in Article 51; for the maintenance of international peace and security, states have come to rely not upon the Security Council, nor upon agencies subject to its control, but upon alliance systems that have been created for the explicit purpose of functioning autonomously. With respect to the principle laid down in Article 52(2-3), that members of regional agencies and the Security Council itself should emphasize the role of those agencies in the settlement of local disputes, the general experience has been quite different; the existence of regional bodies has not, by and large, tended to reduce the case load of United Nations organs by facilitating solutions at the regional level.[22] In short, both of the fundamental concepts of the Charter pertaining to the role of regional agencies have broken down. Neither the negative control nor the positive utilization of such agencies by the Security Council has become a significant feature of recent international relations.

These developments can be explained by the circumstances that

[21] ''A Re-examination of Regional Arrangements,'' *Journal of International Affairs*, Vol. 9, 1955, p. 84.

[22] See Inis L. Claude, Jr., *Swords Into Plowshares* (2nd ed.; New York Random House, 1959), pp. 121-22.

have occasioned the creation and development of most of the regional bodies functioning in the political-security field. These bodies are primarily *external* in their orientation; they exist to provide joint security against potential enemies on the outside. Hence, their members are wary of subjecting them to possible immobilization by the Security Council in which the influence or voting power of the external enemy may be effective. The North Atlantic Treaty Organization, for instance, would be meaningless if the Soviet veto could be used in the Security Council to deny its authority to act. In short, alliances would wither under Article 53 — but they flourish under Article 51. Moreover, the external orientation of the regional agencies helps to explain their relative insignificance as promoters of local peaceful settlement. Their preoccupation with external threat implies the neglect of this internal concern, although this need not be the case.[23] More importantly, the provisions of Article 52 do not emancipate regional agencies from the Security Council's control in the clear-cut fashion of Article 51. As already noted, the ambiguity of the scheme regarding peaceful settlement leaves large opportunities for Security Council intrusion into intraregional difficulties, and an unfriendly outsider with a seat in that body — particularly a permanent seat involving veto power — may be both eager and able to promote such intrusion. On the whole, regional organizations have had greater incentive and ability to eliminate effective Security Council control over their collective self-defense policy than to prevent the Council's involvement in the handling of disputes among their members.

To some extent these generalizations fail to fit the case of the postwar Inter-American regional system, the OAS. This regional agency is, of course, designed to promote collective resistance to armed attack from outside its zone, and, like other such groupings, it relies upon Article 51 as the legal basis for emergency action unencumbered by the requirement of Security Council authorization. However, the OAS is also characterized by a significant degree of *internal* orientation. As is indicated by its basic documents — the Inter-American Treaty of Reciprocal Assistance (the Rio Pact, 1947) and the Charter of the Organization of American States (formulated

---

[23] In a news conference on 22 May 1956, Secretary of State John Foster Dulles described NATO as essentially a military alliance — a collective defense association under Article 51 of the Charter, rather than a regional association. He said it had no "policy or jurisdiction to deal with disputes as between the members," although he recognized that it might be given such a function. *New York Times*, 23 May 1956.

at Bogotá, 1948) — the OAS is concerned with the settlement of disputes and the suppression of conflicts within its ranks. It is in some sense a collective security system on the regional level, as well as an externally oriented defensive alliance. The relationship of the OAS to the United Nations therefore is not reducible to the relatively simple terms of Article 51, but involves also the complexities of Articles 52-54. Unlike such agencies as NATO, which simply capitalize upon Article 51 to remain separate from the United Nations, the OAS finds itself linked to the world organization because of the breadth of its role in political and security matters. This is a unique relationship; only the experience of the OAS provides a thorough test of the practical application of the Charter's formula for the meshing of regional and global political activity.

The problem of working out an acceptable relationship between the United Nations and the OAS can be reduced to two central issues both of which were foreshadowed in the controversies that raged at San Francisco: (1) the "Try OAS first" issue and (2) the issue of the autonomy of the OAS in imposing sanctions upon its members.

The first of these issues relates to the interpretation of the provisions of Articles 33-35 and 52 bearing upon institutional efforts to promote peaceful settlement of intraregional disputes. Following their success at San Francisco in securing reference to the principle of priority for regional modes of settlement in Article 33, and more prominently, in Article 52(2), the American states took pains to insert formal commitments to use the mechanisms of the OAS before resorting to the United Nations in both of the fundamental instruments of their new organizational system.[24] Ignoring the question of the legal effectiveness of these articles within the context of the United Nations Charter, one can readily see that these formulations represented an attempt to reinforce the Charter's ambiguous recognition of regional priority in pacific settlement, and even to give the OAS the clear-cut jurisdictional monopoly of the preliminary stage of pacific settlement that some Latin American delegations had advocated at San Francisco. These OAS provisions laid the basis for a political struggle to interpose the OAS as a barrier to Security Council consideration of Inter-American disputes whenever regional privacy might be particularly desired. The other side of the "Try OAS first" coin reads, "Security Council, stay out!"

The issue of the autonomy of the OAS in imposing sanctions upon

[24] Inter-American Treaty of Reciprocal Assistance, Article 2; Charter of the OAS, Article 20.

its members relates to the interpretation of Articles 53 and 54. Contention on this point has involved the problem of defining the "enforcement action," which the OAS is forbidden to take except with the authorization of the Security Council. . . . A persistent effort has been made to shake off the restraint imposed upon the OAS by the terms of Article 53, leaving that agency only with the obligation, stated in Article 54, of keeping the Security Council informed of its activities and plans.

The most striking fact about this struggle to enhance the status of the OAS is that leadership was belatedly taken over by the United States. At San Francisco, the United States with mixed emotions followed along in the Latin American drive to minimize the universalist bias of the Charter, and, at Rio, it was conspicuous among the states submitting draft proposals for the Inter-American Treaty of Reciprocal Asssistance in its failure to suggest explicit expression of the "Try OAS first" principle.[25] Nevertheless, the great power of the Western Hemisphere has subsequently assumed the captaincy of the battle, with the political forces of Latin America lending support in imperfect and uncertain array.

This shift can only be understood as one aspect of the development of the United States policy of resistance to Soviet expansionism. The United States has led the fight for OAS jurisdiction in certain cases, not because it regarded them as local matters, but precisely because it believed they involved communist intrusions into hemispheric affairs; for the United States, the campaign on behalf of the OAS has been, in reality, a struggle against the Soviet Union.

.   .   .

CONCLUSIONS

Analysis of the episodes in which the status of the OAS has been treated by argument and hammered into shape at the United Nations forge demonstrates above all the malleability of the Charter under the impact of political considerations and political forces. For an understanding of what has happened, the analytical skill of the student of international politics is vastly more relevant than that of

[25] *Inter-American Conference for the Maintenance of Continental Peace and Security, Quitandinha, Brazil, August 15-September 2, 1947: Report of the Delegation of the United States of America,* U.S. Dept. of State Pub. 3016 (Washington: GPO, 1948). Cf. the United States proposal, p. 82, and those of Brazil, p. 77; Chile, p. 78; Guatemala, p. 79; Mexico, p. 81; Panama, p. 82; Bolivia, p. 112.

the international lawyer. The cold war has prevailed over the Charter; the latest adaptation of the Monroe Doctrine has relegated Article 53 to the ash heap of politically charred legal provisions; the fear of the Soviet veto has taken precedence over the principle that regional agencies should be subordinated to the United Nations.

Most of the political impetus for this transformation of the status of the OAS has been provided by the United States, which lagged behind and held back its fellow members of the Inter-American system in their drive for regional autonomy during the formative stages of the United Nations. The record shows a mixed pattern of victories and defeats for the United States in the pro-OAS campaign. The effort to establish the mandatory "Try OAS first" principle came to naught and was abandoned, in part because of the gradual diminution of Latin American support; after the Guatemalan case [see the article by Gordon Connell-Smith, below, p. 97—ed.], the United States could find few friends, in the OAS or elsewhere, willing to endorse the view that American states were prohibited from appealing to the Security Council, and the Council was barred from heeding their appeals, until the OAS had completed its action or inaction on their complaints. On the other hand, the United States succeeded thanks largely to the steady growth of Latin American support, in emancipating OAS enforcement activity from United Nations control; after the Dominican case [in which the OAS imposed sanctions against the unpopular Trujillo regime and the United States successfully resisted Soviet efforts to have the Security Council approve the sanctions — ed.] the United States found an increasing number of friends, both in the OAS and outside, willing to endorse the view that Article 53 should not be so construed as to inhibit OAS activities against communist intrusions in the hemisphere. In the one case, the Latin American states refused to accept the restriction of their rights; in the other, they rallied to support the expansion of their rights as a regional group.

Fundamentally, this entire struggle over the OAS must be regarded as but a chapter in the larger volume of the cold war. A major feature of the general history of the United Nations is the persistent effort of the United States to deprive the Soviet Union of an effective veto power and of the Soviet Union to retain that power. In this instance of the conflict over the veto, as in many others, the United States has succeeded. It may well be that the United States was able to attract greater support for releasing the OAS from the restriction of Article 53 than for expanding its jurisdictional rights under

Article 52, precisely because the former did, and the latter did not, involve an attack upon the Soviet veto power. The Soviet Union's position in regard to the "Try OAS first" issue supported the competence of a majority in the Security Council to take action; its position with respect to Article 53 represented its claim of competence to veto action by the Council, and implied that all regional organizations were subject to the paralyzing impact of the veto power. Hence, it is not surprising that the Soviet Union was rebuffed in the latter case, rather than the former.

Throughout these cases, the Soviet Union appeared in the unusual role of champion of the rights and competence of the United Nations, while the United States was cast, in equally significant deviation from normal character, as the prime opponent of a strong and active world organization. No more striking demonstration can be found of the inexorable subordination of principle to policy in the operations of statesmen than was revealed by the United States in this set of cases. The United States did not repudiate the principle of the paramountcy of the United Nations in the international system but it subordinated that principle to the necessity of gaining a free hand for combating communist infiltration in the Western Hemisphere. It did not renounce the principle of nonintervention, or of nonviolence except in self-defense, but it made these yield to what it regarded as vital policy considerations. It did not deny the principle of truthfulness and good faith, but, under the pressure of policy commitments, it misstated both its acts and its intentions with respect to communist-oriented regimes in the Caribbean area. It did not renounce the principle of the rule of law, but it protected its policy by constricting the provision of Article 53 that expressed the authority of the Security Council over the OAS, and insisted upon avoiding a judicial inquiry into the meaning of that provision.

The development of the relationship between the OAS and the United Nations confirms the proposition that the original project of permitting and encouraging regional agencies to operate within a framework of United Nations supervision and control has broken down. The OAS has failed to achieve a monopolistic jurisdiction over disputes within its area, but, more importantly, the Security Council has lost any meaningful capacity to regulate or restrict the enforcement operations of the OAS. Broadly, these observations apply as well to other regional organizations dealing with political and security problems. These organizations have exhibited little interest in establishing jurisdictional priority over local disputes, and their members would probably resist any effort to restrict the right of access to the United Nations, just as the Latin Americans have done. With regard to enforcement measures, however, members of all regional agencies have an interest in escaping the control of the Security Council, and it is unlikely that the superior authority of the Council can be effectively applied to any regional body. In the era of the cold war, regional organizations are the chosen instruments of the great antagonists locked in political conflict. Those antagonists will not permit their instruments to be held in check by the United Nations.

APPENDIX

CHARTER OF THE UNITED NATIONS

CHAPTER VI. PACIFIC SETTLEMENT OF DISPUTES

Article 33

1. The parties to any dispute, the continuance of which is likely to endanger the maintenance of international peace and security, shall, first of all, seek a solution by negotiation, enquiry, mediation, conciliation, arbitration, judicial settlement, resort to regional agencies or arrangements, or other peaceful means of their own choice.

2. The Security Council shall, when it deems necessary, call upon the parties to settle their dispute by such means.

CHAPTER VII. ACTION WITH RESPECT TO THREATS TO THE PEACE, BREACHES OF THE PEACE, AND ACTS OF AGGRESSION

Article 51

Nothing in the present Charter shall impair the inherent right of individual or collective self-defense if an armed attack occurs against a Member of the United Nations, until the Security Council has taken the measures necessary to maintain international peace and security. Measures taken by Members in the exercise of this right of self-defense shall be immediately reported to the Security Council and shall not in any way affect the authority and responsibility of the Security Council under the present Charter to take at any time such action as it deems necessary in order to maintain or restore international peace and security.

Chapter VIII. Regional Arrangements

Article 52

Nothing in the present Charter shall impair the inherent right of regional arrangements or agencies for dealing with such matters relating to the maintenance of international peace and security as are appropriate for regional action, provided that such arrangements or agencies and their activities are consistent with the Purposes and Principles of the United Nations.

2. The Members of the United Nations entering into such arrangements or constituting such agencies shall make every effort to achieve pacific settlement of local disputes through such regional arrangements or by such regional agencies before referring them to the Security Council.

3. The Security Council shall encourage the development of pacific settlement of local disputes through such regional arrangements or by such regional agencies either on the initiative of the states concerned or by reference from the Security Council.

4. This Article in no way impairs the application of Articles 34 and 35. . . .

Article 53

1. The Security Council shall, where appropriate, utilize such regional arrangements or agencies for enforcement action under its authority. But no enforcement action shall be taken under regional arrangements or by regional agencies without the authorization of the Security Council, with the exception of measures against any enemy state, as defined in paragraph 2 of this Article, provided for pursuant to Article 107 or in regional arrangements directed against renewal of aggressive policy on the part of any such state, until such time as the Organization may, on request of the Governments concerned, be charged with the responsibility for preventing further aggression by such a state.

2. The term enemy state as used in paragraph 1 of this Article applies to any state which during the Second World War has been an enemy of any signatory of the present Charter.

Article 54

The Security Council shall at all times be kept fully informed of activities undertaken or in contemplation under regional arrangements or by regional agencies for the maintenance of international peace and security.

John Pinder

EEC and Comecon

The most important development in the political economy of the West since the war may well have been the creation of effective multilateral organisations that transcend the nation-state. Gatt, OECD, and Efta have all helped to secure freer trade and better economic cooperation, and to prevent the destructive international competition that characterised the inter-war years. But, as far at least as relations between its members are concerned, the EEC, the European Economic Community, has induced more progress towards these ends than any other organisation. Its members have created a single market as populous as that of the United States; they have developed a system for the formation of common economic policies; and they have transformed a secular hostility between their members into a relationship that places war between them beyond the bounds of possibility. The implications of these facts for the countries of eastern Europe are clearly of great interest; and, even if the new methods of collaboration have now been called in question by General de Gaulle, they have already shown such remarkable results that it is pertinent to ask whether they contain any lessons that could be relevant to the future evolution of eastern Europe.

PROBLEMS OF INTEGRATION IN COMECON

While the nations of the West, and particularly those of the Community, have been in the process of moving beyond national sovereignty, those of eastern Europe have been either standing pat on that

Reprinted from *Survey*, No. 58 (January, 1966) with the permission of the author and the publisher.

concept or moving in the reverse direction. The name Council for Mutual Economic Assistance, and still more its abbreviation Comecon, somewhat resembles that of the Common Market, and this leads some people to believe that the two organisations are therefore similar. But this is a superficial judgment. For entirely understandable historical reasons, their nature is fundamentally different.

The difference is clearly expressed in the treaties that established the two bodies. The members of the EEC were "determined to establish the foundations of an ever closer union among the European peoples,"[1] while CMEA "is established on the basis of the principle of the sovereign equality of all the member countries of the Council."[2] The EEC has a strong and independent Commission as its executive and the treaty lays down that the members can take certain important decisions by majority vote; CMEA has a relatively weak Secretariat and all recommendations or decisions must be adopted by the unanimous vote of those members interested in the question under consideration.

The intractable nationalism of the economic arrangements in communist countries stems from the experience of Russia under Stalin, who created a highly centralised system of national planning that concentrated on independence from outside economies (i.e. on basic industries) and rigidly controlled all foreign trade transactions: a system of extreme economic autarky.

When the greater part of eastern Europe fell into Stalin's hands at the end of the war, this system became the stereotype for the countries concerned. Each of them established a highly centralised system of national planning, concentrating on independence from outside economies and insulated from them by means of the control of foreign trade. Stalin's power and prestige were so great that he could doubtless have imposed a unified economic policy on eastern Europe over a long period, even though the systems he had created were so inherently autarkic and recalcitrant to outside pressures. But after his death the logic of the system began to tell. The political expression of this trend is polycentrism (which seems to be a new word for national sovereignty, as far as countries ruled by communist parties are concerned). The economic implications have been trenchantly expressed by the Rumanians. Thus a Rumanian editorialist,

---

[1] Preamble to the Treaty establishing the European Economic Community.
[2] The Comecon Charter, 1960, Article 1. This and the three following quotations are taken from Michael Kaser's *Comecon: Integration Problems of the Planned Economies* (London, 1965).

rejecting the concept of an interstate development of the lower Danube region, insisted that Rumania was "an independent and sovereign state. On this territory nobody has anything to study, neither in detail nor in lesser detail, without authorisation from the Rumanian government, for both the efficient use of resources and the location of objectives, as well as any other problems, big or small, are of the exclusive competence of the Rumanian government and people." General de Gaulle might speak in similar terms about France in relation to the European Community; but in this he would contradict the letter and spirit of the Rome Treaty, whereas the Rumanian attitude is perfectly consistent with the CMEA Charter and with the communist insistence on national sovereignty. This attitude, which originally served to safeguard the unity and strength of the communist world when it consisted of a single state, has become, with the emergence of a number of communist states, a sorcerer's apprentice that washes away their unity by encouraging them to pull in different directions.

Consistent though this position may be with the post-patristic communist doctrine and the CMEA Charter, however, it is widely recognised in eastern Europe that it flies in the face of modern technology. It is not possible for countries ranging in population from thirty million down to seven million, with much lower purchasing power than those in western Europe, to enjoy a full development of modern industries on the basis of their separate markets, and this applies in particular to the basic industries that began to be established, on the Stalinist pattern, in each east European country. Khrushchev was among those who saw that this pointed in the direction of a single integrated market. Speaking at Leipzig in 1959, he said ". . . the further development of the socialist countries will in all probability proceed along the lines of reinforcing a single world system of the socialist economy. One after another the economic barriers which separated our countries under capitalism will disappear." In 1962 he tried to translate this idea into action by his relatively supranational proposal for a unified planning organ in Comecon.

It is well known that this proposal for "shifting some functions of economic management from the competence of the respective state to the attribution of super-state bodies or organs" (Declaration of the Rumanian Central Committee, April 1964) was strongly and successfully opposed by the Rumanians, whose Declaration went on to say "these measures are not in keeping with the principles which

underlie the relations between socialist countries.'' But if the touchy
Rumanian nationalism had been the only obstacle, a way might have
been found around it. In fact, there are fundamental difficulties
stemming from the autarkic national economic systems that Stalin
bequeathed to the Soviet bloc, which are in direct conflict with any
attempt to integrate their economies.

These difficulties have been well described in Mr. Kaser's book on
Comecon. They relate partly to the problem of the prices at which
goods are to be exchanged. In the absence of a linked system of
market economies such as exists in the West, which provides an
'objective'' procedure for price formation, each east European
country has its own idiosyncratic set of prices. The east Europeans
therefore had to adopt ''world'' (i.e. capitalist) prices for their
trade; yet this system has been severely criticised in eastern Europe,
particularly when the trend of world prices was adverse for a particular country, as it was for Bulgaria for example when the world
market for raw materials was weak. Indeed, it is hard to see how the
east European governments could agree that major decisions about
the structure of their economies should be taken on the basis of prices
set by a system of which they disapprove and quite different from
the prices according to which they each make their internal decisions
on production and investment. An integrated east European economy, giving full scope for large-scale production by centralising the
decisions on many of the most important investments, would surely
have to wait on the development of a common system of prices that
is accepted by each country and by and large applied for purposes
of national economic planning as well as for intra-east European
trade.

Even if a uniform system of prices were to be applied in eastern
Europe, however, there are further conditions that would have to
obtain before the centrally-planned economies could be integrated.
Thus each country would have to apply the same profit criterion to
the production of export goods; it would be no use for each country
to apply the same prices if some allowed their exporting enterprises
to run at a loss (in effect subsidising them) while others insisted that
their enterprises break even or make a profit. Given the same price
system and profit criterion, moreover, there would still have to be a
procedure for assessing rival investment projects. There would clearly
be many occasions when more than one country wished to construct
plant to manufacture a product for which the market was large
enough to justify only one new production unit. The feasibility

studies would have to be vetted objectively — it is too easy for engi neers to produce cost figures and economists market projection optimistic enough to bias the choice in favour of their own country' project. Investments of great importance of economic developmen would sometimes be involved, and those who had to decide on th merits of the competitive projects would be in the position of supranational planning authority.

In short, it is hard to see how a number of monolithic nationally planned economies could be integrated unless they were subsume in a monolithic supranationally-planned economy. But the national ism of the east European states and their autarkic economic structur have been too strong to allow this to happen. Only a militantly im perialist Russia, intent on unifying the communist bloc, would hav been powerful enough to force it through; but as we have seen it wa Khrushchev's Russia, not Stalin's, that perceived the technocrati necessity of integration, and Khrushchev was either unwilling o unable to apply the pressure that would have been required. Thi being so, the preponderant strength of Russia in Comecon was positive deterrent to integration, not a motive force; fo Russia whatever its intentions might be, would be bound to dominate any supranational planning authority in Comecon: the Russian govern ment would in fact virtually be the supranational authority. Th status of the other members of Comecon would be equivalent to tha of provinces of the Soviet Union. Even if they were ready to accep the principle of a supranational economic community, this state o subordination to one of its members would clearly be unacceptable.

The obstacles to economic integration in Comecon, stem from tw basic differences between it and the EEC. The decentralised marke economies of the West are more amenable to a process of gradua integration than the centralised economies of the East, based o imperative target planning (the problems presented by the Commo Market to France's relatively mild indicative target planners an their efforts to extend their planning system to the Community leve are a further indication of this). And the balance of power withi the Community helps to preclude domination of the others by an one member while that within Comecon does not. Where there is desire on the part of the members for a fair share of democratic con trol of the integrated economy, or at least for avoiding absorption b a more powerful state, this kind of balance is absolutely necessary Professor Hallstein has stressed this aspect of the EEC: "the Com munity system, the constitution of the Community, is of itself negation of any hegemony, the organised and methodical rebuttal of hegemony.''[3] Integration within Comecon is, by contrast, hamstrung by the tendency towards hegemony that is built into the structure of its membership because of Russia's predominant size.

The existence of Comecon does not, then, imply that there is, or will be in the next few years, an integrated economy in eastern Europe that negotiates, like the EEC, as a single unit in its external trade. The east European countries will retain, during this period, their centralised, nationally-planned economies, and the institutions of Comecon do not seem likely to make more than marginal differences to this form of organisation.

It is, however, well known that there has recently been some evolution of the east European systems, under the pressure of their transition to consumer societies, in the direction of decentralisation and a market economy. The current reforms, if they become fully effective, will take Yugoslavia far in that direction. In Russia the Liberman experiments and the Kosygin reforms, bringing criteria of competition and profit, are certainly significant, and the Czechs, Hungarians, and Poles are all engaged in implementing some degree of economic decentralisation. In these circumstances it has become less fanciful to suppose, even if the possibility of full integration among east European economies is still a long way off, that a rapprochement with the western economies may become feasible. Thus Mr. Kaser says that ''Renewed efforts to create a multilateral programme may not necessarily be kept within the bounds of [Comecon's] group. Soviet ideology has recently buried the hatchet which, at the time of Comecon's foundation, struck down Varga for discerning the feasibility of planning in the west European mixed economies, and a shared economic language is at least evolving as western Europe and the developing countries embody some of their policies in plans, nationally and internationally. One way for Comecon to enlarge this potential communication would be by the partial transposition of its multilateral programming to a wider area, such as Gatt, or the proposed United Nations Trade and Development Board, where the plans of developed and developing countries could best be confronted.''[4]

Some go farther than this and envisage an association of east European countries with west European free trade systems. This

---

[3] Statement made to the European Parliament, 5 February 1963.
[4] Michael Kaser, op. cit., p. 4.

possibility appeals strongly, for example, to many people in the British Labour Party, and their sentiments have often been echoed in sections of the press, notably *The Observer*. The fear that any prospect of such an association would be thwarted if Britain were to join the "tightly organised" EEC is one argument used by those in the Labour Party who oppose British entry; they contend that Efta with its much looser institutional system, would be able to make such arrangements with the east European whereas the EEC would not In order to assess the validity of this argument in particular, therefore, as well as some of the more general economic implications of rapprochement between East and West, it is worth examining the possibilities and the limits of economic cooperation between eastern Europe and the western trading systems.

EASTERN EUROPE AND GATT

The negotiations about Polish membership of Gatt (General Agreement on Tariffs and Trade) and the discussions on East-West trade in the UN Conference on Trade and Development[5] have brought out many of the problems of closer economic cooperation between East and West, even though no more was being considered than to conduct this trade on the same basis as normal trade between western countries, that is to say with most-favored-nation tariffs and with the use of quotas limited to certain defined emergencies.

From the point of view of the West, the difficulties derive first from the fact that the trade of communist countries (apart from Yugoslavia) is monopolised by state trading corporations which are subject to the orders of the governments. This means that trade could be used for purposes that were either strategic (e.g. the withholding of oil at a critical moment) or political (e.g. buying elsewhere unless a western country or firm complies with certain political stipulations). Since the governments of most communist countries are by no means friendly to the West, this argument causes western countries to feel the need to hold trade controls in reserve in case they should approach in any sector of their economies a condition of undue dependence on communist countries (which would be hard to define but not so hard to recognise).

---

[5] The UNCTAD material on this subject is contained in UN Document E/Conf. 46/ PC.47 and UN Document E/Conf.46/34. The problem of the relations between state-trading countries and Gatt is considered in PEP, *East-West Trade* (1965), pp. 156-61.

Second, it is believed that state monopolies could use their bargain-ng power to exploit those with whom they trade for purely economic ends: to buy cheaper or sell dearer. It is important to get this argu-ment into proportion. The state monopolies of the smaller communist countries occupy such a tiny corner of the world market for most of the things they buy or sell that they have little scope for any such exploitation. They are much less powerful than a large western firm. But, while there are very few products of which a communist state monopoly is a dominant supplier, the orders that the trading corpora-tions of the larger communist countries, and of Russia in particular, can place are so big that the West is right to regard this power as a potential danger to a degree that does not apply with respect to international trade in general.

Third, western countries fear that the trade with communist countries may lead to harmful economic disruption. This is because it is not possible to ascertain whether exports by the state trading corporations are being subsidised; even if they are not, the pricing systems of communist countries have no logic by the standards of market economies, and exports at domestic prices can therefore represent "unfair" competition; and even if the communists stick to world market prices, their planning system is such that large surpluses can appear that would swamp the market. There is a further cause of economic disruption that is present in any trade between more and less developed countries, and that is worth stress-ing because it appears to those brought up on the static theory of classical economies as an unfortunate aberration rather than a fact of fundamental importance in contemporary world trade. This is that the more developed countries have an overwhelming advantage in the capital-intensive (i.e. modern) industries, while the more efficient of the less developed cannot be beaten in the labour-intensive (i.e. old-fashioned) industries. Thus if trade between the two is reasonably free, with low tariffs and no quotas, the old-fashioned industries will disappear in the more developed countries while the modern indus-tries will never take root in the less developed countries. This applies whether the trade is between Asia and Europe, between western Europe and the United States — or between eastern Europe and the West. Now the loss of old-fashioned industries may be uncomfortable for those sectors of an advanced economy, although the process of change can be eased by government help in reconversion, and is also generally eased and often actually prevented by means of high tariffs or special import controls; but the shove in the direction of modernisation is beneficial provided the transition is organised well. To the less developed country, on the other hand, the bargain seems likely to be one-sided: its modern industries will be nipped in the bud and it will be indefinitely relegated to industrial backwardness. It is eastern Europe, therefore, and not the west that has cause to fear the consequences of freer trade between regions at widely different economic levels.

In fact the east Europeans would have no such fear because (except perhaps the Yugoslavs) they have no intention of abandoning the planned growth of their industries or of accepting the criterion of international competition. The Poles offered to erect a tariff if this would enable them to negotiate like other members of Gatt; but it would not, because there is no reason to suppose that their choice whether to manufacture at home or to buy from abroad (which is the choice which nations negotiating about tariffs are essentially concerned) would be altered in proportion to any change in the level of their tariff. Nor are they prepared to let their exports compete freely with those of other countries, by making their currency convertible. This would force them to devalue to a realistic exchange rate and would, even if this were done, introduce a new dimension of uncertainty into what is already a very uncertain sector of their national plans.

The Poles therefore favour an arrangement whereby, in return for a tariff cut that enabled them to sell more to another member of Gatt, they would increase their purchases from that member by an equivalent amount. But this, while it is a sensible and useful proposal, has little in common with the most-favoured-nation (mfn) system of tariff cuts employed by market economies in Gatt: the reciprocal advantage offered by the Poles would not be extended to benefit all other suppliers of the product in question, as is the case with a mfn tariff cut, nor would the arrangement be in any way multilateral.

This is not to say that closer Polish involvement in Gatt, or a special form of membership for Poland, would be a bad thing. It might, perhaps, slightly weaken the organisation by adding to those special categories, such as agriculture, textiles, and developing countries, that now escape the rigour of its rules; but the Czechs are in any case already members, and for the Poles to join them would be a step towards better relations between East and West, and favour any convergence of the two systems that might follow from a continued trend towards decentralisation and the introduction of market principles in the East. The lesson is, rather, that the differences between he economic systems of East and West are still such that trade has to be subject to special procedures that are not compatible with full membership of even an organisation like Gatt, which demands no element of integration. The Executive Secretary of Gatt has put it in a nutshell: "If a free enterprise country comes into the Gatt it accepts a number of commitments. It makes an agreement as to the level of its tariff protection. . . . It agrees not to use import restrictions as a means of protection. It agrees to certain rules relating to subsidies, to dumping, to customs administration, all of which are designed to afford to its trading partners clearly ascertainable and agreed terms of access. . . . None of these conditions exist in a state-trading country."[6] Even if the present members of Gatt deviate from these principles to a greater or lesser degree, it can hardly be denied that the organisation would be undermined by the introduction as full members of important countries from eastern Europe that deviate from them wholesale. This is not to say that the difficulties are absolute or eternal. The structure of the Yugoslav economy may soon be decentralised enough to justify full membership of Gatt; and the other east European countries may well later follow suit. Liberal policies on the part of western countries can moreover help to encourage such developments. But it is not wise to minimise the difficulties or to expect fundamental changes in the near future. The problems of economic relations between East and West are not going to be so quickly or easily solved.

Eastern Europe and Efta

It would be hard to envisage a free-trade grouping under modern conditions with looser institutional arrangements than Efta. Yet the problem of a free trading relationship between Efta and eastern Europe would be those of the Gatt relationship writ large. The economies of the existing Efta members would be wide open to the possibilities of strategic or political pressure, to exploitation by state-trading monopolies, or to disruption due to the difference of economic systems or economic levels. Special controls could doubtless be maintained on trade with the eastern countries, but in this case there would not be a lot of point in pretending that they were a part of Efta. They, for their part, would find the rules of the association

---

[6] E. Wyndham White, *International Trade; Challenge and Response* (Gatt, 1959), pp. 18, 19.

more stringent and therefore still harder to accept than those of Gatt
As in relation to Gatt, such difficulties are neither absolute no
eternal; a decentralisation of the eastern economic systems may
eventually change the situation, and Yugoslavia may even now be
evolving a system that would make associate membership of Efta
possible.

There is however a further, and more important, reason why the
association of state-trading countries with Efta would be the detri
ment of the existing members. There are grounds to believe that free
trade between modern economies must be accompanied by a high
degree of coordination of economic policies. The classical economists
the government's duty was to keep out of economics, and its only
part in free trade was to remove national barriers that should never
have been there in the first place. But now that almost all govern
ments plan and intervene in economic life in a variety of ways, a free
trade area can hardly be sustained unless the plans and interventions
of the member governments pull together instead of clashing with
each other.

In order that the competition between free-trading partners can
be fair, for example, it is necessary for them to enforce similar com
petition policies (with respect to monopolies and restrictive prac
tices); there is no point in removing the import duty if imports are
still excluded by a market-sharing agreement, or by the buying
policy of a state-owned monopoly. What may be called "market
planning" is widely practised in certain sectors such as agriculture
energy, and transport: subsidies are granted or prices fixed by
governments, and competition will be distorted unless government
policies are brought into line. Target planning, whereby industries
are compelled to adhere to production targets rather than to aim at
profitably under market conditions, is a variant of market planning
with particular importance in eastern Europe. "Welfare planning"
can affect the conditions of competition by changing the distribution
of resources as between different income groups, between labour and
capital, or between different regions.

Thus competition, market, target and welfare planning all need
to be coordinated in order to secure fair competition. In a free trade
area, moreover, in which the several national economies are open
to the economic forces generated in the economies of other members
failure to fulfill the objectives of full employment (or growth) and
price stability in any one member can directly affect all the others
A common economic and financial policy therefore becomes necessary

based on a shared doctrine regarding the relative importance of these objectives and the merits of such different instruments of policy as monetary policy or price controls.

It will readily be seen that these fields in which common policies appear likely to be needed by a free trade area are those in which the EEC has from the outset had provision for the formation of common policies, and institutions in which they can be decided upon and by which they can be executed. Together with the free movement of people and of capital, and a common external commercial policy, which are also held to be necessary to the fair and effective functioning of a single market, these comprise the essential differences between the EEC and Efta. Failing a coalescence of the two organisations, it will be difficult enough in any case for Efta to evolve these attributes of economic union. The preponderant weight of Britain has the same inhibiting effect on supranational integration as does the presence of Russia in Comecon. If east European countries, with their sharply divergent economic systems and policies, were associated with Efta, its evolution towards economic union, whether on its own or by joining with the EEC, would become still more problematic. Thus the reasoning of those who oppose British entry into the EEC on the ground that this route towards free trade in the West would cut across the possibility of free trade with the East may be turned on its head: so far from being an unnecessarily divisive factor, supranational institutions and provision for common policies such as those of the EEC are a necessary concomitant of free trade among modern economies, and this makes it still harder to envisage any fruitful form of membership or associate membership for centrally-planned state-trading countries in the free trade systems of the West.

Eastern Europe and the EEC

The idea that the centralised state-trading economies of eastern Europe in their present form could become members or associate members of Efta, let alone of the European Community, is then an example of wishful thinking that a little cold logic will dispel. But this does not mean that, pending structural changes in the east European systems, trade cannot increase and other forms of economic cooperation develop. They have been, and they can, should, and seem likely to go on doing so.

Trade between eastern and western Europe has greatly increased in the last ten years. It is, however, still a smaller percentage of the

European countries' total trade than it was before the War; the east Europeans are anxious to buy more from the West; the economic development of eastern Europe seems likely to produce more goods that are saleable in western Europe (shortage of which, and poor marketing, being among the main brakes on trade at present); and western restrictions on imports from the East are likely to be relaxed rather than tightened. Thus the growth of trade seems likely to continue.

Although western investment in eastern Europe is precluded by communist doctrine, technical cooperation has been developing to a point where the distinction is almost becoming blurred. Sales of know-how have been important for some time. The trade agreement between France and Rumania provides for extensive technical aid in agriculture and other fields. And many instances of industrial collaboration between western firms and Polish or Hungarian state enterprises, have taken economic partnership a stage farther. With abundant labour and capital shortage in eastern Europe, such arrangements seem likely to flourish so long as the political climate is favourable.

Members of the EEC have played a leading part in this development of economic relations with the East (it was natural to mention France and Germany in the last paragraph as pioneers of two forms of technical cooperation). But although the EEC has a common tariff and an obligation to develop a common commercial policy, there have as yet been no negotiations between the Community as such and east European state-trading countries.

This is largely the fault of the East. Displeased, for political and strategic as well as certain economic reasons, at this new initiative towards unification in the West, the east Europeans at first treated the Community as if it did not exist. Khrushchev was the first to suggest in public that it might be advisable to do business with this vast new economic unit. The Poles have sent a delegation to visit the European Commission in Brussels. But officially the east Europeans still do not recognise the Community as the authority that deals with the tariffs of the Six, and they still claim most-favoured-nation tariff treatment, i.e. the extension to them of the Community's internal tariff cuts that will shortly have reduced the tariffs to zero. This is foolish both in theory and in practice: in theory because, as has been explained above, genuine and fair free trade between a centralised state-trading country and a modern free enterprise country would be incompatible with both systems; and in practice because the Com munity is the body that fixes the tariffs of the Six, and no amount of wishing otherwise will change this situation (the only agency that might do so is General de Gaulle, and this is unlikely, seeing what France would lose by the destruction of the Common Market). The east Europeans will undoubtedly have to come to terms with reality and accept that, if they want to negotiate on tariffs with the Six, they will have to do so through the institutions of the European Community.

The Community has tried to tempt eastern Europe into recognising the existence of the common external tariff by offering the Soviet Union a tariff cut on the oddly *dolce vita* items of caviar, crab (tinned), and vodka. So far this offer has been ignored. Apart from this, the Six have not been successful in forming a common policy towards eastern Europe. This is too important a part of the foreign policies of both France and Germany for them to have been able to sink their different approaches in a common policy; and while General de Gaulle is the head of the French Government it will probably remain true that these difficulties "make the prospect of any real progress on this front in the near future very remote."[7]

It is possible that the Community, because of de Gaulle's opposition to its institutions, will remain unable to form a common commercial policy towards eastern Europe. De Gaulle may either break the Community, whose members might then join in a general west European free trade area; or, and more probably, he might take all the power of decision out of its institutions, leaving it unable to negotiate changes in its tariff — like a huge and helpless whale stranded on the shores of world trade. In either of these circumstances the relations of east European countries with those of western Europe would be likely to continue to develop as in the recent past, with increasing trade and technical cooperation on a bilateral basis. The east Europeans would remain as a number of small or medium-sized states poised between Russia and the West, attracted by the technical superiority of western Europe and feeling the pull of the centralised military and economic power of Russia. It is, however, still probable that the Community will outlive de Gaulle and resume its progress towards common policies and the strengthening of its institutions. In this case the weight of western Europe in the international economic system will greatly increase, for the Community will negotiate as a unit of population not far short of 200 million with its present

[7] Miriam Camps, *What Kind of Europe?* (London, 1965), p. 68.

membership, at a high level of technology and living standards, and accounting for over a quarter of world trade. The balance of economic power in Europe would tilt towards the West and, in their balancing between Russia and western Europe, the east Europeans would lean more towards the latter than would otherwise be the case.

If this were the end of the story, it would still be a matter of great significance in the structure of European power politics and economics. The small and medium-sized states of eastern Europe have traditionally been pulled in opposite directions by Russia on the one hand and by western Europe, represented mainly by Germany, on the other. With the destruction of German power at the end of the war, the pull towards Russia became irresistible, and it is still sufficiently strong for it to be legitimate to classify in the east Europeans as belonging to the "Soviet bloc." The existence in western Europe of an economic unit (and, in all probability, eventually a political unit too) nearly as populous as the Soviet Union and much richer and more advanced would, in the long run, redress this balance. Ideology and fear of Germany now stand in the way, but they are likely to fade with the passage of time. Eastern Europe's economic relations with western Europe might well become more important than those with Russia.

There is, however, a still more interesting possibility: that the chemistry of the Community's efforts to transcend the nation-state by means of economic integration and supranational institutions might induce a similar chemical reaction in eastern Europe. The establishment of the Common Market has stimulated "a veritable rash of treaties and proposals for the creation of common markets all over the world." Though "various groups of underdeveloped countries have reasons of their own for wanting to create regional common markets — reasons quite independent of the integration movement in western Europe . . . every new plan for regional cooperation among the underdeveloped countries includes as one of its principal objectives the need to strengthen the hands of these countries in dealing with western Europe."[8] The same arguments appear to hold good for eastern Europe as for the underdeveloped countries. In making his proposal for a unified planning board in Comecon, Khrushchev made it clear that the idea was derived from the supranational EEC. Partly by force of example, more in order to countervail its power

---

[8] Sidney Dell, *Trade Blocs and Common Markets* (London, 1963), pp. 11-13
[9] See Michael Kaser, op. cit., p. 93.

the successful development of the Community will provide a pressure in the direction of unification in eastern Europe. Some people see the Community, in the long run, not so much causing the east Europeans to unite, as attracting the several east European states into its orbit, whether as full members when they have evolved fully-functioning market economies or as associate members when they are on the way to doing so (as Yugoslavia may well now be). This possibility, which depends on radical changes taking place in the economic systems of east European countries, does of course refer to a longer term than that being considered in the analysis, above, of the problems of associating eastern and western countries given their present systems.

Yet other observers envisage that the process of union in eastern Europe will be accompanied by a special relationship with western Europe, leading eventually, perhaps, to a union of the two: "A larger conception of a cooperative community, involving eventually four major units, America and Russia as the peripheral participants, and West Europe and East Europe as the two halves of the inner core (in time perhaps becoming even more closely linked), would provide a more constructive and politically appealing image of tomorrow than a troubled Western partnership implicitly based on the notion of continued European partition."[10]

It is the prospects outlined in the last three paragraphs that are of the greatest interest: those implying that the European Community may represent not only a bloc (or a new federal state) but also a process, a chain reaction that induces unification in other parts of the world and eventually, perhaps, between itself and other similar units. It is not only Professor Brzezinski who, in the last quotation and with reference to eastern Europe, discerns such a possibility; the idea of the Community as a catalyst of integration rather than a great power is implicit in the thinking of M. Jean Monnet, the 'father of Europe," as expressed in a number of his speeches and articles: "The natural attitude of a European Community based on the exercise by nations of common responsibilities will be to make these nations also aware of their responsibilities, as a Community, to the world. . . . European unity is the most important event in the West since the war, not because it is a new great power, but because the new institutional method it introduces is permanently modifying relations between nations and men": and, again, the union of Europe

---

[10] Z. K. Brzezinski, "Peaceful Engagement: a Plan for Europe's Future." *Encounter*, April 1965.

is "not an end in itself. It is the beginning of the road to the more orderly world that we must have if we are to escape destruction."[11] This concept of integration as a process that, starting in Western Europe, will induce integration in other parts of the world and perhaps in the world as a whole may become one of the great contemporary myths (the word is used in no pejorative sense — it is only fair to state that it is a myth with which this writer is in full sympathy). As such it deserves examination in relation to the problems of unity in eastern and western Europe.

EAST EUROPE AND WEST EUROPE: PROBLEMS OF UNION

The experience of the European Community as well as of earlier attempts to create unions indicates that certain conditions are conducive to union and that a majority of them must be present in a certain degree if union is to take place.[12] These conditions will now be considered in relation to the various possibilities of integration within eastern Europe or as between eastern and western Europe.

One set of conditions has already emerged during the examination of eastern Europe in relation to Gatt and Efta. There has to be a broad similarity of economic institutions if close association or, still more, if integration is to be feasible. Not only is it extremely hard to see how fair competition can be ensured between free enterprise economies on the one hand and highly centralised state-trading economies on the other; but the integrating economies must, as explained earlier, have enough similarity in their objectives and instruments of economic policy to strike a similar balance between such objectives as full employment and price stability, and between such instruments as monetary policy and price controls. This argues against union between East and West so long as their economic systems are radically different. It does not count against integration within eastern Europe, but here another factor must be recalled. It was shown earlier that there are serious obstacles to the fusion of economies based on centralised and imperative target planning rather than on the criteria of markets and profits. A union of centrally

[11] Speech by Jean Monnet at the Second World Congress on Man-made Fibres, 1 May 1962, and at Dartmouth College, 11 June 1961.

[12] The conditions are considered in more detail in the writer's chapter on the EEC in Evan Luard et al., *Evolution of International Organisations* (London 1966). In this chapter the writer has drawn heavily, with respect to the earlier union, on K. C. Wheare, *Federal Government* (London, 1951).

planned monoliths appears as an all-or-nothing process of absorption in a large unit; that of decentralised market economies can, as the EEC has shown, take place gradually and without any vast and sudden surrender of sovereignty. Effective integration in eastern Europe will therefore probably have to wait on far-reaching progress towards a system of market economy, which is by no means out of the question; Yugoslavia, it may be repeated, appears to be well on the way towards this. The introduction of market principles in the other east European countries will, however, take time, though less time than would be required for a similarity with west European economic institutions and objectives to develop, such as would be required before any integration of eastern and western economies would be possible.

A broad similarity of economic levels (living standards, productivity, level of technology) was also found earlier to be desirable if different economies are to be associated in a single market. This condition is on the whole satisfied with respect to a union of eastern Europe, which has a long way to catch up before it could be said to have reached a level similar to that of western Europe.

It is often stated that a political union is likely to follow from the economic union of the European Community. This is a rather misleading statement, because the Economic Community is already charged with the formation of common policies on questions of great political import. Those who speak in these terms ignore the fact that a large part of politics concerns questions of economic policy. It would be more correct to say that the Economic Community is a political union whose responsibilities might eventually be extended to other political questions such as defence. But whatever the terminology, it will readily be understood that the members of an economic union must together undertake a variety of exacting political tasks, and in this they are not likely to be successful unless they have broadly similar political institutions and ideas. This has been true in the European Community: when the Treaties were made each member was a parliamentary democracy centred on Christian-Democrat, Socialist, and Liberal parties. It is true of eastern Europe. It is hardly likely to be true of eastern and western Europe together for a long time to come.

The question of balance between the members has also been considered earlier. Union is not likely to take place if it would be dominated by one member who is much more powerful than the others. The presence of Russia therefore precludes the integration of all the existing members of Comecon. Likewise a United Europe "from the Atlantic to the Urals" is an abortive concept, unless it is based on the pre-condition of a federal union of western Europe, which is hardly what de Gaulle has in mind; European Russian alone, with over 150 million people, is three times as populous as any other European state. It may be said in passing, though it is not the subject of the essay, that an Atlantic Common Market of North America and western Europe is for similar reasons ruled out at least until the unity of western Europe has been firmly consolidated (and even then it is hard to envisage a union consisting almost entirely of two giants). On this score, a union of the east European countries except Russia would be practicable. As far as the possibility of eventual entry of eastern Europe into the EEC is concerned, the east European countries separately would not be likely to unbalance it, but they would be hard to accommodate if they were to enter as an already formed unit.

It has also been found necessary that, at least during the time of formation and consolidation of the union, the largest members should be in close alliance. The individual countries have been all too prone to adopt attitudes of narrow nationalism, such as would render union out of the question.

It is, finally and perhaps obviously, necessary for the prospective members of a union to desire it strongly. Many forces will act against it: nationalism, vested interests, inertia. Without powerful motive such as the desire for independence, for defence against an outside power, or for economic gain, and without a profound dissatisfaction with the existing state of affairs, these reactionary forces are not likely to be overcome. In the case of eastern Europe, it is not difficult to envisage the existence of these conditions. Dissatisfaction with the existing state of affairs has erupted at intervals; independence from Russia is deeply desired by many; a need for economic defence against the Common Market is likely to be felt; and the economic gain from large-scale production for a large market was already seen in most of the countries when the negotiations took place about integration in Comecon. If the other political and economic conditions were already fulfilled, some of these motives might well apply to a union of east European countries with the European Community, in addition to which would be the East's need for capital, the West's need for labour, and the need of both sides for a solution of the German problem.

This analysis has shown that the necessary conditions for union in

astern Europe might well be present in the coming years, provided
hat the countries there can both overcome their excessive nationalism
nd find a way of uniting alongside, but apart from, Russia. Union
etween eastern and western Europe, on the other hand, would have
o await a political and economic convergence that will probably be
 long time coming, and if eastern Europe has by then already united,
uestions of balance will make it hard to fuse this unit with western
Surope, except within a wider framework.

If a union of the east European countries apart from Russia is
ndeed possible the West should welcome and encourage it. Poly-
entrism is an improvement on the hegemony that went before it;
ut if taken to its logical conclusion it is no more than balkanisation.
he geographical connotations of the term are too evocative for the
nstability of such a system — or rather non-system — to be ignored.
Vhat is needed is an "organised rebuttal" of hegemony, as Profes-
or Hallstein described the European Community, rather than the
isorganised rebuttal that polycentrism represents. A united eastern
Surope, standing between Russia and the West and too strong to be
ominated by either side, would be a much more stable arrangement:
either hegemony, nor polycentrism, but perhaps oligocentrism.

Such a union would have to come about with Russian agreement —
ne Red Army is stationed in some of the countries concerned. It
ould, however, be necessary in any case to proceed by stages, with
or example an intensification of bilateral economic relations between
ne prospective members and specific projects like the lower Danube
cheme. This would reassure the Russians that no sharp and sudden
ealignment was contemplated. It cannot, indeed, be the case that the
ussians would oppose all schemes for union: The Czechs and Poles
ave discussed a far-reaching plan of economic association, and it
as not Russian opposition but the Czech's fear of Poland's larger
ze (absence of that balance which is a desirable condition of union)
nat prevented agreement. There is no reason to suppose that the
ussians would stand in the way of a wider union in eastern Europe;
at people in the West would have to avoid seeing the process as a
efeat for Russia than the establishment of the European Community
as a defeat for the United States.

If this union were realised, then Nato and Warsaw Pact areas
ould contain four major units — western Europe, eastern Europe,
merica, and Russia: what might be called a Greater Europe divided
to four main parts. These units would themselves be of sizes that
ould constitute a reasonable balance should political and economic

conditions evolve so that closer relations between them were possible
At the appropriate time their association could be cemented by a
political settlement that would include arms control, agreement on
economic collaboration, and a solution of the German problem (which
would then be, in relation to the whole of the area and the problems
involved, of the order of magnitude of the Saar problem in th
fifties).

It would be possible for the West to encourage this whole process
not only by means of better trading relations through, for example
closer east European involvement in Gatt, but also by judicious as
sistance such as has been suggested by Professor Brzezinski. The
transport system of eastern Europe might be a suitable object of aid
in the first instance, with stress on provisions to facilitate traffic be
tween the east European countries whose union it is desired to pro
mote, although communications through these countries from western
Europe to Russia should at the same time be improved. A ''Marshal
Plan'' for the east European economies as a whole might follow a
the time of the political settlement.

It may be objected that the sketching out of such grand designs
is not a realistic exercise : useless and perhaps harmful. Some of th
precedents are discouraging. Dulles's concept of roll-back, the Bolshe
viks' world revolution, and de Gaulle's concert of European power
have all been potent sources of dangerous actions. But all political
acts are based on a view of the future, and the most dangerous view
of all, the one that is absolutely certain to be wrong is that nothing
will change. No more is claimed for the view put forward here than
that it is possible, it is desirable, and it is therefore worth trying t
bring about.

David Mitrany

The Prospect of Integration:
Federal or Functional?

. . .

The six partners in the EEC . . . have stated unambiguously
ow they saw the end-product of "closer political integration." All
he student has to go by are the Fouchet-Cattani proposals and the
esiderata of the Political Committee of the European Parliament as
ffering such formal evidence as there is; and all one can do is to
ee how these relate to accepted patterns of political theory and
xperience. But even that is only half the problem. There are two
ides to any political picture — its form and its fitness. Form is the
isible and classifiable element, but what makes it right or wrong is
he second component of any political system, the social ambience in
·hich it has to operate. If the Governments, who must carry the
onsequences of their words, have shrunk from being more precise
n what they had in mind, the "Europeans" through years of
isistent pressure have failed to probe into the utterly new social
limate for which with unquestioning assurance they have offered
n old transatlantic plant. As Mr. Thornton Read remarked recently,
ith a touch of impatient sharpness, "In politics as in war certainty
a symptom of blindness."[1]

THE REGIONAL FALLACY

The restlessness which now makes life uneasy all the world over
rings from a combination of two revolutionary currents: (i) the

Reprinted from *Journal of Common Market Studies*, IV (December 1965),
th the permission of the author and publisher.

[1] *Military Policy in a Changing Political Context*, Center for International
udies, Princeton, N.J., December 1964, p. 11.

end of the colonial era and the mass-making of new states; (ii) at th
same time, a universal social revolution which through economic plan
ning for social security and welfare is hardening every state int
something more truly "organic" than anything known before; (iii
and all that has to be fitted into the high effort to build up a lastin
international system of law and order. This is the world we face nov
To pass the test of historic fitness any political experiment will hav
to take in the first two verities, which seem irreversible, and help t
contain and guide them towards the third, so that we may comple
the democratic ladder of responsible government. Perhaps in 191
this ideal was premature; nuclear power and the opening up of spac
have now made it the foremost priority within which every oth
human aspiration — communal and individual, material and moral -
is inescapably enmeshed. The reaction to the Second World Wa
brought up pleas for world government and world federation, whi
others retreated into ideas for regional union as an intermediate stag
between the national state and the world.[2] It all depends whether
is meant to promote closed and exclusive regional unions or simpl
for administrative devolution within a universal system. "Given th
complexities of modern life and the restlessness of the mass of ne
states, it is evident that the demands likely to be made upon an
central international authority are bound to be very heavy, an
perhaps excessive. It might be all to the good if that burden could b
relieved by entrusting regional groups with the right and duty
deal in the first instance with any local issues through regional cou
cils and regional courts, with the right of appeal to the central counc
and court should the local effort fail." "Such a scheme of devoluti
would also have politically an educational value in that it wou
encourage the local groups . . . through the exercise of direct respo
sibility to learn the need for and the habit of give and take in the
mutual relations" — as proximity and likeness have not always bre
political tolerance among them. It might also, as a secondary adva
tage, help to ease the problem of representation at the centre.[3]

The possible use of such regional devolution has hardly been e
plored so far. But the regional idea would have vastly differe
consequences if used to set up closed political units. "The new uni

[2] Already the League of Nations had been dismissed by Coudenhove-Kaler
in his *Pan-Europa* as having an "abstract character" because it lacked su
intermediate regional unions.

[3] David Mitrany, "Delusions of Regional Unity," in B. Landheer (ed
Limits and Problems of European Integration, The Hague, 1963, pp. 40-1.

ould then not support but would cut across the jurisdiction and
uthority of any international system. The argument about the need
: an intermediate step is obviously only valid if the regional unions
re to be open unions; whereas if they are to be closed and exclusive
nions, the more fully and effectively they are integrated the deeper
ust in fact be the division they cause in the emergent unity of the
orld.''[4] Most of its ''European'' champions have seen their regional
nion as leading, from the start or by speedy stages, to a federal
ate; and experienced men like MM. Robert Schuman, Spaak, Mon-
:t and others, have urged a Western union also as an essential base
r any global unification. So had Mazzini and his friends been
:voutly convinced that the nation-state was the essential gateway
 a world at peace. But it is curious, and perhaps suggestive, that
e idea should find favour now when it no longer makes sense politi-
lly or economically, and certainly not historically. It did not pre-
nt itself at all to the mind of the two Hague conferences at the turn
' the century, and the Covenant of 1919 touched it but cautiously;
 regional emendation was suggested in 1923 but was quickly rected; it was tried in the Locarno treaties of 1926 but achieved even
cally no more than a momentary easing of strain. Miss Sarah
ambaugh, the American jurist, pointed out some years ago that
ter the first World War Europe and Asia on the one side and the
.S.A. on the other, tried two opposite approaches to security based
 differing philosophies: the League system could not be tried out
lly as long as America remained neutral, the American system had
free run, but insofar as they were regional systems neither worked.
The League system did not fail because it was not regional, but
ther because it was regional in effect.''[5] ''Geographical association
 longer corresponds to the actual interests of neighbours'' — a
ew echoed later in the group appointed by the Council of Europe,
at the interests of Western countries now overflow in all directions;
d she quoted from Carl Hambro that ''it is the sea and air lanes,
t overland continental traffic, that holds us together in close asso-
ation.''

From an international standpoint this is merely quoting the ob-
ous. But even from a regional position it seems strange that it
ould spring into favour in Western Europe. The early European
eamers of world peace — Crucé and St. Pierre, Kant and Rousseau,

D.M., ib., p. 41.
''Regional and Universal Solutions'' in *Regionalism and World Organiza-
n*, Washington, D.C., 1944, pp. 49-50.

and the rest — never thought of it: to them Europe was their un
verse. In later days of trade and colonial expansion Europe wante
to be the universe, and the Concert of Europe was the controllin
voice of the political world. Is there some meaning in the fact tha
this urge for European union should have come when Europe n
longer dominates? Europe created "nationality," but out of th
same fount of liberating principles it also created internationalism
Yet now, when its ideas have spread to the four quarters of the glot
and the prospect seems ripe at last for a general system, Europe
being urged to shrink back within the narrow comforts of her ow
walls. Western union — like Great Britain's eventual connection wit
it — has been urged above all as essential for economic well-bein
through the creation of a large-scale common market. A paper fro
the Council of Europe had summarized the economic case in th
simple proposition that national markets were too small, while worl
integration was impracticable.[6] The argument thus relies (i) on a
outdated physical-political antithesis; and from that it proceeds
(ii) the "specious" assumption that national markets were th
normal economic working unit, ignoring the immense web of inte
national trade and also the numerous intra-national links in all th
main sectors of production.

It seems a doubtful issue, but I am neither competent to discuss
nor am I concerned with economic regionalism except in its politic
repercussions.[7] And as to these, whatever the material results, th
mercantilist practices of economic planning will of necessity have
be applied still more forcefully in a regional union, which will ha

[6] Research Directorate of the Secretariat-General of the Council of Euro
The Present State of Economic Integration in Western Europe, Strasbourg, Ju
1955, p. 94.

[7] As references to the economic success of the United States are especia
persistent, one may refer to the paper by S. Dell, "Economic Integration a
the American Example," *The Economic Journal*, March, 1959 — (i) It quo
the studies of the late L. Rostas to the effect that "relative productivity is
no way related to the size of the market. This points to the fact that t
optimum plant (or firm) and specialization can be achieved within the lim
of a smaller market" (e.g. Swedish and Swiss metallurgical achievement). (
It quotes as "particularly damaging" the findings of Erwin Rothbarth a
others that United States industry was more efficient than British industry
long ago as 1870, if not earlier, when its internal market was smaller than t
English market. (iii) It doubts whether regional *per capita* income differen
are now any smaller in the United States, with its vast integrated economy, th
in Western Europe, with its patchwork of independent states. — It thus refu
the assumption that economic integration by itself leads to greater productiv
and to uniform development throughout a "large" region.

many more strands to re-adjust and pull together, than in any one ate.[8] There must be something in the fact that whereas in England co-ordinating Ministry of Economic Affairs was set up only in the itumn of 1964, by a new Labour Government, the Common Market six sovereign states was from the outset placed under the management of an essentially "bureaucratic" Commission. The same considerations apply with even greater force to the political factors. In eir case the common interest cannot be visibly defined, while they ten touch imponderable and fugitive sentiments. To build up a hesive loyalty national movements have often had to disinter or vent all sorts of historical, social and emotional affinities, above all keep alive the fear of some common external danger. Regionalism, arting with more differences than affinities, would have to go even rther in that. Western Union has been argued all along as vital for tting Europe in a state of economic and political self-defence, "to oid coming under Russian domination without at the same time cepting permanent American overlordship";[9] though some supporters might wish to reverse the order of precedence of the two ghtmares. Western man used to pride himself on his humanistic smopolitan outlook, but now even men of standing have come to talk the need to develop a "European personality." It would not be fair saddle them with the aberrations of the Count Coudenhove-Kalergi, e first recipient of the Charlemagne prize,[10] but what is that "European personality"? Does it begin and end at the limits of the Common Market? Even the formal Martino Report can say that "there is question of dissolving Europe in a wider *ensemble* in which her rsonality would be lost"![11] In the nature of things, it must be mething that both binds and divides, and by implication also something which is not there but has to be brought into being. Indeed, one

See David Mitrany, "The International Consequences of National Planning," *Yale Review*, September 1947 — which argued, incidentally, that as dical reformers would be the foremost practitioners of planning, and as planing must be guided and controlled by the state, Socialists and Labour — even re Marxists — will of necessity find themselves state-bound, will themselves "nationalized."

Letter from a Liberal parliamentary candidate to *The Guardian*, August 1961.

0 In his search for a binding element he has discovered a "Western nationty," a European "race," and even a "European soul" which was emphatily different from the "American soul." "The cultural goal of Europe is to ke the European race conscious of its Western nationality," and many ilar exhortations can be found in *Pan-Europa* and throughout his writings.

1 P. 8, para. 47.

general reason for demanding an elected parliament seems to be belief that "direct elections are the best, perhaps the only way stimulating mass interest and participation in European unific tion."[12]

The making of "Europe" is not to be kept merely to economi and politics, but has to bring into relief also *"l'unité du patrimoi spirituel et culturel de l'Europe."*[13] A strange argument in a serio source, in view of the long sad history of Europe's political and re gious divisions, many more and fiercer than the conflicts with As and the Americas, and now again cut in half ideologically. If the is a "unique characteristic of European civilization, in contrast wi Eastern and other civilizations, it is that it always has been an op civilization . . . [and so] able to permeate the whole world with h political, social and cultural outlook and experience. . . ."[14] When o thinks of the past humanistic glories of the ancient universities Paris and Oxford, of Prague and Bologna, how strange it is to faced now, just when science is opening up the farthest ways to out space and the planets"[15] — and when with our Ariel-like means communication all knowledge is instantly "universalized" — to faced with a proposal for a "European University where things a to be taught from a specifically 'European' angle, so as to reinfor Europe's cultural and scientific potential."[16] Perhaps it is not o but in character that this narrowing scheme should have been p into the Euratom Treaty — although the new University is to tea also economics and politics, sociology and psychology!

Will the new "third world" so eager for knowledge and develo ment, and in which we have to compete with new revolutionary i fluences, not suspect any cultural product labelled as distinct "European"? The very concept of a closed regional union is a cc

[12] Hugh Beesly, "Direct Elections to European Parliament" in *Limits o Problems of European Integration*, The Hague, 1963, p. 85. He would also some of the armoury of the P.R. man: "The European flag, a European U versity, a European satellite, goods-trains marked 'Europe' — all these will h in the gradual growth of a European patriotism" (ibid., p. 87).

[13] Martino Report, p. 6, para. 38. (Report to the European Parliament, Ma 22, 1965.)

[14] Europe has had "an unusually dynamic history"; "the end of the Eu pean Age in history is not necessarily the end of Europe, or of a civilizat which, though inseparable from the European heritage, has ceased to be exc sively European." — Oscar Halecki, *The Limits and Divisions of Europe History*, London, 1950, p. 21.

[15] David Mitrany, "Delusions of Regional Unity," p. 44.

[16] *The Observer*, London, May 28, 1961.

adiction of the historic European idea; and the farther it moves
·om the sheer material sector, the more does its synthetic nature
and exposed.[17] But even if these inbreeding efforts and devices —
·osed economic planning, exclusive political institutions, the cultiva-
·on of a regional patriotism — even if all this were to serve the goal
· a (limited) European union, it can hardly bear the argument that
· also is the highway to a wider international unity.

"Whatever proclaims a difference creates a division," said Dr.
·hnson. The "ecumenical" argument for European union has car-
·ed least conviction of all, and not only among outsiders. One may
·ote a few points of doubt from within the movement, not because
·ey are critical but because they are evident and restore the balance
· view. As to "inwardness," it seems likely that in its first period
· would be "so concentrated on the task of keeping a precarious
·nion together and creating an identity of its own that it would have
·ttle time and energy left for acquiring a global vision and tackling
·obal tasks. It would not be the first time in history when a new
·ation would seek strength in isolation."[18] Dr. Hallstein in fact sees
·is to be inevitable: "There is no public association, no State and
· association of States which does not begin by attending to the
·elfare and security of its own members. [This is] the *raison d'être*
· every political community."[19] As to outlook, "the very penetration
·to these fields [foreign policy and defence] tends to divert atten-
·on among the Six from the aim of being a stepping-stone for better
·ternational co-operation, to that of merely becoming a new 'big
·ower' "[20] — Dr. Hallstein's "sovereign voice." "There is no special
·ason to believe that a federal Europe would suddenly be guided
·xclusively by sweet reasonableness and self-restraint."[21] "In the per-
·ective of the next ten or twenty years the idea of Europe as a
·hird force' will look even more unrealistic than it does to-day."[22]
· s to the limits of the union, the search for a true European solution
· requires more than a solution of little Europe within the framework
· the six, the seven, or the fifteen. The task which the European

---

[17] Hermann Jahrreiss dealt closely and sharply with the "European" idea,
·pecially Coudenhove-Kalergi's *Pan-Europa*, from the standpoint of interna-
·nal legal development. *Europa als Rechtseinheit*, Leipzig, 1929, pp. 28 ff.

[18] J. L. Heldring, *Internationale Spectator* (special issue, The Hague, April 8,
·65), p. 545.

[19] Op. cit., p. 20.

[20] Dr. Alting von Geusau, *Internationale Spectator*, p. 488.

[21] J. L. Heldring, ibid., p. 542.

[22] G. M. Nederhorst, *Limits and Problems*, p. 67.

federalists set themselves in the resistance movement during the fir
post-war years to create in Europe the political and social conditio
for an all-European peace still remains to be solved. This is a pr
gramme which does not accept as inevitable the *status quo* thrust up
us by Soviet policy."[23]

THE FEDERAL FALLACY

Of the many assumptions which have gone into the making of t
"European" creed the most persistent has been the idea of feder
tion; and the federal idea in fact traverses most aspects and issues
European union, both in its internal organization and in its relatic
to the wider international problem. It is an old idea which has a
peared often in plans and literature, but all that has little to say
the substance of the present appeal; except that it always express
some antagonism. The Republican call in the middle of the nineteen
century, with Victor Hugo in the lead, for an European union
"free peoples" was little beyond a Radical "holy alliance" in t
struggle against autocracy; and Cobden's shrill call in 1856 w
pointedly aimed at Russia. The Pan-Europa vicariously urged aft
the First World War was both anti-Bolshevik and anti-Anglo-Saxo
but it never had any solid outline or more than a dubious and chang
able support; the only British politician of rank to have favoured
openly, Leo Amery, was also the only one to have joined Beave
brook's Imperial Crusade — a position as "puristically consistent
that of the anti-Semites who applaud the Zionist ideal of a Jewi
return to Palestine."[24]

Of the inter-war schemes, that proposed by Briand in 1929 was t
only solid one, and also the only one to offer some comparison wi
the present ideas. Though it came before the nuclear explosion ar
the mass of new states, the overwhelming view was that any Eur
pean union must avoid all exclusiveness and must remain an organ
part of the League of Nations;[25] and at Geneva most governmen

[23] Ibid., p. 67. Even M. Jean Monnet, who among "Europeans" stands on
distinguished level of his own, could claim through the recent declaration of l
Action Committee that European union was the best way to achieve Germa
re-unification. Does it not seem obvious instead, as Russia refuses to recogni
the EEC, fears the consolidation of a Western political union in which s
believes Germany would be dominant, that she would be less likely to give
her hold on the buffer formed by Eastern Germany?

[24] D.M. "Pan-Europa — A Hope or a Danger?" *Political Quarterly*, Londo
Sept.-Dec. 1930.

[25] See, e.g., Edouard Herriot, *Europe*, Paris, 1930.

ared that, "no matter what the intentions of its promoters, the
ontinental union might drain the League of Nations of its substance
nd compromise its universality" — therefore they favoured eco-
omic but not political action.[26] The idea of European union could
ardly have been a natural product as it never led to actual unity.
he present call for a federal union is something quite new; it goes
irther in scope, but as a consequence it also is narrower in outlook.
s its advocates hope to make Europe free of the new American
ower by emulating its successful federal formula, a brief look at
1e American analogy should throw light on the fitness of the idea
or international integration under the conditions of our time.

When in spite of the crisis the Supreme Court threw out the
'ational Recovery Act, in 1935, President Roosevelt pointed out that
1 the "horse and buggy" days when the Constitution was written
ome 90 per cent of the population lived in self-sufficient local com-
unities. Even more to the point, the view of democracy then ruling
'anted government to do as little as possible, and the federal system
'as shaped to that outlook. It was an invention meant to deal with
revolutionary situation and to unite thirteen undeveloped states in
1 isolated continent, and with "more common problems coming to
1em in the future than they had separate history binding them to
1e past." The revolutionary situation of the nuclear age hardly
1swers to a pattern which gave every citizen an absolute "right to
irry arms." To be at all valid the analogy would have, in the first
lace, to reflect not what happened nearly two hundred years ago,
ut whether if the forty-eight states had each developed to full sep-
rate political and economic independence they could be induced to
3derate now.[27] Concrete evidence for an answer is supplied by the
ifficulties which all the old federal governments have met since the
Var in the everyday performance of their tasks — in such non-
olitical matters as highways and banking and health services, etc. —
Canada and Australia as in America; even in placid Switzerland
1ost of the referenda since the War have gone against the federal
overnment. They have even been faced with threats of secession
·om Quebec and Western Australia, and in the U.S.A. after two
undred years and a bloody civil war, the issue of State rights still
3mains a perennial irritant.

Sometimes these federal governments have actually been helped by
1ternational commitments in matters in which they were obstructed

[26] Mirkine-Guetzevitch and Georges Scelle, op. cit., pp. 16-17.
[27] See D.M., "Functional Federalism," *Common Cause*, Chicago, Nov. 1950.

by their own internal constitutions.[28] All that can still happen i
federations which by now are well-established national societies. Ye
the reaction is not unnatural. A federal system rests upon a settle
balance of power: any addition to the central functions alters tha
balance, and with cumulative and permanent effect. But wider ev
dence shows that it is not merely a matter of holding on to the lette
of an old compact, but more generally a reaction to the new tende₁
cies of government. We have not sufficiently noted the centrifuga
internal regionalism which in recent years has arisen or hardene
also in old unitary states — in Belgium as in Italy, in France and i
Great Britain; and, significantly, in the new federation of Indi₁
India had been provided with a more modern constitution and ha
inherited a unified administration and a strong sense of national unit
forged in the struggle for independence; yet since then she had bee
troubled by cross-regional strains which had not existed before an
has had to accept new anachronistic sub-divisions in the shape c
language and such states. This widespread experience must mean tha
one effect of centralized planning is to repel local sections with
marked interest or characteristic of their own, and that the reactio
inevitably turns the mind to dis-union. It should be obvious that th
wider the limits of association and the more disparate the parts, th
more difficult it must prove to accommodate the marginal elements.[2]

The "European" federalists have been so fascinated by a readil
convenient formula that they have neither asked how it works wher
it exists, nor whether its origins bear any relation to the problem c
uniting a group of states in the present social ambience. It is thi

[28] The point is developed with some typical illustrations in D.M., "The Fun
tional Approach to World Organization," *International Affairs*, London, Jul
1948. — Indirect proof was offered a few years ago by the attempt of U.
Senator Bricker to make such international acts subject to separate approval b
the States.

[29] It should also be obvious that the "federalizing process" (see below) wi
remain very brittle until fully accomplished. In the interim period nothing
agreed beyond an intention, as in the Rome treaty; and any change of gover₁
ment in the participating states may bring changes of outlook and intentio
"Experience shows that political trends often change in certain countries wit
disconcerting swiftness" and sharply alter policy, "merely as a consequence c
the normal working of democratic institutions and not because of any calculate
Machiavellism" (Jan Hostie, in *Regionalism and World Organization*, pp. 5;
8). Political attempts must remain exposed to "politics"; the late Dr. Hug
Dalton, e.g., insisted that British Labour could join in a European union on₁
with other Socialist governments. Therefore, says Mr. Hostie, "internation₁
institutions must be built to withstand at least the likeliest of the politic₁
shifts" — which seems possible only through functional arrangements.

lestion of sociological fitness which is at issue here. But once again
le has first to interpolate a theoretical clarification, because the
ctical vagueness of the ''Europeans'' has now been fed by a new
lesis from Professor Carl Friedrich, who has a close knowledge of
le European experiment and is a reputed authority on the federal
lea. In two recent papers[30] Professor Friedrich has tried to replace
le established meaning of federation as a particular type of political
nion with the idea of a ''process by which a number of separate
olitical organizations, be they states or any other kind of associa-
ons, enter into arrangements'' for doing various things jointly.
ny and all of these actions belong into a general ''federalizing
rocess.'' Even in old federations, he says, there is never a constant
osition between unifying and diversifying forces, rather an oscil-
ting process with sometimes one sometimes the other in the ascend-
it. That is no doubt true, but it is true of all government; and it
least true of federal government. A new union or association is not
inceivable without some formal compact, whose main purpose is
recisely to delimit the competence of the various organs. That is
hy it has to provide for an arbitral Court, which Professor Fried-
ch lists among the essentials of a federal framework, and why it
inerally puts stiff obstacles in the way of that ''process'' of change
- which Professor Friedrich thinks should be not as difficult as it is
l the U.S.A., but neither ''so easy that the federation will not hold
igether.'' The very purpose of any such written compact or statute
precisely to introduce the factor of fixity in the index of power;
id nothing is so fixed as a federal constitution. It is intended to
ithstand the constant pressures from the ordinary claims of govern-
ent as from sectional interests, and so ''hold together'' the whole.
has been far easier to change the position and powers of the British
rown by what one may fairly call a functional adaptation than it
is been to change the position and powers of the federal authority
l the U.S.A. or Canada or Australia by amendment of their written
institutions.

''The function of a true political thinker,'' said the late Professor
obhouse, ''is not to predict events, but to point out causal connec-
ons.'' With all political systems now shaken by a social revolution
is all the more the part of the political scientist to try to project the

---

[30] Papers for an Oxford meeting on Federation, Sept. 1963, quoted also by
iriam Camps, *What Kind of Europe?*, pp. 126-7; and for the Sixth World
ingress of the IPSA, Geneva, Sept. 1964.

true implications of the schemes and expedients of the practisin
politician; whereas the likely effect of such permissive teaching
illustrated by Dr. Hallstein's lecture — to use an experienced an
authoritative case. He starts from a correct statement of establishe
theory: "The position is that federation is one state but the confe
eration is a league of states" (p. 15). After that his thought becom
elusive. The Community would leave to "each member its ultima
sovereign power," but it had to be a "firm union" (p. 13) and
must speak with "a 'sovereign' voice in world politics" (p. 14). 1
that end, after economic and social life, trade and foreign policy an
"the sinews of war must be made Community matter," leading
the "integration of defence policy" (pp. 16-17). "Integration
thus a process and not a static thing, and this process is one th
tends towards complete federation, that is to a federal state." An
the argument ends in the dismantling of the initial statement: "T
conclusion is that there is no hard distinction between federation an
confederation, obliging us to choose" (p. 17).[31]

We have not been helped by such recent inflationary usage
"democracy," yet that is an abstract generic term which might l
filled with any content, from *laisser faire* to Socialist planning. B
terms of specific constitutional classification are meant to tell
within fairly clear limits what kind of political prospect we are calle
upon to underwrite with our votes. That is all the more proper in
new and far-reaching political adventure; and for an electora
which so far has nowhere been faced yet by a special "European
party or by a special election on a clear issue of European unio
Could an election for an European parliament ask the electorate fro

[31] Professor Friedrich's "any kind of association" presumably could me
that OEEC and COMECON, EFTA and NATO and the Arab League are a
engaged in a "federalizing process," whether they mean it or not. — The kir
of confusing guidance which such terminological licence can bring was offer
to the Oxford Conference by Prof. W. H. Morris-Jones, as quoted by Pro
Friedrich (Geneva paper, Note 10): "The Commonwealth, although as a who
it is no kind of federalism, can usefully be regarded as a collection of parti:
functional, intermittent federations, composed of different members at differe
times for different purposes." Perhaps in fairness to M. Denis de Rougemo
one should note that years ago he had anticipated this free-wheeling "federali
ing" conception in a pamphlet which said that European federation would gro
by "here an economic agreement, there a cultural affinity," two Church
sharing Communion, above all by private individuals creating "a series of ne
works for the exchange of ideas"; indeed, there was apparently nothing poli
cal about "federalizing," a federation is formed "not by working from t
centre outwards or through the medium of governments" (*Totalitarianism a*
Federalism, London, 1950).

remen to Brindisi simply to "Vote for our federalizing process"?
he thesis is all the more dubious from such a learned source[32] be-
use at the same time Professor Friedrich prescribes (with one
ception) all the orthodox ingredients as necessary for a federal
amework: an arbitral Court and provision for amendments — both
' which imply not only a written but a firm Constitution — and a
int working executive; and if a federal executive no doubt also a
deral parliament. And here we come to those matters which are at
e heart of the European problem, as of any political system,
amely, the range of its functions and the conditions under which
ey have to be performed. Fortunately there is one aspect on which
l students of politics are likely to be agreed — the vast change in
e nature of government and, as a consequence, in the respective
ositions of executive and parliament. The original intent of the
emocratic idea was "that Government should be kept to a minimum,
nd that minimum was to be guided by an informed and sensible
ectorate and controlled by its independent representatives." In all
ese respects we have gone far towards the opposite pole, even in
emocratic countries. "Government now tends to be omnipresent
nd, where present, almost omnipotent, if we accept, as we must, Sir
rnest Barker's definition that government authority is 'the sum
f its functions.' "[33] For any new federal experiment, if meant to be
ee to develop the modern attributes of a welfare society, the work-
g prototype is likely to be not the U.S. Constitution of 1787 but
mething nearer to the federal system of the U.S.S.R.

The two functions always conceded as belonging to a federal ex-
utive have been defence and foreign policy (and trade). Defence
recently as 1914 was still a matter of a limited force with a limited
rmoury; but which part of resources and of industrial potential
uld now be said to remain outside the range of Dr. Hallstein's
sinews of war" — and not only in time of war, but throughout the
nger periods of peace? Which part of economic and financial policy
now outside the scope of foreign policy? Nor is it possible to en-
isage any limit to the spread of centralized public action; the con-
nuous pressure for new inventions and discoveries, on which the

---

[32] No other authorities have suggested such an inflation of the federal idea.
ne need not go back to the classical work of Jellinek, but among leading con-
mporary writers neither Prof. C. K. Wheare, in general theory, nor Prof. A.
. Goodhardt, as an authority on the American system, has propounded any-
ing of the kind.

[33] D.M., "Parliamentary Democracy and Poll Democracy," *Parliamentary
ffairs*, London, Winter 1955-6, p. 17.

economic sector is as dependent as defence, can generally be co
trolled and provided for only by some central authority. The politic
balance-sheet of these considerations should be self-evident. If t
all-inclusive union which the "Europeans" want were to be base
on a restrictive federal balance-of-power it will not be capable
growing freely into the kind of planned welfare society which mar
our time; whereas if it were to be set up without the tradition
federal restraints, it must grow — as it will have more, and mo
mixed, elements to weld together — into a more unitary politic
system than any existing federation.[34]

"The sum of these functions," not any preconceived formula, mu
in the end shape the character of an eventual European executiv
and hence also of an European parliament. As executive and parli
ment will be the pivotal organs of any fully-fledged union — we ma
ignore for this brief review the piquant question of who would be i
head, an elected President with hereditary Kings and Queens und
him, or perhaps the several national rulers by rotation — it is stri
ing how perfunctorily they have been examined in the prolific liter
ture on European union; indeed, the nature of the executive h
been given hardly a glance.[35] Most of the recent argument has e
pressed an anxiety to give the European parliament some real pow
of control over policy as against that which now falls to the Counc
of Ministers — the "popular" as against the "governmental" facto
The argument has been put with cogency and urgency in the Martir
Report and may be justified in itself — as long as the present a
rangements last.[36] But it is dubious as a general argument, an

[34] Dr. J. W. Beijen, Dutch financial expert and diplomat, has recently insiste
on the importance of the social task, saying that a modern government could n
give up its freedom to use economic and financial policy for social ends unle
that responsibility were taken over by some common authority. "The Europe
Communities were conceived to do just that. . . . Too often the Communiti
are still considered as merely a means to increase the economic strength of t
area. In essence, their task in the social field is fundamental." The inclusion
agriculture enhances that aspect, for everywhere agricultural policy is "for
most social policy and only secondary economic policy. It is the conduct of soci
policy which makes the Community into something different in essence fro
other forms of economic co-operation between Governments." — *Internationa
Spectator*, pp. 466-7.

[35] Dr. Nord in *Internationale Spectator* mentions the need for "an executi
sufficiently independent and strong," but he had no occasion to go beyond tha
— One of the Reports to the European Parliament mentioned a curious pr
posal, later abandoned, for an autonomous Secretary-General with powers li
those of the United Nations Secretary-General and with the sole task of pressi
for integration.

[36] Op. cit., especially pp. 5-6.

eculiar in its immediate assumptions. It is peculiar that a body of elegated parliamentarians should think it possible to be trans-ormed, and fairly speedily, into a representative Parliament, with ommensurate powers, without making it clear that this could not be ntil an equally representative common executive had taken charge f affairs — of affairs intended to spread quickly and widely into ew fields. The making of a comprehensive union could hardly be left o an amorphous "popular" assembly and a Commission of "tech-ocrats." And in a more general way, the expectation of command-ng powers for such a parliament overlooks the strong contrary cur-ent, and one bound to prevail if the wish for full union is fulfilled; ne could almost lay it down as a law of modern politics that the owers of executive and parliament are bound to move in inverse atio to each other. There are three general reasons for this. First, he enormous increase in government activity reduces the possibility f parliamentary initiative and control; that is bound to be more cute in a multi-state union with its wider jurisdiction and therefore reater complexity in policy-making. Second, the same conditions ave added weight to party organization and constricted the indepen-ence of individual members (both admitted and justified by the late ord Morrison in his book *Government and Parliament*). As one annot foresee how party alignments and organization would develop n an elected European parliament that is one particular point that ust remain open.

The third reason is the most active and relevant. The "wider the ctivity of the state the wider its direct contacts and relations with rganized groups of interest, a trend as conspicuous in Scandinavia s in U.S.A. Many points of economic and social policy are now ttled, or modified in application, through private bargaining be-veen government departments and professional and other organized roups, without benefit of Parliament."[37] A whole new system of olicy-making has thus grown up, not through any arbitrary imposi-on but through the inescapable sweep and urgencies of planned overnment, a system of "government by committee."[38] This particu-ar tendency, above all others, would inevitably be strongly at work a new multi-state union. Its administration could hardly work un-

[37] D.M., *Parliamentary Affairs*, Winter 1955-6, p. 19. — A few years ago an merican observer of the British administrative scene, Prof. Samuel Beer, of arvard, went so far as to describe what he had seen as "quasi-corporatism."
[38] PEP study, "Advisory Committees in British Government," London, 1960. K. C. Wheare, "Government by Committee," Oxford, 1953.

less it were preponderantly "bureaucratic."[39] The wider and mor
varied the jurisdiction to be encompassed, the firmer will its plan
ning have to be, and in the same measure less amenable to protracte
debate and detailed control by a motley parliamentary chamber a
the centre. Local variations in claims and interests, and the multi
plicity of organized groups, could not be attended to in any othe
way so as to gain acceptance for uniform legislation and administra
tive rules. While, therefore, it is a fair claim that the present Com
munities (though it was not true of ECSC) fall short in democrati
content as long as they lack a representative assembly, it is a
illusion to think that in a "more perfect union" an elected parlia
ment will gather unto itself more power than is now left to nationa
parliaments even in the best of democratic states. It is likely to b
less: it will have neither the cohesion nor the acquired traditions o
a national parliament; while the executive will be under greate
pressure of public business but also less exposed to the watchfulnes
of parties and press and popular opinion. Warning that "Europ
is not a nation," the Secretary-General of the European Parliamen
Dr. H. R. Nord, went on to say that "It follows that attempts shoul
not be made to solve the problem of European parliamentary contr
merely by trying to make the European Parliament look more lik
a national one. We are faced with a new and original phenomeno
and the future role of the Parliament should be assessed in the ligh
of the distribution of power within the Community."[40]

Because of the neglect of such an assessment some other derivativ
aspects of the parliamentary problem have been passed by altogethe
The European Parliament has for some years pressed for direc
elections with universal suffrage so as "to associate the peoples" i
the work of political integration, though as members of their hom
parliaments they must be aware of the spreading apathy of mas
electorates everywhere. Constituencies are too large for close contac
and persuasion, and the public issues too many and too technical t
allow for more than very broad party appeals at election time. Wha
range of constituencies could serve for an oversize Continental elec
tion — a million, two million names on the electoral roll? What kin
of concrete "European" issues could be put by candidates to so vas

[39] Camps, op. cit., p. 115. — It has been noted by several observers that th
attitude of the EEC Commission towards political union had acquired a sug
gestive ambivalence; it now seems to distrust moves towards fuller politica
union, with some dominant executive organ at the head, but favours greate
powers for the European Parliament.

[40] *Internationale Spectator*, p. 689.

nd mixed an electorate to make as good sense in Sicily as in Brabant, n the Ruhr and in Brittany, so as to produce that common "Euro- ean consciousness"? That brings up a final and a more serious issue han the awkwardness of electoral mechanics. A fair "European onsciousness" has been achieved at Strasbourg by the simple device f keeping the anti-Europeans out. It was perhaps not unnatural to end to Strasbourg party members who at least were in general sym- athy with the institution.[41] But it was a drastic act to exclude the Communists altogether when they are such a formidable electoral orce in Italy and in France. What is to be done about this in a eneral election? Only two alternatives seem possible: (i) submit to he fundamentals of universal suffrage and so let in from the start a owerful element opposed to the very idea of Western union and llied ideologically to the hostile Communist world; or (ii) exclude he Communists and so pollute the democratic claim from the start. This, moreover, may make them the gathering core for other dissident lements and so, paradoxically, on this issue help to widen their ational appeal and make their outcast status still more indefensible.

Perhaps there is no more curious sidelight into the state of mind, r the tactics, of the "Europeans" than the way they have all along ssumed that direct elections by universal suffrage must bring them opular support. The probability has simply been ignored that such direct electoral challenge would also provide the first occasion when he various, now still disjointed groups and sections who, for one eason or another, dislike or doubt the idea of Western union, would e brought together into something like an organized opposition.

THE FUNCTIONAL ALTERNATIVE

So much of what precedes had to be given to a critical examination f the federal idea because what matters here is not its theoretical irtues but its fitness for multi-national association — even within he arbitrary limits of a region. That people should have turned to it s not unnatural: it seemed the only available formula, because our olitical thinking has been so long rooted in the notion that every uthority must be linked to a given territory.[42] For the rest, it is

[41] French extreme groups have been kept away and even Italy in effect ex- ludes the Opposition. — Murray Forsyth, *The Parliament of the European 'ommunities,* PEP, London, 1964, p. 21. — Even M. Monnet's Action Com- ittee for a United States of Europe, supposed to include heads of parties and f trade unions in the six countries, has excluded Gaullists and Communists.
[42] This came out partly in the criticism of M. J. Petot, that the experience of

plain that European federalism has been a blend of myth and som
very mixed sentiments.[43] That is proved in another way by th
readiness of moderate "Europeans" for something more flexible
"The majority of us do not regard the unification of Europe with th
emotions of people acquiring a new fatherland," writes Prof. Sam
kalden; there is a need for "a diversity of new organizations fo
specific needs and interests," and a "plurality" of them is already
available in which the value of the European communities, "but als
theïr necessary limitation, find clear expression."[44]

"New and original phenomena" demand as at other crossroads i
history suitable changes in the government of societies, and thre
such phenomena may be singled out as governing the present problen
of international peace and development. (i) The new scientific in
ventions and discoveries have raised political, social and moral issue
which can be dealt with only on their own global scale. Not one o
them is peculiar to Europe; in the nuclear field all that Wester
Europe can do is to add its own pile of nuclear bombs, but not t
halt their fearful menace. (ii) At the same time we face the contrar
prospect of twice the number of independent states entitled by thei
sovereign status to follow their own will, and many tempted by a
revolutionary mood to do so. (iii) The third factor, cutting across th
other two and confusing their relation, is the trend to neo-mercantil
ist "planning." It has injected the political element into well-nigl
all the manifold international activities and relations which formerl
grew freely across most frontiers. That is the given equation. Th
key we have to find is how in these conditions "to harmonize th
actions" economic and social, in the words of the UN Charter, "in th

the European communities shows the unreality of the "functionalist" thesi
that starting from small, autonomous specialized authorities one could build a
complete state! A "complete state" and its introverted nature happens to b
the very idea which functionalism seeks to overcome internationally. — "De
Communautés Européene à la Fédération," *Revue Générale de Droit Inter
national Public*, Paris, 1960, vol. 64(2).

[43] "The fallacy starts when it is believed that the motives for political inte
gration are as rational as those for economic integration." The first are "mainl
mythical, which does not deprive them of a certain driving force. But this forc
is soon spent when it clashes with the deeper and older myths and loyalties o
the national states." — J. L. Heldring, *Internationale Spectator*, p. 544.

[44] *Internationale Spectator*, pp. 641-2. — This trend of thought runs through
out the contributions from people like the Secretary-General of the Europea
Parliament, a former Secretary-General of NATO, the Dutch members of th
executives of ECSC and Euratom, the Rector of the College of Europe, th
Secretary-General of the European Trade-Union Secretariat, a former Dutcl
foreign minister and lately ambassador to France; of the others, several ar
professors of international law and organization.

attainment of common ends.'' To have lasting effect the solution must be global. In theory it could be done through a world state or federation, but even if desirable such a monstrous construction could hardly come about except through conquest. Or it can be done by making use of the present social and scientific opportunities to link together particular activities and interests, one at a time, according to need and acceptability, giving each a joint authority and policy limited to that activity alone. That is the functional way.

Let it be said at once that there is nothing new in that. It has been the natural mode of Western international relations, some public and many private, before the two World Wars, but since then we have moved backwards from the liberal nineteenth century. ''Before 1914 world integration was proceeding steadily by means of firm treaties and relationships, open-door arrangements and so on. In addition, a great number of pre-1914 agreements created what might be termed abstract regions' through multi-lateral contracts under the authority of international law.''[45] Now, as in former autocratic times, economic, social and even cultural relations have fallen under the control of the state — ''the State has almost become an organization for the prevention of free international intercourse and the growth of a normal human society.'' Fichte's eighteenth-century academic aberration, *Der Geschlossene Handelstaat*, is looming before us as a twentieth-century contingent reality. The trend is general, varying only in manner and degree, and informed with a ruthless pragmatism which permits any government in the name of its ''plan'' to change policy and practice abruptly without regard to the effect on the interests and plans of other peoples and the hurt to international goodwill. As their problems are more acute and their ways less staid the new undeveloped states are especially apt to resort to such planned licence; and as at the same time they are now protected by the incipient collective system of the UN, they can indulge — as no Great Power would have dared in the days of so-called ''international anarchy'' — in what is also a new phenomenon and can only be described as ''total sovereignty.''

That is the new world which somehow has to be brought back into working relationships, to open up a prospect and provide the elements for international government. We do not know what kind of inter-

---

[45] Adolf Drucker, in *Regionalism and World Organization,* 1944, p. 102. — One should note the erudite work of Prof. Francois Perroux, who uses the conception of *éspaces économiques* freed from ''the servitudes of localization.'' See e.g. *L'Europe sans Rivages,* Paris, 1954.

national government will work. But we do know that as governmen
is only a framework which enables a social community to live its lif
well, international government can have little sense or body withou
a living international community. One new phenomenon at leas
opens up a positive and remarkable prospect in that direction. As wa
said before, the immediate impact of planning, with its spreading
concern for social welfare and rights, is nationalistic. But in it
"external aspect one central characteristic is that it is *universal*.
believe this to be a novel, a unique historical situation. In the tradi
tional category of 'human rights' there have always been difference
from place to place in attitude, conception and practice. But now
whatever their constitutional form or cultural tradition, *all* countrie
have adopted the philosophy and claims of social security; and hence
inevitably, also similar machinery of administrative practice and
controls."[46] If this reading be correct, two practical factors are al
ready at work, and on a world scale, to which strands of functiona
co-operation could be made fast. One is the indispensable factor of a
common outlook and purpose, which in this case puts into strong re
lief an evident identity of everyday social aims and policy. The othe
is the useful factor of close similarity of ways and means. Adminis
trative law is implicitly "functional" law, and so is administrativ
practice. Every functional link helps to build up a common lega
order — as the ILO well exemplifies — specific but also concrete an
cumulative, one which does not stay aloof in the atmosphere of dip
lomatic and juridical pacts but which enters everywhere into th
daily life of the peoples themselves.

Two general considerations may be cited in support of this thesis
A general wish for a collective security system was natural after th
shock of two World Wars and of the atom bomb; but new and re
markable were the first signs "of a sense of world community, o
international responsibility for local conditions everywhere. The ide
of the welfare state, new as it is even in our own countries, is alread
broadening into a sentiment for a welfare world."[47] The substantia
and manifold efforts and contributions generally known as "technica
assistance" are tangible proof of that; not as in the past occasiona
charity in some emergency, but a continuous programme of aid now
accepted almost as a responsibility by the richer countries. On th

[46] D.M., Comment in the Human Rights section, 6th IPSA World Conference
Geneva, September 1964.

[47] D.M., "International Co-operation in Action," *Associations*, Brussel
September 1959.

ther side, the new states, politically tangled up in aggressively
"uncommitted" groups and leagues, have shown themselves eager
o join the UN's special agencies and other such bodies "because the
alance of considerations is in favour of such participation," and
hey have come to look upon it "as an international asset and a
trengthening of their position in the world." In spite of their ex-
reme sensitiveness the new states have shown little mistrust of such
odies, "even where the activities of the international organization
vithin the State's territory is concerned."[48]

Considerations such as these show why one can find both opportu-
ity and promise in working arrangements as a way of building up an
nternational community. But it also is a natural, not a contrived idea
ressed into an existing political mould. Generically speaking it
epresents a general turn grown out of the living complexities of
wentieth-century society. Both devolution and integration tend to
o that way, within states as between states. Socialist theory had
ontemplated some form of centralized control (state socialism or
yndicalism or guild socialism) for economic sectors taken over from
apitalist enterprise, but when it came to "nationalization" Labour
urned instead to the non-political device of autonomous boards and
uthorities. That has become the normal way for activities which are
ltogether new — aviation, atomic energy, and so on. The use made
f it in existing federations is of special relevance here. In America,
a spite of an old and hard-set regionalism, departments of state
war, agriculture, the Federal Reserve Board, etc.) make use in their
dministration of functional regions ("single-purpose areas") which
ary freely from service to service and seldom coincide with State
nes. And so do the hundred or so executive agencies which have come
ato being especially since the New Deal — which itself was "not
ashioned theoretically out of economic or social creeds" but was the
holly pragmatic response to the "felt necessities" of a pressing
.tuation. The clearest evidence can be found in the great experi-
.ent of the TVA.

Because its own task could not be performed unless allowed to cut
cross the sovereign jurisdiction of seven of the United States, the
VA offers a good prototype for possible inter-state arrangements.
ut for this reason it is as well to deal first with a general point
iised in this connection. To the argument that even in established
ederations reforming activities have often had to be diverted into

[48] Benjamin Akzin, "New States and International Organizations," *UNESCO*,
aris, 1955, pp. 170-2.

functional by-paths, instead of moving along the direct formal way
of constitutional amendment, it has often been retorted that func
tional experiments have been possible and effective in America
precisely because they worked within a federal system.[49] It is a
plausible point, but fortunately one to which one can get closer from
concrete experience. For the past century-and-a-half a growing num
ber of international unions and services have worked well without
reference to political supervision or protection. More specifically, in
North America, and apart from the war-time combined boards with
Canada, the U.S. since then has become a party to substantial joint
activities with neighbouring states — the Alcan Highway (a likely
model for an eventual Channel tunnel), the St. Lawrence Waterway
the Rio Grande project with Mexico — all of them without any
offence to or intrusion by the three federal constitutions.

On the other side, as mentioned before, there are a great many
cases where a federal constitution has stood in the way of interna
functional developments. The TVA indeed itself provides a complete
answer. In the face of a pressing social need for such river contro
repeated efforts by several Presidents since the beginning of the
century went astray, until the calamity of the great depression gave
Franklin Roosevelt a chance to push through the bill which created
the autonomous Authority. It was all done by May, 1933, within a
few weeks of his taking office; but then the TVA had to fight of
forty-one legal suits over a period of five years and on a variety of
constitutional objections before it was allowed to settle down to its
great work. "The TVA really introduced a new dimension into the
constitutional structure of the U.S., without any change in the Con
stitution; but it could do so only because it was a new administrative
and not a new political dimension."[50]

This is not the place to restate the political philosophy which in
forms the functional idea beyond saying that to prefer it to the
constitutional approach is not to be timid, much less to be haphaz
ard.[51] "It rests indeed squarely upon the most characteristic idea o

[49] See, e.g., Andrea Chitti-Batelli, "Functional Federalism," *Common Cause*
Chicago, April, 1950; and D.M.'s reply, November 1950.

[50] D.M., *American Interpretations*, London, 1946, pp. 18-20. — As against thi
one must note that President Roosevelt's only "attempt at direct constitutiona
revision, to increase the membership of the Supreme Court from nine to fifteen
was bitterly disputed and defeated; though in effect it would have meant much
less of a constitutional inroad than the experiment of the TVA and the body o
new federal executive agencies." — ib., p. 22.

[51] See D.M., *A Working Peace System*, 4th ed., London, 1944, and late

ie democratic-liberal philosophy, which leaves the individual free
) enter into a variety of relationships — religious, political and pro-
essional, social and cultural — each of which may take him in dif-
erent directions and dimensions and into different groupings, some
f them of international range. Each of us is in fact a 'bundle' of
inctional loyalties; so that to build a world community upon such a
onception is merely to extend and consolidate it also between na-
onal societies and groups.''[52] The argument has grown out of a
efinite view of the dilemma of our time: that we can neither ignore
ie deep roots of nationality in the search for material efficiency, nor
eny the urgent cry for social betterment for the sake of a hollow
idependence. In the face of this dilemma one may look briefly at the
elative merits of the functional idea in regard to some of those issues
hich have been shown to raise difficulties for any comprehensive
olitical union.

In the first place, the functional approach does not offend against
ie sentiment of nationality or the pride of sovereignty. Instead of a
ctitious formal equality it offers even to the weakest of countries
ie assurance of non-domination and of an equality of opportunity
i the working benefits of any functional activity in which it partici-

---

ritings. — A useful chapter on international functional bodies in Max Sørensen,
us Gentium (Danish), 1949, pp. 83-104.

Some valid theoretical definitions and observations were given already in Georg
ellinek's classic on federalism. *Die Lehre von den Staatenverbindungen*, 1882.
.part from confederations and federations he paid some attention to ''adminis-
-ative unions,'' with their own organs and a common purpose, which made them
joint administrative area for that task. Thus the International Postal Treaty of
874 made all treaty states into one vast postal territory in respect of those
rvices. The oldest such unions were set up to ensure free navigation on inter-
ational rivers, like the Rhine and especially the Lower Danube. The European
anube Commission had greater powers as it was created for the collective
terest of Europe and had thus a general international character; it issued
gulations and could impose penalties which the member states were bound to
force, performing in this respect ''acts of international legislation,'' and
ithin its sphere it also had the character of an ''international court.'' Though
reaties creating these unions were for limited periods and members had the
ght to withdraw, in effect the nature of their activity made them perpetual
s no state could, e.g., want the dissolution of postal and telegraph services
hich served the common interests of civilized communities (pp. 158 ff.). (These
ineteenth-century precedents suggest how much political trouble they would
ave saved themselves, while doing service to the whole world community, if at
ie end of the First World War the Allied Powers had acted not ''strategically''
ut ''functionally'' and internationalized the Dardanelles and the Suez and
anama canals; now the first is in effect dominated by Russia, whom they
leant to keep out, the second in the not too reliable hands of Egypt, and the
ist a source of friction between the U.S. and the new temper in Latin America.)

[52] D.M., *Associations*, 1959, p. 647.

pates. And these assurances can be the more readily accepted eve
by touchy ex-colonial states, as Professor Akzin has shown, becaus
functional arrangements have the patent virtue of technical sel
determination: the range of their task can be clearly defined and thi
in turn, makes plain the powers and resources needed for its pe
formance. Internationally speaking, political self-determination i
this way is translated into functional co-determination. Allowing fo
suitable variations, Mrs. Camps has concluded that even for th
Common Market "this pattern is likely to be followed in the futur
and to be reinforced by the fusion of the Communities, the gover
ments being willing effectively to shift authority to the Commissio
only when the limits within which the Commission can act have bee
fairly strictly defined."[53]

This bears closely on the central difficulty of democratic contro
As we have said, even in democratic states control over executive an
administration has slipped away from Parliament; in England (an
elsewhere) we have indeed enacted the paradox that industries an
services nationalized into public ownership have been exempted fro
the public control of Parliament, except for a general debate on thei
annual Reports. In this respect at any rate international develop
ment would seem to show an advance on national practice. For th
discussion of general policy the UN has the Economic and Socia
Council; but the significant innovation is that everyone of the spe
cialized agencies, including the ILO, has its own little functional as
sembly, varying with the work of the agency, which meets periodicall
to review the work done and to lay down policy and fix a budget fo
the next period. Moreover, Art. 71 of the UN Charter has give
certain private international bodies, the non-governmental organiza
tions (NGOs), a formal right to be consulted or an informal righ
to be heard in their particular sphere of interest, and so has estab
lished a sort of functional constituency which can influence th
agency's policy, but also brings back to the members of their associa
tion an insight into the reasons why that policy should be sup
ported.[54] In that way an effective process of democratic representa
tion can be restored; while the doings at Brussels have practicall
been taken out of the hands of the national Parliaments, both th

[53] Op. cit., p. 131.
[54] Lyman B. White, *International Non-governmental Organizations,* Ne
Brunswick (U.S.A.), 1951. Each association "constitutes a segment of worl
unity for the particular interest with which it deals, and an accumulation o
such segments would serve to create a living world community" (p. 12).

elegates to these functional assemblies and the non-governmental
ssociations know what it is all about and can judge whether a policy
s valid and whether it has been carried out fairly.[55]

Bodies such as these may "diminish the orthodox sovereignty of
he states, but the power and sovereign rights of the people would
ncrease, because they would have a direct voice through their own
elegates in all the agencies handling some of their affairs."[56] "Peo-
le are bad judges of general considerations," was said already by
Iachiavelli, "but good judges of detail." Apart from these special
odies, the same trend has developed in recent years through national
epartments negotiating and acting together, for many purposes of a
echnical or practical nature, directly with their opposite branches
n other countries; and very often these contacts continue despite
olitical friction. The extent to which the whole practice of foreign
olicy and relations has thus been revolutionized, in step with the
weep of technical developments and the extension of public controls
vithin each state, can be seen in the mere fact that while three inter-
ational conferences met in 1853, and about a hundred in 1900, their
umber had increased to some two thousand by 1953 and now pos-
ibly is nearly twice as high. "And it is not merely a matter of num-
ers. We have travelled far from the glittering parade of princes at
he Congress of Vienna to the sober meetings of civil servants, scien-
ists and technicians who through their work now link together
ectors of their national life and sections of their national depart-
nents into a vast and growing network of peaceful and beneficial
nternational relations."[57]

The same reasons also help to hem in the present inevitable tend-
ncy to bureaucracy, both through the clear definition of the scope
nd powers of a functional authority and through the watchfulness
f people who know the work as well as the "technocrats" and have
direct interest in its good performance. The ECSC was organized
nd worked well on such a basis; whether mixing the three com-

---

[55] D.M., "An Advance in Democratic Representation," *Associations*, March,
954. — These functional assemblies have sometimes been confused by critics
vith functional representation in general bodies, like the economic parliaments
opular for awhile after the First World War; but in economic parliaments the
everal groups were there to fight for sectional interests, as in any ordinary
arliament, whereas functional bodies represent one interest and one purpose
ommon to them all, and the debate is about ways and means.
[56] Hans E. Fried, "The Frontiers of the Future," *Free World*, August 1943,
. 11.
[57] D.M., Review in *International Affairs*, RIIA, September 1960, p. 228.

munities will keep these advantages unimpaired remains to be see
But having pressed out of sheer political zeal for the fusion of tl
three, many "Europeans," as the Martino Report admits, are no
afraid lest the clear supra-nationality of the ECSC should in tl
process be diluted to the inter-governmental level of the others. Y
it cannot be otherwise: the wider and vaguer the range of its activit
the less is the likelihood that a technical organization would be giv
the freedom of supra-national autonomy.[58]

The question of membership provides one final point of compar
son. A federal system is bound to be closed and exclusive; a fun
tional system is as naturally open, as changes in membership can l
absorbed without doing violence to policy and administration. A fe
eral constitution is a balancing act in regard to a whole range
social and political factors: with any change in membership tl
whole structure may have to be re-organized and probably to l
re-negotiated[59] — rather like the Austro-Hungarian *Ausgleich,* whic
Viennese wits dubbed "Monarchie auf Kündigung" because of tl
inevitable crisis at each ten-yearly renewal. In fact, Mrs. Camp
brings up this very point: at Brussels, too, "there is too much rel
ance on crises as a technique for forcing decisions."[60] Professo
Friedrich's recent thesis is particularly dubious on this point. H
would like federal rules to be so easy as to make it possible for son
members to leave or for others to be added without breaking up tl
whole federation. From a wide international experience, on tl
other hand, Dr. Beijen gives the clear warning that if one reall
wants to extend the membership of the Common Market "it is bette
not to speak of federation."[61] Even with the EEC, far as it is fro

[58] Under their several treaties the powers of the European Parliament a
lower in matters appertaining to the Rome Treaties than those of the ECSC, e.g
in treaty revision. In fact, as the PEP pamphlet, "Direct Elections and Eur
pean Parliament" (Oct. 1960) pointed out, the ECSC Assembly, encouraged b
the High Authority, had greatly enlarged the part given it in the Treaty an
instead of being only a *post facto* critic it actually helped to shape the policy o
the Community.

[59] That this may happen even in old federations was shown at the Canadia
Federal Provincial Conference in July, 1965. The Federal Government ha
decided to refer to the Supreme Court the question of title to seabed resource
on the Pacific Coast, but the Premiers of British Columbia and of Quebec "le
a furious attack on the Federal Government, claiming that the matter was on
for political negotiations and not for judicial settlement." The Premier o
Quebec declared that he would not respect a Supreme Court decision, or allo
exploration in the Gulf of St. Lawrence on the strength of a Federal permi
(*The Guardian,* London, July 24, 1965).

[60] Op. cit., p. 93.

[61] *Internationale Spectator,* p. 470.

deration, the clause that leaves open the door for "any European untry" willing to join implies, according to Mr. Nederhorst, ull acceptance of "existing economic institutions and political rinciples";[62] and it was not unnatural in the discussions on the 'ouchet plan for the French to insist there, too, on unanimity for ew admissions. As under the Rome Treaty the Commission has a rominent voice in this matter. There is much to be learnt from the markable change of mind from its Memorandum of February,)59, which urged "very great flexibility" so as to allow "associa-on" according to the needs and wishes of any likely candidate, to s recent hardened position against anything short of full member-iip.[63]

On a minor scale the contrast stands out clearly even within the xisting Communities. The ECSC and Euratom are straight func-onal bodies and can get on with their allotted task without offend-ig the position of other countries, while remaining open to link up ith them. The scope of EEC is by comparison diffuse and subject to continuous temptation to self-inflation (which the "Europeans" eem a virtue); with a bureaucratic tendency because it is diffuse, nd an expansionist tendency because it is bureaucratic. The more elds of activity it actively enters, e.g., agriculture, the more acquisi-ve it tends to become;[64] and in the degree to which it is rounded ut it also hardens into a segregated entity. (One might have pre-icted this even without the repulsion of the Seven into the EFTA rouping, and without the later rupture of negotiations with Great ritain.) The point is that for service units like the ECSC and 'uratom, as for all the specialized agencies of the UN and any future inctional bodies, wider association means more points of co-opera-ve contact; for a self-inflating organization like the EEC, more elds of control must mean internationally more points of competi-ve contact.

Federation was an advance on empire as a way of joining under common government a group of separate territorial units. But

[62] *Limits and Problems,* p. 59.

[63] Camps, op. cit., p. 65.

[64] "The General, despite his dislike of integration, has done much to reinforce e Commission's powers, by pressing for a common agricultural policy which alone can administer." On its part, using the argument that it would be democratic to handle the large agricultural funds without democratic control, e Commission has put forward a scheme "which would transfer much of the uncil's powers to the Parliament, and, even more, to the Commission." — *'ie Economist,* May 8, 1965, p. 638.

federation is not only inadequate but irrelevant when the genera
task is not to consolidate but to loosen the hold of the territorial
sovereign conception of political relations, and find a way to worl
peace through the revolutionary pressures of the time. Even earlie
neither the British Empire nor Latin America, with their many socia
and historical affinities, had turned to the federal idea for politica
comfort. It has not served any of the post-war problems and situa
tions. It has not proved acceptable to neighbouring groups in Eas
Africa or the Middle East or the Caribbean in spite of pressing com
mon needs and paucity of resources; alone the Nigerian federatio
survives, not too easily, in the wake of a unitary administration. :
has not suggested itself as a remedy for healing the split betwee
parts that had been formerly united. Some years ago, Mr. Nehru an
the Pakistani President agreed that their countries had many pract
cal interests which could with advantage be managed in commor
and now the leaders of the two parts of Ireland are working to en
an old enmity by doing just that. But would either case have had
better prospect if one of the parties were to have said, "We mus
federate first"? Quite a number of practical activities are carrie
out in common by or for the British Commonwealth, but would an
mere hint that they needed a political underpinning not cause a
once a flight from this functional association?

When it comes to the new scientific inventions and discoveries -
aviation, wireless, atomic energy, space exploration — their own tecl
nicalities defy any arrangement below the global scale. So muc
so that, e.g. in broadcasting, states have to respect the mutual intere
even where there is no formal agreement. Flying may still claim fc
awhile sovereign rights in the air above a state's territory; but wit
satellites and space travel we have in truth reached the "no man
land of sovereignty." Nor is there any workable dividing line b
tween military and non-military usage of space: no means of sel
protection is left, only all-round protection through some commo
authority. The programme for space exploration adopted by th
General Assembly in 1962 was only a first step towards taking
out of politics; and the same intent clearly informed the Antarctic
Treaty signed by twelve countries, including Soviet Russia, in 195'
which suspended all territorial claims and disputes for a period c
thirty years and instead provided for scientific co-operation, and als
for mutual inspection to prevent any military activities. These ar
if one may be allowed the expression, not "federalizing" but "fun

onalizing" actions; they could never lead to any political union,
t alone federation between the parties, but the Antarctica treaty —
nsidered as a type — which now amounts to a temporary neutral-
ation under a joint agreement, could well lead to permanent neu-
alization under a joint international authority.

Before concluding, there are two points that need to be mentioned
; they recur in almost every critical account of the functional ap-
roach. One is the central and difficult question of co-ordination. To
degree, insofar as it is raised as an abstract assumption, it expresses
e difficulty which our political thinking finds to conceive of author-
y, as part of the tradition of sovereignty, without a territory; even
ie Roman Pontiff had to be allowed the Vatican territory as a base
or sovereign status, though it is less than a speck on the Pontiff's
ast expense of influence and authority throughout the world. But
ie criticism also has a core of evident truth in the fear that a variety
f autonomous organs might work at cross-purposes with each other.
t is a real problem, but is it not better to wait till the need arises
nd experience shows what the need is? To prescribe for the sake of
aditional neatness something more definite than the guidance and
ipervision of, e.g., the Economic and Social Council, would be to
istort the whole conception from the start. To try to fit the functional
odies into a common mould would take away some of their special
ierits in working efficiency and flexibility of membership; while to
ipose upon them a "co-ordinating" authority, with anything like
ntrolling status, would be to move again towards that accumulation
f power at the centre which is in question here. We would be drifting
ack onto the political track and so miss the way to possible univer-
ility.

The second point is one of doubt, not infrequently heard: "Where
ill the political will for such functional union come from?" It
ems a curious question. If there should be no will for working to-
ether on such lines, limited to evident self-interest, can one assume
iat there might be a better will for wider unlimited political inte-
ration? The question is not so much a criticism of the functional
lea as a great doubt whether peaceful international co-operation is
ossible at all. It is perhaps an open question whether in 1945 we had
een too hopeful or too form-bound in our approach. In the view of
enator J. W. Fulbright, the UN has in a manner broken down
ecause it was based on the assumption of a unity of outlook among
he Great Powers; now we had to turn to a functional approach to

build up an international community, to tackle concrete problem
instead of spectacular attempts at world constitution-making.[65] Th
same question, whether they were too hopeful or too form-tie
applies to the "Europeans" who gathered at The Hague in 194
Many of them now feel the need for "a more cautious conception
integration"; "if Europe is to pursue its fundamental goal, fun
tional integration appears to be the only practical method of c
operation."[66] And the "fundamental goal" here means not loc
peace and strength, but world peace and well-being. As to this ult
mate goal, in the concluding volume to the series of inquiries initiate
by the Carnegie Endowment for International Peace, *The Natior
and the United Nations*,[67] Prof. Robert MacIver himself conclud
that the UN's main service to the cause of peace may lie not in i
political activities, but in the development of the common or c
operative interests of the peoples in areas which lie outside or on th
margin of the usual play of power politics.

CONCLUSION

This paper has been written from the standpoint of a student
political science (with an evident international bias). It has in r
way been concerned with the question whether a European unic
would, or would not, bring prosperity to its populations, or wheth
it would be a good thing or not for Britain to join it. As a student
have sought an answer to two questions: What kind of political cor
struction was a European union likely to be, and what would be i
temper — for if, as I think, function determines structure, this als
means that structure must affect practice. And therefore, in th
second place, what would be its relevancy to the prospects for
general international system?

Admittedly, to try to examine the "European" idea thus is lik
trying to hold a line on a political rainbow with its many fleetin
hues — a rainbow with one horizon among those who are clear tha
they were not seeking "a new fatherland" and wanted Europ
united that it may work the better for international union, and th
opposite horizon falling in Dr. Hallstein's camp. For Dr. Hallstei
is no less clear that they were after "awakening a new Europea
patriotism"; and that — while the old nations may be left to drea

[65] *Foreign Affairs*, New York, October 1961.
[66] Prof. Alting von Geusau, *Internationale Spectator*, p. 488.
[67] New York, 1959.

heir national dreams (and after dismissing any idea of supplanting he national with the supra-national as "another illusion") — that perhaps it is true that only States can act politically. Then let us reate the European State — or is Europe finally to abdicate?"[68]

If the aim is political union, a "United States of Europe," Dr. Iallstein's picture, with all its tactical tergiversations, is clearly earer the mark. Both lines of inquiry have led to the same point, hat by its nature and tendency a political union must be na-ionalistic; and that as such it must impede, and may defeat, the reat historic quest for a general system of peace and development. Jnder the pressures of a planned and radical social transformation t is bound to shape towards a centralized system — closed, exclusive, ompetitive; and whatever else it may do, such a system would ardly be suited to mediate between the new ideological divisions, or emper the raw nationalism of the new states so as to steer them >wards the greener pastures of a mutual international community.

More likely it is that it will cause the tentative "blocs" that have lready confused policy at the UN, out of distrust of the old world, > harden into other "unions" in emulation of it. Could a European nion, in the long run, benefit its own peoples if it tends in the least > split the world afresh into competing regional sovereignties? Is not reaking through that dour barrier of sovereignty the ultimate test? n a world of a hundred and more states sovereignty can in simple act never be dismantled through a formula but only through func-ion, shedding national functions and pooling authority in them; nless we are to give up all purpose of wide all-round international haring in the works of peace.

SUGGESTIONS FOR FURTHER READING

rmstrong, Hamilton Fish, "Regional Pacts: Strong Points or Storm Cellars?" *Foreign Affairs,* 27 (April 1949), pp. 351-68.

arr, E. H., *Nationalism and After* (London, 1945).

laude, Inis L., Jr., *Swords into Plowshares* (New York, 3rd ed., 1964), Chapter 6.

'eutsch, Karl, et al., *Political Community and the North Atlantic Area* (Princeton, 1957).

'tzioni, Amitai, "The Dialectics of Supranational Unification," *American Political Science Review,* LVI, 2 (1955), pp. 927-35.

———, *Political Unification* (New York, 1965).

riedrich, Carl J., "International Federalism in Theory and Practice," in

---

[68] Op. cit., p. 15.

Elmer Plischke (ed.), *Systems of Integrating the International Community* (Princeton, 1964).

Furniss, Edgar S., Jr., "A Re-examination of Regional Arrangements, *Journal of International Affairs,* IX,2 (1955), pp. 79-89.

Haas, Ernst B., "Regional Integration and National Policy," *International Conciliation,* 513 (May 1957), pp. 381-442.

———, "The Challenge of Regionalism," *International Organization,* XI (Autumn 1958), pp. 440-58.

———, "International Integration: The European and the Universal Process," *International Organization,* XV (Summer 1961), pp. 366-92.

Herz, John, "The Rise and Demise of the Territorial State," *World Politics* IX (July 1957), pp. 473-93.

Korbonski, Andrzej, "COMECON," *International Conciliation,* 549 (September 1964), pp. 3-62.

Lawson, Ruth C., *International Regional Organizations: Constitutional Foundations* (New York, 1962).

Mangone, Gerard J., *The Idea and Practice of World Government* (New York, 1951), Chapter 3.

Padelford, Norman J., "Regional Organization and the United Nations, *International Organization,* VIII (May 1954), pp. 203-16.

Russett, Bruce M., *International Regions and the International System* (Chicago, 1967).

Streit, Clarence K., *Freedom's Frontier: Atlantic Union Now* (New York, 1961).

van Kleffens, E. N., "Regionalism and Political Pacts," *American Journal of International Law,* 43 (1949), pp. 666-78.

Wilcox, Francis, "Regionalism and the United Nations," *International Organization,* XIX (Summer 1965), pp. 789-811.

Yalem, Ronald, *Regionalism and World Order* (Washington, 1965).

PART TWO

REGIONALISM AND THE QUEST FOR SECURITY

Linda B. Miller

Regional Organization
and the Regulation
of Internal Conflict

I

Are regional and global approaches to world order compatible or ompetitive? Policy-makers and scholars pose this question with in-easing frequency. Yet too often assessments of the relative capabili-es of regional and general international organizations fail to distin-uish the different demands such issues as threats to the peace or odernization create for widely divergent institutions. Enthusiasm r regionalism waxes and wanes with events. As Inis Claude ob-rves, "The advocacy of regionalism can be, and often is, as doc-inaire and as heedless of concrete realities as the passion for all-ncompassing organization."[1]

The realities of contemporary internal violence suggest that inter-ational regulation intrastate disorder is desirable. Internal dis-ders, in the form of armed insurrections, bloodless military coups, olonial revolts, or factional disputes, are prevalent in the less in-ustrialized sectors of Asia, Latin America, Africa, and the Middle ast. The attempts of countries in these regions to modernize their ocieties generate social and political unrest and invite violent or abviolent civil strife.

These disorders may reveal a desire to achieve political change

Reprinted from *World Politics*, XIX, No. 4 (July 1967), with permission of e Princeton University Center of International Studies and the author.

[1] *Swords Into Plowshares* (New York 1964), 95.

when previously legitimate means of effecting change have broke
down or when the goals of dissident groups cannot be realized b
legitimate means.[2] Revolutions, civil wars, coups, or mere threats c
force attest to issues of policy or ideology; disagreements ove
foreign-policy, constitutional, ethnic, racial, or economic question
may spark violence that creates new issues for domestic and extern
parties.[3] Nation-building and insurgency are closely linked: the lac
of a basic national consensus about the means and ends of gover
ment may raise doubts as to the legitimacy of the formal governmer
in power; or bureaucratic inefficiencies may call into question th
capacity of ruling groups to govern.[4]

Different kinds of internal violence create different internation
concerns. Conflicts that subside quickly or remain confined withi
national boundaries may arouse some interest on a regional basis an
little or no attention on a global scale. Protracted disorders that ma
spill over territorial boundaries stimulate global interests in peacef
change and human rights. When struggles for internal supremac
are seen by local and foreign participants as parts of larger conflic
of a racial or ideological character, the potential or actual threat 1
global and regional stability is increased.

Competitive external interventions have become the familiar moc
for larger powers who view internal conflicts as a means of extendir
their own national influence at the expense of cold-war adversaries
regional competitors. Thus the steadily expanding war in Vietna
has dramatized the extent to which the line between internation
and internal conflicts may be erased by the actions of third parti
who regard civil disorders as threats to political values. The lack
substantive rules of conduct in civil strife increases the likelihood
unregulated third-party interventions. The specter of unilateral mil
tary responses to internal violence raises the most serious issues f
world order. Few would disagree with Richard A. Falk who argu
that "civil strife constitutes the major challenge to those convinc
that decisions to use military power in world affairs should not I
matters of national discretion."[5] Nevertheless, since the effecti

[2] Cyril E. Black, in Cyril E. Black and Thomas P. Thornton, eds., *Communis
and Revolution* (Princeton 1964), 7 ff.

[3] *Ibid.*, 9-12.

[4] Lucian Pye, in Harry Eckstein, ed., *Internal War: Problems and Approach*
(New York 1964), 158, 164.

[5] "The International Regulation of Internal Violence in the Developi
Countries," American Society of International Law, *Proceedings* (April 196(
59.

ontrol of force remains on the national level, the prospects for in-
ernational regulation of internal conflict depend upon the self-
estraint of third parties.

Such a fragile basis for world order is unsatisfactory to those who
vould give primacy to transnational interests. Therefore it is not
urprising that some scholars have attempted to postulate a series of
legal" restraints that might serve as guides for policy-makers.
'alk, for example, has proposed that the legitimacy of particular
iterventions be based on whether they rest on prior principles that
xpress "patterns of general community consent or merely reflect
d hoc political majorities of the moment." Thus unilateral inter-
entions in which one nation intervenes in the internal affairs of
nother, as did the Soviet Union in Hungary, would rank lower on
ie scale of legitimacy than regional interventions in which a group
f states forms a juridical entity and imposes a combined will on a
issenting member, as did the OAS with Cuba. Still higher on the
ale would come collective interventions under the aegis of the UN,
s in the Congo or Cyprus.[6] Falk would give to the UN greater legis-
tive competence to intervene in domestic affairs, authority that
ould enable the Organization to move into *any* civil disorder threat-
ning world peace or abusing human rights. In some instances the
N might become the sole authority in modernizing countries ex-
riencing civil upheaval.[7] Regional interventions would occupy a
iddle position between undesirable unilateral interventions and
esirable, but perhaps unattainable, UN interpositions.

The structural and political realities of regional organization in-
cate that the possibilities for attaining effective management of civil
rife through regional efforts are limited. Nevertheless, it is useful
stipulate the *feasible* responses for regional actors even if these re-
onses fall short of *desirable* ones.

II

It is important to differentiate both types of internal conflict and
tterns of regional organization. The term "internal war" is not
lpful in this context, since many internal disorders are not "wars"
a traditional sense. Moreover, "internal war" is rendered still less
ecise by its occasional use as a description of conflicts in which

---

[6] Falk, in Roland Stanger, ed., *Essays on Intervention* (Columbus 1964),
-41.
[7] *Ibid.*, 40-44.

"Communist" states participate.[8] It would be advantageous if scho
ars could develop categories that permit clear distinctions betwee
diversified internal conflicts.[9] In the absence of widely accepted cat
gories, observers must select those pertinent to the scope of a parti
ular inquiry. From the standpoint of international organizatio
three types of internal conflict are significant: colonial wars, intern
conflicts involving a breakdown of law and order, and proxy wa
and internal conflicts involving charges of external aggression or su
version.

Two types of regional organization are of potential consequence i
the regulation of internal conflict: (1) groupings of states such as tl
Organization of American States and the Organization of Africa
Unity, with a continental or hemispheric basis, a set of decisio
making institutions, and established procedures for pacific settleme
of disputes; and (2) collective defense arrangements such as NAT(
SEATO, and the Warsaw Pact, whose geographical bases conform '
strategic needs rather than natural boundaries and whose nonmilita
functions are virtually undeveloped. Regional organizations of bot
types are arenas in which competing governmental interests are act
out. When these interests converge, a consensus may emerge on a
propriate responses to internal violence. These responses, wheth
they involve attempts to isolate an internal conflict, to foster n
gotiations between disputants, or to impose a settlement, devel
pragmatically in each case. The British Commonwealth is a mo
anomalous type of "regional" organization. Despite the fact th
the Commonwealth is unlike other organizations, it may attem
similar functions when internal strife breaks out in a member stat
if political circumstances permit. The Commonwealth's lack of c
hesion, apparent throughout Rhodesia's conflict with Britain, is
major impediment to effective action.

Few precedents are discernible in the practice of regional organiz
tions in civil disorders, but some frequently observed deficienci
have proved to be highly relevant. In Asia, there is no region
grouping of stature and comprehensive authority. The recent
formed Asian and Pacific Council (ASPAC) has no institution
structure and is limited to a few countries in the area. Even mo

[8] See, for example, Roger Hilsman, "Internal War: The New Commun
Tactic," in Franklin Mark Osanka, ed., *Modern Guerrilla Warfare* (New Yc
1962), 452-63.
[9] For an extended discussion of this point, see Linda B. Miller, *World Ord
and Local Disorder: The United Nations and Internal Conflicts* (Princet
1967), Introduction.

stricted is Maphilindo, a grouping that has remained an expression of intent rather than a viable foundation for regional activities.
Africa, the existing OAU lacks military resources and is torn by
periodic ideological splits. In the Middle East, the Arab League's
membership is incomplete and the competition for dominance between Egypt and Saudi Arabia affects every regional undertaking.
Latin America, the U.S. continues to dominate the OAS and seeks
to have American conceptions of Communists threats to the hemisphere prevail. Similarly, preeminent American power plus divergent
attitudes toward the degree and quality of Communist involvement
have characterized the responses of NATO and SEATO to intraregional civil strife.

Past attempts of regional organizations to regulate varieties of internal violence illustrate these deficiencies and others that preclude
effective contributions to world order.

III

The chief colonial wars since 1945 have unfolded in parts of the
world where regional organization is either precarious or nonexistent.
Throughout the postwar period, the organizational focus of decolonization has remained the United Nations. The destabilizing effects of
the new nations' transition to self-rule have colored the relations of
the European nations with the Soviet Union and its allies, as well as
intra-alliance relations in the West. The lengthy struggles of indigenous groups in Indonesia, Algeria, and Angola have involved
third-party states and international organizations in asymmetrical
conflicts in which incumbents have enjoyed an initial preponderance
of power. These revolutionary wars have taken place in territories in
which the metropolitan power remained distant, geographically and
politically. Each European power in turn has confronted nongovern-
mental cliques determined to end foreign domination. The Dutch,
French, and Portuguese governments sought to isolate these conflicts
in hopes that concessions short of outright independence would be
sufficient to quell disorder. Each colonial power vigorously opposed
formal internationalization of the conflict, fearing that the UN (and
later the OAU, in the case of Angola) would serve to confer status on
the rebelling faction and to expose repressive administrative policies.
Insurgent groups in Indonesia, Algeria, and Angola have favored
UN involvement (and now OAU participation) for the reasons the
European states opposed it: first, as a means of enlisting sympathy

for rebel goals; and second, as a means of enhancing bargainir
positions and compensating for military weaknesses. In all three col
nial wars, the UN's efforts (and those of the OAU) to confine host
ities, to restore order, to foster self-determination, and to encoura₃
viable political settlements have been hampered by the reluctance
incumbents and insurgents to legitimize each other, to accord t₁
recognition implied in acceding to negotiations. In each case, t₁
international organizations have expressed a definite preference f
change favorable to insurgents.

The vestiges of white rule in southern Africa constitute the la
barrier to an independent continent. A "colonial" war that cou
dwarf the violence of preceding African conflicts is a distinct po
sibility. Can the OAU be expected to play a constructive role
securing the black majority's rights and in preventing uncontroll₁
bloodshed? The record of the OAU in the Angolan revolt is instru
tive.

Unlike many of the intra-African issues, the Angolan colonial w
has served to unite the states of Black Africa on policy. The form
tion of the OAU in 1963 provided new impetus for a sanctioni
approach to Portugal, but African leaders have sought a wider foru
for their denunciation of Salazar's administration — hence their co
centration on securing UN resolutions and UN investigations rath
than exclusive OAU discussions. Lacking the military capabilities
intervene with force in Rhodesia, Angola, Mozambique, or Sou
West Africa, the African states have tended to act individually
such matters as training rebels or recognizing a specific indigeno
regime as the *de jure* authority. The OAU as an organization, apa
from the actions of certain of its members, has not "regulated" t₁
Angolan conflict in any sense; in fact, the revolt has diminished. T₁
OAU members have cast themselves as a group in the role of negoti
tors for the rebels in their dealings with Portugal. These talks, urg₁
in numerous UN resolutions, have foundered on the issue of se₁
determination for Angola. But the fact that the OAU has consider₁
itself a party to the conflict and has been accepted as such by the U
may be a valuable precedent.

In view of the ideological splits that have plagued the OAU sin
its establishment and the continuing military weakness of the orga
ization, it is difficult to foresee a more interventionary OAU r₁
even in circumstances of policy agreement. It would appear that bo
regional and global approaches to change in southern Africa a
dependent on shifts in the commitments of Western states, notab

e United States and Britain. The African states continue to lack
fficient power to "impose" a settlement on Portugal or South
frica, even if the combined will of the OAU membership would
vor an attempt to do so. Moreover, the pattern of settlement in the
donesian and Algerian wars indicates a bilateral framework for
entual solutions rather than a regional one. Feasible OAU re-
onses would involve continued diplomatic pressure on other UN
embers in presentations that stress violations of human rights and
e compatibility of regional and global concerns. In addition, the
irty-eight members of the OAU might adopt more uniform pro-
dures for urging all African states to refrain from trading with
ther Portugal or South Africa. The many examples of extensive
ade between the new states and the "colonial" powers are impres-
ve. Only if other economic arrangements can be devised so that the
sses from an end to such trade are shared will the new African
ates be willing to adopt firm practices.

A severe outbreak of organized resistance to the South African reme, rather than sporadic incidents of civil disobedience, would in-
lve the UN as well as the OAU. A potential source of disagreement
tween the two organizations might develop over the question of
rder-sealing. From the UN's perspective, such a move might in-
ease the chances for isolating the disorder. But from the OAU's
ewpoint, border-sealing would favor the police actions of the in-
mbents and prevent the external assistance needed to topple the
ite government. Thus border-sealing, while feasible, might not be
sirable. In this instance, competitive means might mask compatible
als.

The role of security pacts in colonial wars appears even more re-
ricted. In the Indonesian and Algerian conflicts, NATO served as a
nor channel through which the United States could direct pres-
res against the Netherlands and France when it wished to do so.
the Angolan rebellion, the United States shifted its initial posi-
n in the UN and came to accept the *principle* of an arms embargo
ainst its NATO ally Portugal. But since the alliance itself is in
ronic disarray, it is unrealistic to expect "NATO" policies on
lonial matters that appear less critical now than in the 1950's.

IV

The declining importance of prolonged struggles for independence
s been accompanied by an upsurge in virulent forms of post-

colonial civil disorder. These conflicts, often characterized by breakdown of law and order, create a complex set of policy choice for third parties, both individual states and regional or global organizations. A compatibility of ends and means between the UN and the interested regional association cannot be assumed. Friction or tension between field operations of the UN and those of regional organizations may be the price of a mutual concern for stability. The Congo, Dominican, and Cyprus disorders have found international organizations deeply involved in seeking to halt violence and to promote political solutions.

The relatively uncomplicated roles played by these organizations in the colonial wars contrast sharply with the intricacies of the prolonged participation in the breakdowns of law and order. The conflicts have confronted international organizations with an array parties whose interests transcend the colonial pattern of incumbent and insurgents. In countries as diverse as the Congo, the Dominican Republic, and Cyprus, a common instability arising from a lack adequate preparation for full self-rule (as opposed to colonial dictatorial rule) has marked the disintegration of political process

To an important extent, regional organizations and the UN have shared compatible goals in these disorders. Both have tried to restore and maintain international peace and security, pursuant to the principles and purposes. Both have tried to prevent external interventions from escalating local violence into superpower conflagrations. In attempts to realize their goals, both have been limited inadequate means and by the attitudes of individual member states with narrower national interests in the outcome of internal strife. Similar limitations have plagued the efforts of international organizations in colonial wars and internal conflicts involving charges external aggression or subversion. But special hazards have accompanied the involvement of international institutions in upheavals that have exposed the weaknesses of the social fabric in developing societies with minority groups of a mixed racial or linguistic heritage. The nature of the breakdowns of law and order has required the formation of a consensus within each organization. In each case commitment to a definite outcome has developed within each institution when local and external parties have evaded political solution

By the time the Organization of African Unity was formed in May 1963, the post-independence breakdown of law and order in the Congo had passed through several critical stages. From the beginning tribal violence and the subsequent collapse of central authority

₃opoldville, African statesmen individually and collectively had
ught to exercise some influence on events. Hammarskjöld and later
resident Kennedy and U Thant expressed the hope that the Black
frican states might play a constructive role in securing a political
ttlement of the Congo's turmoil. But the expectations of these
ficials rested on two assumptions, both of which proved unrealistic:
at the African states could unite sufficiently to take a concerted
proach toward the rival Congolese leaders, especially Tshombe and
umumba, and that in matters of tactics and strategy African polit-
al figures would step aside in favor of U.S.-UN management. The
itial response of the Africans to Hammarskjöld's principles for
e operation of ONUC was favorable. Lacking military capabilities
d a continental organization through which to act, African leaders
dorsed a UN peacekeeping operation as a means of preventing
rect superpower exploitation of the situation. Individual African
atesmen took the lead in drafting Security Council resolutions that
d to ONUC's establishment, and they contributed contingents
ickly.

The Congo crisis soon threw the disagreements among African
aders into sharp relief. A central issue concerned the appropriate
titude for the UN to adopt toward Katanga's continued seces-
on, and toward Tshombe personally. Severe differences separated
krumah and Touré, who wished to see the secession crushed, from
presentatives of the former French colonies, who were prone to
gard the rebel leader as a bulwark against communism in Africa.
his early divergence between the "conservative" Brazzaville group
d the more "radical" Casablanca group proved to be the precursor
other cleavages that threatened to prevent the formation of an
frican regional organization. Neither grouping proved to be rigid
structure; the Brazzaville group itself split in August 1961. The
ilitary coups in Africa in 1965-1966 have produced new configura-
ons, with Ghana now a "conservative" state in contrast to its
rlier "radical" posture.

As conflict in the Congo persisted in 1961-1962, the activities of a
ore moderate group of African states, among them Nigeria, began
be prominent in Hammarskjöld's Advisory Committee and later
the UN Conciliation Commission. By the time the Addis Ababa
nference convened to chart the course of the new African organiza-
on, it was apparent that the "bloc" configurations represented by
asablanca, Monrovia, and Brazzaville had become dysfunctional.
nked by the common but negative bond of anticolonialism, eager for

a distinctively African association that would replace the impose
decentralization of the colonial era, the thirty-six states adopted
charter that revealed the need to avoid extreme positions. Faced wi
problems of internal security as well as of economic underdevelo
ment and the absence of a historical tradition of cooperation, tl
assemblage approved a constitutional document that placed emphas
on the legitimacy of existing regimes in Black Africa and the ''
legality'' of white-dominated governments in southern Africa.

Barely a year after its founding, the OAU was strained by tl
establishment of the Kasavubu-Tshombe government in July 196
While Tshombe's return as head of a ''Government of Nation
Reconciliation'' had been accomplished by legitimate means, l
remained, for some African leaders at least, a ''Belgian lackey'' ar
a ''white man's puppet.'' The Belgian-American airlift in Novemb
intensified the views of these dissenters. Prior to the rescue missio
the OAU's Conciliation Commission had failed in its efforts to n
gotiate the release of rebel-held prisoners in Kwilu and Kivu pro
inces. The vituperative Security Council debates on the airli
exposed cracks in the facade of African unity. The impotence of tl
OAU in circumstances of intraregional civil conflict was demo
strated unmistakably as Ghana, the UAR, and Algeria intervened c
behalf of the rebels, while other African states urged a recognition
Tshombe's government. The Security Council's compromise resol
tion called for a conciliatory role for the OAU.[10] But as the time fe
ONUC's withdrawal neared, the African organization did not col
mand enough respect to make its influence felt, despite its pacit
settlement procedures. African leaders, in failing to agree on tl
choice of a regime to govern the Congo or to endorse leaders alreac
selected, prevented effective OAU participation.

V

In the Dominican Republic's lengthy civil strife the America
military intervention shaped not only the course of the upheaval b
also the responses of the OAS and the UN. The role of the Unite
States throughout the course of the disorder was so pronounced,
predominant that some observers may question the utility of di
cussing the Dominican instance in the context of regional control
internal conflict. Yet it is precisely the way in which the U.S. use

[10] Security Council Resolution S/6129, December 30, 1964.

e OAS in an attempt to legitimize its own actions that gives the
isode its importance.

From the initial stages, different characterizations of the cir-
mstances leading to the American intervention were advanced by
resident Johnson, former Dominican President Juan Bosch, and
mpeting Dominican forces engaged in the struggle.

The dispatch of American airborne units and Marine reinforce-
ents to the Dominican Republic on April 28, 1965, was explained
 President Johnson on that day as a measure to "give protection
 hundreds of Americans who are still in the Dominican Republic
id to escort them safely back to this country."[11] The same reason
as cited in a letter dated April 29 sent to the President of the UN
ecurity Council explaining the American action.[12] But on May 2,
resident Johnson, in answering widespread criticism of the inter-
ntion, stated that "the revolutionary movement took a tragic turn.
ommunist leaders, many of them trained in Cuba, seeing a chance
 increase disorder, to gain a foothold, joined the revolution. They
ok increasing control. And what began as a popular democratic
volution, committed to democracy and social justice, very shortly
oved and was taken over and really seized and placed into the
ands of a band of Communist conspirators."[13] The President pro-
uced no evidence to support his assertion; but on May 5, the State
epartment released a list of fifty-five "Communist and Castroite"
ames to support the Johnson administration's claims of Communist
keover. The list, denounced by Bosch and rebel leaders, was also
diculed by other governments and individuals critical of the Amer-
an action.

The extent of hemispheric hostility to the unilateral American
tervention emerged when the United States sought to involve the
AS in a peacekeeping role. An American draft resolution calling
r a cease-fire was adopted on April 30 by the Council of the OAS
ith no negative votes.[14] Similarly, a second draft resolution intro-
uced by the U.S., in conjunction with Argentina, Brazil, Colombia,
uatemala, Mexico, and Peru, at the Tenth Meeting of Consultation
 Ministers of Foreign Affairs, a resolution calling for the establish-

[11] White House press release, April 28, 1965; reprinted in *Department of State
ulletin*, LII (May 17, 1965), 738.

[12] U.N. Doc. S/6310, April 29, 1965.

[13] White House press release, May 2, 1965; reprinted in *Department of State
ulletin*, LII (May 17, 1965), 744.

[14] Resolution of the Council of the Organization of American States, April
, 1965, U.N. Doc. S/6315, May 1, 1965.

ment of an OAS committee to investigate "all aspects of the situ
tion in the Dominican Republic" and to assist in the arrangement
a cease-fire, was adopted on May 1.[15] But prolonged negotiatio
were required to secure the adoption of an American draft resolutic
to establish an inter-American peacekeeping force. The creation of
regional military force, endorsed by the five-nation peace committ
sent to Santo Domingo pursuant to the May 1 resolution, was oppose
by Mexico, Uruguay, Chile, Ecuador, and Peru, states with social ar
political systems more advanced than those in many other Lat
American states. These states, fearful that the American interve
tion might be a foretaste of other U.S. interventions in Latin Amer
can states experiencing domestic unrest, condemned the America
action in the Dominican Republic and voted against the resolutio
They decried the intervention as illegal under Article 17 of the OA
Charter[16] and scored the United States' failure to consult the OA
before taking its action. Their negative votes were not sufficient
defeat the plan; intensive behind-the-scenes discussions produced
bare two-thirds majority for the American proposal, as amended b
five other Latin American states who recorded the view that approv
of OAS intervention in the Dominican Republic should not be co
strued as approval of the initial American intervention. Venezue
abstained on the resolution.

Approved by thirteen states plus a representative of the Dominica
Republic (although the country had no legitimate government at th
time), the resolution provided for an international force to be esta
lished incorporating United States forces present in the Dominica
Republic and units to be contributed by other members of the OA
The resolution stipulated that the force would operate under th
authority of the Tenth Meeting of Consultation and would have a
its purpose "that of co-operating in the restoration of normal co
ditions in the Dominican Republic, in maintaining the security of i
inhabitants and the inviolability of human rights, and in the esta
lishment of an atmosphere of peace and conciliation that will perm
the functioning of democratic institutions."[17] The Security Counc

[15] Resolution of the Tenth Meeting of Consultation of Ministers of Forei
Affairs, Organization of American States, May 1, 1965, U.N. Doc. S/631
May 3, 1965.

[16] Article 17 of the OAS Charter states: "The territory of a state is i
violable; it may not be the object, even temporarily, of military occupation
of other measures of force taken by another state, directly or indirectly, und
any grounds whatever."

[17] Resolution of the Tenth Meeting of Consultation of Ministers of Foreig

der Article 54 of the Charter,[18] was informed of passage of the
AS resolution, as it had been informed of other actions taken by
e regional body in the Dominican conflict.

The preference of the United States government for OAS con-
eration of the Dominican disorder rather than United Nations
volvement stemmed from America's dominant position in the OAS
d its disinclination to encourage the Soviet Union or Cuba to exit the American military presence on the island for propaganda
rposes. Thus when the Security Council debated the Dominican
estion in sixteen meetings from May 3 to May 25, the American
presentative argued that the OAS should continue to exercise pri-
ry responsibility for attaining a permanent cease-fire and pro-
oting a political solution to the disorder. In a series of statements
the Council, Adlai Stevenson defended the American intervention
necessary: "When hours and even minutes counted — there was
time for deliberate consultation and for the organization of
ernational machinery which did not yet exist."[19] He repeated the
ims of the U.S. government that its intervention was justified on
manitarian and legal grounds and stressed its interest in securing
settlement in accord with the wishes of the Dominican people.

The predictable Soviet and Cuban denunciations of the American
sition were echoed by British, Bolivian, and French criticisms. The
ited States succeeded in preventing the passage of a Security
uncil resolution that would have condemned its actions and given
Thant and the Council more extensive responsibilities in the Do-
nican conflict. While debate in the OAS and the UN continued, the
ited States shifted its support from the military junta it had
aced in power to a coalition regime, in a belated acknowledgment
the depth of non-Communist endorsement of the rebel cause.
roughout the next few months, the rebel forces continued to press
r an enlarged UN role rather than OAS mediation, which they re-
rded as partial to the Dominican military forces manipulated by
e United States. Each local party to the internal conflict sought to
e one of the interested international organizations to advance its
use against its opponents.

---

airs, Organization of American States, May 6, 1965, para. 2, U.N. Doc.
5333, Rev. 1, May 7, 1965.

8 Article 54 states: "The Security Council shall at all times be kept fully
ormed of activities undertaken or in contemplation under regional arrange-
nts or by regional agencies for the maintenance of international peace and
urity."

9 U.N. Doc. S/P.V. 1200, May 5, 1965, 12.

The eventual settlement of the Dominican conflict, the establis
ment of a provisional government after a cease-fire, and the inquiri
into violations of human rights took place under OAS aegis. Fr
quent reports of "confusion" between the regional body's functio
and those of the UN observer on the scene were voiced in Securi
Council debates and in the press. U Thant on several occasions e
pressed concern over the precedents that the OAS actions might s
for relationships between the UN and regional organizations. T'
Charter articles setting forth the desirable balance between region
and UN activities are ambiguous. They emphasize the need f
Security Council authorization when regional enforcement acti
is undertaken, but they do not clarify what kinds of action shall l
considered "enforcement." The United States, arguing that t'
OAS actions in the Dominican Republic did not constitute "enforc
ment," claimed the primacy of the regional organization. Apa
from legal questions, the conflict raised, but did not resolve, a pra
tical issue: the compatibility of functions between regional organiz
tions and the UN in civil strife. Might it be desirable to consid
allotting *peacekeeping* functions to one organization and *peacema*
ing functions to the other? What function should each organizatic
assume? Can a feasible combination be found?

The widespread distaste for the American intervention was evide
as few Latin American countries endorsed a United States plan for
permanent inter-American peace force. Aside from Brazil, only t'
military dictatorships of Honduras, Nicaragua, and Paraguay co
tributed troops; Costa Rica contributed police. The initial interve
tion raised doubts about the purposes of regional organization in t'
hemisphere; the subsequent establishment of the inter-America
force and the OAS assumption of responsibilities for securing
specific settlement ran the risk of hindering the organization in t'
performance of other political tasks.

VI

The capabilities of security pacts in circumstances of intraregion
civil strife remain untested. When disturbances between the Gree
and Turkish communities erupted on Cyprus in December 1963,
appeared that NATO might lead in the search for a settlement of t'
internal conflict. The British and American governments clearly pr
ferred a regional approach to a global one. The British proposed
three-month, NATO-recruited peacekeeping force of 10,000 men u
der British command with political guidance from a committee •

ambassadors, as well as the appointment of a mediator from a North
Atlantic non-NATO country.

Turkey reluctantly assented to the plan, Greece accepted it with
some reservations, but the Greek Cypriots rejected it. American support for the British plan was subject to temporary suspension of the
two contested treaties and avoidance of any Security Council control.
The U.S. hoped to prevent Soviet intrusion into the affair via Council
votes. The Cypriot president, Archbishop Makarios, then demanded
that the proposed force be made responsible to the Security Council,
that Turkish troops be excluded from its composition, and that mediation be confined to Britain, Greece, and Turkey (with the Turkish
Cypriot minority barred from the talks). He also urged that a Commonwealth force be established rather than a NATO one. Shortly
thereafter, the United States yielded to Makarios' demand that the
force be "linked" to the UN via "reports." After additional negotiations between U Thant, American and British officials, and the Archbishop, the U.S. abandoned its earlier position and, with Britain,
endorsed an appeal to the Security Council.

Speculation on alternatives to the course adopted are worth pon-
dering. Could the U.S. and British negotiators have given Makarios a
choice of a NATO force or no force at all and risked Soviet intervention in the Cyprus dispute? Would Makarios have invited the Soviets
to intervene directly, and would they have done so? Could the two
Western powers have arranged to have the Council meet in order to
authorize a force whose composition and instructions were agreed
upon in advance by the parties? The Archbishop's refusal to accept
a regional peacemaking force or continuation of the British force
in Cyprus marked a defeat for Anglo-American diplomacy. It was
clear that his rejection did not derive from the military deficiencies
of these proposals but from his conviction that the UN would serve
as the most reliable mechanism for realization of his internal political
goals. Controlling eighty percent of the island's population, the Archbishop defined the problem as one of "self-determination" in an attempt to court the sympathies of the new states who might be expected
to support anticolonialist positions in the General Assembly.

The evidence suggests that instances of a breakdown of law and
order may pose the most intractable problems for regional organizations and for the UN. One issue that remains unsettled is the character
of the desirable relationship between the two types of organization.
Since it can be assumed that political rather than legal considerations
are uppermost in the minds of policy-makers, any clarification of these

ill-defined relationships that would require advance commitments
use one or the other type of organization first or exclusively appea
remote. The demands placed on the UN in breakdowns of law a
order are comparable to those placed on regional organizations wh
they become involved in similar conflicts. It is clear that rival lo
factions will attempt to use these organizations, against one anoth
if necessary, in order to realize internal political aspirations. Also,
is apparent that the different members of regional organizations m
disagree on the nature of outside threats or external control in in
vidual conflicts and may withhold the support needed to promc
collective peacekeeping actions or negotiations between disputan
As a result, it is possible that a regional organization may beco
overcommitted, politically, if its members cannot agree on a sing
candidate or group of individuals among many to perform the ord
giving functions of government.

The efforts of regional organizations to foster peaceful solutions
internal disorders may be unrewarding if the type of settlement p
posed ignores the fact that the very outbreak of violence indicates t
lack of a national consensus needed for orderly government. Reco
mendations that call for the establishment of new political structur
must take national histories and traditions into account. If a soluti
is proposed in regional decision-making councils that is not suited
the politics of the country in disorder, tensions may be exacerbat
rather than eased. The more extensive the role of the internation
organization, the greater the uncertainties that hamper attempts
secure cease-fires and lasting accommodation between local adve
saries. Less ambitious but no less desirable tasks for regional acto
to perform in breakdowns of law and order include adequate fac
finding procedures and selective border-sealing or supervision whi
violence works itself out. These activities would be extremely valuab
given the frequent inability of the UN to undertake them. In additio
such responses would underscore the compatibility of regional a
global approaches, a compatibility threatened by elaborate peac
keeping operations that appear competitive.

VII

The interests that have limited the effectiveness of international o
ganizations in colonial wars and in conflicts involving a breakdown
law and order have assumed still greater proportions in proxy wa
and conflicts involving charges of external aggression or subversio

e actions of third-party states — the superpowers in Greece, Guate-
la, Hungary, Lebanon, Laos, and Vietnam, and Egypt and Saudi
abia in Yemen — have heightened the threat to regional and global
bility when internal violence has erupted in these countries. Inter-
tional organizations as political institutions have represented at
st a partial embodiment of national objectives for third parties.
ey have served chiefly as forums for debate and propaganda. Occa-
nally, the UN and regional organizations have undertaken inves-
ations or observation missions, but patterns of response have
veloped excluding large-scale peacekeeping operations or respon-
ilities for obtaining political settlements.

The policy preferences of the United States and the Soviet Union
ntinue to be crucial in determining whether regional and global ap-
oaches to these conflicts are perceived as compatible or competitive.
roughout the postwar period, American, Soviet, and, more recently,
inese policy-makers have exercised wide discretionary powers in
ssifying internal conflicts as externally initiated, abetted, or con-
olled. Major U.S. foreign policy "doctrines" — the Truman, the
senhower, and the Johnson-Rusk — have had as a prime purpose
e delineation of "subversive" threats or "aggressive" intentions
at the United States commits itself to combat by whatever means —
ilateral, regional, or multilateral — it selects. Similarly, Russian
d Chinese policy statements have argued that "wars of national
eration" or "people's wars" against "imperialist oppressors" are
t subject to international review procedures that might assess the
gitimacy of interventions and counterinterventions. Since the Chi-
se leadership is not represented directly in the UN or in regional
ganizations, its doctrines and actions are removed still further
om review than are those of the United States and the Soviet
nion.

The superpowers, both in the UN and in their respective alliances,
ve adopted flexible criteria for estimating the dangers created by
ch other's interventions in internal conflicts. Understandably, secu-
ty pacts have served as the most convenient vehicles for the super-
wers in their efforts to legitimize interventionary courses of action.
t the internal stresses and strains of their defense systems —
ATO, SEATO, and the Warsaw Pact — have confronted the U.S.
d the Soviet Union with the need to "go it alone" if they choose to
tervene on a massive scale in conflicts like Vietnam. The increasing
luctance of formal allies to support superpower interventions in in-
rnal conflicts, of which Vietnam is the most notable example, has

reduced one value of security pacts to the superpowers. At the sam
time, the lessened tension between the superpowers themselves h
called the rationale of such alliances into question.

Throughout the postwar period, the superpowers have used a va
ety of instrumentalities to secure endorsement of their own poli
goals as well as to prevent unfavorable shifts in the world balance
power. When internal conflicts involving charges of subversion
external aggression have appeared to presage detrimental shifts, t
United States and the Soviet Union have employed security pacts a
the UN to explain the selection of direct intervention, lesser forms
manipulation, or, in some cases, abstention. The United States us
the UN, prior to NATO's formation, as the mechanism for exposi
what it termed a Soviet-inspired foreign challenge to Greek inc
pendence and sovereignty. The announcement of the Truman Dc
trine reaffirmed the already evident U.S. policy of meeting su
challenges with unilateral or collective defense responses rather th
with UN measures.

In the 1954 Guatemalan disorder, the U.S. successfully used t
OAS as a Latin American NATO, while the Soviet Union argued f
Security Council primacy. In the 1956 Hungarian uprising, the U.S
preoccupied with intra-NATO ramifications of the Suez crisis, us
the UN as an instrument for expressing its desire to avoid interve
tion. The Soviet Union, defending its unilateral intervention
Hungary, cited the Warsaw Pact in a transparent effort to addu
"regional" legitimacy for its actions. In Lebanon, the U.S. approv
UN observation, while it supported the incumbent Chamoun regin
with a unilateral intervention.

Repeatedly, the superpowers have denounced each other's inte
ventions or defended their own by referring to Article 51 of the U
Charter.[20] In no disorder has the tendency to allege "self-defense
against "armed attack" produced greater controversy than in tl
Vietnam war.[21] In no instance has the failure to develop mandato

[20] Article 51 states: "Nothing in the present Charter shall impair the i
herent right of individual or collective self-defense if an armed attack occu
against a Member of the United Nations, until the Security Council has tak
the measures necessary to maintain international peace and security. Measur
taken by Members in the exercise of this right of self-defense shall be i
mediately reported to the Security Council and shall not in any way affect t
authority and responsibility of the Security Council under the present Charter
take at any time such action as it deems necessary in order to maintain
restore international peace and security."

[21] For a lucid analysis of the legal aspects of American intervention
Vietnam, see Falk, "International Regulation of Internal Violence," 63-67.

view procedures for arguments based on Article 51 been more dan-
rous. The United States, in asserting that infiltration from North
ietnam to assist insurgents constitutes "an armed attack" that
stifies its large-scale intervention on behalf of incumbents in South
ietnam as "self-defense," has underscored the impotence of regional
curity pacts as well as the UN in proxy conflicts. Despite American
tempts to place its intervention in a SEATO context, many states
the region, as well as outside it, have denied the validity of this
aaracterization. Apart from the legal ramifications of such question-
ɔle arguments, the political consequences for international organiza-
ons are serious.

The absence of agreement on definitions of aggression, self-defense,
ɪd armed attack hinders, but need not preclude entirely, the devel-
ɔment of review procedures in the UN or in regional organizations
hereby member states might subject to careful scrutiny the claims
ɪd counterclaims made under Article 51. Without such scrutiny,
nilateral interventions can continue to transform internal disorders
to proxy wars with no chance of effective international regulation.
Tith such procedures, the salience of regional organizations as cen-
rs for debate, conciliation, negotiation, or even selective interposi-
ons would be enhanced.[22]

Clearly, it is in the interest of the developing countries to press for
ɪe institutionalization of review procedures since the larger powers
ɪnnot be expected to do so. Relevant discussion in the OAU and the
AS might demonstrate the compatibility of regional and global ap-
roaches in enforcing a pause in fighting during which parties could
ove toward negotiations. Collective defense arrangements, by defini-
ɔn, will tend to favor a revision or maintenance of the status quo
ɪvorable to one or the other superpower, an objective that may be
ɪcompatible with the aims of international organizations in specific
ɪstances. The Afro-Asian states and the Latin American states who
ish to avoid client status may improve their chances by forming
·ganizations that avoid alliance connotations.

VIII

The preceding discussion has emphasized the internal and external
mitations that characterize the responses of regional organizations
ɔ civil strife. Some limitations — for example, restricted member-

[22] For a provocative discussion of this point, see Oran R. Young, *The Inter-
ediaries: Third Parties in International Crises* (Princeton 1967), chap. 3.

ships, jurisdictions, and resources — are equally significant in a tempts to regulate the three types of internal conflict considere Others, especially ideological splits, may be more relevant to one ty of conflict than to the other two. Colonial wars, internal conflicts i volving a breakdown of law and order, and proxy wars and intern conflicts involving charges of subversion or external aggression co front regional organizations with demands they are not well equipp to meet. The line between the three types of disorders is fluid, course. A colonial war may be but the first step toward a breakdov of law and order, and then a proxy war. The perceptions of leaders third-party states rather than objective tests may be most importa in determining the classification of internal conflicts and, hence, t compatibility or competitiveness of regional and global approach These approaches appear to be most compatible in the colonial wa and potentially most competitive in the breakdowns of law and ord

The coincident interest of global and regional organizations proxy wars is the maximization of pressures that will restrain t superpowers, China, or smaller revisionist powers in the modernizi areas from counterinterventions in civil strife. The present resourc of regional groupings like the OAU and OAS permit investigato activities that present little risk and, too often, are of little value civil strife. The resources of security pacts, on the other hand, a impressive militarily but of peripheral political value in promoti peaceful change in modernizing countries.

Barring desirable changes in the direction of stronger autonomo regional groupings, the prevailing pattern of *ad hoc* responses to i ternal conflict is likely to persist. A restructuring of regional orgar zation would facilitate the regulation of internal conflict on a su global basis. As already suggested, the smaller states, whose territori are targets for competitive unilateral interventions, might well tal the lead in establishing new organizations that exclude the supe powers from membership. But if countries in disorder are to avo foreign interventions, third-party states must exercise greater r straint in using internal conflicts for the achievement of nation policy goals. Both changes in the international system are desirab for purposes of conflict management. Both are feasible only if a lar number of states give priority to them.

Gordon Connell-Smith

The OAS and the
Dominican Crisis

On 28 April 1965, following a revolt against the ruling junta in Santo Domingo, and without prior reference to the Organization of American States,[1] detachments of U.S. marines were sent into the Dominican Republic. This was the first time the United States had taken such action since Franklin Roosevelt launched the Good Neighbour policy in 1933. Moreover, it was in clear violation of the OAS charter which declares that the territory of an American State "may not be the object, even temporarily, of military occupation or of other measures of force taken by another State, directly or indirectly, on any grounds whatever" (Article 17). The only exception lies in "measures adopted for the maintenance of peace and security *in accordance with existing treaties*" (Article 19, author's italics). U.S. intervention has thus been a severe blow to the inter-American system which, only two weeks earlier, had celebrated seventy-five years of "peace and progress."

Yet the United States sets some store by the inter-American system. She brought it into existence in the late 1880s and very largely finances its activities. Her self-image requires that relations with her weaker neighbours should appear different from those traditionally existing between Great and small Powers — and, of course, those

Reprinted from *The World Today* (June 1965), with the permission of The Royal Institute of International Affairs and the author.

[1] The OAS is the central organization of the network of principles, agreements, and institutions which form the inter-American system. For a brief description see the present writer's "The Organization of American States," in *The World Today*, October 1960.

between the Soviet Union and *her* neighbours. The OAS is, theoreti
cally, an association of equals, based on the principle of one natio
one vote, with no member enjoying a power of veto. It has been sai
that in her relations with Latin America "Pan-Americanism was th
choice of the United States rather than imperialism."[2]

This self-image is an extremely important factor in U.S. foreig
policy. It is closely linked with what George Kennan has called he
"legalistic-moralistic approach" to international problems. Th
United States has sought from the inter-American system "th
legitimacy of multilateralism," or, to put it more simply, an OA
label for her hemispheric policies. Such was the OAS Council resolu
tion of 23 October 1962 calling for the dismantling of the Sovie
missiles in Cuba and authorizing whatever measures might be neede
to secure their withdrawal. President Kennedy's proclamation of
naval "quarantine" of the island cited this resolution, and such lega
case as the United States could advance to justify her measures o
"anticipatory self-defence" referred to the Inter-American Treat
of Reciprocal Assistance signed in Rio de Janeiro in 1947. The U.S
representative in the U.N. General Assembly declared his countr
had a "mandate" from the OAS to protect the Western Hemisphere

Again, since the OAS is described in its charter as "within th
United Nations . . . a regional agency," the United States has bee
able to claim that hemispheric questions should be dealt with by th
inter-American body. Although she has not been entirely successfu
in preventing Latin American countries in dispute with her fro
appealing to the United Nations, her great influence has made th
OAS virtually autonomous in the field of international peace an
security in the region. Sanctions under the Rio treaty have been im
posed upon the Dominican Republic (in 1960) and Cuba (in 196
and 1964), the United States contending that measures short o
armed action do not constitute "enforcement action" requirin
authorization by the U.N. Security Council. At the Ninth Meeting o
Consultation of American Foreign Ministers (July 1964) the Cuba
Government was threatened with "armed force" should it "persis
in carrying out acts that possess characteristics of aggression." Ar
ticle 51 of the U.N. Charter permits such action only against arme
attack.

But the basic reason for U.S. sponsorship and continuing suppor

[2] Joseph Byrne Lockey, *Essays in Pan-Americanism* (Berkeley, University o
California Press, 1939), p. 158.

f the inter-American system has been to secure hemispheric accept-
nce of her own national policy of excluding from Latin America
xtra-continental influence inimical to her own interests. This has
een of increased importance since growing commitments in other
egions of the world have made it difficult for her to justify the
Ionroe Doctrine, which in any case has never been popular with her
outhern neighbours. The existence of the inter-American system has
aade it possible for the United States to claim that her own under-
akings in other continents give no cause for other Powers to inter-
ene in the Western hemisphere. Such intervention would be not
ierely against her, but against all the American republics, who share
community of interests. Since the challenge from international com-
iunism poses the most serious threat ever offered to her interests in
atin America, the United States has seen the OAS in recent years
rimarily as an instrument to assist her in combating this challenge.

It has not proved an entirely satisfactory instrument, however.
Iany Latin Americans have not accepted the U.S. position on the
old war, and reject the idea of the OAS as an anti-communist alli-
nce. Indeed, they look to the inter-American system to impose re-
traint upon their powerful neighbour: to maintain the principle of
on-intervention. Latin Americans believe, not without justification,
hat the United States tends to view any movement for substantial
ocial reform as communist-inspired, and they are extremely reluc-
ant to give OAS support to what would in practice be action by the
United States. In spite of all the pressure she has been able to exert,
he United States has received only qualified Latin American support
1 meeting the communist challenge in the hemisphere. So, from time
) time, she has taken unilateral action. A pattern of appeal to the
OAS and subsequent unilateral action may be observed. It is only
gainst this background that President Johnson's decision to inter-
ene in the Dominican Republic — and Latin American reaction to
— can be evaluated.

First, there was the Guatemalan experience. At the Tenth Inter-
merican Conference (Caracas, 1954), the United States endeavoured
) obtain Latin American agreement to the proposition that:

. . the domination or control of the political institutions of any American
tate by the international communist movement, extending to this hemi-
ohere the political system of an extra-continental power, would constitute
threat to the sovereignty and political independence of the American
tates, endangering the peace of America, and would call for appropriate
tion in accordance with existing treaties.

This was, in effect, an endorsement of the Monroe Doctrine, which would be violated by the mere existence of a communist government in the Western hemisphere. The Latin Americans were not prepared to accept this, and most of them supported a modified version only with reluctance and in the fact of great pressure; warm support came only from right-wing dictatorships. Argentina and Mexico did not vote for the Caracas anti-communist resolution; Guatemala, against whose Government it was directed, opposed it. The subsequent removal of the Arbenz Government was effected by the Central Intelligence Agency, not by action of the OAS, though the latter's existence was used by the United States to prevent the Security Council acting on Guatemala's complaint to the United Nations.

Cuba presented a much graver challenge to the United States, for Castro eventually aligned himself with the Soviet Union. The Seventh Meeting of Consultation of American Foreign Ministers met at San José, Costa Rica, in August 1960 to consider the question of communist intervention in the hemisphere. But, although the Eisenhower Administration joined in condemning the Trujillo Government of the Dominican Republic for aggression against Venezuela at the immediately preceding Sixth Meeting of Consultation, it failed to secure a specific condemnation of the Cuban Government.

So President Kennedy permitted the CIA to attempt a repetition of its Guatemalan achievement by launching an invasion of Cuba by Cuban exiles: the Bay of Pigs fiasco of April 1961, based upon a sad misappraisal of the situation on the island. Following this bitter setback, the President warned Latin America that "if the nations of this hemisphere should fail to meet their commitments against outside Communist penetration — then I want it clearly understood that this Government will not hesitate in meeting its primary obligations, which are to the security of our nation."

Then, in the following November, occurred an interesting episode — of greater significance in the light of more recent events. Trujillo had been assassinated in the previous May and his heirs overthrown. A threat of further upheaval in the Dominican Republic provided the occasion for a show of force avowedly to discourage an attempt by the Trujillo family to seize power again. Without preliminary reference to the OAS, the United States dispatched eight naval vessels with 1,800 marines on board to cruise three miles off the Dominican coast. The U.S. Government clearly was encouraged by the general absence of Latin American criticism of this action (due doubtless to the unpopularity of the Trujillo regime). It was applauded at home s at last taking a firm line in the Caribbean region; the loudest acclaim came from those hoping it would prove a preliminary to strong measures against Castro. Perhaps the Kennedy Administration was preparing the ground for such measures should an opportunity arise.

At all events, under strong domestic pressure "to do something about Castro," the U.S. Government took the Cuban issue once more to the OAS. At first it hoped for sanctions against Castro, but it soon became clear that this would not receive the necessary Latin American support. At the Eighth Meeting of Consultation, held at Punta del Este, Uruguay, in January 1962,[3] all members of the OAS (except Cuba) agreed "that adherence by any member of the Organization of American States to Marxism-Leninism is incompatible with the inter-American system." But only a bare two-thirds majority supported the exclusion of "the present Government of Cuba" from the inter-American system. The six which did not do so (and, in fact, had not favoured holding the Meeting) were Argentina, Bolivia, Brazil, Chile, Ecuador, and Mexico. They thus included the most important countries of Latin America and represented more than two-thirds of the total population of the region. Nor did Cuba's exclusion from the OAS noticeably improve the prospects of removing Castro from power: the U.S. objective — however long-term.

In the following October there was the Cuban missile crisis. The U.S. appeal to the OAS and her success in obtaining its support have already been noted. Of course, the OAS was faced with a *fait accompli:* the proclaimed determination of the United States to take certain measures and the knowledge that she had already initiated them. The other members of the inter-American system had no significant voice in either the formulation or execution of the decisions taken; they accepted U.S. policy, and the OAS acted, on this occasion, as the "rubber stamp" its critics have always described it as being. The support of Bolivia, Brazil, and Mexico, however, was qualified; their delegates stated that they did not support an armed invasion of Cuba to accomplish the purposes of the resolution. Moreover, the degree of support the United States obtained was to meet the immediate crisis, not for her general policy towards Castro. This soon became evident when attempts were made to strengthen inter-American machinery for combating subversion. The Latin Americans were more apprehensive of U.S. intervention in their internal affairs.

[3] See the present writer's "The Future of the Organization of American States: Significance of the Punta del Este Conference," in *The World Today,* March 1962.

The death of President Kennedy awakened Latin American fear of a hardening of U.S. policy. In particular, it appeared that the new Administration was less concerned than its predecessor had been over the recent incidence of military *coups* in Latin America. The successor governments generally were more strongly anti-communist than those they had overthrown, and more co-operative with the United States on the Cuban issue. President Johnson seemed to be insensitive to Latin American feelings. For example, he did not conceal his satisfaction with the overthrow of President Goulart of Brazil in April 1964, which was soon followed by the severance of diplomatic relations with Cuba.

When the Ninth Meeting of Consultation met at the Pan-American Union in July to consider Venezuelan charges of aggression and intervention by the Cuban Government, the situation seemed much more favourable for severe measures against Castro than on any previous such occasion. By this time only four Latin American countries still maintained relations with Cuba: Bolivia, Chile, Mexico, and Uruguay. Although they did not support sanctions at the Ninth Meeting all except Mexico did so subsequently in the face of renewed U.S. pressure. The most significant result of the Meeting was a warning to Cuba:

. . . that if it should persist in carrying out acts that possess characteristics of aggression and intervention against one or more member States of the Organization, the member States shall preserve their essential rights as sovereign States by the use of self-defense in either individual or collective form, which could go so far as resort to armed force, until such time as the Organ of Consultation[4] takes measures to guarantee the peace and security of the hemisphere.

This could form the basis of some future action by the United States against Castro, and appears the more ominous since her intervention in the Dominican Republic. The Ninth Meeting also called upon the non-American allies of the United States to help make its resolution effective: that is to say, to stop trading with Cuba. There was very little more the OAS could do about Castro unless he offered more obvious provocation. Yet the United States was determined not to co-exist with a communist government in the Western hemisphere.

Meanwhile, it would hardly be surprising if Mr. Johnson concluded from the Cuban experience that the only way to prevent the emergence of "a second Castro" was for the United States to act swiftly

[4] Under the Rio treaty, this is the Meeting of Consultation of American Foreign Ministers or the OAS Council acting provisionally in that capacity.

any situation where a communist take-over of another Latin American country seemed likely. The United States could not rely upon er allies to accept her judgment as to when that situation had arisen, ut few would oppose her once she was committed. Specifically, she ould secure the two-thirds majority needed in the OAS to give some orm of legality to her position. Those Latin American countries un-illing to endorse her intervention would in any case have raised bstacles to prompt action had she sought prior agreement from the AS.

At all events, the marines were landed in the Dominican Republic. hey had been sent, it was said at first, to safeguard the lives of U.S. itizens and other foreign nationals following the breakdown of law nd order. Even so, this action was painfully reminiscent of the days efore Franklin Roosevelt, and was viewed with anger and dismay roughout Latin America: anger among the vast majority as yet nother manifestation of "Yankee imperialism," and dismay among atin American leaders seeking to co-operate with the United States the face of widespread anti-Americanism. When the United States ppealed for OAS assistance in carrying out her self-appointed task, any member governments were very reluctant to accommodate her.

Moreover, it became clear almost at once that the real purpose of e U.S. intervention was to prevent a communist take-over of the ominican Government. President Johnson declared that the United tates had evidence that the rebel movement had come under com-unist control. It is of interest that he endeavoured to justify his tion by reference to the unanimous resolution of the Eighth Meet-g of Consultation declaring the incompatibility of Marxism-Lenin-m with the inter-American system. But the U.S. appeal to the OAS as not to assist in meeting a communist threat, but to provide an ter-American peace-keeping force.

Convened in secret session "at the ministerial level," the OAS ouncil is reported to have heard considerable criticism of the U.S. tervention; Chile, Mexico, and Venezuela openly accused her of olating the OAS charter. The most the United States could obtain first was the appointment of a five-man conciliation commission onsisting of representatives of Argentina, Brazil, Colombia, Guate-ala, and Panama) to visit the Dominican Republic and try to nego-ate a cease-fire between the rebels and the military junta. In the eantime, the United States protested that she was not taking sides, hile accusing the rebels of being communist-dominated! It was veral days before she was able to muster the necessary Latin Amer-

ican vote for an inter-American military force. In spite of the im
mense pressure the United States exerts on a crucial issue, he
proposal (somewhat modified) obtained only the bare two-third
majority required for its adoption. Chile, Ecuador, Mexico, Peru, an
Uruguay voted against it, and Venezuela abstained. Some of thes
countries are important, and their opposition is indicative of muc
wider Latin American dissatisfaction with what had occurred. Uru
guay, one of the two Latin American members of the Security Coun
cil, joined France in condemning the U.S. intervention when th
Soviet Union brought the matter before the world organization.

The Dominican crisis is not yet over, but certain conclusions ca
be reached concerning it. Tens of thousands of U.S. marines hav
been sent into a small Caribbean country: a show of force designe
to demonstrate U.S. determination that another communist satellit
shall not be established in the Americas. An OAS presence will giv
a façade of internationalism while the United States resolves th
Dominican political situation to her own satisfaction. The Securit
Council will prove no obstacle to the fulfilment of this objective, an
the result will appear on the surface as a triumph for what is comin
to be called the ''Johnson Doctrine.'' Latin American feelings ma
have suffered, but these must be subordinated to more urgent con
siderations; so must widespread criticism of the intervention in othe
regions of the world.

But this is not the end of the matter. It is possible that the marine
will have to remain in the Dominican Republic a long time if a gov
ernment is to be sustained there which satisfies U.S. requirement
A comparable situation may develop elsewhere in the hemispher
perhaps in one of the larger Latin American countries. Colombia i
already being mentioned. Meanwhile, the United States is not recor
ciled to the continued existence of the present Cuban Government
indeed, the next logical step for the Johnson Doctrine would surel
be to overthrow Castro. This would be a further blow to the inter
American system already weakened by the Dominican crisis. Th
possibility of such action is a threat hanging over inter-America
relations.

U.S. relations with Latin America are intrinsically delicate becaus
of the vast disparity of power between them. Perhaps the most im
portant function of the inter-American system has been in som
measure to mitigate this Great Power-small Powers relationship
Because of her overwhelming might — and her past policies — th
United States is unpopular in Latin America, and therefore it i

xtremely difficult for Latin American governments to avoid charges
f subservience if they are friendly towards her. Hence the unpalat-
ble fact that, generally speaking, right-wing dictatorships, un-
sponsive to public opinion, have been the most co-operative with
e United States, especially on the question of combating commu-
ism in the hemisphere. But the U.S. preference for such dictator-
ips over what she calls "leftist" governments has further increased
er unpopularity in Latin America. Only by exercising more restraint,
nd showing greater understanding of the problems of the region and
atin American efforts to solve them, can the United States hope to
ut inter-American relations on a less precarious basis.

One obvious way to further more harmonious inter-American rela-
ons is to strengthen the Organization of American States as a body
which Latin American governments are genuinely consulted on the
ital issues of the hemisphere and may hope to have influence on the
ecisions taken. This the United States has tried to do until a crisis
rises in which her leaders consider it necessary either to force the
ecessary degree of support for her policies or to ignore the OAS
together. Unfortunately, Latin America is a critical area and likely
become more so. This has been heavily underlined by the crisis in
e Dominican Republic, and will continue to be the case whatever
e immediate outcome. Under these circumstances, in spite of much
seful work which it promotes in many fields of inter-American co-
peration, the Organization of American States can make only a
arginal contribution to a solution of the great issues which confront
e Western hemisphere today.

Bernard K. Gordon

Regionalism and Instability
in Southeast Asia

Will some new organizational structure for Southeast Asia spee
economic development, encourage Cambodians to get along bett
with Thais, contain Chinese ambitions, and maybe even bring lastir
peace between Indonesia and Malaysia? At different times, many
Asia's leaders have asserted that all these noble goals — and othe
too — would be promoted by regionalism, or ''regional cooperation.

A plethora of proposals on regionalism has afflicted Southeast As
for almost twenty years, and little that is tangible or significant h:
come to pass. Despite that, new proposals for regional cooperatio
and revisions of old ones, continue to be pressed at high levels: t!
Asian Development Bank, established early in 1966, and proposals
organize an Asian and Pacific Council (ASPAC), set forth at mee
ings held in South Korea in June 1966, are only the most rece:
illustrations. Two questions immediately arise: why has so little bee
achieved, and why, in the face of so little success, have so mar
continued to advocate regionalism?

The first question has two answers. Regionalism has not taken ro
in Southeast Asia, first, because of the many political conflicts amor
the nations there, and second, because there is so little agreemen
even among its advocates, on what ''cooperation'' would mean i
practice. That same imprecision also helps to answer the secor
question. In large part, regionalism continues to attract supporte
because the concept, vaguely defined, seems to promise differe:
benefits to different national leaders. To many, regionalism has mea:

Reprinted from *Orbis,* X, No. 2 (Summer 1966), with the permission of t'
University of Pennsylvania Foreign Policy Research Institute and the autho

revival of cultural, and perhaps political, ties among Asian
brothers," long divided during the period of European colonialism.
or many others regional cooperation has offered hope for a more
ficient path to national economic development. To another group,
gionalism has seemed to offer small nations a stronger guarantee
' defense and security.

Conceivably, regional cooperation might serve all these purposes,
1d the result would be to make that part of the globe more cohesive,
1d less unstable, than it is today. But if we want to judge whether
egionalism has a future we must first understand Southeast Asia's
ivisive elements, particularly the intraregional conflicts that are so
mmon.

THE MAJOR DIVISIVE FORCES

Aside from the war in Vietnam, which now involves forces whose
iterests go beyond those of the Southeast Asian nations, conflicts
i Southeast Asia seem to fall roughly into two categories: those that
ave roots deep in Asia's history, before the period of European
olonialism, and those that stem primarily from much more recent
vents. The disputes between Cambodia and her neighbors, Thailand
id both Vietnams, illustrate the first type: old fears and animosities
einforced by modern events. The argument between the Philippines
nd Malaysia over the sovereignty of North Borneo is more clearly
i illustration of the second type. It reflects no long-standing interest
f Filipinos or Malaysians in the affairs of the other, nor is it accom-
anied by that centuries-old mutual dislike and distrust which exists
etween Cambodians and Vietnamese (or Thais). In contrast, the
ontroversy between Indonesia and Malaysia is a combination of
oth types. It is modern, in terms of the sources of Indonesia's ideo-
gical attitude toward Malaysia, and very old too, because of some
istorical relationships among the territories that make up Indonesia
nd Malaysia today.

Indonesia and Malaysia: Temporary Quarrel? One of the most
romising recent developments in Southeast Asia is the decision of
idonesia's new leaders, which became apparent soon after the eclipse
f President Sukarno, to call off the "confrontation" with Malaysia.
y the early summer of 1966 the new government in Djakarta was
eking actively to terminate this conflict, which had led to small-
ale guerrilla actions in Borneo and Malaya. Finally, after several
onths of searching for a mutually face-saving accommodation, the
vo parties brought confrontation to a close in August 1966.

Yet Indonesia's "crush [ganjang] Malaysia" policy, had, sin late 1962, caused a serious disturbance in an unstable area. It important to understand what led to the hostility toward Malays in the first place. Indonesia is, after all, the fifth most populous sta in the world, the largest state in the region; any lasting effort stability or regional cohesion in Southeast Asia must take Indones into account.

The view that the policy was essentially Sukarno's has been wide accepted. Thus it has been argued that Indonesia's hostility to Mala sia derived from Sukarno's need to provide circuses rather tha bread, and from his "balancing" position between the army and th Indonesian communists. Confrontation, in this view, was a perfe issue on which nationalists, soldiers and communists could readi agree, and just another of Sukarno's "nation-building" methods.

While there are elements of truth in this view, it misses a vit point: Indonesia's attitude toward Malaysia goes much deeper tha Sukarno's immediate requirements of the 1962-1965 period. Thu while Sukarno's successors seek an end to the policy of confrontatio because it is tactically expedient to end it, the attitudes that gene ated the policy will continue. This is because Indonesian leade share a number of ideas and attitudes about their nation's role i the region, most of which envisage some sort of Indonesian influen and dominance in Southeast Asia.

Among the most important ingredients of Indonesia's Southea Asia policy is a body of thought which advocates a "Greater Ind nesia." Evidence of this thesis is found as early as 1945 in the stat ments of Indonesia's nationalist leaders, including Sukarno. Ove the objections of Mohammad Hatta[1] and others, two-thirds of th leaders who proclaimed an independent Indonesia in 1945 believe that their country's territory should include Malaya, all of Borne and parts of southern Thailand. Sukarno himself went further whe he said:

I have on one occasion in my life dreamt of a pan-Indonesia, which wi include not only Malaya and Papua (New Guinea) but also the Philip pines. . . . I myself am convinced that the people of Malaya feel themselve [to be] Indonesians, belonging to Indonesia and as one of us. . . Indonesia will not become strong and secure unless the whole Straits o Malacca is in our hands.[2]

---

[1] Hatta shared with Sukarno the leadership of Indonesia's independence move ment, and served as Indonesia's Vice President until 1956.

[2] "The Territory of the Indonesian State," in *Background to Indonesia Policy Towards Malaysia* (Kuala Lumpur, 1964), pp. 20-21. This consists c

early, this sort of thinking can support a crude territorial expan-
onism — which in Indonesia has been reinforced by other pre-
alaysia attitudes concerning Malaya.

First, Singapore, included in the Malaysia concept, represented to
any leading Indonesians a host of negative symbols. To them, this
hinese-run entrepôt, with its banking and processing facilities, bore
large share of the responsibility for the historic and, in their mind,
ntinuing economic "bleeding" of Indonesia. Add to this resent-
ent the bitterness that many Indonesian leaders have felt toward
e Malayan government of Tunku Abdul Rahman since 1958-1959,
hen, according to them, both Malaya and Singapore shielded and
sisted Indonesian rebels during the insurrection against the central
vernment. Indeed, events during that period strained Djakarta's
plomatic relations with Kuala Lumpur and reinforced Sukarno's
nviction that control of the "whole Straits of Malacca" is a require-
ent of Indonesian security.

Then, too, there is the curious mixture of contempt and apprehen-
on with which many Indonesians regard Malaya, and which has
ntributed to hostility. "Contempt" is perhaps too strong a term,
t there is definitely an attitude in Djakarta that Malaysia is an
upstart" as a spokesman for Malay peoples; that Indonesia is cul-
rally superior to Malaya; and that Indonesia is the natural leader
all ethnic Malays. The other side of the coin, a certain Indonesian
prehension about Malaya, derives from the latter's economic pros-
rity and its relative political stability. This has occasionally led
jakarta to fear that some Indonesians (particularly those on
matra) might attempt to emulate their neighbors' example, and
ply in Indonesia the free-enterprise model so successful in Ma-
ya's economic development. There has even been concern in Indo-
sia regarding Sumatran secessionist feelings, which tend toward
her independence or association with Malaysia.

The final element that contributed to hostility toward Malaya
rived from Indonesia's heavily ideologized politics. This was of
urse most apparent in the last years of Sukarno's "guided democ-
cy." During that period the official Indonesian world view in-
easingly regarded all nations as divided into two camps: the old
tablished forces and the new emerging forces. Indonesian leaders
nsidered Malaysia to be one of the old established forces, or at least

---

ranslation of part of the records of the 1945 meetings which laid the founda-
ns for Japan's grant of independence to Indonesia.

a product of those forces,[3] and frequently asserted that a fund⌐
mental tenet of Indonesia's ideology was to work for the dissoluti⌐
of those forces. Even General Jani, among the officers slain by co⌐
munist activists during the night of the attempted coup on Septemb⌐
30, 1965, maintained that Indonesians have an obligation to a⌐
national liberation movements — particularly those along their ov⌐
borders.[4] As a result of this conviction, Indonesians of many politic⌐
persuasions were perfectly willing to give both overt and covert su⌐
port to measures designed to disrupt the government of Malaysia a⌐
replace it with one more inclined to the views of Indonesia's leade⌐
General Nasution, who barely escaped assassination that same nig⌐
and disagrees with Sukarno on many other matters, also spoke fr⌐
quently of the need to destroy Malaysia. Before the confrontati⌐
was announced he issued orders that led (as he later disclosed)⌐
the training of "more than 6,000 anti-British, anti-Malaysia reb⌐
in the Northern Borneo territories."[5]

All these factors combined to form an anti-Malaya political base⌐
Indonesia that could support the foreign policy goals of the "Great⌐
Indonesia" thesis. Since "Greater Indonesia" implied Indonesi⌐
dominance over the territories slated for Malaysia, and since ma⌐
Indonesians were already unfriendly to the Kuala Lumpur gover⌐
ment that was spearheading the Federation idea, it was not diffic⌐
for Indonesian leaders to fashion a "ganjang Malaysia" policy. T⌐
opportunity came in December 1962, as a direct result of an aborti⌐
revolt in Brunei, which Indonesia may or may not have initiated b⌐
certainly supported. The Brunei revolt set back, at least temporaril⌐
the plans for the Malaysian Federation, and Djakarta responded ⌐
dropping any restraint previously shown with regard to its ultima⌐
goals concerning the Malaysia territories. At that point Sukar⌐
launched the confrontation and declared his intention to "ganja⌐
Malaysia."

The thesis that Indonesia's decision was mainly the product⌐
internal forces operating on Sukarno — that "components of t⌐
Indonesian ruling group were eager to embrace some new forei⌐
crisis"[6] — must be rejected. Had a "foreign crisis" indeed be⌐

[3] On this point see Donald E. Weatherbee, "Indonesia and Malaysia: C⌐
frontation in Southeast Asia," *Orbis*, Summer 1962, p. 339.

[4] See Jani's statement reported in the *Washington Post*, February 2, 19⌐
that his troops were "awaiting the order" to move in support of people⌐
Borneo "struggling for independence."

[5] *New York Times*, September 3, 1963.

[6] Donald Hindley, "Indonesia's Confrontation with Malaysia: A Search⌐
Motives," *Asian Survey*, June 1964, p. 909.

quired — which some leading authorities doubt[7] — Indonesia had
her targets from which to choose. Portuguese Timor, surrounded
Indonesia, would have been an ideal candidate for "liberation,"
rticularly considering the negative image of Portugal in the United
ations and elsewhere. Certainly no important group inside Indonesia
d no major foreign power would have strongly opposed a campaign
"liberate" Timor. Indeed, on every conceivable ground a con-
ontation over Timor, rather than against Malaysia, would have
tter served Indonesia's "need for a foreign crisis" — if that had
en Indonesia's need. But that was not the case, for Timor can be
ized at any time, while the instability surrounding the Malaysia
oposal in 1962 presented an opportunity not to be missed. Indo-
sia's confrontation decision resulted, not from any alleged internal
need," but from a set of external goals reinforced by the conditions
its internal environment.

Indonesia's leaders expected their opposition to Malaysia would
d with relative ease to important changes in the nature of the
oposed new state. Djakarta had two goals. The immediate one no
ubt was at least to delay the formation of Malaysia. The second
s probably to assure that Malaysia, if it had to come, would be
ore loosely constructed than the federation then planned. This was
t an unreal goal, because the fear of Kuala Lumpur's domination,
pecially in Sarawak, Singapore and Brunei, was well known
Brunei never did join, while Singapore later left Malaysia). If such
looser Malaysia had been established, its separate parts might then
ve been attracted into some sort of *confederation* with Indonesia
d the Philippines, and that in turn would have provided Indonesia
ith an opportunity eventually to incorporate all or parts of Malay-
. Singapore would have been the only difficult pill to swallow, but
could have been effectively "sugar-coated" by the other, more
early "Malay," communities.

But Malaysia, as proposed by London and Kuala Lumpur, proved
be more difficult to undermine than President Sukarno anticipated.
nfrontation did not achieve success in delaying significantly, alter-

---

[7] Herbert Feith, weeks before confrontation was launched, wrote that Indo-
sia's territorial ambitions had been satisfied by the New Guinea settlement,
d the army leaders "would almost certainly oppose an agitational campaign"
Timor or Borneo. Finally, he wrote, Indonesia's need for "functional equiv-
nts" to the New Guinea campaign could be met by tackling internal prob-
s. ("Indonesia's Military Hardware," mimeo., 1962, p. 4. A slightly
rtened version of this article was published in *Nation* [Sydney], November
1962.)

ing the nature of, or "crushing" Malaysia. Indeed, Indonesia herse
ran into difficulties during the second half of 1963 in her pursuit
these goals. Sukarno's several efforts to negotiate with Malaysia aft
mid-1963, as we will see below, strongly suggests that he realized t
price of confrontation — the decidedly negative economic and pol
ical effects within Indonesia — might be too high. Therefore,
resolved, probably by June 1963, to attempt to end the confrontatic

By that time, however, the policy had developed a dynamism of
own within Indonesia, particularly among Indonesia's communis
and their associates. To the Indonesian Communist Party (PKI
confrontation combined many advantages. First it meant that ec
nomic stabilization could not be undertaken in Indonesia. Second,
provided a legitimate method for opposing Malaysia, and for foste
ing national liberation movements in Borneo. Finally, of course, co
frontation had once again placed the PKI at the forefront on
Indonesian movement championed by Sukarno.

For these reasons, Sukarno's wish to modify the confrontation w
obstructed by its very dynamism, and the efforts he and Subandi
exerted were faltering and in the end unsuccessful. Neverthele:
during 1963 and 1964, they tried on at least three occasions,
Manila, Bangkok and Tokyo, to extricate themselves, and each tir
Sukarno's dilemma became more clear: how to give in without a
pearing to. The records of the final effort, the Tokyo meetings wi
the Tunku and the Philippines President, show that Sukarno eve
seized upon a vague proposal for an Afro-Asian commission to ei
the conflict.[8] But on each occasion Indonesia insisted upon conditio
— for example, prolonging Indonesian guerrilla activities while neg
tiations were in progress — that were intolerable to Malaysia.

When Sukarno lost power, the effort that he began, to reach
compromise settlement, was resumed, but under far better conditior
With the PKI demolished, and with men in office who are committe
to more rational economic measures, the difficulties that Sukar
believed he faced no longer impede the process of ending confront
tion. Indeed, the first moves to restore a measure of stability came
the heels of Singapore's separation from Malaysia in 1965, an eve
caused by reasons internal to Malaysia. Almost immediately, Ind
nesia offered to resume trade and other ties with Singapore. Soc
afterward, Indonesia's new Foreign Minister, Adam Malik, made

---

[8] For a full discussion on this point and extracts from the Tokyo and oth
"summit" meetings, see Bernard K. Gordon, *Dimensions of Conflict in Sout
east Asia* (Englewood Cliffs, N.J.: Prentice-Hall, 1966), pp. 98-116, especial
the section called "Hypothesis For Sukarno's Tactics."

ear that he would do more than simply normalize trade with Singa-
re. He wanted to find some way to hold talks with Malaysian
aders, end the embarrassing confrontation, and direct Indonesia's
ergies to economic development, which confrontation had helped
sabotage for three years.[9]

But it should be stressed that the end to confrontation at this time
not a "good guys, bad guys" proposition. Indonesia's anti-
alaysia policy was not an invention of Sukarno and Subandrio,
hich automatically disappears as they leave the scene. Sukarno him-
lf attempted to find an end to confrontation because it brought
ore liabilities than assets *at the time*, but he would have continued
pursue certain foreign policy goals even had he been able to termi-
ate confrontation. Sukarno's successors are seeking to end confron-
tion, and will probably succeed because it is expedient, not because
ey like, more than Sukarno does, today's Malaysian regime. A dis-
ste for and distrust of the whole Malaysia concept will continue,
r the genesis of the "crush Malaysia" campaign lay in Indonesia's
jective goals and subjective attitudes. Those goals do not neces-
rily call for the extension of formal Indonesian sovereignty over
ljoining territories. They do imply, however, a dominant Indone-
an influence in Malaya, and, in the view of some leading Indone-
ans, Djakarta's dominance in all of insular Southeast Asia.

With the end of confrontation, those objectives and attitudes will
ot cease to exist. Should another opportunity arise under circum-
ances again susceptible to a catalyst (like the Brunei revolt), Indo-
esia may be expected to resume a foreign policy which seeks to
tablish regional dominance. At first glance, therefore, the policies
 Indonesia would appear inconsistent with any hopes for greater
gional cohesion; there are, however, certain circumstances in which
idonesian policies might reinforce or serve regional cohesion. That
ossibility will be discussed later in this article, for it still remains
 examine certain of the other disruptive forces in the region.

Filipino Adventurism: The Claim to North Borneo. The Philippines
ve also been involved in a dispute with Malaysia since 1962-1963.
his controversy, too, seems now to be coming to an end. But the
hilippines-Malaysia dispute differs from Indonesia's confrontation
 two important respects. First, it is unlikely to be revived, and

[9] By May 1966, press stories from Kuala Lumpur confirmed what had been
officially rumored for some time: that with the aid of Japanese and Thai
ficials, senior officials of the Indonesian and Malaysian governments had al-
ady been in direct contact in order to bring an end to confrontation. *Washing-
n Post,* May 12, 1966.

secondly, it does appear to have revolved heavily around a sing
person: former Philippines President Diosdado Macapagal.

The controversy arose because of a Philippine claim to Nor
Borneo, now the Malaysian state of Sabah. While the claim deriv
from conflicting interpretations of a grant of land made by the Sulta
of Sulu in 1878, it had to all intents and purposes lain dormant un'
the election of President Macapagal in 1961. At about the same tim
a group of the Sultan's heirs gave notice that a formal claim to tl
territory would be presented to Great Britain, which still exercis
sovereignty in North Borneo. A well-known Manila attorney, "Nick
Osmeña, represented them, and he reportedly let it be known that h
clients would accept compensation in cash for their rights to Saba
Estimates of the asking price run between \$20 and \$40 million.

Soon afterward, in early 1962, a series of colorful Manila pre
stories appeared demanding the "return" of North Borneo to tl
Philippines. Precisely at this time, when the proposals to establir
Malaysia — which would incorporate North Borneo — were bei
discussed throughout Asia, President Macapagal made a famo'
declaration. He announced that the Philippines government had su
ceeded to the Sultan's claim, and was going to press for ownersh
of North Borneo, or Sabah, as a matter of sovereignty and nation
security. Ever since, relations between Kuala Lumpur and Mani
have been troubled.

The claim itself has met with no success, but there have been sever
important consequences for international politics in Southeast Asi
First, in order to weaken the proposal for formation of Malaysia, ar
Malaysia itself once it became a reality, the Philippines entered in
a year-long embrace with Indonesia. This step aggravated many lea
ing Filipinos, some of them leaders of Macapagal's own party. Whe
Malaysia was established, Manila refused to recognize the new go'
ernment and recalled the Philippines Ambassador; this led to a bre
in diplomatic relations with Kuala Lumpur. These strained relatior
in turn forced the cessation of all activities in the Association f
Southeast Asia (ASA), the group which the Philippines, Malaya ar
Thailand had set up in 1961 as Southeast Asia's first indigenous effo
at practical regional cooperation.

Since that time, there have been a number of efforts to improv
Philippines-Malaysia relations,[10] including some while Macapag
was still President, for he must have realized that his anti-Malays
posture had not received wide support at home. The new Preside

[10] Consular ties were resumed after a year.

the Philippines, Ferdinand Marcos, even while he was a leader of capagal's party and President of the Senate, became increasingly ter in his denunciations of Philippines policy during this period. rcos, former Vice-President Pelaez, and many others felt that nila's suddenly warm relationship with Indonesia was a particuly foolish move. As a result, it is very likely that with Marcos as sident, the Philippines will attempt to restore the previously good ationship with Kuala Lumpur, and it is likely too that ASA activi will be resumed during 1966.[11]

Nevertheless, leading Malaysian officials feel that the Philippines vernment, during former President Macapagal's term of office, rificed those formerly good relations in favor of two charlatans: karno and Osmeña. The Tunku and his associates regarded nila's efforts to cooperate with Indonesia during 1963-1964 as a iical attempt to bring pressure on the Borneo claim. This policy of nsparent expedience sorely distressed the Tunku, and some Philipies officials were in turn irritated by Malaysia's attitude that the rneo claim was simply not negotiable. Thus, while ties between the countries will be resumed soon, it is clear that the dispute over rth Borneo eroded a large portion of the mutual trust that had eloped between the two governments. It may not be quickly uilt.

Thailand and Cambodia: Diplomacy by Recrimination. Unlike the ilippines and Malaysia, Thailand and Cambodia have had relations h each other for centuries, and between them nothing like mutual st has ever been present. While there are few material issues iding them today, a legacy of historical enmity embitters their ry contact. Cambodia fears, for example, that Thailand still covets least two Khmer provinces, lands which were in fact "returned" Thailand by her Japanese allies in World War II.[12] On top of this, ince Sihanouk of Cambodia has long suspected Thai involvement attempts to overthrow him. Almost daily he charges that Thailand

ASA completed its first meeting in three years in Kuala Lumpur on April 1966 with recommendations for 29 economic and cultural projects to be ertaken by the revived three-nation association. On August 3, 1966, ASA vened its third meeting of Foreign Ministers, a strong indication that the up is no longer moribund.

On April 1, 1966 a new twist was added when Cambodia's official broadcast-station charged that "As everyone knows, the Bangkok leaders are not tent with only coveting Khmer provinces and trying to nibble portions of territory, they also look hungrily at Laos, Burma and Malaysia. These ansionists, the Thais of Southeast Asia, have always tried to expand their ntry at the expense of . . . all their neighboring countries."

harbors his enemies and permits an anti-Sihanouk radio station broadcast from Thailand. This has led him to launch venomous tacks on all Thai leaders; when Thailand's former Premier, Mars Sarit, died in 1963, Sihanouk decreed that Cambodia should begin period of "national rejoicing." These days the Prince's favorite t get is Thailand's Foreign Minister, Thanat Khoman, who genera returns the barbs with the implication that the Prince is no lon sane.

In addition to this personal bitterness, Thai leaders, already anxi about communist gains in Laos and Vietnam, believe that Sihano will turn Cambodia over to the communists without a struggle. T is unlikely, for Sihanouk has made his distrust of Asia's communi very clear, yet the relations between the two countries are not i proved by their mutual public recriminations and threats. For ample, General Praphat, nominally second in command in Thaila but in the view of many the real power in the country, has decla that "we must . . . put an end to the most vile acts of Si nouk. . . ."[13]

Against this background it is difficult to envisage any significa improvement in Cambodian-Thai relations — especially under th present leaderships. It is true that Cambodia has participated, und UN auspices, in the Mekong River project, but it is also true tl Cambodia has steadfastly declined to participate in other, perh more immediately important, efforts at cooperation in the region. S did not, for example, join ASA, and her bitter relationship with Th land may inhibit Sihanouk from participating in other practical operative undertakings. Part of his reason may indeed be his des to avoid too close a connection with Western-associated states like Philippines and Malaysia, for fear of alienating Peking, but so part of his thinking will continue to derive from the historic Ca bodian fears of Thailand.[14]

THE OTHER SIDE OF THE COIN:
EFFORTS AT COOPERATION

We have discussed up to this point some, but by no means all, Southeast Asia's many conflicts; they suggest that the obstacles

[13] From a press conference statement of Praphat, reported by the Cambod government on March 20, 1964.

[14] For a full discussion see Bernard K. Gordon, "Cambodia: Where Fore Policy Counts," *Asian Survey*, September 1965.

peration are not negligible. But as we remarked at the beginning,
ltheast Asia's leaders do nevertheless continue to devote a remark-
e amount of time and energy to the concept of cooperation in their
ion. Even Prince Sihanouk has commented, almost wistfully, on
potentially major economic benefits that would be available if
os, Cambodia and all of Vietnam came together again, as they had
n joined economically under the French-inspired "Associated
ites of Indochina."

Once again we ask: why, in the face of so little success, has region-
sm continued to be stressed? That it does continue to attract sup-
rt is indicated by the establishment of two important — though
tering — steps toward cooperation, ASA and MAPHILINDO
(alaysia-Philippines-Indonesia), created in 1961 and 1963, and by
ner measures such as the Asian Development Bank. In addition, the
economic commission in the region, ECAFE, has for years pro-
ted studies and plans which attempt to point the way toward
peration in intraregional trade and coordinated development.
cently, the Japanese government sponsored meetings designed to
ter some form of economic cooperation in Southeast Asia,[15] and
s was followed by the Korean sponsored conference for Asian and
cific Cooperation (ASPAC).

The Essential Elements for Cooperation. None of these efforts has
t resulted in a durable entity, although both ASA and MAPHIL-
DO went further than earlier undertakings — especially in the
ise that both were truly Asian and that ASA in particular promised
-tain practical economic advantages. But like all other efforts
vard regionalism, since Aung San and Quirino gave voice to the
ncept soon after World War II, ASA and MAPHILINDO lacked
e or more of the essential elements that might convert regionalism
:o reality.

Some of those early calls for regionalism were impressive at the
ne; a few seemed quite far-sighted. But often they were merely
gue, as in the case of the "pan-Malay" idea which has long in-
.enced a number of intellectuals in Malaya, Indonesia and the
iilippines. President Sukarno has been attracted to that notion,
t many others, too, have looked toward the day when all the peoples
the Malay race would be united, as ostensibly they had been in
ecolonial times. Rizal, the Philippines' national hero, was among

---

[15] See the statement of Aiichiro Fujiyama, Director of Japan's Economic
inning Agency, Tokyo Ministerial Conference for Economic Development of
itheast Asia, April 7, 1966.

these, and Manuel Quezon also "dreamed of a larger federation e
bracing Burma, Thailand, and Indochina."[16]

It seems fair to say, however, that in the early postwar years, wl
some of these sentiments for Asian unity were expressed, the Asi
governments themselves were not ready for the concept of region
ism. Some leaders may have spoken of Asian "brotherhood," but
notion of cooperation seemed unrelated to their more immedi.
domestic needs. Those were times when the struggle for independer
and the first difficult steps that must follow the removal of coloni
ism's yoke had priority. And the big powers, the United States
particular, had their interests focused elsewhere; or, as in the ca
of Japan, were themselves emerging from the destruction of w
Thus, two elements — Asian interest in regionalism and great-pov
support for the idea — were out of phase with each other.

Later, when the big powers did turn their attention to the potent
benefits that might lie in regional cooperation (as Britain did
Colombo in 1954 and the United States at the Simla Conference
1955), the nations of Southeast Asia seemed to have lost even th
early vague interest in cooperation. They were in the midst of me
ing the pragmatic requirements of independence, when the first flu
of freedom gave way to recognizing the hard facts of making sta
hood work. To most it meant "full steam ahead" with *natio*
economic development. In turn, this meant that prior attention h
to be given to the capital and technical assistance that only l
powers could provide. Thus in 1955 at Simla, few in Asia were rea
to listen to American talk of multilateral planning and offers
"regional" assistance, if those offers implied any reduction in wl
each of the recipient Asian states might expect by acting alone.

Today, however, the Asian nations seem once again interested
regional cooperation, particularly in the economic sphere. Inde.
officials in Washington who are involved, for example, in Preside
Johnson's recent offer to $1 billion for Asian regional developme
and who were also involved in U.S. plans for regional assistance
1955, must wonder what has changed that might permit the idea
regionalism to work now when the same good idea could not get
the ground a decade earlier.

The answer is a simple one: Much has changed, in that the th
"essential elements" for regional cooperation might now, for the fi
time, be in phase with one another. Those elements are the th

[16] Arnold C. Brackman, *Southeast Asia's Second Front* (New York: Praeg
1966), p. 179.

roups of nations whose interest and support will be essential for the
ccess of any effort toward regionalism: (1) the more developed and
efficient" states in the area, such as Malaysia, Thailand and the
hilippines, whose participation can provide a regional effort with
ractical experience in economic planning and a record of past
complishment; (2) the "uncommitted," though important, nations
Asia (like Indonesia) whose support is vital if a future regional
rouping is to be truly "regional" and a force for stability in the
gion, though initially they can add little in material terms; and
3) the world powers, such as the United States and Japan, whose
aterial support is indispensable if regional economic development
to approach the take-off stage. In the next pages we will examine
o of those elements in detail, namely, the interest of the Asian
tions in regionalism.

ASA and MAPHILINDO. Among the most important manifesta-
ons of this interest was the formation of ASA in 1961. ASA's short
t interesting history has been characterized by an increasing move-
ent away from big, grandiose notions (like a regional airline) in
vor of smaller but more practical efforts. Thailand, for example,
ressed before entering ASA that the new group should be a "prac-
cal organization." And it should not be forgotten that one of the
st measures accomplished by ASA before it went into suspended
imation was the series of steps — taken by each of the three govern-
ents — to appropriate $1 million each to a joint "ASA Fund."
his Fund was designed to support joint ventures, largely in re-
arch, that would aid the national goals of each member. Other ASA
rojects examined trade problems, and their studies indicated that
rtain cooperative measures — in the fields of joint marketing and
dustrial planning, for instance — could assist domestic economic
als. This is not to say that ASA was ready to accomplish all the
ings its most fervent supporters hoped for, but only that ASA was
ginning to come to grips with the pragmatic tasks of regional
operation precisely when the Association's activities were sus-
nded.

ASA foundered in 1963 on the shoals of the Philippines' claim to
bah. The events which followed that claim, particularly Manila's
metime support for Djakarta, led directly to the establishment of
APHILINDO. But MAPHILINDO was in no important way a
ccessor to ASA, for they represent fundamentally different con-
ptions of regionalism. ASA was formed in 1961 partly because both
e Tunku and President Garcia of the Philippines shared a deep

aversion to communism, and concluded that regional cooperati‹ could accelerate the economic progress they felt essential to count the appeals of communism. MAPHILINDO, in contrast, develop‹ out of the simply cynical and tactical motives of Presidents Mac pagal and Sukarno (as well as Subandrio). President Macapag‹ sponsored MAPHILINDO because it provided hope for keeping ali the North Borneo claim; Indonesia joined because it supported co‹ frontation, while at the same time recognizing that it was "good d‹ mestic politics for Macapagal";[17] and the Tunku acquiesced in it order to buy time. With those beginnings, it is not surprising th‹ nothing practical resulted.

Yet MAPHILINDO did bring one important accomplishme‹ It showed that President Sukarno was willing to submit the Malays dispute to a regional grouping and join a clearly regional organiz‹ tion. For Indonesia, this decision represented an important bre‹ from her past preference for the global level of diplomacy, partic‹ larly in the Afro-Asian framework. Indonesian membership MAPHILINDO could signal the coming into phase of that seco‹ element — the participation of the uncommitted though importa‹ nations in Southeast Asia — for Indonesia is without question t‹ most important of those states, both by virtue of her population a‹ resources, and also because the direction of her policies thus far h‹ been so destabilizing.

One Approach to Stability: "ASANEFOS". One can make strong case for the thesis that stability in the region would be e‹ hanced if Indonesia became regularly associated with almost any so‹ of regional organization. Even without material benefits from su‹ an association — and Indonesia's participation, with her econom‹ and administrative weaknesses, could mean some initial net loss the other states — the political gains could be major. Conversely, a‹ effort toward regionalism that does not include Indonesia will be se‹ as unreal by Asian leaders, who also hope for Djakarta's involv‹ ment in region-wide efforts as one way to improve stability in t‹ area.

For example, an organizational affiliation — such as ASA pr‹ vided for Malaya and the Philippines when they were most at od‹ over North Borneo — might similarly provide Indonesia's leade‹ with a rationale for smoothing the roughest edges of her regional

---

[17] Based on interviews in Djakarta, including one with Dr. Subandrio of Ju‹ 4, 1963.

stabilizing foreign policies. In the Philippines-Malaysia dispute, SA served both as an organizational entity — a value — that each tion hoped to preserve, and as a communications link. Thailand, SA's third member, performed this communications function, rgely in the person of Foreign Minister Thanat Khoman.

Of course, to suggest that the "rough edges" of Indonesia's poli-es might be smoothed by participation in some regional organiza-on implies that Indonesia's proclivity for expansionism can be oderated. Sukarno, we should recall, attempted to use MAPHIL-DO to end the confrontation. He and Subandrio saw MAPHIL-DO as a framework for influencing Malaysia and for claiming that donesia's "voice" had been listened to in Southeast Asian affairs. he new leadership in Indonesia is no more likely than Sukarno ould have been to forget about the policy goals that gave rise to nfrontation in the first place. Those goals derive from a perception Indonesia's place in Southeast Asia which holds that Djakarta ould exercise a major influence regarding the territories now part Malaysia, and that Indonesia's views must be taken seriously ithin the region as a whole.

Recognizing this Indonesian outlook, there are several ways that her nations might attempt to deal with it. One was attempted in 58-1959 when several countries encouraged the dissolution of In-nesia, at least as presently constituted. Another way may be to ndemn Indonesia as a "trouble maker," and strive to build untervailing strength around her. But for a variety of reasons, nong them the many weaknesses of Malaysia, such hopes would pear doomed to failure.

A third approach is to *internalize* the role of Indonesia within the stem of Southeast Asia's international relations. This approach ould try to involve Indonesia in a new regional or subregional sociation. If such an association effectively combined the political-plomatic character of MAPHILINDO with ASA's goals of prac-al economic cooperation, we might look for benefits in improved ability for the region as a whole, as well as improvements in In-nesia's internal well-being. What we are proposing, therefore, is new MAPHILINDO-*cum*-ASA which would have two advantages: irst, it would provide Indonesia with the framework for a grand reign policy role in Asia, thus helping to satisfy her need for a ajor voice in world and regional affairs. Second, to the extent that ch a body developed into an association for practical projects in chnological and economic cooperation, it could contribute signifi-

cantly to development and stability within Indonesia. That woul
itself add to the stability of the region.

Such a group might be called "ASANEFOS" — to designate tl
"Association of Southeast Asian New Emerging Forces." AS
NEFOS would include Indonesia, the ASA members, and hopeful
could attract even Cambodia and Burma. But the main feature of tl
group is that it would combine the membership of both ASA an
MAPHILINDO, and could thereby secure Indonesia's participatic
in practical cooperative undertakings. Moreover, ASANEFOS woul
provide a rationale, for the first time, within which the developmer
plans of Indonesia's "administrators" and "economists" could l
legitimized.

Up to now, such a rationale has been missing. A central malaise
Indonesian politics has been that practical and moderate men, who:
overriding concern is with economic development, have lacked
grand ideological design and symbol with which to attract intern
support for their efforts. Without such a grand design, the dichotom
between "nation-building" and "economy-building" has not bee
bridged. Under Sukarno, with the nation-builders dominating, I
donesia's economy suffered and she undertook foreign policies fru
trating both to herself and her neighbors. The new leadership, on tl
other hand, seems to have embarked on a more moderate progran
emphasizing pragmatic steps to bring economic stabilization and
clearly less adventurous foreign policy. Nevertheless, a country
diverse and divided as Indonesia continues to need the cementin
forces which Sukarno provided with his dramatic posturings an
grand ideological symbols.

That requirement could be met, in part, by a new regional grou
in Southeast Asia in which Indonesia plays a leading, even uniqu
role. By putting her energies to work in an organization which coul
bring economic benefits, Indonesia would have a stake in its succes
If so, this would help to attenuate the forces that might again pr
duce a disruptive Indonesian foreign policy in Southeast Asia. A
organization such as the proposed ASANEFOS would also help t
bridge the dichotomy not spanned in Sukarno's time, for it woul
give Indonesia's economy-builders a legitimate and attractive al
Asian symbol, to be invoked and cited as a reason for taking soun
economic steps.

In sum, ASANEFOS should be seen as a potential stabilizin
force for Southeast Asia as a whole and Indonesia specifically. If
carefully provided for Indonesian nuances (as in its name, its state

als, and perhaps in headquarters location), it could satisfy certain
the foreign policy aspirations of many leading Indonesians.
multaneously, it could provide a new incentive and rationale for
mestic efforts in Indonesia toward economic development.[18]

Conclusions

A regional effort along these new lines will have to combine two
ite different perspectives on "regionalism." Both outlooks already
ist simultaneously in each of the ASA and MAPHILINDO coun-
ies. There are on the one hand many leaders, pragmatic about the
quirements of economic and political development, who see region-
ism in instrumental-economic terms: a means to help achieve de-
lopmental goals. On the other hand, a strident and sometimes flam-
yant Asian nationalism sees regionalism as a format for asserting
sia's identity and recapturing an "Asian unity" that ostensibly
is upset by colonialism. Any new cooperative effort will have to
mbine the appeals and energies of both. It will have to reflect more
Asia's new nationalism than ASA, but will also have to be far
ore practical than MAPHILINDO.

The formation of a group like the proposed ASANEFOS would
present two of the three essential elements for regionalism. It
uld mean that the interest in regionalism of the colorful but less
osperous states (like Indonesia) had begun to converge with the
terests of the more efficient small states (the ASA group). The
ird essential element, the interest and support of the great powers,
becoming more apparent. This was signaled in two ways: first, by
esident Johnson when he spoke in 1965 of a $1 billion contribution
ward cooperative developmental efforts in Southeast Asia, and
cond, by the Japanese and American promises to subscribe $200

[18] This would be especially true if practical aspects of the new group were
deled after ASA, and one would expect that if Thailand participated the ASA
del would exercise a major influence. ASA, once its "shakedown" phase was
mpleted, showed a marked change. It grew away from its early attachment to
gional cooperation almost as an end in itself to a more practical instrument
thin which to press ahead with the economic development of each participat-
; state — in ways that required multinational cooperation. Again, ASA's
perience suggests that the model for regional cooperation in Southeast Asia
ll emphasize joint projects to improve commodity production, as in rubber
1 probably in rice; planning on industrial development, so as to avoid need-
s redundancies and duplication; educational exchanges, in order to utilize
rce skills more efficiently; and efforts that can help to bring greater levels
intraregional trade among Southeast Asian countries. These are some of the
ections in which ASANEFOS might move.

million each to the Asian Development Bank. As these three eleme
move into place — for the first time in history — they provide
practical basis for making regionalism work in Southeast Asia.

However, whether the dream will become reality will depend p
marily on the actions of Southeast Asian states. Their policies w
help to determine whether the material support of outside states
in the form of capital investment — will flow into Southeast As
That support will look for a greater measure of political stability
the region than has existed up to now. Stability requires that politi
sores, such as Indonesia's confrontation against Malaysia and t
Philippines' claim to North Borneo, be healed. While these goals a
difficult, recent changes in Manila and Djakarta indicate that th
can be achieved. If conflicts can be resolved and some measure
stability thereby restored, the climate for great-power support f
regionalism in Southeast Asia will have been greatly enhanced. T
states in the region have increasingly begun to feel a sense of regior
consciousness and identity, in part because of their common con
tion and the common problems of development that they face. It
also because they recognize that they are impotent in world politics
except on a regional scale. As one scholar has noted, "the extreme
limited international capacities of these countries is a major influen
for regionalism."[19]

The sense of common interest goes beyond the economic plight
the developing nations of Southeast Asia, and is today foster
even in Japan, by the growing power of Communist China. He
mann puts it this way: "actual and potential security threats .
rather than common cultural heritage . . . have laid the foundati
for a sense of regional identity."[20] We have in this circumstance
convergence of interests between Japan on the one hand and the we
and poor states of Southeast Asia on the other, which can devel
into the most formidable of all incentives toward Asian regionalis
Japan has, of course, the resources to assist not only in the develo
ment but in the defense of Southeast Asia; yet until now China h
been the "political king and Japan the passive, economic queen"
Asia's international politics.[21]

This pattern is changing, and Japan is again turning her attenti

---

[19] Donald C. Hellmann, "East Asia: The Evolving Postwar Internatio
Order," Paper read at the 18th Annual Meeting, Association for Asian Studi
April 6, 1966, p. 5.

[20] *Ibid.*, p. 4.

[21] *Ibid.*, p. 2.

Southeast Asia. In April the Japanese government convened an
economic conference of Southeast Asian states for the purpose of encouraging among them better industrial planning, sounder development programs and greater economic cooperation. Tokyo suggested
that there are potential "concrete projects of economic cooperation,"
and promised to submit detailed proposals.[22] These steps represent a
marked change in the direction of postwar Japanese behavior toward
the region, and they are being undertaken now because Japan once
again frankly recognizes its "special bond" to Southeast Asia.[23] As
Prime Minister Sato remarked at the time, Tokyo would soon significantly expand its aid to the area, because Japan is "resolved to
engage in positive cooperation for the development of Southeast
Asian countries."[24]

Is Japan, with its reputation for circumspection and caution,
likely to renew and expand this investment in Southeast Asia without
at the same time concerning itself with the long-term security of the
region? Probably not. Instead, Japan will probably intensify not
only its economic interest, but also its emphasis on defense and security in Southeast Asia, and that is a very hopeful sign in the process
of developing cohesion and stability in Southeast Asia.

[22] Joint Communiqué of the Tokyo Ministerial Conference for Economic Development of Southeast Asia, April 7, 1966.
[23] Statement of Aiichiro Fujiyama, the Tokyo Conference, April 6, 1966.
[24] Joint Communiqué, *op. cit.*

Henry A. Kissinger

Coalition Diplomacy
in a Nuclear Age

For several years now disputes have rent the Atlantic Alliance
They have focused on such issues as nuclear strategy and control, t
organization of Europe and the nature of an Atlantic Communit
However, the most fundamental issue in Atlantic relationships
raised by two questions not unlike those which each Western socie
has had to deal with in its domestic affairs: How much unity do w
want? How much pluralism can we stand? Too formalistic a co
ception of unity risks destroying the political will of the members
the Community. Too absolute an insistence on national particulari
must lead to a fragmentation of the common effort.

One does not have to agree with the methods or policies of Pres
dent de Gaulle to recognize that he has posed an important questio
which the West has yet to answer. There is merit in his contentio
that before a political unit can mean something to others, it mu
first mean something to itself. Though de Gaulle has often acted
if he achieved identity by opposing our purposes, our definition
unity has occasionally carried overtones of tutelage.

There is no question that the abrupt tactics of the French Pres
dent have severely strained the pattern of allied relationships whi
emerged after the war. But no one man could have disrupted t
Alliance by himself. Fundamental changes have been taking place
the nature of alliances, in the character of strategy and in the rel
tive weights of Europe and the United States. A new conception
allied relationships would have been necessary no matter wl

Reprinted by special permission from the author and *Foreign Affairs,* 42 (Ju
1964). Copyright by the Council on Foreign Relations, Inc., New York.

overned in Paris or in Washington. The impact of particular states-
en aside, a farsighted policy will gear itself to dealing with these
nderlying forces. It will inquire into the degree to which objectives
re common and where they diverge. It will face frankly the fact that
ifferent national perspectives — and not necessarily ignorance —
an produce differing strategic views. It will examine the scope and
mits of consultation. If this is done in a new spirit on both sides of
le Atlantic, a more vital relationship can take the place of the pre-
ious U.S. hegemony.

II. The Change in the Nature
of Alliances

Since the end of World War II an important change has taken
lace in the nature of alliances. In the past, alliances have been
reated for three basic reasons: (1) To provide an accretion of power.
ccording to the doctrine of collective security, the wider the alli-
nce, the greater its power to resist aggression. (2) To leave no
oubt about the alignment of forces. It has often been argued that
ad Germany known at the beginning of both World Wars that the
nited States — or even England — would join the Allies, war
ould have been averted. (3) To provide an incentive for mutual
ssistance beyond that already supplied by an estimate of the na-
onal interest.

To be sure, even before the advent of nuclear weapons, there was
me inconsistency among these requirements. The attempt to com-
ne the maximum number of states for joint action occasionally con-
cted with the desire to leave no doubt about the collective motiva-
on. The wider the system of collective security, the more various
ere the motives animating it and the more difficult the task of ob-
ining common action proved to be. The more embracing the alliance,
e more intense and direct must be the threat which would produce
int action.

This traditional difficulty has been compounded in the nuclear age.
he requirements for tight command and control of nuclear weapons
e to some degree inconsistent with a coalition of sovereign states.
he enormous risks of nuclear warfare affect the credibility of tradi-
nal pledges of mutual assistance.

As a result, most of the theories of nuclear control now current
thin the Western Alliance have a tendency either to turn NATO
to a unilateral U.S. guarantee or to call into question the utility of

the Alliance altogether. American strategic thought verges on th
first extreme; some French theorists have hinted at the second.

As for the United States, official spokesmen have consistently em
phasized that the European contribution to the over-all nuclea
strength of the Alliance is negligible. European nuclear forces hav
been described as "provocative," "prone to obsolescence" an
"weak." For a considerable period after the advent of the Kenned
Administration, some high officials held the view that on nuclea
matters the President might serve as the Executive Agent of th
Alliance. Since then the United States has made various proposa
for nuclear sharing, the common feature of which has been th
retention of our veto over the nuclear weapons of the Alliance.

However sensible such schemes may appear from the point of vie
of the division of labor, they all would perpetuate our hegemony i
nuclear matters within the Alliance. Allies are considered necessar
not so much to add to over-all strength as to provide the possibilit
for applying power discriminately. In these terms, it is not surprisir
that some allies have considered their conventional contribution a
actually weakening the over-all strength by raising doubts about th
nuclear commitment of the United States.

According to the contrary view, alliances have lost their signi
cance altogether. The French theorist, General Gallois, has argue
for example, that nuclear weapons have made alliances obsolet
Faced with the risk of total destruction, no nation will jeopardi
its survival for another. Hence, he maintains, each country mu
have its own nuclear arsenal to defend itself against direct attac
while leaving all other countries to their fate.

This formula would mark the end of collective security and woul
be likely to lead to international chaos. Under conditions of growir
nuclear power on both sides, it would be idle to deny that the thre
of nuclear retaliation has lost some of its credibility. The Gallo
theory would, however, transform a degree of uncertainty into
guarantee that the United States would *not* come to the assistan
of its allies, thus greatly simplifying the aggressor's calculatio
Moreover, in order to protect itself in this new situation, ea
country would need to develop not only a nuclear arsenal of its ov
but also foolproof procedures for assuring the Soviets that a giv
nuclear blow did not originate from its territory. If Gallois is righ
and each country is unwilling to risk nuclear devastation for a
ally, it will also want to prevent itself from being triggered in

uclear war by a neighbor. Thus each country will have a high incentive to devise methods to protect itself from a counterattack based on a misapprehension. The Gallois theory would lead to a multiplication of national nuclear forces side-by-side with the development of methods of surrender or guarantees of non-involvement.

When views such as these carry influence on both sides of the Atlantic, it is no accident that much of the debate on nuclear matters within NATO turns on the question of confidence. We tend to ask those of our allies possessing nuclear arsenals of their own: If you trust us, why do you require nuclear weapons? Our nuclear allies reply: If you trust us, why are you concerned about our possession of nuclear weapons? Since the answer must inevitably emphasize contingencies where either the goals or the strategy would be incompatible, the debate on nuclear control within NATO has been inherently divisive.

The concentration of nuclear power in the hands of one country poses one set of problems; the range of modern weapons raises another. In the past, a threatened country had the choice either of resisting or surrendering. If it resisted, it had to be prepared to accept the consequences in terms of physical damage or loss of life. A distant ally could be effective only if it was able to bring its strength to bear in the area of conflict.

Modern weapons have changed this. What each member country wants from the Alliance is the assurance that an attack on it will be considered a *casus belli*. It strives for deterrence by adding the strength of a distant ally to its own power. But, equally, each state has an incentive to reduce damage to itself to a minimum should deterrence fail. The range of modern weapons provides an opportunity in this respect for the first time. In 1914 Belgium could not base its defense on a strategy which transferred to Britain the primary risks of devastation. In the age of intercontinental rockets this technical possibility exists.

Part of the strategic dispute within the Alliance, therefore, involves jockeying to determine which geographic area will be the theater of war if deterrence fails (though this obviously cannot be made explicit). A conventional war confined to Europe may appear relatively tolerable to us. To Europeans, with their memory of conventional wars, this prospect is not particularly inviting. They may find a nuclear exchange which spares their territory a more attractive strategy and the threat of nuclear retaliation a more effective deter-

rent. The interests of the Alliance may be indivisible in an ultima
sense. But this does not guarantee the absence of sharp conflicts
methods to reach these objectives.

In short, the destructiveness and range of modern weapons ha
a tendency to produce both extreme nationalism and neutralism.
wise alliance policy must take care that in dealing with one of the
dangers it does not produce the other.

The nature of alliances has changed in yet another way. In t
past, one of the reasons for joining an alliance was to impose .
additional obligation for assistance in time of need. Were ea
country's national interests completely unambiguous, it would kn
precisely on whom it could count; a formal commitment would
unnecessary. Both the aggressor and the defender would understa
what they would confront and could act accordingly. Wars could n
be caused by a misunderstanding of intentions. They would occ
only if the protagonists calculated the existing power relationshi
differently.

Traditionally, however, the national interest has not been una
biguous. Often the aggressor did not know which countries wou
ultimately be lined up against it; Germany in 1914 was genuine
surprised by the British reaction to the invasion of Belgium. Occ
sionally the defenders could not be certain of the extent of the
potential support — as was the case with the Allies in both wa
regarding U.S. participation. Historically, the existence of an u
derstanding on this point, tacit or explicit, has often been the d
termining factor in the decision to go to war. In the decade prior
World War I, the staff talks between Britain and France, which l
to the transfer of the French fleet to the Mediterranean, were one
the key factors in Britain's decision to go to war in August 191
(Thus the talks achieved one objective of traditional alliances:
commit Britain to the defense of France. They failed in another:
make the opposing alignment clear to the potential aggressor.)

One of the distinguishing features of the nuclear period is tha
the national interest of the major powers has become less ambiguou
In a bipolar world, a relative gain for one side represents an absolu
weakening of the other. Neither of the major nuclear countries ca
permit a major advance by its opponent regardless of whether t
area in which it occurs is formally protected by an alliance or no
Neutral India was no less assured of American assistance when t
Chinese attacked than allied Pakistan would have been in simil

rcumstances. In these conditions, the distinction between allies and
eutrals is likely to diminish. A country gains little from being allied
id risks little by being neutral.

This inevitably results in the weakening of allied cohesion, pro-
icing what some have described as polycentrism. But polycentrism
ies not reflect so much the emergence of new centers of actual power
i the attempt by allies to establish new centers of decision. Poly-
entrism is virulent not because the world has ceased to be bipolar,
it because it essentially remains so. Far from doubting America's
ilitary commitment to Europe, President de Gaulle is so certain
: it that he does not consider *political* independence a risk. He thus
lds American power to his own in pursuit of his policies.

No matter how troublesome a major ally may be, it cannot be
lowed to suffer defeat. France's policy is made possible by our
iclear umbrella — a fact which adds to the irony of the situation
id the annoyance of some of our policy-makers. Our frequent in-
stence that in the nuclear age an isolated strategy is no longer possi-
e misses the central point: for this precise reason allies have un-
recedented scope for the pursuit of their own objectives. And the
ore the détente — real or imaginary — proceeds, the more momen-
im these tendencies will gather. We live in a curious world where
eutrals enjoy most of the protection of allies and allies aspire to
ive the same freedom of action as do neutrals.

These conditions turn coalition diplomacy into an extraordinarily
elicate undertaking. Appeals which were effective in the past
ther work no longer or turn counterproductive. Thus the warning
iat certain European actions might lead the United States to with-
raw is bound to have consequences contrary to those intended. If
elieved at all, it demonstrates that there are at least *some* con-
ingencies in which the United States might abandon its allies, thus
agnifying pressures for European autonomy.

The scope for real Third Force policies is vastly overestimated.
ealism forces close association between Europe and the United
tates whatever the vagaries of individual statesmen. But it has
ippened often enough in Western history that an underlying com-
unity of interests was submerged by subsidiary rivalries. Ancient
reece foundered on this discord. Western Europe nearly tore itself
iart before it submerged its rivalries. And now the Atlantic area
ices the challenge of how to combine common action with a respect
ir diverse approaches to the central problem.

III. The Abstractness and Novelty
of Modern Power

The destructiveness of modern weapons gives the strategic debat unprecedented urgency. The speed with which they can be delivere complicates the problem of command and control in a way unimagir able even a decade and a half ago. Doctrinal and technical dispute occur within each government. It is not surprising, then, that the should rend the Alliance as well.

The novelty of modern weapons systems gives the disputes metaphysical, almost theological, cast. Never before in history has s much depended on weapons so new, so untested, so "abstract." N nuclear weapons have been exploded in wartime except on Japai which did not possess means of retaliation. No one knows how goverr ments or people will react to a nuclear explosion under condition where both sides possess vast arsenals.

Moreover, modern weapons systems are relatively untested. Durin the debate in this country over the nuclear test-ban treaty, a grea deal of attention was focused on the adequacy of our warheads. I fact, the other components of our weapons systems contain man more factors of uncertainty. The estimated "hardness" of Minute man silos depends entirely on theoretical studies. Of the thousand of missiles in our arsenal, relatively few of each category have bee thoroughly tested. There is little experience with salvo firing. Ai defense systems are designed without any definite knowledge of th nature of the offense. A high proportion of the phenomena discovere in nuclear testing have been "unexpected."

The situation is further complicated by the fact that the purpos of modern weapons is deterrence: to prevent — by a particula threat — a certain course of action. But deterrence is primarily psychological problem. It depends on the aggressor's assessment o risks, not the defender's. A threat meant as a bluff but taken seriousl; is more useful for purposes of deterrence than a "genuine" threa interpreted as a bluff. Moreover, if deterrence is successful, aggres sion does *not* take place. But it is impossible to demonstrate wh; something has not occurred. It can never be proved whether peac has been maintained because NATO pursues an optimum strategy o a marginally effective one. Finally, the longer deterrence lasts th more color will be lent to the argument that perhaps the Communist never intended to attack in the first place. An effective NATO de

:rrent strategy may thus have the paradoxical consequence of
:rengthening the arguments of the quasi-neutralists.

Even if there is agreement about the correct weapons system, there
.ay be disagreement about how it can best be coupled with diplomacy
ɔ produce deterrence. How does one threaten with solid-fuel missiles?
.s these are always in an extreme state of readiness, how then does
ne demonstrate an increase in preparedness such as historically
erved as a warning? From a technical point of view it is highly
robable that missiles can perform most of the functions heretofore
.ssigned to airplanes. The shift to missiles and the elimination of
irplanes envisaged by the former Deputy Secretary of Defense
{oswell Gilpatric[1] makes a great deal of sense technically. But has
dequate attention been given to the kind of diplomacy which results
– particularly in crisis situations — when the retaliatory threat de-
ends on solid-fuel missiles in underground silos? During the Cuban
.issile crisis, dispersing SAC planes to civilian airports proved an
ffective warning. What will be an equivalent move when our stra-
egic forces are composed entirely of missiles?

These questions do not permit clear-cut answers. Yet they are at
.e heart of many of the disputes within NATO. The United States
as held the view that deterrence was best achieved by posing a
redible threat. And it has related credibility to whether the risks, if
.eterrence failed, were tolerable. The Europeans for a variety of
easons have generally been of a different opinion. They have main-
ained that deterrence depended on posing the most extreme risks.
hey have been prepared to sacrifice a measure of credibility in
avor of enhancing the magnitude of the threat. This debate has been
.conclusive because it ultimately depends on a psychological, not a
echnical, judgment.

The controversy originated in an attempt by the United States in
961 to change the relative weight to be given to conventional and
.uclear weapons in NATO doctrine. The method of effecting this
hange was not new — though it was urged with new insistence.
JATO had been presented many times before with American blue-
rints and had seen its consultative role limited to discussing the
echnical implementation of an American conception. What gave the
.ispute its particular urgency was that the advent of a new, highly
.nalytical American Administration coincided with the growing
trength and self-confidence of Europe and the deliberate policy of
'resident de Gaulle to assert a more independent role.

[1] "Our Defense Needs: The Long View," *Foreign Affairs*, April 1964.

In the process, many of the issues that had been obscured in th previous decade by the curious, somewhat one-sided, nature of th transatlantic dialogue came for the first time into sharper focus. Th highlighted a difference in perspective between the American and th European conception of NATO which had existed since its beginnin

When the Korean War raised the spectre of Soviet military aggre sion, both sides of the Atlantic made a serious effort to turn NAT into a more effective military instrument. However, given the eno mous disparity in military and economic strength between the Unite States and Europe, the primary concern of the European countrie was to commit the United States to their defense. They saw in NAT above all a means to obtain American protection, by which was mear American nuclear protection.

However, the Europeans had too much experience with the ten ousness of formal commitments not to strive for more tangib guarantees. This led to pressures for the stationing of America troops in Europe. European reasoning was similar to that ascribe to a French marshal in 1912 when he was asked how many Britis troops he wanted for the outbreak of a European war. He is reporte to have replied: "We need only one, who we will make sure is kille on the first day of the war." In the nuclear age, the price of guarantee has risen to something like five divisions.

With so many American troops permanently stationed in Europ it was only sensible to try to give them some meaningful militar mission. Even during the period of the doctrine of massive retalia tion, NATO forces were larger than the prevailing strategic concep seemed to demand. Indeed, the number was somewhat inconsisten with it. Despite our commitment to a retaliatory strategy, we con stantly pressed for a European contribution of ground forces. Th Europeans, though they agreed to a succession of NATO force goal never really believed in the doctrines used to rationalize them. Rathe they saw in their military contribution a form of fee paid for Unite States nuclear protection. The Europeans agreed to our request But they tried to see to it that their actual contributions would b large enough to induce us to keep a substantial military establishmen in Europe, yet not so high as to provide a real alternative to nuclea retaliation. They were opposed to giving the conventional forces central military mission; but they also resisted any hint of America withdrawal.

This ambivalence was brought into the open by the shift i United States strategic doctrine in 1961. The American attempt t

engthen the forces for local defense had the paradoxical conse-
ence of bringing to the fore the issue of nuclear control which for
ny Europeans had always been the crux of the matter. For the first
ne, U.S. strategic views were publicly challenged, at first hesi-
atly, then ever more explicitly. Europe had now gained sufficient
ength and confidence so that the mere enunciation of an American
icy no longer guaranteed its acceptance. The peremptory way in
ich the United States proceeded only sharpened the controversy.
d France added fuel to the flames by giving European misgivings
ir most extreme formulation.

But if French policy has deliberately sharpened conflicts, the
ited States tendency to turn an essentially psychological issue into
echnical one has unintentionally exacerbated disagreements beyond
ir intrinsic significance. Our spokesmen often leave the impression
t disagreement is due to the ignorance of our allies, and that it is
stined to yield ultimately before extensive briefings and insistent
teration. Faced with opposition, we are less given to asking whether
re may be some merit in the arguments of our allies than to over-
elming them with floods of emissaries preaching the latest version
our doctrine.

But the real problem is not that the Europeans fail to understand
r quest for multiple options. They simply reject it for themselves.
hen the issue is Asia or Latin America, Europeans favor an even
re flexible response than we do; with respect to the defense of
rope, their attitude is more rigid. As long as the United States
ains ultimate control over nuclear weapons, the European incen-
e is bound to be exactly the opposite of ours. Rather than permit
'pause'' for ''appreciating the wider risks involved,'' Europeans
fer to force us to make our response as automatic as possible.

This problem has little to do with whether the United States could
ord to give up Europe. It is rooted in the nature of sovereignty
1 made more acute by the destructiveness of nuclear weapons.
bert Bowie, one of the most eloquent spokesmen of the dominant
ool of U.S. thought, criticized British nuclear policy before the
sembly of the Western European Union as follows: ''Britain has
ained its national command structure and the right to withdraw
m at its option. This means that they *certainly* could not be
nted on by any of the others to be available in case of need.''[2]
alics supplied.] If this concern is real regarding British nuclear

Proceedings of Western European Union Assembly, Ninth Ordinary Session,
ember 3, 1963.

forces, which are, after all, assigned to NATO, it must be eve
stronger regarding U.S. strategic forces which remain under e
clusive American control.

The problem can then be summed up as follows: Exclusive U.
control of nuclear strategy is politically and psychologically inco
patible with a strategy of multiple choices or flexible response. T
European refusal to assign a meaningful military mission to conve
tional forces in Europe is incompatible with the indefinite retenti
of large U.S. forces there. If the United States prizes a convention
response sufficiently, it will have to concede Europe autonomy
nuclear control. If the Europeans want to insist on an automat
nuclear response, a reconsideration of our conventional deployme
on the Continent will become inevitable. Refusal to face these fac
will guarantee a perpetuation of present disputes and increasi
disarray within NATO.

The United States-European dialogue on strategy is confus
further by the nature of the intra-European debate. Many of the
who applaud our views do so for reasons which may not prove ve
comforting in the long run. We must be careful not to take eve
agreement with us at face value. Acquiescence in our opinion c
have two meanings: It can represent either a sincere commitment
Atlantic partnership or disguise a neutralist wish to abdicate respo
sibility. For the American nuclear umbrella, now sometimes exploit
by President de Gaulle for his own purposes, can also be used — a
more dangerously for the West — to support policies amounting
neutralism. In many countries it is the leaders and groups traditic
ally most committed to national defense who have developed views
strategy which challenge American concepts; while some of the
most ready to accept U.S. strategic hegemony have in the past be
the least interested in making a serious defense effort. We may the
fore have to choose between our theories of nuclear control a
Atlantic cohesion, between the technical and the political sides
Atlantic policy.

IV. DIFFERENCES IN HISTORICAL
PERSPECTIVE

Some of the strains in Atlantic relationships have resulted fr
factors outside anybody's control. Many reflect the growth in Eurc
of the very strength and self-confidence which American policy I
striven to promote since the end of World War II. Others have be

used by the tactics of President de Gaulle, whose style of diplomacy
not really compatible with the requirements of coalition. We share
e responsibility through too much insistence on technical solutions
d too little allowance for the intangibles of political judgment and
ll.

But perhaps the deepest cause of transatlantic misunderstandings
a difference in historical perspective. Americans live in an environ-
ent uniquely suited to an engineering approach to policy-making.
s a result, our society has been characterized by a conviction that
y problem will yield if subjected to a sufficient dose of expertise.
ith such an approach, problems tend to appear as discrete issues
thout any inner relationship. It is thought that they can be solved
on their merits'' as they arise. It is rarely understood that a ''solu-
n'' to a problem may mortgage the future — especially as there is
fficient optimism to assume that even should this prove to be the
se, it will still be possible to deal with the new problem when it
aterializes.

But Europeans live on a continent covered with ruins testifying to
e fallibility of human foresight. In European history, the recogni-
n of a problem has often defined a dilemma rather than pointed to
answer. The margin of survival of European countries has been
ore precarious than ours. European reasoning is likely to be more
mplicated and less confident than ours. This explains some of the
rains in Atlantic relationships. Americans tend to be impatient
th what seems to them Europe's almost morbid obsession with the
st, while Europeans sometimes complain about a lack of sensitivity
d compassion on the part of Americans.

In the fall of 1963, our newspapers were filled with derisory
mments about French manœuvres then taking place. The scenario
these manœuvres supposed that an aggressor force was attacking
ance through Germany. France's allies had surrendered. As the
gressor's armies were approaching her borders, France resorted to
r nuclear weapons. It is, of course, easy to ridicule this scenario
contrasting the small size of the French bomber force with the
agnitude of the disaster envisaged. But the crucial issue is not
chnical. It arises from the fact that France has undergone shatter-
g historical experiences with which Americans find it difficult to
entify. The scenario of the French manœuvres recalled importantly
perhaps too rigidly — France's traumatic experience of 1940, when
reign armies attacked all along the Western front and France's
lies collapsed. The British Fighter Command remained in England;

the fact that this critical decision was wise does not affect the bas
psychological point. Moreover, the French disaster came at the end
two decades in which France almost single-handedly shouldered t
responsibility for the defense of Europe while her erstwhile alli
withdrew into isolation or offered strictures about France's obsessi
with security. The nightmare that some day France might aga
stand alone goes far deeper than the obstinate illwill of a sing
individual.

A comparable problem exists in Germany. Washington has
times shown signs of impatience toward the German leaders and the
constant need for reassurance. Secretary Rusk has been report
more than once to be restless with what he has called the "pledgi
sessions" which the Germans seem so often to demand. However, i
security is endemic in the German situation. A divided country wi
frontiers that correspond to no historical experience, a society whi
has lived through two disastrous defeats and four domestic upheav
in 40 years, cannot know inward stability. The need to belong
something, to rescue some predictability out of chaos, is overwhel
ing. The memories of our allies should be factors as real in the discu
sions of our policy-makers as the analysis of weapons systems.

The importance of this difference in historical perspective
compounded by the continuing disparity in strength between t
two sides of the Atlantic. While it has become fashionable to speak
Europe's new-found equality, it is important not to take it t
literally. Europe *has* gained in strength over the past decade and
half. It can and should play an increasingly responsible role. But i
the foreseeable future we are likely to be by far the stronger partn

It is important to be clear about this because it requires us to sh
unusual tact and steadiness. Many of our allies have been guilty
unilateral actions far more flagrant than ours. But when we a
unilaterally, disarray in the Alliance is almost inevitable. Dras
changes in U.S. strategic doctrine or action without adequate co
sultation — such as the removal of I.R.B.M.s from Italy and Turk
or the withdrawal of troops from Germany — create either a sense
European impotence or increase the pressure for more autonom
Bilateral dealings with the Soviets, from which our allies are e
cluded, or about which they are informed only at the last moment, a
bound to magnify Third Force tendencies. When our allies res
such U.S. policies and practices, it is not necessarily because they d
agree with our view but because they are afraid of creating a prec
dent for unilateral changes in other policies. (Even statements

bstantive disagreement may be a smoke-screen for deeper con-
rns.) Moreover, many allied leaders who have staked their prestige
certain U.S. policies can suffer serious domestic consequences if
e change them drastically.

Thus the voice of Europe reaches us in extremely distorted form.
resident de Gaulle sharpens all disputes and even creates them in
rsuit of his policy of independence. But some other leaders do not
ve full expression to their disquiet because they do not want to
dermine further the solidarity on which their security is thought
 depend. Whereas France exaggerates her disagreements, some
her countries obscure theirs. Thus the dialogue with Europe is
ten conducted on false issues, while real issues — like the future of
ermany, or arms control, or the role of tactical nuclear weapons —
e swept under the rug in order not to magnify the existing discord.

We, in turn, are faced with the problem that technology and politi-
l conditions are changing so rapidly that no policy can be main-
ined over an indefinite period of time. How to shape policies that
e responsive to change while maintaining the confidence of our
lies? The future vitality of the Western Alliance depends on under-
anding the possibilities and limits of the consultative process.

V. The Limits and Purposes
of Consultation

The always difficult problem of coalition diplomacy is magnified
 three factors:

(1) The fact that the two superpowers are committed to the ex-
ting balance provides their European allies with wide scope for
rely national actions.

(2) The internal workings of modern government are so complex
at they create a variety of obstacles to meaningful consultation.
ations sometimes find it so difficult to achieve a domestic consensus
at they are reluctant to jeopardize it afterwards in international
rums. The tendency of the United States to confine consultation to
aborating its own blueprint reflects less a quest for hegemony — as
me of our European critics occasionally assert — than a desire to
oid complicating still further its own decision-making process.

(3) As governments have found in their domestic experience,
cess to the same technical data does not guarantee unanimity of
derstanding. In an alliance of states very unequal in size and
rength, and with widely varying histories, differences are almost

inevitable. And they are likely to be made all the more intractable b
a technology of unprecedented destructiveness and novelty.

Thus consultation is far from being a magic cure-all. It will n
necessarily remove real differences of geography, perspective or i
terest. Nevertheless, an improvement in the consultative proce
should be one of the chief concerns of the Alliance.

The dominant American view has been that consultation woul
be most effective if there were a division of labor within the Allian
according to which the United States retained control over nucle
weapons while Europe specialized in conventional forces. Similarl
it has been suggested in Great Britain that the independent Briti
nuclear deterrent could be given up in return for a greater voice
American policy.[3] The proposed NATO Multilateral Force on whi
the United States increasingly stakes its prestige is basically a devi
to make its nuclear hegemony acceptable.[4]

In other words, the thrust of our policy is to create a structu
which makes it physically impossible for any of the allies (exce
the United States) to act autonomously. This raises the followin
problems: (a) How effective will consultation based on such premis
be? (b) Is such a system as useful for the long-term political vitali
of the Alliance as it is for the conduct of a general nuclear war?

With regard to the first of these, any process of consultation mu
be responsive to the following three questions: Who has a right to
consulted? Whose voice carries weight? Who has enough comp
tence?

These three levels are not necessarily identical. Many agencies
our own government have a right to express their views, but not
carry the same weight. When some of Britain's Labor leaders sugge
that they want a greater voice in our decisions in return for givi
up British nuclear weapons, the answer has to be: Like whose voic
Like that of the Arms Control and Disarmament Agency? Or t
Joint Chiefs of Staff? Or the State Department? Or the Commer
Department? In our interdepartmental disputes, clearly, the outcor
often depends on the constituency which the agency or departme
represents. The weight given to advice is inevitably related to t
competence that it reflects.

---

[3] See ''The Labor Party's Defense and Foreign Policy,'' by Patrick Gord
Walker, *Foreign Affairs*, April 1964, pp. 391-398.

[4] For the author's view on the NATO Multilateral Force see, ''NATO
Nuclear Dilemma,'' *The Reporter*, March 28, 1963.

If the United States retains indefinitely an effective monopoly of
ıclear power, we would probably find in time that Europe simply
)es not have sufficient technical competence for its views to carry
eight. And this in turn is likely to breed irresponsibility on both
des of the Atlantic. A right of consultation without the ability to
ake a serious judgment may, in fact, be the worst possible system.
ver a period of time it is bound to reduce Europe's voice in Wash-
gton; while in Europe it must produce a sense of impotence or
:treme nationalism. Indeed, it may enable neutralists to focus all
urope's anti-nuclear sentiment against the United States. Some
uropean autonomy on nuclear matters — preferably growing out of
:isting programs — seems therefore desirable.

The emphasis placed on a unitary strategic system for the Alliance
ıs reversed the proper priorities. The real challenge to the consulta-
ve process is less in the field of strategy than in diplomacy. The
ıility to fight a centrally controlled general war is useful; but the
ıility to devise common policies in the face of a whole spectrum of
ʼentualities is much more important.

If the Alliance cannot develop procedures for a common diplomacy
- or at least an agreed range of divergence — it seems contradictory
» insist on a system of unitary strategic control. When NATO has
roved unable to develop even a commọn trade policy toward the
ommunist world, it is not surprising that countries are reluctant to
ıtrust their survival to a NATO ally, however close. Policies on a
hole range of issues such as Suez, the Congo, negotiating tactics
ʼer Berlin or the defense of Southern Arabia have been unilateral
ʼ divergent. The United States is now in the curious situation of
aking a great deal of its prestige on establishing the NATO Multi-
,teral Force and a system of unitary strategic control while East-
Ʒest negotiations or the war in Southeast Asia or arms control are
ealt with more or less unilaterally.

In re-assessing these priorities, it may be important to ask how
ıitary a system of control for strategy and diplomacy is in fact
esirable. What kind of structure is more vital in the long run: An
tlantic system that automatically involves all partners? Or one
ıat permits some autonomy? On many issues — particularly East-
Ʒest relations — united action is essential. With respect to others,
»me degree of flexibility may be desirable. Over the next decades the
ʻnited States is likely to find itself increasingly engaged in the Far
ast, in Southeast Asia and in Latin America. Our European allies

will probably not consider their vital interests at stake in these area
President de Gaulle's views on this subject are far from unique i
Europe, even if his methods are.

If the Atlantic system is absolutely centralized, policy may b
reduced to the lowest common denominator. The Soviets may use ot
involvements elsewhere to blackmail Europe. This, combined wit
the lack of interest among Europeans in the issues involved, ma
strain the Alliance beyond the breaking point. On the other hand,
Europe is accorded some capacity for autonomous action — militar
and political — its concern would be no greater, but the temptatio
for Soviet adventures might be reduced. Put positively, a structu
which permits a variety of coördinated approaches toward the ne
nations could enhance the vigor of our policies, the self-confidence
our allies and the long-term vitality of the Alliance. Paradoxicall
the unity of the Atlantic area may well be furthered by a structu
which grants the possibility of autonomous action while reducit
the desire for it.

VI. What Structure for the Atlantic Area?

The most delicate problem faced by the United States in i
Atlantic policy, then, is to promote cohesion without underminin
the self-confidence and the political will of its allies. Formal stru
tures can help in this effort. But when they become ends in them
selves they may cause us to beg the key question by the very terms
which we state it.

Some of the current theories of Atlantic partnership run precise
this risk. According to the dominant U.S. view, shared by such wi
Europeans as Jean Monnet, there is only *one* reliable concept
Atlantic partnership — that described by the image of "twin pillar
or a "dumbbell," composed of the United States and a united E
rope organized on federal lines with supra-national institutions. Th
is, of course, one form of Atlantic partnership. But is it wise
stake everything on a single approach? History is rarely such
linear and simple process.

Every European state is the product of some process of integrati
at some time over the past four centuries; and Germany and Ita
achieved unity less than one hundred years ago. European histo
suggests that there is more than one way to achieve integration.
Italy, it came by way of plebiscite and annexation abolishing the i

idual states. In Germany, unification occurred under the aegis of
e state but as the act of sovereign governments which remained in
stence after unity was achieved. The resulting structure clearly
l not lack cohesiveness.

Moreover, how valid is a concept of European integration which
rejected by *both* France and Great Britain? In the outrage over
itain's exclusion from the Common Market, it has not always been
ced that Britain's view (shared by both major parties) of the
ganization of Europe is almost identical with that of France. Both
untries would find it difficult, if not impossible, to commit them-
ves now to a federal structure and a common parliament. It only
ls to the irony of the situation that many of the most ardent advo-
es of Britain's entry into the Common Market both here and in
rope are also dedicated proponents of a federal Europe. How do
y propose to reconcile these two objectives?

There may be various roads to European coöperation. The one
ced by the Fouchet Plan — calling for institutionalized meetings
foreign ministers and sub-cabinet officials — is not the least plau-
le, and indeed it is the one most consistent with British participa-
n. It has the advantage of producing some immediate progress
hout foreclosing the future. It would also permit a more flexible
angement of Atlantic relations than the "twin pillar" concept
v in vogue.

While the United States should welcome any European structure
t reflects the desires of the Europeans, it would be unwise to stake
rything on one particular formula. A very rigid conception of
antic partnership can easily fail to do justice to the richness and
iety of relationships possible within the Atlantic context. Is it
lly possible or useful to lump the countries of Europe together
all issues? Are they always inherently closer to one another than
 of them is to the United States? Do the Dutch inevitably feel a
ater sense of identification with the French, or the British with
 Germans, than either does with the United States? If we separate
 question into political, military or economic components, is the
wer always uniform and does it always point in the same direc-
n? Would it not be wiser to retain some flexibility? There is a
ve risk that too doctrinaire an approach will produce either a
lapse of political will, or more likely, a new and virulent form of
ionalism, perhaps even more intense than the nationalism of the
ries. A Europe largely constructed on theoretical models might be
ced into an anti-American mold because its only sense of identity

will be what distinguishes it from America. Our bent for structu
remedies sometimes blinds us to the fact that institutions prod
their own momentum and that this cannot be foreseen from
proclamations of their founders.

In assessing our own Atlantic policy, we must cut through sloga
to such questions as: Is it wise to insist that the only road to Eu
pean unity is by institutions unacceptable to both France a
Britain? Is the best way to solve the strategic problem by staki
our prestige on a device — the Multilateral Force — which comp
us to oppose the existing nuclear programs in Europe while bringi
a host of presently non-nuclear countries (among them Germa
Italy, Greece and Turkey) into the nuclear business, occasiona
with only their reluctant assent? Can it be in the interest of NA1
of the Federal Republic, or of the United States, to make Germa
the senior European nuclear partner in the Multilateral Force a
to create an institution which can rally all anti-U.S., anti-Germ
and anti-nuclear sentiments against us?

European history teaches that stability is unattainable exc
through the coöperation of Britain, France and Germany. C
should be taken not to resurrect old national rivalries in the na
of Atlanticism. The United States should not choose a special part
among its European allies. The attempt to woo one, or to fo
European countries to choose between us and France — a tende
which despite all disavowals is real — must magnify the Europ
nationalism which French policy has already done so much to fost

Our concern thus returns to the somewhat out-of-scale figure
President de Gaulle. A sense of frustration resulting from his p
cies, and even more from his style, has caused many to see him
individually responsible for the failure to realize many deeply
objectives. This is not the place to attempt an assessment of
character. Conceivably he is as petty, as animated by remember
slights, as some of our commentators suggest. It is also possible t
a man so conscious of his historic role has larger purposes. At a
rate, we will not know until we have had a real dialogue with h
In a period of détente with Soviet Russia, is it impossible to cond
a serious conversation with a traditional ally? President de Gau
has repeatedly expressed his willingness to coördinate strategy rat
than to integrate it. We should make new efforts to explore what
means. His 1958 proposal of a Directory is not acceptable when c
fined to Britain, France and the United States. Do we know
attitude toward a wider forum?

Irritation with de Gaulle's tactics does not change the fact that in
proposals of 1958 for a Directory he put his finger on perhaps the
problem of NATO. In the absence of a common foreign policy —
at least an agreed range of divergence — the attempt to devise a
mmon strategy is likely to prove futile. Lord Avon and Dean
heson have come to the same conclusion. The time seems ripe to
ate a political body at the highest level — composed perhaps of
United States, the United Kingdom, France, the Federal Re-
blic and Italy — for concerting the policies of the nations border-
the North Atlantic. Such a body should discuss how to imple-
nt common Atlantic purposes and define the scope of autonomous
tion where interests diverge. It should also be charged with develop-
a common strategic doctrine.

Conceivably this could end the sterile scholastic debate over the
ative benefits of integration as against coördination. It might heal
ift which if continued is bound to hazard everything that has been
infully built up over 15 years. Both the United States and France
able to thwart each other's purposes. Neither can create an
ernative structure — France even less than we. As in a Greek
gedy, each chief actor, following a course that seems quite reason-
e, is producing consequences quite different from what he intends.
This should not happen. The problems will become insuperable only
technique is exalted above purpose and if interest is too narrowly
ceived. The West does itself an injustice by comparing its dis-
reements to the rifts in the Communist bloc. In the Communist
rld, schisms are inevitable and unbridgeable. Western societies
ve been more fortunate. Their evolution has been richer; they have
ged unity by drawing strength from diversity. Free from the
ckles of a doctrine of historical inevitability, the nations of the
est can render a great service by demonstrating that if history has
neaning it is up to us today to give it that meaning.

Suggestions for Further Reading

l, M. Margaret, *NATO and the European Union Movement* (New York,
959).

ufre, Andre, *NATO and Europe* (New York, 1966).

tros-Ghali, Boutros, "The Addis Ababa Charter," *International Con-
iliation*, 546 (January 1964), pp. 5-62.

nell-Smith, Gordon, *The Inter-American System* (New York, 1966).

ier, John C., *The Organization of American States and the Hemisphere
Crisis* (New York, 1962).

Fox, William T. R., and Annette B. Fox, *NATO and the Range of Americ Choice* (New York, 1967).

Furniss, Edgar T., Jr. (ed.), *The Western Alliance: Its Status and Pre pects* (Columbus, Ohio, 1965).

Gordon, Bernard K., *The Dimensions of Conflict in Southeast Asia* (Eng wood Cliffs, N.J., 1966).

Gordon, Lincoln, "Economic Aspects of Coalition Diplomacy — The NAT Experience," *International Organization,* X (November 1956), pp. 529-

Hoffmann, Stanley, "De Gaulle, Europe, and the Atlantic Alliance," *Int national Organization,* XVIII (Winter 1964), pp. 1-28.

Kissinger, Henry, *The Troubled Partnership* (New York, 1965).

Macdonald, Robert W., *The League of Arab States* (Princeton, 1965).

Manger, William, *Pan-America in Crisis: The Future of the OAS* (Was ington, 1961).

Mazrui, Ali A., *Towards a Pax Africana* (Chicago, 1967).

Modelski, George, *SEATO: Six Studies* (Melbourne, 1962).

Richardson, James, "The Concept of Atlantic Community," *Journal Common Market Studies,* III (October 1964), pp. 1-22.

Slater, Jerome, *The OAS and United States Foreign Policy* (Columb Ohio, 1967).

Tevoedjre, Albert, *Pan Africanism in Action: An Account of the UA* (Cambridge, Mass., Harvard University Center for International Affa Occasional Paper, 1965).

Thomas, Ann Van Wynen, and A. J. Thomas, Jr., *The Organization American States* (Dallas, 1963).

Touval, Saadia, "The Organization of African Unity and African Border *International Organization,* XXI (Winter 1966), pp. 102-27.

Wallerstein, Immanuel, "The Early Years of the OAU: The Search Organizational Pre-eminence," *International Organization,* XX (Autu 1966), pp. 774-87.

Wilcox, Francis O., and H. Field Haviland, Jr. (eds.), *The Atlantic Co munity* (New York, 1963).

Wild, Patricia Berko, "The Organization of African Unity and the Algeri Moroccan Border Conflict: A Study of New Machinery for Peacekeepi and for the Peaceful Settlement of Disputes Among African State *International Organization,* XX (Winter 1966), pp. 18-36.

Zartman, I. William, *International Relations in the New Africa* (Englewe Cliffs, N.J., 1966).

PART THREE

WESTERN EUROPE: BEYOND THE NATION-STATE?

Ernst B. Haas

Technocracy, Pluralism
and the New Europe

The practices associated with regional integration in contemporary
stern Europe correspond to a type of society and economy vari-
sly labeled "post-industrial," "post-bourgeois" or merely "the
w Europe."[1] This New Europe evolved historically from the inter-
nnected strands of capitalism, industrialism and pluralistic democ-
cy. It resembles in any respects the type of economy and society
niliar to us in North America. Regional government in such a
ciety is thus merely an adaptation on the scale of half a continent
forms of social and economic organization which evolved histori-
ly at the national level. Regional government in the New Europe
the institutional and political recognition that societies have
anged dramatically since 1945, so dramatically that they cannot
adequately described in the doctrines and ideologies made familiar
nineteenth- and early twentieth-century political thought. Hence

Reprinted from Stephen Graubard (ed.), *A New Europe?* (Boston: Houghton
flin Company, 1964) with the permission of *Daedalus*, The American Academy
Arts and Sciences, and the author.

The term "the New Europe" was made familiar by George Lichtheim, *The
w Europe — Today and Tomorrow* (New York: Praeger, 1963), whose gen-
l view of things I share almost completely. The economic and sociological
soning and analysis which underlie the concept are developed in the following
lications: Ralf Dahrendorf, *Class and Class Conflict in Industrial Society*
anford: Stanford University Press, 1959); Raymond Aron, "Fin de l'age
ologique?" in Adorno and Dirks (eds.), *Sociologica* (Frankfurt: Europäische
lagsanstalt, 1955); Daniel Bell, *The End of Ideology* (Glencoe: The Free
ss, 1960); Gunnar Myrdal, *Beyond the Welfare State* (New Haven: Yale
versity Press, 1960); S. M. Lipset, "The Changing Class Structure and
temporary European Politics," *Daedalus* (Winter, 1964).

the New Europe and its regional government is the future of th
part of history which has also been aptly described as "the end
ideology." It owes so little to the visions of the Abbé de Saint-Pierr
of William Penn, of Immanuel Kant and of Victor Hugo that the
oft-invoked precursors of the contemporary movement could scarce
be expected to recognize their brainchild.

Yet the news of the last few months seems at variance with th
extreme view of things. Disintegration and nationalist *immobilisn*
appear to dominate, rather than the advance of regional governmei
France's veto of January, 1963, stopped not only the entry of Brita
into the European Community of the Six, but in effect postponed t
merger of the Europe of Seven with the Community. EFTA, aft
appearing to be on the threshold of dissolution, acquired a new lea
on life as a result. In agriculture, the Community has succeeded
translating the general policy adopted a year ago only to some co
modities; but disagreement on target prices and levies continues wi
respect to others, while interest group representatives, parliamenta
ians and government experts continue to squabble about the prop
compromise. In the field of energy, the Council of Ministers is n
considering the fourth "interim memorandum" of the Communi
executives regarding the proper role and pricing of oil, coal, natur
gas and hydroelectric power. Again, the interest groups press th
claims and governments support or reject them in line with natior
perceptions of interest, thus far to the detriment of a coherent 1
gional policy. During the summer of 1963, the special political agr
ment between Bonn and Paris went into effect, thus symbolizing
some Europeans that special Franco-German relationship whi
might institutionalize the hegemony of de Gaulle over the Communi
of the Six. The General's offer of a lilliputian French nuclear u
brella to his five partners has done nothing to dispel this impressic
If the Fouchet Plan for a political confederation, a *Europe c
patries,* superimposed on the existing regional government w
turned down by four of the Six, its institutionalization among t
of them is still perceived as disturbing.

Nor are things any better outside the framework of the Six. Lor
standing efforts to refurbish NATO as a dynamic agency for wor
ing out common Atlantic defense and foreign policies have achiev
little. The American proposal to share control of the safety catch
the nuclear deterrent by means of the NATO Multilateral Nucle
Force has been cold-shouldered by France and greeted with reser

Britain. Only Germany seems fully committed to the idea. The
ganization for Economic Cooperation and Development, for all its
omising work on the sharing of aid to the non-western world, has
ne little to smooth the incipient United States-Common Market
riff war, of which the chicken rather than the rooster or the bald
gle is the symbol.

The unfortunate image of the dumbbell has been invoked to de-
ribe the desirable relationship between North America on the one
nd and a united western Europe on the other, an image more
spectfully labeled "partnership" by President Kennedy as well as
President Hallstein of the EEC Commission. Partnership con-
tes close cooperation tied to mutually respectful distance; hence
ople affiliated with the Atlantic Council of the United States pre-
r to speak of "community," or of close institutional and quasi-
derative ties, to take the place of the current Atlantic structure,
ich merely perpetuates disarray. Yet the notions of partnership
community among two equal and allied blocs have begun to comte with rival images invoking a vision of concentric circles with the
tropean Community at the core or of an even looser system of
lycentrism in which both Britain and France would retain inde-
dent relations inside as well as outside the Atlantic world.

These events and the prescriptions for reform bespeak disintegra-
n rather than a shiny New Europe or New Atlantis. Have they
dermined the system of regional government which has developed
the Community of the Six, the system which goes under the label
"supranationality"? To answer this question the nature of supra-
tionality must first be well understood.

General de Gaulle equates supranationality with a federalism
ich he detests; Jean Monnet identifies it with a federalism of
ich he is a leading partisan. Both gentlemen mistake the essence
the phenomenon, even though Monnet is rightfully considered its
nding father. British statesmen were repelled by the European
mmunity for a long time because they could conceive only of federal
traditional intergovernmental international institutions, and they
ld the Community to be almost federal. Supranationality, however,
neither federalism nor intimate intergovernmental cooperation,
n though the institutions it employs resemble those of a federation
re than the United Nations or NATO. Supranationality is a unique
le of making international decisions, unique because of the nature
the participants, the context in which decisions are made, and the
ality of the decisions produced.

The participants in the supranational decision-making process i
clude of course "governments"; indeed, governments theoretical
dominate it because their representatives constitute the Councils
Ministers which rule the three communities. But these representativ
are for the most part high civil servants meeting in almost continuo
confrontation with their opposite numbers and working out comm
policies on the basis of their perception of the technical possibilit
inherent in whatever is being discussed. Only exceptionally are de
sions wholly made by the ministers themselves, and then only on t
basis of suggestions and proposals prepared by the European Co
mission or the High Authority; that is, by experts whose job it is
find common ground among the six nations. Other participants
clude spokesmen for all major national and European inter
groups, who confer almost all the time with the specialists in t
Community executives. Proposals by the executives to the minist
always take into account the demands of the major interest grou
Finally, the legislatures of the six countries participate in the fo
of the European Parliament, which makes its wishes known a
which demands to be consulted by the commissions and the Hi
Authority. If it is still true that the representatives of the six gove
ments dispose, this is so only because the European executives,
consultation with private and parliamentary groups, propose. T
alternative dispositions in areas subject to regional jurisdiction a
defined and limited by the range of proposals stemming from ext
governmental sources.

The context of supranational decisions is economic, social a
technical. But this should not lead us to conclude that just beca
expressly "political" and military issues are excluded, supranatio
decisions are somehow secondary. The essence of supranationality l
in the tendency for economic and social decisions to "spill over" i
the realm of the political, to arise from and further influence t
political aspirations of the major groupings and parties in democra
societies. The supranational style stresses the indirect penetration
the political by way of the economic because the "purely" econor
decisions always acquire political significance in the minds of t
participants. In short, the kind of economics and social questi
here dealt with are those at the very core of the modern welfare sta

The quality of supranational decisions differs sharply from t
federal and the intergovernmental norms. In intergovernmental neg
tiations differing initial positions are usually compromised on t
level of the lowest common denominator. That is, the least cooperat

rticipant defines the limits of the compromise. In federal systems
nple majoritarianism decides in ultimate situations of conflict, even
this be the majority of one vote on a federal Supreme Court. In
pranational systems, on the other hand, the compromise pattern
en involves "splitting the difference" between the final bargaining
sitions of the participants. More significantly still, supranational
stems feature a bargaining process which I call "upgrading com-
n interests." It occurs when the participants have great difficulty
arriving at a common policy; yet they do agree that they should
ve some common stand in order to safeguard other aspects of inter-
pendence among them. Hence they tend to swap concessions in
lated fields, but outside the specific contexts in which disagreement
evails. Further the swapping takes place on the basis of services
ndered by an institutionalized conciliator with powers of its own,
e European executives; that body is able to construct patterns of
itual concessions from various policy contexts and in so doing
ually manages to upgrade its own powers at the expense of the
ember governments. Yet those governments do not feel as if they
d been bullied: common interests are upgraded also in the sense
at each feels that by conceding something it gained something else.
e final compromise, far from somehow debasing the bargaining
ocess, induces a feeling of commitment, of creativity and of gain in
e participants.

Hence it is a mistake to argue, as spokesmen for the communities
ually do, that "the criteria by which policy decisions are made are
longer purely national criteria: there is also recognized to be a
ommunity' point of view which arises out of a consideration, from
objective standpoint, of the interest of the economic unit as a
ole."[2] In an objective sense there is no demonstrable "Community
ewpoint," if by that we mean a voluntary national subordination
the general interest as defined by the executives. But there is a
mulative pattern of accommodation in which the participants re-
ain from unconditionally vetoing proposals and instead seek to
tain agreement by means of compromises upgrading common in-
rests.

Having defined the supranational style, we can now answer the
estion of the disintegrative effects of recent events. Clearly, General
Gaulle does *not* play the game according to these rules. Supra-
tionality evolved gradually since the inception of the Coal and

[2] Roy Pryce, *The Political Future of the European Community* (London:
arshbank, 1962), p. 19.

Steel Community in 1952 in a manner falling short of Monne
federalism but exceeding British ideas of intergovernmental coope
tion. De Gaulle is coming close to stopping that evolution. This
true despite the admitted fact that the Fifth Republic has honor
its obligations under the treaties establishing the three communit
even though it deplores the surrender of sovereignty implicit in tl
It is true even though the Fifth Republic has taken the initiative
proposing and executing several measures which involved the ι
grading of common interests, as for example in the case of agricultι
and the acceleration of tariff dismantling. The point is that such ste
were taken only when the government felt these steps to be in ι
national — rather than the European — interest, and that it l
adamantly resisted other attempts to upgrade common interests wh
de Gaulle considered the surrender of further sovereignty undes
able.

The Gaullist vision of the New Europe is neither supranatioι
nor federal. It is confederal; it limits the participants to ministe
the contexts to the political in the grand sense and the quality of ι
decisions to unanimous agreement defined by the leading nations.
the words of former Prime Minister Debré:

In Europe, legitimate power is the power which comes from natio
sovereignty and against this power arbitrary outside tyrannies like
so-called "supranational" institutions can do nothing. European unity
becoming, and will continue to become, a reality through the will of th
who legitimately wield power in each of the countries which together m
up Europe.[3]

The appeal is to a pre-modern notion of national sovereignty wh
exalts the political at the expense of the economic and social. T
Fouchet Plan and the bilateral treaty with Bonn exemplify ι
Gaullist conception of a European confederation. Will it successfu
impede supranational integration which reverses the emphasis a
thereby avoids the notion of sovereignty altogether?

This formulation contains the larger question of the ultimate futι
of Europe, the shape of European society and the manner of gove
ing it. De Gaulle agrees with the European Federalists in believι
that the present structure is an impossible halfway house. The Fι
eralist position disdains "mere" economics; or at best it consid
it a necessary area of joint action among nations before the ultimι

[3] Press Conference, Paris, September 5, 1960. PEP, *Occasional Papers*, No.
p. 12. Nothing which has been said by de Gaulle since changes this view
things.

itical stage of constitutional federation is reached, with its pan-
y of directly elected European legislature, federal executive
ioying general powers and federal judiciary. Emphasis is on com-
tment, faith, vision and a certain method of politics. Little is said
ut the content of politics except to stress the mystical superiority
a "political" quality over the humdrum collection of social wel-
e measures. For de Gaulle the supreme element is belief in the
mutable nature of "high politics," of *Grosspolitik* in the expressive
marckian phrase. Economics, military strategy, social welfare,
ricultural prices, relations with underdeveloped countries — all
se are so many substantive subitems in the pursuit of the supreme
stance, the defense of the national interest. It so happens that this
erest is held by de Gaulle to be closely tied to that of the other
itinental European nations. But a confederacy is all that is re-
ired to realize and assert it against others. In short, this argument
erts that the Europe of the three supranational communities can-
t last: it must become either a full-fledged federation or a confeder-
y under the hegemony of the most important constituent nations.[4]
Few people believe that the existing system of regional government,
it supranational method now under French attack, has a claim to
igevity. I believe that it does. Because it corresponds to the nature
the New Europe, the Europe of adaptative interest groups, bu-
iucracies, technocrats and other units with modest but pragmatic
erests resembling the traditional nationalisms of *Grosspolitik* only
ry remotely, it may well be a real system of government rather than
mere temporary style. "There are more things in Heaven and
irth, General de Gaulle, than are dreamt of in your philosophy."
What are these characteristics of the New Europe? Its main eco-
mic component is neither capitalism nor socialism: it is industrial-
n. Industry, under whatever management, easily produces enough
make everybody comfortable. Minimum standards of consumption
e assumed as given for the entire citizenry. If the market mechanism
d freely negotiated wage levels fail to attain the minima the state
tervenes with subsidies, family allowances, social security pay-
ents, educational scholarships and retraining funds. Rising produc-
n and rising consumption are brought into gear by more or less

---

[4] These alternatives are convincingly and perceptively explored by Stanley
iffmann, "Discord in Community: The North Atlantic Area as a Partial Inter-
tional System," *International Organization*, vol. XVII, no. 3 (Summer, 1963),
. 537-538. My understanding and rejection of the newly rehabilitated concept
"confederation" owes much to Max Beloff, "International Integration and
Modern State," *Journal of Common Market Studies*, vol. II, no. 1 (1963).

systematically pursued policies of full employment or inco▮
guarantees. The flow of investment necessary for this is assured
policies of central steering through tax laws, credit policy and dir▮
consultation among government, industry and organized lab▮
Foreign trade policy becomes particularly important in such a c▮
text because it tends to be manipulated to serve the ends of domes▮
production and consumption; this is as true at the regional as at t▮
national level.

The New Europe has worked out a pragmatic synthesis of capit▮
ism and socialism in the form of democratic planning. Nationalizati▮
of industries is sometimes, but not consistently, employed; the pr▮
system and the market remain the central regulatory agents. Pla▮
ning takes place in the form of forecasts of demand for speci▮
products in specific industrial sectors, which are then presented
the form of aggregate forecasts. Planning, unlike the commun▮
variant, avoids fixed production targets. It "programs" desirab▮
investment and production levels in line with predicted demand a▮
interferes with the self-adjusting market only to that extent. F▮
our purposes, the mechanism of this programming process is
central importance. It features the continuous participation, of ▮
major voluntary groups in European society through elaborate s▮
tems of committees and councils. The technical bureaucracies of tra▮
unions, industrial associations, bankers and farmers sit down wi▮
the technocrats from the ministries of finance, labor and economi▮
— or with central government planning offices — to shape the futu▮
Statistics tend to replace ideology and dogma. Permanent negotiati▮
and occasional conciliation tend to replace active confrontation, d▮
trinaire discussion and class warfare. The symbol is compulsory arb▮
tration rather than the general strike. Even in countries in whi▮
"planning" is taboo, such as West Germany, key government offici▮
consistently use techniques of consultation and of fiscal policy
attain results similar to those sought by the planners.

These economic features clearly rest on a social substratum ve▮
different from that portrayed in the inherited western ideologi▮
Relative upward mobility now obtains. Relative social equality,
least as compared to the situation fifty years ago, is in the ascen
ancy. The formerly alienated working class seems to have made i
peace with the industrial system, perhaps because stronger unio▮
in large-scale enterprises give it more scope for participation tha
was true in the earlier period of small family owned and manag▮
plants. Ideology has lost its former relevance in the relations amor

rkers, industrial managers and middle-class professionals. The oups which find it difficult to adjust to industrialism are the ones r whom ideologies remain important. The lower middle-class shop- epers, artisans and inefficient farmers who are hard pressed by the vent of massive industrialism and large-scale bureaucratized enter- ises of all kinds are the main consumers of doctrinaire ideology day, whether this be communism or some form of organic, status- iented fascism. But even here the advent of the regional logic is anifest: contemporary neo-fascist groups in Europe profess a ecies of pan-European nationalism directed against Russia, the iited States and the Afro-Asian world rather than the more miliar Germanic, Gallic or Roman varieties; it is a "white man's" tionalism directed against "inferior" extra-European races. The mmunists, for their part, are beginning to make their peace with e erstwhile "clerical-fascist conspiracy" by encouraging their trade ions to participate as just another interest group in the decision- aking process of the communities.

Ideology, then, is still with us. But it manifests itself in religious, hnic and educational policy confrontations rather than in the realm the economy or the large issues of defense and foreign policy. Thus find its continued role primarily in Belgium, Italy and France ther than in Scandinavia, Britain, Germany or Austria. Ideology muted to the extent that cleavages in the national populations cut ross contexts rather than clustering in firm groups united on a riety of issues. If a citizen can bestow his support — or his in- fference — to differing groups for purposes of education, welfare easures, religion, defense, recreation and ethnic identity the logic a pluralism based on cross-cutting cleavages will continue to mute eology. Only if a citizen relies on his party or association for *all* these aims will the logic of pluralism be defeated. The Communist et Louis Aragon might have spoken for some Socialists and some ristian Democrats when he said:

> mon parti m'a rendu mes yeux et ma mémoire
> mon parti m'a donné le sens de l'époque
> mon parti, mon parti, merci pour tes leçons . . .

the New Europe, however, this clustering of affections and expec- tions seems to be a thing of the past.

Indeed, when we turn to the political style of the New Europe, rhaps indifference is the key term. Political parties remain intact; t they are no longer divided by glaring controversy because all

the major social and economic issues of fifty years ago no long
plague the body politic. Campaigns tend to avoid the great princip
and to stress efficiency in administration. As a Swedish commentat
put it, "as the general standard of values is so commonly accepte
the functions of the state become so technical as to make polit
appear as a kind of applied statistics. . . . Voting in our day is mu
less than in earlier times a proof of political interest; elections shou
rather be considered as a general census."[5] In many European cou
tries cabinets are now formed on the basis of more or less permane
coalitions among powerful parties united in a general consensus
the desirability to preserve and develop industrial society. Moreov
they agree on subordinating most other public questions to t
desire. Industrial society is run by technocrats, inevitably. And
the technocrat has become the *éminence grise* of all governme
public and private, local, national and regional. As the function
a parliamentary opposition has lost its sharpness the average citiz
has lost much of his interest in politics. Politics in such a setting l
been aptly described as the politics of collective bargaining amo
groups, all of whom accept the legitimacy of representation of ea
participant. The argument among the groups, then, is merely ov
the slice of the pie to be given to each. At the European regional le
this image need not undergo any qualitative restatement: the arg
ment is no longer over the slice of the pie to go to each; it is incre
ingly over the means for increasing the overall size of the past
But otherwise the style of moderate accommodation, universal rep
sentation and mediation by technocrats remains as central at t
regional as at the national level. Holland, Belgium, Austria a
Sweden epitomize this trend. In Germany the reunification iss
somewhat blurs the same phenomenon, while in Italy the relative i
maturity of industrialism contributes to the continued presence
the older pattern of politics. In Britain the modal pattern preva
even though it is obscured by the dominance of the two-party syste
which normally makes coalition politics unnecessary. The major
ception to the trend is France, where the towering figure of Gene
de Gaulle imposes an unnatural style on politics which would oth
wise conform to the depoliticized trend, as indeed it did under t
Fourth Republic.

In such a setting there is but little trace of a purely politi
dimension. *Grosspolitik* is merely a phrase left over from a p

[5] Herbert Tingsten, "Stability and Vitality in Swedish Democracy," *Pol
cal Quarterly,* vol. 26 (1955), pp. 140-151.

dustrial setting, national grandeur and national destiny concep-
ons which the upward mobile citizen weighs distrustfully against
e new "telly," Renault, or that trip to the blue Adriatic. In a sense,
erything is political simply because the modern industrial system
genders public concern — if not control — over so many aspects of
onomic and social life. But by the same token there is no longer a
stinctly political function, separate from economics, welfare or
lucation, a function which finds its reason for being in the sublime
ights of foreign policy, defense and constitution-making.

It will have become clear by now that the supranational scheme
government at the regional level bears a very striking resemblance
the prevailing nature of government at the level of the industrial
ition in everything but constitutional terminology. Supranational-
y, not federation, confederation or intergovernmental organization,
ems to be the appropriate regional counterpart to the national state
hich no longer feels capable of realizing welfare aims within its own
arrow borders, which has made its peace with the fact of inter-
pendence in an industrial and egalitarian age. It represents the
ethod adopted to secure maximum welfare, including military
curity, for a post-capitalist state which no longer conceives of its
terests in starkly political and nationalistic terms. The advent of
pranationality symbolizes the victory of economics over politics,
er that familiar ethnocentric nationalism which used to subordinate
tter to guns, reason to passion, statistical bargaining to excited
mands.

Recent history offers a number of instances in support of this
nclusion. Britain's decision to make its independent nuclear
terrent dependent on American Polaris technology was motivated
considerations of cost; that is, by the decision not to sacrifice
elfare. Its ill-fated decision to join the Community of the Six
plied very serious soul-searching and ended with the serious
eakening of a nationalist mood and calculus which had long been
ken for granted. Norway and Sweden have been known for their
oderation in international affairs, but also for their fierce inde-
ndence from entanglements and passionate belief in the value of
eir national ways of life. Notwithstanding these facts Norway
plied for full admission to the inner circle of the Six, with all its
pranationality, and Sweden sought the less binding tie of economic
sociation with the Community. Upon being rebuffed in the crisis
January, 1963, neutral Sweden was in the forefront of those
eking to give EFTA a much more supranational scope than it had

hitherto been permitted to acquire. Even Switzerland, to whic
neutrality and aloofness *is* the national way of life, anxiously di
cusses the alternatives open to it. Like many others, the Swiss wou
prefer a clear-cut distinction between the constitutional and politic
dimension on the one hand, and the politics of economics on the othe
If Europe opted for political unification they would stay aloof; b
if a "mere" economic union were the final plan they could mak
their peace with it. "Only when that decision is made can we distir
guish once more between the two plans whose confusion obstruct
all discussion," complains Herbert Lüthy. "Customs officials wi
cease making policy and statesmen will cease building Europe b
organizing a market for beasts."[6] But it is the essence of the Ne
Europe that the market for beasts and the discussion of ultimat
political destinies can no longer be separated. In a welfare-oriented
industrial and technocratic order ultimate political concerns are eve
more closely intertwined with these more mundane considerations.

Our argument, however, runs into the very obvious obstacle c
active dislike for the supranational method on the part of som
Europeans and of their practical resistance to continued integratior
both among the Six and between the Six and the rest of Europe a
well as North America. This resistance is explained by some scholar
as a manifestation of the reassertion of the political function. Supra
national integration may well take place on the basis of economi
policies spilling over into more and more neighboring fields c
activity, they suggest, until the *economic* potentialities of the proces
are exhausted. As long as we are merely dismantling tariffs, estab
lishing fair pricing rules for steel, harmonizing social security rate
and facilitating the free movement of manpower we remain withi
the logic of the economic spill-over. But once the limits of these task
are reached, once these objectives are attained, we are up agains
the hard core of politics: foreign policy coordination, defense arrang
ments and the ultimate relationship between *national* political pla
ning and *national* economic welfare. When statesmen feel that th
point has been reached — as de Gaulle clearly does — the spill-ov
will trickle away and integration will either stop or take on a pure
political-constitutional hue. Supranationality will then be condemne
to linger listlessly in the economic institutions already created b

[6] Herbert Lüthy, "La Suisse à contre-courant," *Preuves* (October, 1963
p. 27.

reclosed from further development.[7] The Europe of the Six may
e at this point now.

This formulation mistakes the nature of the New Europe. It is
ot only the outer military shell of nations which has become very
enetrable. Self-reliance equals the flirtation with suicide not only
n the realm of defense. The outer shell of nations has become pene-
able even more in terms of trade, travel, investment, values and
elfare in proportion to the degree of industrial pluralism which
revails domestically. The image which characterizes the nation-state
s a warm and self-contained community and juxtaposes it to the
older and more calculating world of nation-states labeled ''inter-
ational society'' is oversimplified and misleading, at least in the
orth Atlantic area. The internal *as well* as the external network
f relations of nations constitute a species of society; both increas-
gly function on the basis of calculated interest and adjustment
mong interests, on the part of voluntary groups as well as of govern-
ents. And the extent of the adjustment is deeply influenced by the
egree of penetrability which the outer shell of the total national
orpus permits.

Armed with this perspective, let us have another look at the spill-
ver process. While it assumes the continued commitment of major
articipants to the process of integration, it does not presume passion-
e enthusiasm and takes for granted opposition to specific items in
e catalogue of integrative ventures. The support for given steps
sts on the convergence of expectations of the participants; com-
eting expectations and goals can be compromised on the basis of
vapping concessions from a variety of sectors, all under the general-
ed purview of supranational institutions and processes. Lack of
greement among governments can thus give rise to increased
elegated powers on the part of these institutions. Dissatisfaction
ith the results of partial economic steps may lead labor and indus-
y to demand new central action. Supranational institutions and
ational groups may create situations which can be dealt with only
rough central action, unless the nations are willing to suffer
privations in welfare. The very penetrability of the national shell
aves the nation open to the lure of intersectorial bargains whereby
e government is willing to take a loss in exchange for a gain in
other sector. Nations outside the economic grouping but deeply
tertwined with it through the activities of their citizens may ex-

---

[7] This argument is fully developed in Hoffmann, *op. cit.*, pp. 526-531.

perience problems which can be solved — if welfare is not to b
sacrificed — only by joining the grouping and upgrading its centra
powers.[8] No statesman, even if he deeply dislikes the process, ca
permanently isolate his nation from a commitment to unity which
already partially implemented, unless he is willing to pay the pric
in diminished welfare. De Gaulle may be willing to pay that price
but I doubt that French society is. Moreover, if de Gaulle expect
Holland, Belgium, Italy and post-Adenauer Germany to endors
certain French goals he will be obliged to pay for this support b
acquiescing to the goal expectations of his allies. And this involve
him willy-nilly in more supranational integration.

What, then, is spilling over in the Europe of the Six despite curren
French policy? Where does the generalized post-national statistica
mood manifest itself even though it does not fit the nineteenth
century national sentiments of the General? Despite a snail's pac
but because of French insistence, the integrated agricultural marke
ing system is beginning to operate for certain commodities, eve
though no single interest group or government seems to be completel
happy with it. The harmonization of turnover taxes is making slo
progress under the active mediation of the EEC Commission. Th
first regulations concerning a harmonized social security system hav
come into operation. Europe has its first modest common regulatio
governing competition, even though the appreciably different ap
proaches of the Common Market and the Coal and Steel treaties ar
creating confusion in this realm. The relative inflexibility of the Coa
and Steel treaty, even though this was supposed to conduce to stronge
supranational powers, also clashes with the more permissive approac
of the Common Market treaty in the fields of transport policy, ai
to redundant industries and national subsidies, with the result tha
very little has been done in these areas. Lack of success in agreein
to a common energy policy is partially attributable to the same caus
even though the governments of France and Italy also have her
shown that so far they are quite unwilling to subordinate the nation
to the European interest. Another reason for lack of success lies i
the adamant opposition between private and public interests identifie
with coal and oil, respectively, in each nation. In the fields, then, th
spill-over has turned into a trickle.

But this does not exhaust the picture. The Court of the Commun

[8] These formulations are developed by Leon N. Lindberg, *The Political D*
namics of European Economic Integration (Stanford: Stanford Universi
Press, 1963), pp. 10-11.

es has recently pronounced its equivalent of Marbury v. Madison
the *Van Gend* Case, laying down clearly the supremacy of Com-
unity law and holding that it applies directly to the individual
tizen. Several European governments were found guilty of violating
ortions of the Treaty of Rome; in all cases they faithfully carried
it the court's rulings. The Netherlands, in exchange for accepting
e Community's association agreement with eighteen African states
in agreement which conduces primarily to the benefit of France),
tracted a promise that in the future single vetoes could not validly
old up the association of additional outside countries. Despite the
clusion of Britain numerous countries still feel sufficiently attracted
or threatened by the Community to demand the opening of nego-
ations for some form of economic association with it.[9] All these
anifestations imply a continuation of the spill-over process despite
e preferences of the most active opponents of supranational integra-
on. There are further such examples. It is the Community which
ecides the criteria of political respectability applied to candidates
r association : Turkey proved respectable, Spain did not. Similarly,
tacitly decided that permanent neutrality was incompatible with
e political goals of union. Because of the logic of intersectorial
rgaining the Six were forced to accelerate their own schedule of
riff dismantling. In addition they were obliged to work out a com-
on economic and commercial position toward the United States,
atin America and Africa earlier than planned in order to be able
present a common front in GATT. The association agreement with
e African nations compelled the preparation of a common policy on
d to underdeveloped countries, even though France had been far

[9] In January, 1963, all members of EFTA had applied either for full or
sociate membership. As of October, 1963, only Austria was conducting active
gotiations for some kind of association, while France was obliged to accede to
s partners' demand for continued contact with Britain by way of the Western
uropean Union. Other nations with whom various types of association were
ing negotiated at the time of writing are: Turkey, Israel, Cyprus, Ireland,
geria and Iran. Greece has become an associate member with the intention
becoming a full member in 1984; its economic ties and obligations to the
mmunity were so defined as to amount to complete union by that date. The
reement of association with the eighteen African nations (all former French,
alian and Belgian possessions, except Guinea) provides for a preferential EEC
riff on some African exports and for a nil tariff on some others, but opens
frica to EEC exports on a preferential basis and confirms the right of estab-
hment. It steps up and diversifies EEC financial aid to African development,
eates a standing institutional mechanism and a system of compulsory arbitra-
on for the settlement of trade and financial disputes. For an official summary
the Convention see *Bulletin of the EEC*, vol. VI, no. 2 (Brussels, February,
63), pp. 21-25.

more interested in development funds from its partners than in a‹ vice and consent on policy.

Still, the events of the year 1963 gave some justification to tho: who dispute the longevity of economic-supranational approaches ¹ regional government. It is therefore natural that the Commission ‹ EEC and the High Authority of ECSC should have fallen back ‹ the very dynamic of the New Europe to advance their cause. And th they did do. The Coal and Steel Community was checked in its e› deavor to work out a common energy policy. But, conscious of tl implications of this problem with respect to upgrading commo interests among governments, consumers, producers and worker the High Authority proposed the amendment of its treaty: "retrenc] ment" cartels for collieries should be authorized, subsidies to perm the conversion of mines should be permitted, and the Communit should be able to conduct its own commercial policy toward thir countries. The administration of these plan-like activities, of cours would rest in the hands of the High Authority.[10] The proposal wa endorsed by all parties in the European Parliament and all sociali: trade unions, except the miners' unions. It was rejected as not su ficiently protective of coal by the European Committee of Coal Pr ducers and opposed by some Dutch interests as too protective. Frenc government and producer spokesmen rejected it because it wou] limit the ability of national governments to adjust the importatic of oil in response to coal production needs. While nothing has bee finally decided, the High Authority has opened the door to a swee] ing compromise conciliating a variety of attitudes.

Even the politics of national grandeur, even when equipped wit Mirage IV nuclear-armed bombers, seems to find the expansion ‹ supranational authority palatable in the New Europe when welfa: planning is at stake. Such, at least, is the conclusion to be draw from the favorable reception the French government gave to tl EEC Commission's audacious program for "medium-term econom coordination." In October, 1962, the commission presented a schen for centralized monetary policy and intensified business-cycle resear‹ with a view toward the evolution of a central antirecession ar income policy. Free enterprise-oriented interests responded b denouncing central economic direction and deliberate economic "pr gramming" of the type already practiced in France, Holland ar Italy. But the governments cooperated in the first systematic cor

[10] European Coal and Steel Community, High Authority, *Résumé du Douziè: Rapport Général* (April, 1963), pp. 29-31.

rison of their national budgets in terms of expected future economic
rformance; however, they were slow to initiate the advance planng of desirable antirecession measures. The commission thereupon
rapped the term "programming" and began to refer to "medium-
rm economic coordination," which is to involve aggregate demand
d supply forecasts for a four-to-five-year period. Since governments
ere already responsible for spending one third of the national
come under medium-term conditions, efforts to coordinate govern-
ent spending for cyclical and developmental purposes would in fact
her in Community-wide planning under a label found acceptable
en by Mr. Erhard. The almost uniformly favorable response of
arly all interest groups and of the major governments presages the
rly implementation of this reaffirmation of the supranational
yle.[11]

The spill-over process, though rooted in the structures and motives
the post-capitalist welfare state, is far from automatic. Our survey
specific areas of decision-making indicated where the slowing down
s occurred. One the initial *élan* of the supranational style was
ssipated (a development also connected with the advent of de Gaulle
d the retirement of Adenauer) the quality of supranational bar-
ining subtly altered. If one important member unit started to
ince reservations it followed that the remaining governments felt
at a proportional amount of caution was required of them. As
illiam Diebold diagnosed matters:

e change will surely be in the direction of giving less weight — though
rhaps not very much less — to agreement for the sake of agreement and
calculating national interests in a more conventional way than that which
d been developing in "the Community method." This is not a matter of
ick and white, of separate national action versus common action, or supra-
tional versus intergovernmental power. . . . It is enough to say that the
ench action and the inevitable reaction to it on the part of the other five
vernments move the Community along the spectrum away from common
ion and towards national action.[12]

[11] The formulation and negotiation of the Commission's approach is under
e direction of Robert Marjolin, who did much the same kind of job in France
der the authority of the Commisariat au Plan between 1946 and 1948. The
ndle of proposals was endorsed by a variety of French officials, including M.
kanowski, Minister of Industries, several German industrial and CDU spokes-
n, all socialist parties and socialist trade unions, and the Dutch employers.
was opposed by the German FDP and cautiously endorsed by Erhard. See
ropean Community, No. 65 (September, 1963), p. 3; *Bulletin of the EEC*, vol.
, no. 3 (March, 1963), pp. 23-26.
[12] William Diebold, Jr., "European Economic Integration in a New Phase,"
per given at Ohio State University, October 24, 1963, mimeographed, p. 15.

Yet the spill-over process does not presume the continuation
enthusiasm so as to produce agreement for the sake of agreemen
Its continued sway is manifest precisely in this hardening of t
bargaining attitude among the Six. On behalf of a Germany f
from eager to implement the agricultural agreement of 1962, Gerhar
Schroeder advanced the new concept of "synchronization" of joi
policies: "we should equalize as far as possible the advantages ar
disadvantages of the measures of the Community as applied to t
separate member states. We cannot embark on a system of advan
concessions to be made notably by those countries which have alread
made considerable concessions up to now."[13] Immediate and propo
tional counter concessions seemed implied rather than deferr
benefits. The upshot of this doctrine was the very supranation
manner in which the agricultural crisis of December, 1963, w
resolved: in exchange for implementing the common agricultur
policy (a German concession to France), the foreign trade policy
the Community was to be so carried out as to offer broad and re
tariff concessions to third countries (a French concession to German
and the Benelux countries).

The loss of *élan* is far from fatal with respect to the operation of t
integrative logic, though it produces a clearly visible decelerati
effect. There remains one admittedly "political" factor which cou
bring the whole process and its underlying logic to a dead stop: t
reunification of Germany. The end of ideology in West Germany
itself partly a function of a recognition of the loss of the old
national power. The interest of Germany's neighbors in compl
integration is in large measure the result of their fear of a stro
Germany and their continued desire to enmesh the Federal Repub
in a web of interdependencies. A Germany of over seventy milli
people and Europe's greatest concentration of industrial might
the soil of one nation would quickly rekindle the older fears a
trigger once more the old stereotypes, whether warranted by
nature of the new German society or not. The continued sway of
spill-over process, therefore, does rest on the indefinite division
Germany and on the tacit recognition of that status in the minds
West German leaders.

To what extent is the future of Europe determined by this vers
of the past? It seems to me incontestable that the future is determi

13 "What is 'Synchronization'?" *European Community* (June, 1963). Quo
in Diebold, *op. cit.*, p. 18.

the sense that the supremacy of welfare-dominated policies is
sured. If supranational institutions already charged with further
netrating this field are firmly anchored in this supremacy, they will
rvive and flourish. Determined is the role of the technocrat, the
chnical expert whose statistics and negotiations fashion welfare
licies, whether this technocrat is on the payroll of a powerful inter-
t group, a national government or a supranational executive. Deter-
ined is the citizen's distrust of simplistic nationalist slogans, the
alization of which would involve him in sacrificing his peace or his
andard of living. Determined, therefore, is indifference to mili-
rism, adventurism and heroics. If by the term "americanization"
merely mean the progressive *embourgeoisement* of tastes and
havior patterns which goes along with industrial society in the
est as well as in the East, then the americanization of the New
irope is equally determined.

What is far from determined by history, however, is the extent of
e region so ruled, the degree of supranationality the rule will imply,
d the region's relationship with the rest of the western industrial-
·d world. Let us consider each of these indeterminate points.

The Europe of the Outer Seven, of EFTA, corresponds to the
ofile of the New European society even more closely than does
e European Community. In principle, and neglecting the current
reign policies of the Community, it would "fit in" perfectly. Ined, the history of EFTA until February, 1963, was mainly one of
iting and watching for the best time and terms for disbanding and
tering the EEC. With the French veto on this step it should not
illy come as a surprise that the supranational-integrative logic
gan to assert itself rapidly within EFTA. Even though the Outer
ven had foresworn any political plans, had shied away from a
stoms union and had kept the politically sensitive issue of agricul-
ral trade out of their constituent agreement, all this began to
ange. Even though the very word "supranational" was taboo in
eir circle, the style of upgrading common interests by means of
ersectorial bargains made its advent in 1963. EFTA became a
ccess by default; it embraced supranationality as an unintended
t inescapable consequence of exclusion from the Community,
spite all earlier British, Swedish and Swiss disclaimers to the
ntrary.

In 1963 EFTA began the discussion of a common commercial
licy against outsiders; it initiated studies and discussions of
ricultural trade and concluded several agricultural and fisheries

agreements; like EEC, it undertook a dramatic acceleration in t
schedule of removing trade barriers among the members, keepi
the schedule closely geared to its rival's. The developed EF?
nations began to study concerted policies of development aid
the underdeveloped members. On the institutional side this, of cour
involved an increase in the powers of the expert; it also called ir
being the need for consulting private interest groups who are n
represented in a consultative committee. And it gave rise to a nucle
parliamentary gathering in the form of meetings of delegates
EFTA parliaments to the Council of Europe. As the spokesman f
this group, Per Federspiel, remarked:

> . . . whereas EFTA has always been considered an economic association, a
> the EEC a political union, we found that the political approach by
> EFTA countries to the problems concerning us was generally coherent a
> that EFTA in itself was capable of developing a political policy.[14]

But how long will this last? Every protestation that EFTA n
is here to stay is balanced with the assurance that no fight with EI
is intended and that all bridges to it must remain intact. While int
EFTA trade took a marked swing upward in 1963, this had not be
true previously and may not remain true indefinitely. And in t
meantime the actual joint policies pursued in EFTA would facilit
an eventual merger with EEC by eliminating many national ru
and practices and substituting therefore unified regional rules wh
resemble those adopted within EEC. Hence we cannot assume t
inevitable, continuous and autonomous evolution of the Outer Sev
since only Sweden seems to be certain that this would be desirable.

The continued uncertainty regarding the extent of the N
European policy increases the doubts regarding the future of sup
nationality as a form of government. Simple federation rema
excluded simply because there is no generalized enthusiasm for
the constitutive federal act in the New Europe of mass politics wo
have to rest on a substratum of passion and devotion which wo
differ from the older nationalism in name only. If a genui
"European sentiment," a sense of vocation and spiritual uniquene
were actually in existence on a mass scale rather than being confin
to the minds of a few intellectuals, such a feeling would be identi
with a new nationalism writ large. But there is little trace of t
sentiment. Without it, formal federation is inconceivable. B
de Gaulle's confederal approach is equally irrelevant because it re

[14] *EFTA Reporter* (No. 82, Sept. 17, 1963), p. 2.

false premises and enjoys few supporters apart from the aged
nrad Adenauer. Both federation and confederation remain tied
the concept of sovereignty and the pre-eminence of the political.
 long as political figures are more interested in concrete problems
d specific administrative tasks, these concepts are anachronisms of
 earlier legal vocabulary. They remain irrelevant to the future
 the New Europe.

A more relevant controversy, however, exists with respect to the
gree to which existing supranational institutions perform satisfac-
rily. Many Europeans complain that they do not because they are
t sufficiently powerful to carry out all the economic tasks wished
 them, because they cannot formulate a strong policy vis-à-vis the
tside world, and because they do not permit continuous democratic
ntrol over technocrats and ministers. All these charges are true
ough, but whether there is any sense in devising institutional
vices for overcoming them is another question. The common for-
ila proposed for perfecting supranationality among the Six in-
lves a modest and pragmatic federalization.

First, the three executive bodies are to be merged into one
iropean High Commission which would enjoy all the powers now
elded separately by the three organs. Second, the three Councils
 Ministers would be fused into one Council of the European Com-
inities, but otherwise undergo no change in competence.[15] Third,
e economic competences of the communities would be extended
rther, following the proposals of the commissions and High Author-
, and approaching gradually a competence over defense and
reign policy. Fourth, democratic control would be provided over
e ever more powerful technocrats by strengthening the powers of
e present European Parliament, whose competence now is confined
 a posteriori review of executive action and dismissal of the
ecutives. Under the new dispensation the Parliament would be
ected directly by the European citizenry, thus for the first time
abling it to participate in regional government; further the com-
tence of the Parliament would be expanded by giving it the power

[15] This is the essence of a Dutch proposal for the fusion of the executives,
esented to the Councils of Ministers on June 27, 1961, the text of which may
 found in Roy Pryce, *The Political Future of the European Community* (Lon-
n: Marshbank, 1962), pp. 100-102. For the text of the Draft Convention for
ect elections to the European Parliament, see *ibid.*, p. 98. The fusion of the
ecutives was accepted in principle by the six governments in 1963, even though
ither the composition nor the administrative structure of the new European
gh Commission has been decided.

of *a priori* review over all executive policy, but not the ability
legislating.

It may be doubted that the direct election of the Parliament, apa
from giving the Communists representation for the first time, w
result in a dramatic change in the personalities now inhabiting t
assembly, or in a change of the party balance. *A priori* review, in
setting of inevitable technocratic dominance, may delay the prepar
tion of policy but not change its content. Public participation ma
confuse rather than accelerate integration by giving the victims
industrialism a European platform. The point is, rather, as the El
Commission's Action Program said, "what we call the econon
integration of Europe is in essence a political phenomenon."[16]
other words, even without formal constitutional change the prese
supranational institutions are likely to acquire the powers necessa
to advance welfare.

In the meantime, the implementation of the reform program
apt to hinder the integration of the EFTA bloc into the New Euro
The outsiders are unlikely to advance as enthusiastically to a
European integration — once this becomes politically conceivable
if they are confronted with an already highly developed set
quasi-federal institutions. This, of course, is a reason for advocat
of an "Inner Europe" to proceed with institutionalization as rapid
as possible. The supranational-integrative logic suggests the tighte
ing of relations *among* the Six and *among* the Seven. It can teach
little about the tie *between* the two blocs, except to suggest that rap
federalization in one is likely to repel the other.

Even more indeterminate is the future relationship between t
New Europe and the North American world. Neither the milita
ties of NATO nor the economic links of OECD have engendered t
kinds of relationships on which a self-sustaining spill-over proce
could thrive. Short of inaugurating a single Atlantic defense ar
arms production policy and an Atlantic customs union, it is doubtf
that the basis for such a process could be created. In the absence
any such trend the competing formulas of federation, partnershi
concentrism and polycentrism all remain equally plausible in ter
of logic, though not in probability of implementation.

The sweeping and audacious institutional formula pressed in t

[16] For a full exposition of this line of thought in the mind of the EEC Co
mission see Walter Hallstein, *United Europe* (Cambridge: Harvard Univers
Press, 1962), pp. 62-66.

mous Declaration of Atlantic Unity is the least probable.[17] It places
e need for an active federalizing impulse in the Atlantic world on
e Communist threat; but the example of the Community of Six
ggests that an external threat is of secondary usefulness among the
any stimuli pushing toward permanent unity. It indiscriminately
ids all strictly European efforts toward unity on the mistaken
sumption that this must necessarily conduce to the greater benefit
North America as well. And it stresses the need for the immediate
eation of new federal Atlantic institutions while saying next to
thing about the concrete tasks facing the Atlantic nations or the
ities these institutions might be expected to perform. Atlantic
deration substitutes institutional gimmickry for efforts at upgrad-
g common interests in substantive and pivotal policy conflicts.

In the military field the substantive task revolves around the active
gemonial role of the United States, especially in the field of nuclear
rategy. The Nassau Agreement and its possible extension to France,
well as the scheme for a multilateral nuclear fleet for NATO, dis-
ise but do not obliterate this hegemony. While these schemes
ultilateralize control over the safety catch they merely perpetuate
e American preponderance as concerns technology, arms procure-
ent and strategic doctrine; the choice left to the European partici-
ants is so limited as to affront their own sense of purpose and
mpetence. In the economic field, the task hinges around the fact
at the interests of the Atlantic nations are neither homogeneous
or equally intense with respect to intra-Atlantic and world-wide
ade and investment. Japan, Latin America and parts of South
sia are more important to the United States; Africa, the Middle
ast and the temperate-zone Commonwealth countries tend to pre-
cupy Europe. No amount of federalizing and invocation of Com-
unist dangers can gloss over the differences in interests regarding
ternational monetary liquidity, price stability for agricultural
mmodities and economic development needs.

Those most impressed by these conflicts consider and sometimes
cept the opposite of the federal formula: the path of western poly-
ntrism, a sort of *sauve-qui-peut* policy under which each major
untry or bloc would seek its own salvation as best it can in terms
heterogeneous and asymmetrical ties within and outside the At-

---

[17] For a summary of the Declaration of Atlantic Unity and a variety of
dorsements see *The Atlantic Community Quarterly*, vol. 1, no. 2 (Summer,
63), pp. 275-276, and the bulk of the articles which appeared in the Spring,
63 issue of the same publication.

lantic world. NATO might well survive here, but its tasks wou
remain confined to the narrow aspects of military policy on whi
interests converge.[18] Both EFTA and EEC would prosper, the Co
monwealth would remain identified with Britain, but Canada a
the United States would have to make the best deal they can.

The concentric approach was devised to head off such tendenci
but it despairs of a real meshing and upgrading of Atlantic interes
This approach grants that the West has a great deal to gain
maximizing its contribution to economic development in the no
western world, through tighter planning and coordination in OEC
It grants further that the confusion in agriculture could logical
be solved only in terms of some joint Atlantic policy geared to th
of the major one-crop exporting nations. Monetary matters also wou
have to be jointly discussed. But the approach takes for granted th
asymmetries between the United States, Britain and the EEC wou
continue just the same. Therefore it conceives of a series of conce
tric circles, with the Community at the center and radiating outwa
in ever weaker ripples to take in the Atlantic world as well as Japa
Coordination could not be expected to proceed beyond the patte
of discussion and confrontation concerning monetary, trade a
aid policies now being carried on leisurely in OECD.[19]

That leaves us with the ''partnership'' formula. It should be not
from the outset that the soul-searching and planning associated wi
this approach is to be taken very seriously, because for the first tin
in the Atlantic setting it proceeds from a concern with internal co
flict rather than merely from a response to a temporary and inte
mittent external threat, such as NATO. If partnership is to unite t
West ''there must be a genuine division of labor between the t
halves of the alliance. The concept of 'interdependence' will not
satisfied by any formula that assumes that advanced technology
an American prerogative, and which attempts to apply a division
effort which is at variance with economic realities and capabilities.'
In short, it must involve a military policy of sharing not on
weapons as end products and joint control over launching them, b

[18] See Max Beloff, ''Britain, Europe and the Atlantic Community,'' *Int
national Organization*, vol. XVII, no. 3 (Summer 1963), pp. 587, 589-591.

[19] The concentric formula is suggested by Livingston T. Merchant, ''Evolvi
United States Relations with the Atlantic Community,'' *ibid.*, pp. 626-627. T
economic issues at stake are discussed by William Diebold, Jr., ''Econom
Aspects of an Atlantic Community,'' *ibid.*, especially pp. 671 ff.

[20] Alastair Buchan, ''Europe and the Atlantic Alliance: Two Strategies
One?'' *Journal of Common Market Studies*, vol. I, no. 3 (1962), p. 250.

so a common policy of research, production, targeting and command. Unless complete rather than fragmentary multilateralization takes place, the Gaullist claim of a "special relationship" between the United States and Britain retains its plausibility. And de Gaulle's offers of a separate continental deterrent, perhaps linked to Britain's way of the Western European Union, will become increasingly attractive to Europe. It has already been partially endorsed by the Western European Union. A mere coordination of national efforts, now in NATO, will not advance Atlantic integration. A true integration under United States leadership will be resented and cause fragmentation. Only complete sharing can set the scene for the upgrading of common interests from which further integrative steps can spill over into other policy contexts. Such an approach is facilitated by the fact that we seem to have reached the political limits in Europe with respect to the size of conventional forces which are to be deployed. Emphasis can therefore be placed on an effective division of labor between these forces, including the equipment they will carry and the auspices under which it will be manufactured and procured. By capitalizing on this point an economic spill-over can be built into military planning. But by the same token the United States would have to agree to a nuclear division of labor not yet officially accepted in Washington.

And so it is in the economic realm. Short-run discussion concerning small steps for easing the United States gold outflow will not create a spill-over. Neither will practices in OECD under which growth rates and economic aid measures are frankly discussed and criticized. Joint policies in the fields of commercial policy, agricultural marketing, labor competition and monetary stability are called for. The nature of the task must define the creation of appropriate institutions. These, since the task bears so much similarity to what has been done by the European Community, will approximate the supranational style no matter by what name they are called.

The Atlantic Institute in Paris took the initiative in exploring these tasks under the general aegis of the partnership doctrine. Further, it devised institutions capable of carrying out the tasks after exploring what ought to be done.[21] The substantive proposals stress the interconnected aspects of tariff policy, trade in agricultural commodities, aid to economic development in non-western countries, and the stability versus liquidity issue in the interna-

[21] Pierre Uri *et al.*, *Partnership for Progress: A Program for Transatlantic tion* (New York, Harper & Row, 1963), especially pp. 96-107.

tional payments system. In the field of tariff reduction in the tran atlantic trade in manufactured goods, the Atlantic Institute propos a fixed method of negotiation tied to a new set of criteria for judgi the protective character of existing duties and the reciprocity concessions. Rules governing dumping and discrimination in t home market would be worked out for the Atlantic nations. In t realm of agriculture, the Atlantic Institute proposes an ambitio formula for multilateralizing the sale of agricultural surpluses underdeveloped countries, stabilizing the terms of trade so as to e the victimization of exporters of primary products and computi development aid in connection with this stabilization. At the sa time the manufactures of underdeveloped countries are to be giv a slowly expanding market in the Atlantic nations. In short, t Atlantic Institute proposes to end competition among the membe of the Atlantic partnership in their relations with third countri a formula which requires a great deal more coordinated and joi action than in the past. The payments problem is to be solved short-term measures of balance-of-payments aid at the Atlantic lev tied to the creation of a Common Market foreign reserves fund Europe.

That these measures would require a high degree of technocra autonomy for the officials called upon to carry them out is cle beyond argument. But following the integrative logic of the EE the Atlantic Institute proposed a modest body of institutions wi vaguely articulated powers, yet flexible enough to develop additior competences by following the functional lines of task-oriented poli making. It is a suggestion which looks forward to an eventual partite Atlantic partnership, transcending the present division Europe.

For the immediate future, a tripartite committee is to be set with the task of exploring and defining the policy areas requiri attention and preparing the necessary negotiations, notably in t "Kennedy round" of tariff cutting. This committee would be co posed of the EEC, the United States and Britain, each representi the nations associated with it in terms of world trade blocs. The m important task of this committee would be the easing of tensio between EEC and EFTA and the eventual merger of the tv Following this development, the bipartite machinery would begin work. At the top there would be a Council of Partnership, made of European and American economic administrators *and* ministe They would enjoy supreme authority to dispose. Power to propo

wever, would be lodged in a Committee of Wise Men responsible
no government and inspired by the example of the executives of
European communities. The prestige of the Wise Men would be
ch as to make the adoption of their proposals by the Council a
rly certain outcome. The power to review and criticize — but not
alter — these decisions would be lodged in an Atlantic Parlia-
ntary Assembly, following the model of the current European
rliament.

The essence of this proposal remains true to the technocratic nature
pluralistic, welfare-oriented modern states. Democratic account-
ility, majority voting and public discussion are balanced at all
els by permanent bodies of experts negotiating away from the
re of public confrontation. OECD is to provide the expert com-
ttees and the secretariat for the entire operation and thereby gain
new lease on life as the technical body charged with unifying
stern economic policy, representing both the enlarged European
mmon Market and North America. As the Atlantic Institute put

shall thus have an organization systematically conceived as a *network*
committees, organized on a functional basis and served by a single secre-
iat. Such a body would prove an invaluable forum for the submission and
ler discussion of the ideas of the two main partners before they are
Illy dealt with in the appropriate international bodies.[22]

We can now restate, at the Atlantic level, the formula of cross-
tting cleavages in popular expectations and loyalties which we
duced in the characterization of post-capitalist and post-ideological
stern society. It is the supreme merit of the Atlantic Institute's
oposals to have grasped this point and to have married the con-
uation of the supranational process of integration in Europe to
splitting of the task so as to prevent Europe's pre-empting the
ture. Integration in any network of autonomous units is ad-
nced if no single unit is the supreme repository of hopes, hates
d tasks. If a united Europe were to become the vessel for the
ultaneous execution of a nuclear military policy and a compre-
nsive economic approach to its internal trade *as well as* to the un-
rdeveloped world, we would have to bury both NATO and
CD and forget about partnership. There would no longer be an
portunity, in terms of tasks and institutions, for technocrats to
pare policy and for voluntary groups to coalesce across national

2 *Ibid.*, p. 106. Italics in original.

boundaries. Hence military matters must be kept out of the hands
purely European and North American agencies, and econom
issues must be divided among those which can be dealt with by
enlarged EEC and others which properly belong to an Atlan
structure. A future confrontation of the autonomous units on bo
sides of the Atlantic — one an old nation and the other in the proc
of making a new one out of established nationalisms — might w
lead to the revival of that very *Grosspolitik* which we dismiss
earlier. The preservation and cultivation of cross-cutting cleavag
at the Atlantic level can prevent this; indeed it is a necessary co
dition for partnership.

Stanley Hoffmann

Obstinate or Obsolete?
The Fate of the Nation-State
and the Case of Western Europe

I

The critical issue for every student of world order is the fate of
e nation-state. In the nuclear age, the fragmentation of the world
o countless units, each of which has a claim to independence, is
viously dangerous for peace and illogical for welfare. The dy-
mism which animates those units, when they are not merely city-
tes of limited expanse or dynastic states manipulated by the
ince's calculations, but nation-states that pour into their foreign
licy the collective pride, ambitions, fears, prejudices, and images
large masses of people, is particularly formidable.[1] An abstract
eorist could argue that any system of autonomous units follows
e same basic rules, whatever the nature of those units. But in prac-
e, that is, in history, their substance matters as much as their
·m; the story of world affairs since the French Revolution is not
·rely one more sequence in the ballet of sovereign states; it is the
ry of the fires and upheavals propagated by nationalism. A claim
sovereignty based on historical tradition and dynastic legitimacy
·ne has never had the fervor, the self-righteous assertiveness which
imilar claim based on the idea and feelings of nationhood presents:
world politics, the dynastic function of nationalism is the con-

Reprinted from *Daedalus*, 95, No. 3 (Summer 1966), with the permission of The
erican Academy of Arts and Sciences and the author.

See Pierre Renouvin et Jean-Baptiste Duroselle, *Introduction a l'histoire des
tions internationales* (Paris, 1964).

stitution of nation-states by amalgamation or by splintering, a
its emotional function is the supplying of a formidable good cc
science to leaders who see their task as the achievement of nationho
the defense of the nation, or the expansion of a national missio

This is where the drama lies. The nation-state is at the same ti
a form of social organization and — in practice if not in every bra
of theory — a factor of international non-integration; but those w
argue in favor of a more integrated world, either under more cc
tralized power or through various networks of regional or functio
agencies, tend to forget Auguste Comte's old maxim that *on
détruit que ce qu'on remplace:* the new "formula" will have to p
vide not only world order, but also the kind of social organization
which leaders, élites, and citizens feel at home. There is curren
no agreement on what such a formula will be;[3] as a result, natic
states — often inchoate, economically absurd, administratively ra
shackle, and impotent yet dangerous in international politics —
main the basic units in spite of all the remonstrations and exhor
tions. They go on *faute de mieux* despite their alleged obsolescen
indeed, not only do they profit from man's incapacity to bring abc
a better order, but their very existence is a formidable obstacle
their replacement.

If there was one part of the world in which men of good w
thought that the nation-state could be superseded, it was Weste
Europe. One of France's most subtle commentators on internatio
politics has recently reminded us of E. H. Carr's bold prediction
1945: "we shall not see again a Europe of twenty, and a world
more than sixty independent sovereign states."[4] Statesmen have
vented original schemes for moving Western Europe "beyond t
nation-state,"[5] and political scientists have studied their efforts w
a care from which emotional involvement was not missing. The cc
ditions seemed ideal. On the one hand, nationalism seemed at
lowest ebb; on the other, an adequate formula and method for bui
ing a substitute had apparently been devised. Twenty years aft

[2] In a way, the weaker are the foundations on which the nation rests,
shriller the assertions become.

[3] On this point, see Rupert Emerson, *From Empire to Nation* (Cambrid
Mass., 1962), Ch. XIX; and Raymond Aron, *Paix et Guerre entre les Nati*
(Paris, 1962), Ch. XI.

[4] E. H. Carr, *Nationalism and After* (London, 1965), p. 51. Quoted in Pie
Hassner, "Nationalisme et relations internationales," *Revue française
science politique,* Vol. XV, No. 3 (June 1965), pp. 499-528.

[5] See Ernst B. Haas' book by this title (Stanford, Calif., 1964).

e end of World War II — a period as long as the whole interwar
a — observers have had to revise their judgments. The most opti-
stic put their hope in the chances the future may still harbor,
ther than in the propelling power of the present; the less optimistic
es, like myself, try simply to understand what went wrong.
My own conclusion is sad and simple. The nation-state is still
re, and the new Jerusalem has been postponed because the nations
Western Europe have not been able to stop time and to fragment
ace. Political unification could have succeeded if, on the one hand,
ese nations had not been caught in the whirlpool of different con-
rns, as a result both of profoundly different internal circumstances
d of outside legacies, and if, on the other hand, they had been able
obliged to concentrate on "community-building" to the exclusion
all problems situated either outside their area or within each one
them. Domestic differences and different world views obviously
ean diverging foreign policies; the involvement of the policy-makers
issues among which "community-building" is merely one has
eant a deepening, not a decrease, of those divergences. The reasons
llow: the unification movement has been the victim, and the sur-
val of nation-states the outcome, of three factors, one of which char-
terizes every international system, and the other two only the
esent system. Every international system owes its inner logic and
unfolding to the *diversity* of domestic determinants, geo-historical
uations, and outside aims among its units; any international
stem based on fragmentation tends, through the dynamics of un-
enness (so well understood, if applied only to economic unevenness,
Lenin) to reproduce diversity. However, there is no inherent
ason that the model of the fragmented international system should
le out by itself two developments in which the critics of the nation-
ate have put their bets or their hopes. Why must it be a diversity
nations? Could it not be a diversity of regions, of "federating"
ocs, superseding the nation-state just as the dynastic state had
placed the feudal puzzle? Or else, why does the very logic of con-
tgrations fed by hostility not lead to the kind of catastrophic uni-
ation of exhausted yet interdependent nations, sketched out by
ant? Let us remember that the unity movement in Europe was
ecisely an attempt at creating a regional entity, and that its origins
d its springs resembled, on the reduced scale of a half-continent,
e process dreamed up by Kant in his *Idea of Universal History*.[6]

[6] See on this point my essay "Rousseau on War and Peace," in *The State of
ar* (New York, 1965).

The answers are not entirely provided by the two factors th
come to mind immediately. One is the legitimacy of national se
determination, the only principle which transcends all blocs a
ideologies, since all pay lip service to it, and provides the foundati
for the only "universal actor" of the international system: t
United Nations. The other is the newness of many of the states, whi
have wrested their independence by a nationalist upsurge and a
therefore unlikely to throw or give away what they have obtain
only too recently. However, the legitimacy of the nation-state d
not by itself guarantee the nation-state's survival in the internatior
state of nature, and the appeal of nationalism as an emancipati
passion does not assure that the nation-state must everywhere rema
the basic form of social organization, in a world in which ma
nations are old and settled and the shortcomings of the nation-sta
are obvious. The real answers are provided by two unique featur
of the present international system. One, it is the first truly *glob*
international system: the regional subsystems have only a reduc
autonomy; the "relationships of major tension" blanket the who
planet, the domestic polities are dominated not so much by t
region's problems as by purely local and purely global ones, whi
conspire to divert the region's members from the internal affai
of their area, and indeed would make an isolated treatment of the
affairs impossible. As a result, each nation, new or old, finds itse
placed in an orbit of its own, from which it is quite difficult to mo
away: for the attraction of the regional forces is offset by the pu
of all the other forces. Or, to change the metaphor, those nations th
coexist in the same apparently separate "home" of a geographic
region find themselves both exposed to the smells and noises th
come from outside through all their windows and doors, and lookir
at the outlying houses from which the interference issues. Comir
from diverse pasts, moved by diverse tempers, living in differe
parts of the house, inescapably yet differently subjected and attracte
to the outside world, those cohabitants react unevenly to their exp
sure and calculate conflictingly how they could either reduce the di
turbance or affect in turn all those who live elsewhere. The adjus
ment of their own relations within the house becomes subordinated
their divergences about the outside world; the "regional subsystem
becomes a stake in the rivalry of its members about the system as
whole.

However, the coziness of the common home could still prevail
the inhabitants were forced to come to terms, either by one of the

by the fear of a threatening neighbor. This is precisely where the
ond unique feature of the present situation intervenes. What
nds to perpetuate the nation-states decisively in a system whose
iversality seems to sharpen rather than shrink their diversity is
e new set of conditions that govern and restrict the rule of force:
amocles' sword has become a boomerang, the ideological legiti-
acy of the nation-state is protected by the relative and forced
meness of the world jungle. Force in the nuclear age is still the
midwife of societies'' insofar as revolutionary war either breeds
w nations or shapes regimes in existing nations; but the use of
rce along traditional lines, for conquest and expansion — the very
e that made the "permeable" feudal units not only obsolete but
llapse and replaced them with modern states often built on "blood
d iron" — has become too dangerous. The legitimacy of the feudal
it could be undermined in two ways: brutally, by the rule of
rce — the big fish swallowing small fish by national might; subtly
legitimately, so to speak, through self-undermining — the logic of
nastic weddings or acquisitions that consolidated larger units. A
stem based on national self-determination rules out the latter; a
stem in which nations, once established, find force a much blunted
apon rules out the former. Thus agglomeration by conquest or
t of a fear of conquest fails to take place. The new conditions
violence tend even to pay to national borders the tribute of vice
virtue: violence which dons the cloak of revolution rather than of
terstate wars, or persists in the form of such wars only when they
company revolutions or conflicts in divided countries, perversely
spects borders by infiltrating under them rather than by crossing
em overtly. Thus all that is left for unification is what one might
ll "national self-abdication" or self-abnegation, the eventual will-
gness of nations to try something else; but precisely global in-
lvement hinders rather than helps, and the atrophy of war removes
e most pressing incentive. What a nation-state cannot provide
one — in economics, or defense — it can still provide through
ans far less drastic than hara-kiri.

These two features give its solidity to the principle of national
lf-determination, as well as its resilience to the U.N. They also give
present, and quite unique, shape to the "relationship of major
asion": the conflict between East and West. This conflict is both
ited and universal — and both aspects contribute to the survival
the nation-state. As the superpowers find that what makes their
wer overwhelming also makes it less usable, or rather usable only

to deter one another and to deny each other gains, the lesser sta discover under the umbrella of the nuclear stalemate that they a not condemned to death, and that indeed their nuisance power impressive — especially when the kind of violence that prevails present circumstances favors the porcupine over the elephant. T superpowers experience in their own camps the backlash of a reb lion against domination that enjoys broad impunity, and cann easily coax or coerce third parties into agglomeration under th tutelage. Yet they retain the means to prevent other powers fro agglomerating away from their clutches. Thus, as the superpow compete, with filed nails, all over the globe, the nation-state comes the universal point of salience, to use the new language strategy — the lowest common denominator in the competition.

Other international systems were merely conservative of div sity; the present system is profoundly conservative of the divers of nation-states, despite all its revolutionary features. The dream Rousseau, concerned both about the prevalence of the general w — that is, the nation-state — and about peace, was the creation communities insulated from one another. In history, where '' essence and drama of nationalism is not to be alone in the world, the clash of non-insulated states has tended to breed both nati states and wars. Today, Rousseau's ideals come closer to reality, in the most un-Rousseauan way: the nation-states prevail in pea they remain unsuperseded because a fragile peace keeps the Ka ian doctor away, they are unreplaced because their very invol ment in the world, their very inability to insulate themselves fr one another, preserves their separateness. The "new Europ dreamed by the Europeans could not be established by force. Left the wills and calculations of its members, the new formula has jelled because they could not agree on its role in the world. The fail (so far) of an experiment tried in apparently ideal conditions t us a great deal about contemporary world politics, about the chan of unification movements elsewhere, and about the functional proach to unification. For it shows that the movement can fail only when there is a surge of nationalism in one important pa but also when there are differences in assessments of the natio interest that rule out agreement on the shape and on the world r of the new, supranational whole.

The word nationalism is notoriously slippery. What I suggest

---

[7] P. Hassner, *op. cit.*, p. 523.

e following threefold distinction, which may be helpful in analyz-
g the interaction between the nation-state and the international
stem:

1. There is *national consciousness* (what the French call *senti-
ent national*) — a sense of "cohesion and distinctiveness,"[8] which
ts one off from other groups. My point is that this sense, which
ads to have important effects on international relations as long as
is shared by people who have not achieved statehood, is rather
neutral" once the nation and the state coincide: that is, the exist-
ce of national consciousness does not dictate foreign policy, does
t indicate whether the people's "image" of foreigners will be
iendly or unfriendly (they will be seen as different — nothing else
implied), nor does it indicate whether or not the leaders will be
lling to accept sacrifices of sovereignty. One cannot even posit
at a strong national consciousness will be an obstacle for move-
ents of unification, for it is perfectly conceivable that a nation
avinces itself that its "cohesion and distinctiveness" will be best
eserved in a larger entity. Here, we must turn to the second cate-
ry.

2. For lack of a better phrase, I shall call it the *national situa-
on*. Any nation-state, whether pulsing with a strong "national con-
iousness" or not — indeed, any state, whether a true nation-state
a disparate collection of unintegrated groups — is, to borrow
artre's language, thrown into the world; its situation is made up
together of its internal features — what, in an individual, would be
lled heredity and character — and of its position in the world. The
ate of national consciousness in the nation is one, but only one,
the elements of the situation. It is a composite of objective data
nside: social structure and political system; outside: geography,
rmal commitments) and subjective factors (inside: values, prej-
lices, opinions, reflexes; outside: one's own traditions and assess-
ents of others, and the other's attitudes and approaches toward
eself); some of its components are intractable, others flexible and
angeable. Any statesman, whether he is a fervent patriot or not,
ust define the nation's foreign policy by taking that situation into
count; even if he is convinced of the obsolescence of *the* nation-
ate (or of *his* nation-state), the steps he will be able and willing

8 Karl Deutsch, *Nationalism and Social Communication* (Cambridge, Mass.,
53), p. 147.

to take in order to overcome it will be shaped by the fact that
speaks — to borrow de Gaulle's language this time — for the nati
as it is in the world as it is. He cannot act as if his nation-state d
not exist, however sorry its shape may be, or as if the world we
other than it is. The national situation may facilitate unificati
moves, even when national consciousness is strong. It may prove
formidable obstacle, even when national consciousness is weak. T
point is that even when the policy-maker tries to move "beyond t
nation-state" he can do it only by taking along the nation with
baggage of memories and problems — with its situation. I do n
want to suggest that the situation is a "given" that dictates polic
but it sets complicated limits that affect freedom of choice.[9]

3. I will reserve the term *"nationalism"* for a specific meanin
it is one of the numerous ways in which political leaders and élit
can interpret the dictates, or rather the suggestions, of the natior
situation, one of the ways of using the margin it leaves. Where
national consciousness is a feeling, and the national situation a co
dition, nationalism is a doctrine or (if one uses a broad definitio
an ideology — the doctrine or ideology that gives to the nation
world affairs absolute value and top priority. The consequences
such a preference may vary immensely: nationalism may imply e
pansion (that is, the attempt at establishing the supremacy of one
nation over others) or merely defense; it may entail the notion of
universal mission or, on the contrary, insulation. It may be peacef
or pugnacious.[10] It is less an imperative determinant of choice th
a criterion of choice and an attitude which shapes the choices mad
But whatever its manifestations, its varying content, it always fo
lows one rule common to all the former, it always pours the latt
into one mold: the preservation of the nation as the highest go
Nationalism thus affects, *at least* negatively, the way in which t
freedom of choice left by the national situation will be used; inde

[9] A more systematic and exhaustive analysis would have to discrimina
rigorously among the various components of the national situation; if t
purpose of the analysis is to help one understand the relations between t
nation-state and the international system, it would be particularly necessary
assess (1) the degree to which each of these components is an unchangea
given (or a given unchangeable over a long period of time) or on the contra
an element that can be transformed by will and action; (2) the hierarchy
importance and the order of urgency that political élites and decision-mak
establish among the components.

[10] See Raoul Girardet, "Antour de l'ideologie nationaliste," *Revue frança
de science politique, op. cit.,* pp. 423-45; and P. Hassner, *op. cit.,* pp. 516-

may collide with, and try to disregard or overcome, the limits
ᴉich the situation sets.

The relation between nationalism and the two other factors is
mplicated. Nationalism (in the sense of the will to establish a
tion-state) is triggered by, and in turn activates, national con-
ɩousness in oppressed nationalities; but nationalism, in colonial
eas as well as in mature nation-states, can also be a substitute for
still weak or for a fading national consciousness. In nation-states
at are going concerns, national consciousness breeds nationalism
ly in certain kinds of national situations. The national situation
ᴉy be assessed by a nationalist leader exactly in the same way as
 a non-nationalist one; however, nationalism may lead the former
 promote policies the latter would have rejected and to oppose
ɩves the former would have undertaken. That bane of international
lations theory, the national interest, could be defined as follows:
N.I. = National situation X outlook of the foreign policy-makers.
It is obvious that the same situation can result in different poli-
ᴉs, depending in particular on whether or not there is a nationalist
licy-maker. It is obvious also that national interests of different
tions will not be defined in easily compatible terms if those re-
ective outlooks are nationalist, even when the situations are not
 different. But the same incompatibility may obtain, even if the
tlooks are not nationalistic, when the situations are indeed very
ferent.[11]

II

Let us now look at the fate of the nation-states in the part of
ɪrope occupied by the so-called Six, that is, the continental part
 Western Europe, first by examining the basic features of their
tional situations, then by commenting upon the process of uni-
ation, later by discussing its results, and finally by drawing some
sons.

Western Europe in the postwar years has been characterized by
ɾee features which have affected all of its nations. But each of
ᴉse features has nevertheless affected each of the six nations in a
ferent way because of the deep differences that have continued
 divide the Six.

---

[1] As will be stated more explicitly in part V, what matters is not the ''objec-
ɟ'' difference detected by scholars or outsiders, but the ''felt'' difference
erienced by political élites and decision-makers.

1. The first feature — the most hopeful one from the viewpoi
of the unifiers — was the temporary demise of nationalism. In t
defeated countries — Germany and Italy — nationalism had beco
associated with the regimes that had led the nations into war, defe
and destruction. The collapse of two national ideologies that h
been bellicose, aggressive, and imperialistic brought about an
most total discredit for nationalism is every guise. Among the n
tions of Western Europe that were on the Allied side, the m
remarkable thing was that the terrible years of occupation and
sistance had not resulted in a resurgence of chauvinism. Amusing
enough, it was the Communist Party of France that gave the mc
nationalistic tone to its propaganda; on the whole, the platforms
the Resistance movements show an acute awareness of the dange
of nationalist celebrations and national fragmentation in Weste
Europe. The Resistance itself had had a kind of supranational
mension; none of the national resistance movements could have su
vived without outside support; the nations whose honor they h
saved had been liberated rather than victorious. All this prevent
the upsurge of the kind of cramped chauvinism that had follow
the victory of World War I, just as the completeness of the disast
and the impossibility of putting the blame on any traitors crush
any potential revival in Germany of the smoldering nationalism
resentment that had undermined the Weimar Republic. There w
in other words, above and beyond the differences in national situ
tions between indubitable losers and dubious winners, the gener
feeling of a common defeat, and also the hope of a common futur
for the Resistance platforms often put their emphasis on the ne
for a union or federation of Western Europe.

However, the demise of nationalism affected differently the va
ious nations of the half-continent. On the one hand, there we
significant differences in national consciousness. If nationalism w
low, patriotic sentiment was extremely high in liberated Fran
The circumstances in which the hated Nazis were expelled and t
domestic collaborators purged amounted to what I have called els
where a rediscovery of the French political community by t
French:[12] the nation seemed to have redeemed its "cohesion a
distinctiveness." On the contrary, in Germany especially, the d
struction of nationalism seemed to have been accompanied by
drop in national consciousness as well: what was distinctive w

[12] See "Paradoxes of the French Political Community," in S. Hoffmar
et al., *In Search of France* (Cambridge, Mass., 1963).

iilt and shame; what had been only too cohesive was being torn
part not by internal political cleavages, but by partition, zones of
ccupation, regional parochialisms blessed by the victors. The
rench national backbone had been straightened by the ordeal,
though the pain had been too strong to tempt the French to flex
ationalistic muscles; the German national backbone appeared to
ave been broken along with the strutting jaw and clenched fist
: Nazi nationalism. Italy was in slightly better shape than Ger-
any, in part because of its Resistance movements, but its story was
oser to the German than to the French.

However, there were other elements in the national situation, be-
des patriotic consciousness, that also affected differently the various
ations' inclination to nationalism. The defeated nations — Ger-
any in particular — were in the position of patients on whom
rastic surgery had been performed, and who were lying prostrate,
ependent for their every movement on the surgeons and nurses.
ven if one had wanted to restore the nation to the pinnacle of values
nd objectives, one could not have succeeded except with the help
nd consent of one's guardians — who were not likely to give
ipport to such a drive; in other words, the situation itself set the
rictest limits to the possibility of any kind of nationalism, expan-
ve or insulating. The lost territories were beyond recuperation;
healing period of *"repli"* comparable to that which had marked
ıe early foreign policy of the Third Republic was not conceivable
ither. One could not get anything alone, and anything others could
rovide, while limited, would be something to be grateful for.

On the other hand, France and, to a lesser extent (because of their
ıuch smaller size), Belgium and Holland were not so well in-
culated. For, although the prevalence of the nation meant little
ı the immediate European context, it meant a great deal in the
nperial one: if the circumstances of the Liberation kept national
onsciousness from veering into nationalism in one realm, the same
ircumstances tended to encourage such a turn with respect to the
olonies. Cut down to size in Europe, these nations were bound to
ct as if they could call upon their overseas possessions to redress
he balance; accustomed, through their association of nationalism
vith Nazi and Fascist imperialism, to equate chauvinism only with
xpansion, they would not be so easily discouraged from a nation-
lism of defense, aimed at preserving the "national mission" over-
eas. The Dutch lost most of their empire early enough to find
hemselves, in this respect, not so different from the German and

Italian amputees; the Belgians remained serene long enough not
have nationalistic fevers about the huge member that seemed
give them no trouble until the day when it broke off — brutall
painfully, but irremediably. The French, however, suffered almc
at once from dis-imperial dyspepsia, and the long, losing battle the
fought gave rise continuously to nationalist tantrums of frustratic
and rage. Moreover, the French inclination to nationalism w.
higher because of an internal component of the national situatic
as well: there was in France one political force that was clear
nationalist, that had indeed presided over the Liberation, given wha
ever unity they had to the Resistance movements, and achieved :
the most impressive way a highly original convergence of Jacob
universalist nationalism and of "traditionalist," right-wing, defe
sive nationalism — the force of General de Gaulle. His resignatic
had meant, as Alfred Grosser suggests,[13] the defeat of a doctrine th.
put not only a priority mark on foreign affairs but also a priori¹
claim on *Notre Dame la France*. The incident that had led to b
departure — a conflict over the military budget — had been symbol
enough of the demise of nationalism referred to above. But his dur.
bility, first as a political leader, later as a "capital that belongs
all and to none," reflected a lasting nostalgia for nationalism; and
was equally symbolic that the crisis which returned him to powe
was a crisis over Algeria.

2. The second feature common to all the West European nation;
situations, yet affecting them differently, was the "political collap;
of Europe." Europe did not merely lose power and wealth: suc
losses can be repaired, as the aftermath of World War I had show
Europe, previously the heart of the international system, the loct
of the world organization, the fount of international law, fell unde
what de Gaulle has called "the two hegemonies." The phrase i
obviously, inaccurate and insulting: one of those hegemonies too
a highly imperial form, and thus discouraged and prevented th
creation in Eastern Europe of any regional entity capable of ove
coming the prewar national rivalries. Nothing is to be gained, ho
ever, by denying that U.S. hegemony has been a basic fact of lif
American domination has indeed had the kinds of "domination e
fects" any hegemony produces: the transfer of decision-making i
vital matters from the dominated to the dominator breeds a kin

[13] *La politique extérieure de la V République* (Paris, 1965), p. 12.

paternalism in the latter, and irresponsibility (either in the form
abdication or in the form of scapegoatism) in the former. But
e consequences of hegemony vary according to its nature. The
culiar nature of this domination has also had unique consequences
better and worse than in the classical cases. One may dominate
cause one wants to and can; but one may also dominate because
e must and does: by one's weight and under the pressures of a
mpelling situation. This has been America's experience: its heg-
ony was "situational," not deliberate.

The effects have been better than usual, insofar as such hegemony
stricted itself to areas in which European nations had become
ther impotent or incapable of recovery by self-reliance. It left the
minated with a considerable freedom of maneuver, and indeed
odded them into recovery, power recuperation, and regional unity;
favored both individual and collective emancipation. But the ef-
cts have been worse precisely because this laxity meant that each
rty could react to *this* common feature of the national situations
hat is, American hegemony) according to the distinctive *other*
atures of his national situation, features left intact by the weight
d acts of the U.S., by contrast with the U.S.S.R. American domi-
tion was only one part of the picture. Hence the following para-
x: both America's prodding and the individual and collective
potence of Western European nations, now reduced to the con-
tion of clients and stakes, ought logically to have pushed them
to unity-for-emancipation — the kind of process Soviet policy dis-
uraged in the other half of Europe. But the very margin of auton-
ny left to each West European nation by the U.S. gave it an array
choices: between accepting and rejecting dependence, between
ity as a weapon for emancipation and unity as merely a way to
ake dependence more comfortable. It would have been a miracle
all the nations had made the same choice; the diversity of national
tuations has ultimately prevailed. To define one's position toward
e U.S. was the common imperative, but each one has defined it
his own way.

At first, this diversity of domestic outlooks and external positions
d not appear to be an obstacle to the unification movement. As
rnst Haas has shown,[14] the movement grew on ambiguity, and
ose who accepted American hegemony as a lasting fact of Euro-
an life as well as those who did not could submerge their dis-

[14] *The Uniting of Europe* (Stanford, Calif., 1958).

agreement in the construction of a regional entity that could
seen, by the former, as the most effective way for continuing to r
ceive American protection and contributing to America's missie
and, by the latter, as the most effective way to challenge America
predominance. However, there are limits to the credit of amibiguit
The split could not be concealed once the new entity was asked
tackle matters of "high politics" — that is, go beyond the purely i
ternal economic problems of little impact or dependence on tl
external relationship to the U.S.[15] It is therefore no surprise th
this split should have disrupted unification at two moments —
1953-54, when the problem of German rearmament was raised; ar
in 1962-65, when de Gaulle's challenge of the U.S. became global.

This is how the diversity of national situations operated. Firs
it produced (and produces) the basic split between those I wou
call the resigned ones, and those I would call the resisters. The r
signed ones were, on the one hand, the smaller nations, aware
their weakness, realizing that the Soviet threat could not be met l
Europeans alone, accustomed to dependence on external protectoi
grateful to America for the unique features of its protection, ar
looking forward to an important role for Europe but not in tl
realm of high politics. Italy had, in the past, tried to act as a gre
power without protectors; yet not only were those days over, b
also the acceptance of American hegemony provided the creak
Italian political system with a kind of double cushion — against tl
threat of Communism, but also against the need to spend too mue
energy and money on Italian rearmament. For the smaller states
well as for Italy, the acceptance of U.S. hegemony was like a
insurance policy, which protected them against having to give pr
ority to foreign affairs. On the other hand, Germany accepted d
pendence on the U.S. not merely as a comfort, but as a necessity

[15] See my discussion in ''The European process of Atlantic cross-purposes,
Journal of Common Market Studies (February 1965), pp. 85-101. The ve
success of internal economic integration raised those external issues far earli
than many expected. (Cf. Britain's application for membership, the problem
external commercial policy.)

[16] The latter case is self-evident; the first, less so, since the crisis over E.D.
was primarily an ''intra-European'' split, between the French and the Germa
over the return of the latter to arms and soldiery. However, there was more
it than this: E.D.C. was accepted mostly by those who thought that Europe cou
and should not refuse to do what the U.S. had demanded — that is, rearm in ord
to share the defense of the half-continent with the U.S., and to incite the U.
to remain its primary defender; E.D.C. was rejected by those who feared th
the Defense Community would freeze existing power relationships forever.

tal as breathing. West Germany's geographical position had turned into the front line, its partition has contributed to imposing secu- ty as the supreme goal, the staunch anti-Communism of its leader- ip had ruled out any search for security along the lines of neu- ality. There followed not only the acceptance of U.S. leadership ıt also the need to do everything possible in order to tie the United tates to Western Europe. Moreover, in West Germany's helpless ɔsition, the recovery of equality was another vital goal, and it could ɔ reached only through cooperation with the most powerful of the ɔcupying forces. Defeat, division, and danger conspired to making ˜est Germany switch almost abruptly from its imperialistic nation- ism of the Nazi era to a dependence which was apparently sub- issive, yet also productive (of security and status gains) under denauer.

As for the resisters, they, like the West Germans, gave priority ɔ foreign affairs — only not in the same perspective. The French ɔading of geography and history was different.[17] To be sure, the ɔresent need for security against the Soviet Union was felt. But ɪere were two reasons that the "tryanny of the cold war" operated ɪfferently in France. One, French feelings of hostility toward ussia were much lower than in Germany, and, although it may be ɔo strong to speak of a nostalgia for the wartime grand alliance, it is ɔt false to say that the hope of an ultimate détente allowing for uropean reunification, for a return of the Soviets to moderation, ɪd for an emancipation of the continent from its "two hegemonies" ever died. The French time perspective has been consistently dif- ɔrent from, say, the German: the urgency of the threat never over- ɪadowed the desire for, and belief in, the advent of a less tense ɪternational system. This may have been due not only to France's ɔcation, but also to other elements in France's national situation. ˜hereas Germany's continuity with its past was both wrecked and ɔpudiated, France (like England) looked back to the days when urope held the center of the stage and forward to the time when urope would again be an actor, not a stake: the anomaly was the ɔresent, not the past. Also, on colonial matters, France (more than ngland) often found little to distinguish America's reprobation ˜om Soviet hostility. Two, France continued to worry not only ɔout possible Soviet thrusts but also about Germany's potential ɪreats: the suspicion of a reborn German national consciousness

[17] There was, however, in France, a minority of ''resigned ones,'' like Paul ɔynaud.

and nationalism has marked all French leaders. An additional reas
for fearing the perpetuation of American hegemony and the free
ing of the cold war, for hoping for a détente that would he
Europe reunite, was thus provided by the fear that any other cour
would make Germany the main beneficiary of America's favors. Ge
many looked East with some terror, but there was only one f
there; when the French looked East, they saw two nations to fear
each could be used as an ally against the other — but for the tim
being the Soviet danger was the greater, and, should Germany I
built up too much against the Soviets, the security gained by Fran
in one respect would be compromised in another.[18]

There was a second way in which the diversity of national situ
tions operated. As I have suggested, situations limit and affect b
do not command choices. A general desire for overcoming the col
war and American hegemony did not mean a general agreement c
how to do so. What I have called "the resistance" was split, and
is this split that has become decisive for an analysis of the obstacl
to European unification. Had all the resisters calculated that the be
way to reach France's objectives was the construction of a powerf
West European entity, which could rival America's might, turn th
bipolar contest into a triangle, and wrest advantages from bot
extra-European giants, the "ambiguity" of a movement led by r
signed as well as resisting forces might not have damaged the ente
prise until much later. However, there was a sharp division ov
methods between those who reasoned along the lines just describe
— like Jean Monnet — and those who feared that the sacrifice
national sovereignty to supranational institutions might entail a lo
of control over the direction of the undertaking. The latter consiste
of two kinds of people: on the one hand, the nationalists who, as i
dicated above, were still very much around, exasperated by th
colonial battles, anxious to preserve all the resources of French d
plomacy and strategy in order, in the present, to concentrate on th
fronts overseas and, later, to promote whatever policies would I
required, rather than let a foreign body decide; on the other han
men like Mendès-France, who were not nationalists in the sense
this paper, but who thought that the continental European constru
tion was not France's best way of coping with her situation — the

[18] There is an impressive continuity in French efforts to preserve the diffe
ence between France's position and Germany's: from the préalables and prot
cols to E.D.C., to Mendès-France's Brussels proposals, to de Gaulle's oppositi
to any nuclear role for Germany.

ought that priority ought to go to more urgent tasks such as the
arch for a détente, the liberalization of the Empire, the reform of
e economy.[19]

The success of the European movement required, first, that the
resisters'' suspicious of European integration remain a minority —
t only throughout the six but in the leadership of every one of the
x, not only in Parliament but above all in the Executive, the prime
cision-making force in every state: a requirement which was met
. 1950-53 and in 1955-58, but not in the crucial months for E.D.C.
. 1953-54, and no longer after 1958. The movement proceeded after
)58 because of the dialectic of ambiguity; however, there was a
cond requirement for success: that the "minute of truth" — when
le European elites would have to ask themselves questions about
le ultimate political direction of their community — be postponed
s long as possible; that is, that the cold war remain sufficiently in-
nse to impose even on the "resisters" a priority for the kind of
curity that implied U.S. protection — a priority for the *urgent* over
le *long-term important* as they saw it. This is precisely what was
ready, if temporarily, shaken by the brief period of nervous de-
obilization that followed Stalin's death, in 1953-54, and then grad-
ally undermined by the third basic feature of Europe's postwar
tuation. But before we turn to it, one remark must be made: in
rench foreign policy, "resistance by European integration" pre-
ailed over "resistance by self-reliance" only as long as France was
ogged down in colonial wars; it was this important and purely
rench element in France's national situation whose ups and downs
fected quite decisively the method of "resistance."[20]

[19] France's "integrationist resisters," like Jean Monnet himself, often chose
t to stress the "resistance" aspect of their long-term vision, but nevertheless
med ultimately at establishing in Western Europe not a junior partner of the
.S. but a "second force" in the West. Mendès-France's political vision never
ut the nation on top of the hierarchy of values; however, in 1954 (especially in
is ill-fated demands for a revision of E.D.C. at the Brussels meeting in August)
s well as in 1957 (when he voted against the Common Market), his actual pol-
ies did put a priority on national reform over external entanglements.

[20] It is no coincidence if E.D.C. was rejected six weeks after the end of the
ar in Indochina, if the Common Market was signed while war raged in Algeria,
de Gaulle's sharpest attack on the "Monnet method" followed the Evian
greements. The weight of the situation affected and inflected the course of even
s nationalist a leader as de Gaulle, between 1958 and 1962. Even he went along
ith the "Monnet method," however grudgingly, right until the end of the
lgerian War. It is not a coincidence either if the French leaders most suspi-
ous of the imprisoning effects of the community of the Six from France were
le ones who labored hardest at improving the national situation by removing

3. The divisions and contradictions described above were shar
ened by the third common feature, which emerged in the mid-195C
and whose effects have developed progressively since: the nucle
stalemate between the superpowers. The impact of the "balance
terror" on the Western alliance has been analyzed so often a
well[21] that nothing needs to be added here; but what is needed
a brief explanation of how the two splits already discussed ha
been worsened by Europe's gradual discovery of the uncertaint
of America's nuclear protection (now that the U.S. could be de
astated too), and how some new splits appeared. For to the exte
to which the stalemate has loosened up a previously very tight situ
tion — tight because of the threat from the East and the ties to t
U.S. — it has altogether sharpened previous differences in nation
situations *and* increased the number of alternatives made availab
to élites and statesmen. Greater indeterminacy has meant great
confusion.

First, the split between French "resistance" and German "resi
nation" has become deeper. The dominant political élites in Ge
many have interpreted the new national situation created by t
balance of terror as merely adding urgency to their previous calcul
tion of interest. The nuclear stalemate was, given Germany's po
tion, deemed to increase the danger for the West: the U.S. w
relatively less strong, the Soviet Union stronger, that is, more of
threat. Indeed, the Socialists switched from their increasingly mo
furtive glances at neutrality to an outright endorsement of the Chri
tian Democratic interpretation. If America's monopoly was broke
if America's guarantee was weakened thereby, what was needed
in a world that was not willing to let Germany rearm with nuclea
weapons, in a continent that could not really develop a nuclear for
of its own capable of replacing America's and of matching Russia
— was a German policy so respectful of America's main concern
and also so vigilant with respect to the Soviet Union, that the U.
would both feel obligated to keep its mantle of protection ov
Germany and not be tempted into negotiating a détente at Ge

the colonial burdens (Mendès-France, de Gaulle) — and if those French rule
who followed Monnet and tried to place the pride of a nation with a sharp b
wounded patriotic sense in its leadership of a united Europe were the men w
failed to improve the national situation overseas (the M.R.P., Mollet). The o
French politician who sought both European integration and imperial "dise
gagement" was Antoine Pinay.

[21] Especially by Henry Kissinger in *The Troubled Partnership* (New Yo
1965).

any's expense. German docility would be the condition for, and unterpart of, American entanglement. The German reaction to a velopment that could, if General Gallois' logic were followed, ad to the prevalence of "polycentrism" at bipolarity's expense was e search for ways of exorcising the former and preserving the tter. On the whole, the smaller nations and Italy, while not at I fearful about the consequences of polycentrism (on the con- ary), were nevertheless not shaken out of their "resignation"; the ere appearance of parity of nuclear peril was not enough to make em anxious to give, or to make them domestically capable of giv- g, priority to an active foreign policy.

In France, on the contrary, the balance of terror reinforced the titude of resistance: what had always been a goal — emancipation - but had in fact been no more than a hope, given the thickness of e iron curtain, the simple rigidity of the superpowers' policies in e days of Mr. Dulles, and Europe's inability to affect the course ' events, now became a possibility; for the giants' stalemate meant creased security for the less great (however much they might mplain about the decrease of American protection and use it as pretext, their lament coexisted with a heightened feeling of pro- ction against war in general). What the Germans saw as a liability as an opportunity to the French. Germany's situation, its low na- onal consciousness, incited most German leaders to choose what ight be called a "minimizing" interpretation of the new situation; rance's situation, its high national consciousness and, after 1958, e doctrine of its leader, incited French political élites to choose a maximizing" interpretation. The increasing costs of the use of force ade this use by the superpowers less likely, American protection ss certain but also less essential, Europe's recovery of not merely ealth but power more desirable and possible — possible since the est for power could be pushed without excessive risk of sanctions y the two giants, desirable since power, while transformed, remains e moving force and *ultima ratio* of world politics. This recovery f power would help bring about the much desired prevalence of olycentrism over bipolarity.[22]

Secondly, as this feud shows, the balance of terror heightened

---

[22] One should not forget that the original decisions that led to the French rce de frappe were taken before de Gaulle, or that the French opposition to a tional deterrent came from men who did not at all object to his argument out the need for Europe as a whole to stop being a client of the U.S., and who ought that, indeed, America's nuclear monopoly in the alliance was obsolete.

the split over method among the "resisters." On the one hand,
provided new arguments for those who thought that emancipati
could be achieved only through the uniting of Western Europ
individual national efforts would remain too ridiculously weak
amount to anything but a waste in resources; a collective effo
however, could exploit the new situation, make Western Europe
true partner of the U.S., and not merely an economic partner a
a military aide-de-camp. On the other hand, those who feared th
the "united way" could become a frustrating deviation reason
that the theory of graduated deterrence justified the acquisition
nuclear weapons by a middle-sized power with limited resources a
that this acquisition would increase considerably the political infl
ence as well as the prestige of the nation. The increased costs
force ruled out, in any case, what had in the past been the mo
disastrous effort of the mushrooming of sovereign states — a warlik
expansionist nationalism — but they simultaneously refloated t
value of small or middle-sized nations, no longer condemned by t
cold, bipolar war to look for bigger protectors or to agglomera
in order to assure their security. Moreover, the "united way" wou
be a dead-end, since some, and not exactly the least significant,
the associates had no desire for collective European power at t
possible expense of American protection. Not the least significa
reason for the prevalence of the second line of thought over the fir
has been one important element of the national situation — the army
almost destroyed by its Algerian experience, it had to be "reco
verted." In the circumstances of 1962, this meant inevitably a co
version to French atomic concerns. Its success builds up in turn
vested interest in the preservation of the new establishment — ar
increases the difference in national situations between France ar
a non-nuclear Germany.

Thirdly, the new situation affected European unification neg
tively not only by sharpening those splits but in two other ways a
well. On the one hand, until then, opposition to a supranation
entity had come only from a fraction of the "resisters"; in the ear
1950's the U.S. had strongly — too strongly — urged the establis
ment of a European defense system which was not considered likely
challenge America's own predominance in the military area. In t
1960's, the U.S. no longer urged the West Europeans to build su
a system. American leadership has developed a deep concern fo
maintaining centralized control over the forces of the alliance, tha
is, for preserving bipolarity, and a growing realization that Europe

petite would not stop short of nuclear weapons. As a result, some
the "resigned ones," instead of endorsing European integration
unreservedly as when the situation of a dependent Europe in a
d-war-dominated world did not allow Europeans to entertain
ughts of genuine military "partnership" with the U.S., now for
e first time showed themselves of two minds — they were willing
pursue integration in economic and social fields, but much less
in matters of defense, lest NATO be weakened. It is significant
at the Dutch resisted de Gaulle's efforts, in 1960-62, to include
fense in his confederal scheme and that the German leaders, in
eir quest for security, put their hopes in the MLF — a scheme that
s European nations one by one to the U.S. — rather than in a
vised and revived E.D.C. Inevitably, such mental reservations of
ose who had been among the champions of supranationality could
ly confirm the suspicions of those "resisters" who had distrusted
e "Monnet method" since the beginning. Thus, the national situa-
n of Germany in particular — a situation in which America's own
licy of reliance on Germany as the anchor of U.S. influence on
e continent plays a large role — damaged the European movement:
e German leaders were largely successful in their drive to entangle
e U.S., but found that the price they had to pay was a decreasing
ility to push for European integration. European integration and
pendence on the U.S. were no longer automatically compatible.[23]
On the other hand, even that minority of German leaders who
gan to read Germany's national interest differently did not really
mpensate for the weakening of the majority's integrating ardor.
creasingly, in 1963 to 1965, suspicions about the value of the pol-
y of docility-for-entanglement were voiced by a group of Christian
mocrats, led by Adenauer and Strauss. They still read the Ger-
an situation in terms of security first; but their faith in America's
titude to provide it was shaken, and they saw that Germany had
fficiently gained from America's support not to have to behave
 a minor any longer. Their nickname of German Gaullists is how-
er totally unsuitable. To be sure, these men are "resisters" in the
ase of turning away from America; they are close to the French
ntegrationist resisters," insofar as they propose a European defense
ort and a joint European nuclear policy (rather than a purely
rman one). Nevertheless, their foreign policy goals are quite dif-

3 Hence the rather vague or embarrassed formulas used by Jean Monnet's
tion Committee for the United States of Europe with regard to defense in
 past two years.

ferent from those of all the French resisters, integrationist or ᵬ
tionalist. The national situation of France made most French leade
agree on a common *vision*, described above, that can be summ
up as the end of the cold war and a continent reunited with a Ge
many placed under certain wraps. That common vision coexists wi
the split on *policies* already discussed — the ''European'' policy (
which the wraps are organic, that is, the net and bonds of integ
tion) *vs.* the ''national'' policy (in which the wraps are contractua
The national situation of Germany has made most German leade
after the Social Democratic switch,[24] agree on a common *visi*
deeply different from the French — a perpetuation of the cold wa
hostility to the Soviet Union, the hope for a reunification tantamou
not merely to the thawing of the Eastern ''camp'' but to its disin
gration, and with as few concessions as possible. Since 1963, tʰ
vision has coexisted with two different *policies:* the majority poli
of reliance on the U.S., the minority policy of substituting a stroʲ
tough Europe for an increasingly less reliable, increasingly déten
happy U.S. At present, ''resisters'' are thus split not only on methᵉ
(French integrationists *vs.* French anti-integrationists) but also
objectives (French *vs.* German).

This long discussion of the different responses to common situ
tions has been necessary in reaction to the dominant approach
European integration which has focused on process. The self-pʳ
pelling power of the process is severely constrained by the as
ciates' views and splits on ends and means. In order to go ''beyoⁿ
the nation-state,'' one will have to do more than set up proceduʳ
in adequate ''background'' and ''process conditions.'' For a proc
dure is not a purpose, a process is not a policy.

III

However, since it is the process of European integration that ᵢ
its most original feature, we must examine it also.[25] We have be
witnessing a kind of race, between the logic of integration set
by Monnet and analyzed by Haas, and the logic of diversity, an
lyzed above. According to the former, the double pressure of nec

[24] The case of Erich Mende's Free Democrats is more complicated.
[25] See my previous discussion in ''Discord in Community,'' in F. Wilcox ᵃ
H. F. Haviland, Jr. (eds.), *The Atlantic Community* (New York, 1963),
3-31; ''Europe's Identity Crisis,'' *Dædalus* (Fall 1964), pp. 1244-97, and
article listed in reference 15.

y (the interdependence of the social fabric, which will oblige
tesmen to integrate even sectors originally left uncoordinated)
d of men (the action of the supranational agents) will gradually
strict the freedom of movement of the national governments by
rning the national situations into one of total enmeshing. In such
milieu, nationalism will be a futile exercise in anachronism, and
e national consciousness itself will, so to speak, be impregnated
an awareness of the higher interest in union. The logic of diver-
y, by contrast, sets limits to the degree to which the "spill-over"
ocess can limit the freedom of action of the governments; it re-
ricts the domain in which the logic of functional integration op-
ates to the area of welfare; indeed, to the extent that discrepancies
er the other areas begin to prevail over the laborious harmoniza-
n in welfare, even issues belonging to the latter sphere may be-
me infected by the disharmony which reigns in those other areas.
e logic of integration is that of a blender which crunches the
ost diverse products, overcomes their different tastes and per-
mes, and replaces them with one, presumably delicious, juice. One
s each item be ground because one expects a finer synthesis: that
ambiguity helps rather than hinders because each "ingredient"
n hope that its taste will prevail at the end. The logic of diversity
the opposite: it suggests that, in areas of key importance to the
tional interest, nations prefer the certainty, or the self-controlled
certainty, of national self-reliance, to the uncontrolled uncertainty
the untested blender; ambiguity carries one only a part of the
y. The logic of integration assumes that it is possible to fool each
e of the associates some of the time because his over-all gain will
ll exceed his occasional losses, even if his calculations turn out
rong here or there. The logic of diversity implies that, on a vital
sue, losses are not compensated by gains on other (and especially
t on other less vital) issues: nobody wants to be fooled. The logic
integration deems the uncertainties of the supranational function
ocess creative; the logic of diversity sees them as destructive past
certain threshold: Russian roulette is fine only as long as the gun
filled with blanks. Ambiguity lures and lulls the national con-
iousness into integration as long as the benefits are high, the costs
w, the expectations considerable. Ambiguity may arouse and
iffen national consciousness into nationalism if the benefits are
w, the losses high, the hopes dashed or deferred. Functional inte-
ation's gamble could be won only if the method and sufficient
tency to promise a permanent excess of gains over losses, and of

hopes over frustrations. Theoretically, this may be true of econom
integration. It is not true of political integration (in the sense
"high politics").

The success of the approach symbolized by Jean Monnet d
pended, and depends still, on his winning a triple gamble: on goa
on methods, on results. As for goals, it is a gamble on the possibili
of substituting motion as an end in itself, for agreement on enc
It is a fact that the trans-national integrationist élites did not agr
on whether the object of the community-building enterprise oug
to be the construction of a new super-state — that is, a federal pote
tial nation, à la U.S.A., more able because of its size and resourc
to play the traditional game of power than the dwarfed nations
Western Europe — or whether the object was to demonstrate th
power politics could be overcome through cooperation and con
promise, to build the first example of a radically new kind of un
to achieve a change in the nature and not merely in the scale of t
game. Monnet himself has been ambiguous on this score; Hallste
has been leaning in the first direction, many of Monnet's public re
tions men in the second.[26] Nor did the integrationists agree
whether the main goal was the creation of a regional "securit
community,"[27] that is, the pacification of a former hotbed of wan
or whether the main goal was the creation of an entity whose po
tion and might could decisively affect the course of the cold w
in particular, of international relations in general. Now, it is pe
fectly possible for a movement to feed on its harboring continent
nationalists as well as anti-power idealists, inward-looking poli
cians and outward-looking politicians — but only as long as there
no need to make a choice. Decisions on tariffs did not require su
choices. Decisions on agriculture already raise basic problems
orientation. Decisions on foreign policy and membership and d
fense cannot be reached unless the goals are clarified. One cann
be all things to all people all of the time.

As for methods, there was a gamble on the irresistible rise
supranational functionalism. It assumed, first, that national sove
eignty, already devalued by events, could be chewed up leaf by le
like an artichoke. It assumed, second, that the dilemma of gover

[26] See, for instance, Max Kohnstamm's "The European Tide," in Stephen
Graubard (ed.), *A New Europe?* (Boston, 1964), pp. 140-73.
[27] See K. W. Deutsch, *et al.*, *Political Community and the North Atlan
Area* (Princeton, N.J., 1937).

nts having to choose between pursuing an integration that ties
eir hands and stopping a movement that benefits their people
uld be exploited in favor of integration by men representing the
mmon good, endowed with the advantages of superior expertise,
tiating proposals, propped against a set of deadlines, and using
r their cause the technique of package deals. Finally, it was as-
med that this approach would both take into account the interests
the greater powers and prevent the crushing of the smaller ones.

e troubles with this gamble have been numerous. One, even an
tichoke has a heart, which remains intact after the leaves have
en eaten. It is of course true that a successful economic and social
egration would considerably limit the freedom governments would
ll enjoy in theory for their diplomacy and strategy; but why
ould one assume that they would not be aware of it? As the arti-
oke's heart gets more and more denuded, the governments' vigi-
nce gets more and more alerted. To be sure, the second assump-
n implies that the logic of the movement would prevent them
om doing anything about it: they would be powerless to save the
art. But, two, this would be true only if governments never put
at they consider essential interests of the nation above the par-
ular interests of certain categories of nationals, if superior exper-
e were always either the Commission's monopoly or the solution
the issue at hand, if package deals were effective in every argu-
nt, and, above all, if the governments' representatives were al-
ys determined to behave as a "community organ" rather than as
e agents of states that are not willing to accept a community under
y conditions. Finally, functional integration may indeed give last-
g satisfaction to the smaller powers, precisely because it is for
em that the ratio of "welfare politics" to high politics is highest,
d that the chance of gaining benefits through intergovernmental
thods that reflect rather than correct the power differential be-
een the big and the small is poorest; but this is also why the
thod is not likely *à la longue* to satisfy the bigger powers as
ch: facing them, the supranational civil servants, for all their skill
d legal powers, are a bit like Jonases trying to turn whales into
lyfish. Of course, the idea — ultimately — is to move from an essen-
lly administrative procedure in which supranational civil servants
ter a dialogue with national ministers, to a truly federal one in
ich a federal cabinet is responsible to a federal parliament; but
at is thus presented as a linear progress may turn out to be a

vicious circle, since the ministers hold the key to the transformati
and may refuse it unless the goals are defined and the results alrea
achieved are satisfactory.

There was a gamble about results as well. The experience
integration would entail net benefits for all, and bring about cl
progress toward community formation. Such progress could
measured by the following yardsticks: in the realm of interst
relations, an increasing transfer of power to the new common ag
cies, and the prevalence of solutions "upgrading the common int
est" over other kinds of compromises; in the realm of transnatioı
society, an increasing flow of communications; in the area of natioı
consciousness — which is important both for interstate relations,
cause (as seen above) it may set limits to the statesmen's discreti
and for transnational society, because it affects the scope and me
ing of the communication flows — progress would be measured
increasing compatibility of views about external issues. The resu
achieved so far are mixed; negative on the last count (see belov
limited on the second, and marked on the first by features that 1
enthusiasts of integration did not expect. On the one hand, the
has been some strengthening of the authority of the Commissi
and in various areas there has been some "upgrading of comm
interests." On the other hand, the Commission's unfortunate attem
to consolidate those gains at de Gaulle's expense, in the spring
1965, has brought about a startling setback for the whole enterpris
moreover, in their negotiations, the members have conspicuou
failed to find a common interest in some vital areas (energy, Eı
land's entry), and sometimes succeeded in reaching apparently "ı
tegrating" decisions only after the most ungainly, traditional ki
of bargaining, in which such uncommunity-like methods as threa
ultimatums, and retaliatory moves were used. In other words, eitl
the ideal was not reached, or it was reached in a way that was bo
the opposite of the ideal and ultimately its destroyer. If we lo
at the institutions of the Common Market as an incipient politi
system for Europe, we find that its authority remains limited,
structure weak, its popular base restricted and distant.[28]

It is therefore not surprising if the uncertainty about results
ready achieved contributes to uncertainty about future prospec

---

[28] Under authority, I include three distinct notions: autonomy (the capac
to act independently of the governments, and particularly the financial capacit
power (control over acts of others), and legitimacy (being accepted as 1
"rightful" center of action).

r the very divisions among the partisans of integration make it
rd to predict where the "Monnet method" would lead, if the pro-
s were to continue along the lines so fondly planned by the French
nspirator.'' Would the enterprise become an effective federation,
idually turning the many into one, or would it lead to a mere
;ade behind which all the divergences and rivalries would con-
ue to be played out? It is at least remarkable that Gaullist and
nerican fears should converge in one respect: de Gaulle has con-
tently warned that the application of the supranational method
the area of high politics would lead not to a strong European
tity, but to a dilution of national responsibility whose only bene-
iary would be the U.S.; incapable of defining a coherent policy,
e "technocrats" would leave the decisions in vital areas to the
S., at least by default. On the contrary, many Americans have
ne to believe, on the basis of some of E.E.C.'s actions in the realm
tariffs and trade, that a united Europe would be able to challenge
S. leadership much more effectively than the separate European
tes ever could. The truth of the matter is that nobody knows: a
thod is not a policy, a process is not a direction; the results
hieved so far are too specialized, and the way in which they have
en reached is too bumpy, to allow one to extrapolate and project
fely. The face of a united Europe has not begun to emerge; there
e just a few lines, but one does not know whether the suprana-
nal technique would finally give to Western Europe the features
a going concern, or those of a Fourth Republic writ large — the
ibitions of a world power, or the complacency of parochialism.
ie range of possibilities is so broad, the alternatives are so extreme,
at the more the Six move into the stormy waters of high politics,
e less not only they but also the outside powers, such as the U.S.,
ich may be affected by their acts are willing to extend the credit
hope and to make new wagers: neither Gaullist France nor the
esent U.S. leadership is willing to risk a major loss of control.
ntrary to the French proverb, in the process of functional integra-
n, only the first steps do not cost much.

There are two important general lessons one can draw from a
idy of the process of integration. The first concerns the limits of
e functional method: its very (if relative) success in the relatively
inless area in which it works relatively well lifts the participants
the level of issues to which it does not apply well any more — like
immers whose skill at moving quickly away from the shore sud-
nly brings them to the point where the waters are stormiest and

deepest, at a time when fatigue is setting in, and none of the qu
tions about ultimate goal, direction, and length of swim has be
answered. The functional process was used in order to "make E
rope"; once Europe began being made, the process collided with t
question: "making Europe, what for?" The process is like a grir
ing machine that can work only if someone keeps giving it son
thing to grind. When the users start quarreling and stop providi
the machine stops. For a while, the machine worked because t
governments poured into it a common determination to integr:
their economies in order to maximize wealth; but with their weal
increasing, the question of what to do with it was going to arise :
technique capable of supplying means does not *ipso facto* provi
the ends, and it is about those ends that quarrels have broken o
They might have been avoided if the situation had been more co
pelling — if the Six had been so cooped up that each one's horiz
would have been nothing other than his five partners. But this h
never been their outlook, nor is it any more their necessity. Ea
one is willing to live with the others, but not on terms too differe
from his own; and the Six are not in the position of the three m
erable prisoners of *No Exit*. Transforming a dependent "subsysten
proved to be one thing; defining its relations to all other subsysten
and to the international system in general has turned out to be qu
another — indeed, so formidable a matter as to keep the transform
tion of the subsystem in abeyance until those relations can be c
fined.

The model of functional integration, a substitute for the ki
of instant federation which governments had not been prepared
accept, shows its origins in important respects. One, it is essential
an administrative model, which relies on bureaucratic expertise f
the promotion of a policy defined by the political authorities, a
for the definition of a policy that political decision-makers are tec
nically incapable of shaping — something like French planning und
the Fourth Republic. The hope was that in the interstices of pol
ical bickering the administrators could build up a consensus; b
the mistake was to believe that a formula that works well with
certain limits is a panacea — and that even within the limits of "w
fare politics" administrative skill can always overcome the disastro
effects of political paralysis or mismanagement (cf. the impact
inflation, or balance of payment troubles, on planning). Two, t
model assumes that the basic political decisions, to be prepared a
pursued by the civil servants but formally made by the government

uld be reached through the process of short-term bargaining, by
liticians whose mode of operation is empirical muddling through,
the kind that puts immediate advantages above long-term pur-
ts: this model corresponds well to the nature of parliamentary
litics with a weak Executive, for example, the politics of the
urth Republic, but the mistake was to believe that all political
zimes would conform to this rather sorry image, and also to ignore
disastrous results which the original example produced when-
r conflicts over values and fundamental choices made mere em-
ical groping useless or worse than useless (cf. decolonization).[29]
The second lesson is even more discouraging for the advocates
functionalism. To revert to the analogy of the grinder, what has
ppened is that the machine, piqued by the slowing down of sup-
, suddenly suggested to its users that in the future the supplying
grinding material be taken out of their hands and left to the
chine. The institutional machinery tends to become an actor with
take in its own survival and expansion. The same thing happens
en enough within a state whose political system is ineffective. But
e we deal not with one but with six political systems, and the
son for the ineffectiveness of the Council of Ministers of the Six
y be the excessive toughness, not the weakness, of the national
itical systems involved. In other words, by trying to be a force,
bureaucracy here, inevitably, makes itself even more of a stake
t the nations try to control or at least to affect. A new complica-
1 is thus added to all the substantive issues that divide the par-
pants — one that provides them with a whole trunkful of screens
4 masks. Thus, the agricultural problem is one that could have
n solved "technically," since the governments had previously
ched basic compromises, and more or less agreed on the relations
ween Common Market and outside agriculture. But the way in
ich these accords had been reached left scars, and the nature of
agreement meant a victory for one state (France) over another
ermany). The whole issue has been reopened, due not to the
es' but to the Commission's initiative. In the crisis of 1965,
Commission's overly bold proposal of a common agricultural pol-
(along pro-French lines) cum supranationality (against French
ermination) has, on the one hand, allowed some of the Six, hos-
in fact to the substantive proposals, to endorse the Commission's
n and stand up as champions of supranationality, while knowing

Along similar lines, see Francis Rosenstiel, *Le principe de "Supranatio-
té"* (Paris, 1962).

that the French would block the scheme; the French have been a
to use the Commission's rashness as a pretext for trying to kill sup
nationality altogether; a German government not too kindly d
posed toward a Commission whose initiatives and economic inspi
tion were hardly in line with Mr. Erhard's views has found its
defending the Commission, whose head, now under French atta
is a German; a French government anxious to get its partners co
mitted to a protected agricultural market has preferred to postpo
the realization of this goal rather than let the Commission's aut
omy grow. The states have found something more to disagree abo
and the Commission, in an attempt to push the car out of the b
has stopped the motor for months. To be sure, the Commissio
dilemma had become acute: either its members resigned themsel
to being merely patient brokers to their quarreling clients, a
letting them set the pace; or else they tried to behave both acco
ing to the ideal-type of the Monnet method, and as if a genu
community had already been established; but if prudence mea
sluggishness, anticipation has meant delay. In the immediate futu
the settlement of the various substantive issues — "the uniting
Europe, what for?" — is likely to be postponed while the Six try
repair the damaged machinery; in a way, haggling about the ki
of grinder one wants is a polite method for appearing to want
keep grinding together, while really disagreeing completely on wl
one wants to put in and get out.

IV

We must come now to the balance sheet of the "European
periment." The most visible aspect is the survival of the nations.
be sure, they survive transformed: first, swept by the advent of t
"age of mass consumption," caught in an apparently inexora
process of industrialization, urbanization, and democratization, tl
become more alike in social structure, in economic and social p
cies, even in physical appearance; there is a spectacular break
tween a past which so many monuments bring to constant memo
and a rationalized future that puts these nations closer to the pr
lems of America's industrial society than to the issues of their o
history. Second, these similarities are promoted by the Comn
Market itself: it is of no mean consequence that the prospect of
collapse of the Market should have brought anguish to various
terest groups, some of which had fought its establishment: the tra

tional linkages of businessmen and farmers are part of the trans-
mation. Third, none of the Western European nations is a world
wer any longer in the traditional sense, that is, in the sense either
having physical establishments backed by military might in var-
is parts of the globe, or of possessing in Europe armed forces
perior to those of any non-European power.

And yet they survive as nations. Let us go back to the criteria
integration listed above. On foreign and defense policies, not only
s no power been transferred to common European organs, but
ance has actually taken power away from NATO, and, as shown
part two, differences in the calculations of the national interest
ve, if anything, broadened ever since the advent of the balance
terror. As for intra-European communications, research shows
t the indubitably solid economic network of E.E.C. has not been
nplemented by a network of social and cultural communica-
ns;[30] the links between some of those societies and the U.S. are
onger than the links among them. Indeed, even in the realm of
nomic relations, the Common Market for goods has not been
npleted by a system of pan-West European enterprises: enter-
ses that find themselves unable to compete with rivals within
.C. often associate themselves with American firms rather than
rge with such rivals. Finally, views about external issues, far
m becoming more compatible, appear to reflect as well as to
port the divergent definitions of the national interest by the
tesmen. French élite opinion puts Europe ahead of the North
antic partnership, deems bipolarity obsolete, is overwhelmingly
ifferent or even hostile to the U.S., and is still highly suspicious
Germany; only a minority comes out in favor of a genuine polit-
federation of Western Europe and thinks that U.S. and French
erests coincide. German élite opinion puts the North Atlantic
ente ahead of Europe, believes that the world is still bipolar, is
rwhelmingly favorable to the U.S., deems U.S. and German
erests in agreement, is either favorably inclined toward France
at least not hostile, and shows a majority in favor of a European
eration. There is no common European outlook. Nor is there a
mon ''project,'' a common conception of either Europe's role in
ld affairs or Europe's possible contribution to the solution of the
blems characteristic of all industrial societies.

t is important to understand where the obstacles lie. To some

I am using here unpublished studies done under Karl Deutsch, especially
Donald J. Puchala.

extent, they lie in the present condition of national consciousne
I mentioned earlier that there were at the start considerable diff
ences from country to country. In two respects, similarities ha
emerged in recent years. There has been a rebirth of German
tional consciousness, largely because the bold attempt at fasten:
Germany's shattered consciousness directly to a new European
did not succeed: the existence of a German national situation
gradually reawakened a German national awareness, and thus
duced the gap between Germany and France in this area. Mo
over, all the national consciences in Western Europe are alike
one sense: they are not like Rousseau's general will, a combinat
of mores and moves that define with a large degree of intellect
clarity and emotional involvement the purposes of the national co
munity. Today's national consciousness in Europe is negative ratl
than positive. There is still, in each nation, a "vouloir-vivre collecti
But it is not a "daily plebiscite" *for* something. It is, in some pan
a daily routine, a community based on habit rather than on comn
tasks, an identity that is received rather than shaped. Thus G
many's sense of "cohesion and distinctiveness" is the inevitable res
of the survival and recovery of a West German state in a world
nations, rather than a specific willed set of imperatives. In otl
parts, national consciousness is a daily refusal rather than a da
creation, a desire to preserve a certain heritage (however wani
and less because it is meaningful today than because it is one's ow
rather than a determination to define a common destiny, an ident
that is hollow rather than full and marked more by bad humor
ward foreign influences than by any positive contribution.

To be sure, the negative or hollow character of national co
sciousness need not be a liability for the champions of integratio
general wills *a la* Rousseau could be formidable obstacles to a
fusion of sovereignty. However, the obstacle resides partly in t
common nature of the present state of national consciousness, par
in the remaining differences. A patriotic consciousness that survi
in a kind of nonpurposive complacency may not be a barrier
efforts at transcending it, but it is a drag: it does not carry forwa
or push statesmen in the way in which an intense and posit:
"general will" prods leaders who act on behalf of national goals,
in the way in which European federalists have sometimes hop
that enlightened national patriotisms would propel Europe's natio
leaders into building a new European community, into which th
enlightened patriotisms would converge and merge. Moreover, t

the "national consciences" have raised obstacles: the French one
cause it remains too strong, the German one because it remains
) weak. The French may not have a sense of national purpose,
.t, precisely because their patriotism has been tested so often and
long, because the pressures of the outside world have continued
roughout the postwar era to batter their concerns and their con-
its, and because modernization, now accepted and even desired,
so undermines traditional values still cherished and traditional
thority patterns still enforced, French national consciousness op-
ses considerable resistance to any suggestion of abdication, resig-
tion, *repli* — so much so that the "Europeans" themselves have
d to present integration as an opportunity for getting French views
ared by others instead of stressing the "community" side of the
terprise.[31] Germany's national consciousness, on the other hand,
mains marked by a genuine distaste for or timidity toward what
ght be called the power activities of a national community on the
rld stage; hence a tendency to shy away from the problems of
igh politics" which a united Europe would have to face and whose
oidance only delays the advent of unity; a tendency to refuse to
ake policy choices and to pretend (to oneself and to others) that
such choices are required, that there is no incompatibility be-
een a "European Europe" and an Atlantic partnership. In one
se, a defensive excess of self-confidence makes unity on terms other
an one's own difficult, and obliges integrationist leaders to use
nning and flattery and deceit (with often lamentable results —
e the E.D.C. crisis); in the other case, an equally defensive lack
self-confidence projects itself into the external undertakings of the
tion and weakens the foundations of the common European enter-
ise.

And yet, if the "national consciousness" of the European nations
uld be isolated from all other elements of the national situation,
e would, I think, conclude that the main reasons for the resistance
the nation-state lie elsewhere.

They lie, first of all, in the differences in national situations, ex-
erbated by the interaction between each of the Six and the present
ernational system. Earlier, we have looked at concrete instances
such differences; let us return to them in a more analytic way.
e part of each national situation is the purely *domestic* com-
nent. In a modern nation-state, the very importance of the politi-

---

[1] On this point, see Raymond Aron and Daniel Lerner (eds.), *France Defeats
C* (New York, 1957).

cal system, in the triple sense of functional scope, authority, a
popular basis, is already a formidable obstacle to integration. It
comparatively easier to overcome the parochialism of a politi
system which, being of the night-watchman variety, has only
slender administrative structure, whose power consists of punishi
rather than rewarding, with the help of a tiny budget, and wh
transmission belts to the mass of the people are few and narrow, th
it is to dismantle the fortress of a political system which rests
"socially mobilized" and mobilizing parties and pressure grou
and handles an enormous variety of social and economic servi
with a huge bureaucracy. To be sure, it was the hope and tactic
Monnet to dismantle the fortress by redirecting the allegiance
parties and pressure groups toward the new central institutions,
endowing the latter with the ability to compete with the natio
governments in the setting up of social services. In other words, 1
authority of the new European political system would deepen as
scope broadened and its popular basis expanded. The success
this attempt at drying up the national ponds by diverting th
waters into a new, supranational pool depended on three prer
uisites which have not been met: with respect to popular basis, 1
prevalence of parties and pressure groups over Executives; w
respect to scope, the self-sustaining and expanding capacity of 1
new central bureaucracy; with respect to both scope and popul
basis, the development of transnational political issues of inter
to all political forces and publics across boundary lines. The mode
Executive establishment has one remarkable feature: it owes mu
of its legitimacy and its might to the support of popularly bas
parties and pressure groups, but it also enjoys a degree of autono
that allows it to resist pressures, to manipulate opposition, to mar
facture support. Even the weak Fourth Republic has evaded pr
sure toward "transnationalism" and diluted the dose of "bargaini
politics" along supranational lines. The civil servants' careers a
still made and unmade in the national capitals. Above all, each
tion's political life continues to be dominated by "parochial" issu
each political system is like a thermos bottle that keeps warm,
lukewarm, the liquid inside. The European political process h
never come close to resembling that of any Western Europe
democracy because it has been starved of common and distincti
European issues. It is as if, for the mythical common man, t
nation-state were still the most satisfying — indeed the most

rding — form of social organization in existence.[32] As for what it
1 no longer provide him with by itself, the state can still provide it
thout committing suicide, through cooperation, or the citizens can
and find it across borders, without any need to transfer their al-
·iance — or else there is, in any event, no guarantee that any form
social organization other than a still utopian world state could
ovide it. If we look at the issues that have dominated European
litics, we find two distinct blocs. One is the bloc of problems
culiar to each nation — Italy's battle of Reds *vs.* Blacks, or its
1cern for the Mezzogiorno; Belgium's linguistic clashes; Ger-
1ny's "social economy" and liquidation of the past; France's con-
tutional troubles and miraculously preserved party splintering.
·re, whatever the transnational party and interest group align-
·nts in Luxembourg, the dominant motifs have been purely na-
nal. The other bloc of issues are the international ones (including
1ropean unity). But here is where the *external* component of the
tional situation has thwarted the emergence of a common Euro-
an political system comparable to that of each nation.
It is here that the weight of geography and of history — a history
nations — has kept the nation-states in their watertight compart-
·nts. It is no accident if France, the initiator of the process, has
:o been its chief troublemaker: for in those two respects France's
sition differed from everyone else's in the community, and was
tually closer to England's. Historically first: for Germany, in-
;ration meant a leap from opprobrium and impotence, to re-
ectability and equal rights; for the smaller powers, it meant ex-
anging a very modest dose of autonomy for participation in a
tentially strong and rich grouping. France could not help being
1ch more ambivalent, for integration meant on the one hand an
enue for leadership and the shaping of a powerful bloc, but it
:o meant on the other the acceptance of permanent restrictions
an autonomy that was indeed quite theoretical in the late 1940's,
t whose loss could not be deemed definitive. For a once-great
wer, whose national history is long, and therefore used to rise
d fall, inherits from its past a whole set of habits and reflexes
1ich make it conduct its policy as if it were still or could again
come a great power (unless those habits and reflexes have been
ashed, at least for a while, as completely and compellingly as

[32] See Rupert Emerson, *op. cit.*, Ch. XIX.

were Germany's); for this once-great power showed, as describ
above, a still vigilant national consciousness, often the more virule
for all its negativism; for the international system itself seemed
open vistas of increased freedom of action to middle-sized states.
other words, integration meant an almost certain improvement
the national situation of the other five, but for France it could be
deterioration or an adventure.[33] There is no better example th
the nuclear problem: integration here meant, for France, giving
the possibility of having a force of her own, perhaps never ev
being certain that a united Europe (with no agreement on strate
and diplomacy in sight) would create a common deterrent, at b
contributing to a European force which would put Germany in t
same position as France; but the French decision to pursue t
logic of diversity, while giving her her own force, has also made
European nuclear solution more difficult and increased Franc
distance from Germany. Moreover, a geographical difference h
corroborated the historical one: France had lasting colonial invol
ments. Not only did they, on the whole, intensify national co
sciousness; they also contributed to France's ambivalence towa
European integration. On the one hand, as indicated above, t
worse France's overseas plight became, the more integration w
preached as a kind of compensatory mechanism. But, on the otl
hand, this meant that integration had to be given a "nationa
rather than a "supranational" color, to be presented as a new care
rather than as a common leap; it meant that the French consisten
tried to tie their partners to the prevalence of France's overse
concerns, much against these partners' better judgment; above a
it meant that there was a competition for public attention and i
official energies, between the "load" of integration and the burd
of the overseas mission. The great power reflex and the colonial lega
combine today in the policy of cooperation with the former imper

[33] England's refusal to join European integration, before 1961, could not f
to increase French reticence, for integration thus meant equality with Germa
and a clear-cut difference between France's position and England's, that is
reversal of French aspirations and traditions. England has on the whole rejec
the "resignation-resistance" dilemma — and as a result, both the aspects of
foreign policy that appeared like resignation to U.S. predominance and
aspects that implied resistance to decline have contributed to the crisis of Eu
pean integration: for France's veto in January 1963 meant a French refu
to let into Europe a power that had just confirmed its military ties to the U
but Britain's previous desire to play a world role and aversion to "fading i
Europe" encouraged France's own misgivings about integration.

ssessions, despite its costs: cooperation is presented as a trans-
uration of the legacy, and a manifestation of the reflex.[34]
Thus, the national situations have multiplied the effects of dif-
rences between the shapes of the various national consciences. But
e resistance of the nation-state is not due only to the kind of loan
life that its inevitable entanglement in international affairs and
e idle motion left by its past provide even to nations with a low
tional consciousness. It is due also to the impact of the revival of
tionalism in France. Even without de Gaulle the differences ana-
zed above would have slowed down integration and kept some fire
the nation's stoves. But the personal contribution of de Gaulle
the crisis of integration has been enormous. Not only has he raised
estions that were inescapable in the long run, earlier and more
ngently than they would have been otherwise, but he has also pro-
led and tried to impose his own answers. His impact is due to his
yle as well as to his policies. The meaning of de Gaulle has been a
ange in French policy from ambivalence toward supranational
tegration to outright hostility; from a reluctance to force one's
rtners to dispel the ambiguities of "united Europe" to an almost
eeful determination to bring differences out into the open; from a
ndency to interpret the national situation as oppressively difficult
a herculean effort at improving all its components in order to push
ck limits and maximize opportunities. The meaning of de Gaulle
s also been a change in the national situations of the others, lead-
g to a sharpening of antagonisms and to a kind of cumulative
treat from integration. Each one of those meanings must be briefly
amined.

Insofar as France is concerned, the key is provided by de Gaulle's
ncept of grandeur.[35] Greatness is a mixture of pride and ambition
the nation shall not at any point leave the control of its destiny
others (which does not mean that he does not acknowledge the
istence of irresistible waves with which the ship of state must roll,
t, precisely, it fall in the hands of others who would rush to a
edatory rescue or to a plunder of the wreck). The nation must try
any point to play as full a role in the world as its means allow.
e consequences are clear: First, the kind of supranational integra-

[34] See Alfred Grosser, *op. cit.*, Ch. IV.
[35] For a more detailed analysis of this concept, see my article: "De Gaulle's
emoirs: The Hero as History," *World Politics*, Vol. XIII, No. 1 (October
50), pp. 140-155.

tion which would leave decisions on vital issues to majority votes
to executive organs independent of the states is out of the questio
even if the interests and policies of France should happen to prev
for a while (as indeed they did as long as the Commission, in
drive for economic integration, remained very close to French idea
there would be no assurance against a sudden and disastrous revers
Second, extensive cooperation is not at all ruled out: on the contra
such cooperation will benefit all participants as long as it correspon
to and enhances mutual interests. Third, however, it is part of t
very ambition of grandeur that in such schemes of cooperation whi
aim not merely at exchanges of *services* but at the definition of co
mon *policies,* France will try to exert her leadership and carry c
her views: the degree of French cooperativeness will be measured
the degree of responsiveness of the others.

It is true that the General is an empiricist, and that his analy
of the European situation is to a large extent irrefutable. What cou
be more sensible than starting from what exists — the nation-state
refusing to act as if what does not yet exist — a united Europe — h
already been established, and refusing to forget that each of t
European nations is willy-nilly engaged in an international comp
tition that entails a fight for rank and power? But pragmatism
always at the service of ends, explicit or not (the definition of a b
foreign policy could be: that which uses rigid means at the serv
of explicit ends, as well as that whose flexible means are not servi
clearly-thought-out ends). De Gaulle's empiricism is a superb displ
of skill, but on behalf of a thoroughly non-empirical doctrine. It
obvious that his distrust of supranational integration, which, witl
Europe, could submit French interests to the dictates of others, a
could expose Europe to the dictates of the "hegemonists," while
is perfectly comprehensible as a starting point, nevertheless resu
in a kind of freezing of integration and perpetuation of the natic
state. If his chief foreign policy objective were the creation of
European entity acting as a world power, his "empirical" *starti
point* would be a most unrealistic *method.* But the fact is that su
a creation is not his supreme objective, and Europe not his supre
value.

His supreme value remains the nation-state; his supreme politi
objective is the creation of a world in which the "two hegemonie
will have been replaced by a multipolar international system, whe
"first floor" would be the numerous nations, endowed with and e
titled to political integrity and independence, and whose "seco

or'' would be inhabited by the nuclear powers, in a role comparable
that of the late European concert. Again, the implications are
ar: de Gaulle's doctrine is a "universalist nationalism," that is, he
s France's mission as world-wide, not local and defensive; but
s means that Europe is just one corner of the tapestry; Europe is
neans, not an end. "Things being what they are," it is better to
ve separate nation-states (whose margin of freedom is undoubt-
ly smaller than when the use of force was not so costly, whose
pacity to shape history is also undoubtedly limited if their size,
pulation, and resources are mediocre, but whose ability to behave
self-determined actors on the stage is enhanced precisely by the
anting of force and by the opportunities opened to other instru-
nts of power and influence) than it is to have a larger entity,
doubtedly more able to act as a forceful competitor in the world's
ntests should it be coherent, but more likely to be incoherent, given
e divisions of its members and the leverage interested outsiders
ssess over some of the insiders. The size of the unit is less important
an its "cohesion and distinctiveness," for its effectiveness is not
rely a function of its material resources: if the unit has no capacity
turn these to action, because of internal cleavages and strains, the
ly beneficiaries would be its rivals. In a contest with giants, a
nfident David is better than a disturbed Goliath. This is a choice
at reflects a doctrine; the refusal to gamble on European unity goes
ong with a willingness to gamble on the continuing potency of the
ench nation-state; the determination to accept only the kind of
rope that would be France writ large[36] corresponds to a conviction
at French policies could be made to prevail whether Europe con-
butes its support or not: "with Europe if they follow, without
rope if they do not," Europe is just a card in a global game.
humpeter had defined imperialism as an objectless quest; de
ulle's nationalism is a kind of permanent quest with varying con-
it but never any other cause than itself.

As I suggested above, a nationalist leader is one whose reading of
e national situation is likely to be quite different from the reading
her leaders would give. De Gaulle's brand of nationalism being
iat it is — universalist, aimed at overcoming the "two hegemonies,"
ploiting both of the somewhat contradictory trends that dominate
e present world (the conservation of the nation as its basic unit,

36 Grosser, *op. cit.*, pp. 112-113, draws attention to Prime Minister Pompidou's
tement: "France is condemned by geography and history to play the role of
rope."

the concentration of what one might call "final power" among ᵗ
nuclear states) — it is not surprising that he has altogether liquidaᵗ
a colonial burden that kept France away from every one of the rou
he wanted to travel, and replaced it with an ambitious policy of
operation with the "Third World." In a way, it is true, as so
critics have charged, that this policy is a kind of self-consolation pr
for the failure of his European policy; but in another sense it c
forms deeply to his most vital designs and to his most constant ha
of never relying on one line of policy only: In the first place, coope
tion manifests France's universal destiny; in the second, it aims
consolidating a system of independent, if cooperating, nations;
the third, it tries to use the prestige thus gained as an elevator to ᵗ
floor of the "big five," to which access has been denied so far by ᵗ
"big two." It is clear that the first two missions rule out a concent
tion on Europe alone, that the second prevents in any case his puttᵢ
any passion into overcoming the nation-state in Europe, that ᵗ
third is precisely a substitute for the "elevator" Europe has fai
to provide. As a result, all that has made France's historical heritᵃ
and geographic position distinctive has been strengthened.

Every great leader has his built-in flaw, since this is a world
which roses have thorns. De Gaulle's is the self-fulfilling prophe
Distrustful of any Europe but his own, his acts have made Eurᵒ
anything but his. Here we must turn to the impact of his policy
France's partners. First of all, there is a matter of style: wantiᵢ
cooperation not integration, de Gaulle has refused to treat ᵗ
Community organs as Community organs; but, wanting to force
views about cooperation on partners still attached to integratiᵒ
and attempting to impose his views about a "European Europe"
associates who might have settled for cooperation but only on behᵢ
of another policy, de Gaulle has paradoxically had to try to achiᵉ
cooperation for a common policy in a way that smacked of confᵢ
not cooperation, of unilateralism not compromise. Thus we hᵃ
witnessed not just a retreat from the Monnet method to, say, ᵗ
kind of intergovernmental cooperation that marks O.E.C.D., but
a kind of grand strategy of nonmilitary conflict, a kind of politᵢ
cold war of maneuver and "chicken." With compromises wrested
ultimatums, concessions obtained not through package deals ᵇ
under the threat of boycotts, it is not surprising if even the Cᵒ
mission ended by playing the General's game instead of turniᵢ
whatever other cheek was left; its spring 1965 agricultural plan ᵛ
as outright a challenge to de Gaulle as de Gaulle's veto of Janu

53 had been an affront to the Community spirit. Just as de Gaulle
d tried to force Germany to sacrifice her farmers to the idea of a
ropean entity, the Commission tried to call de Gaulle's bluff by
cing him to choose between French farmers' interests and the
ench national interest in a "European Europe" for agriculture,
the one hand, and his own hostility to supranationality and the
ench national interest (as seen by him) in the free use of French
ources, on the other. Playing his game, the Commission also
yed into his hands, allowing him to apply the Schelling tactic of
f you do not do what I ask, I will blow up my brains on your new
it," and in the end buying his return at the price of a sacrifice of
egration.[37] In other words, he has forced each member to treat the
mmunity no longer as an end in itself; and he has driven even its
stituted bodies, which still insist it is that, into bringing grist to his
ll.

Second, his impact on his partners is a matter of policy as well.
ere we must examine Franco-German relations. As long as he hoped
at Germany would follow his guidance and provide the basis for the
European Europe" of his design, his attitude toward West Ger-
any was one of total support of her intransigence toward the
mmunists. As soon as the increasing clarity of his own policy
alf-veiled until the end of the Algerian ordeal and his triumph in
e constitutional battle of October-November 1962) provoked Ger-
an suspicion and reticence, as soon as the U.S., in response to his
allenge, consolidated its ties with a still loyal Germany and even
omised her substantial rewards for her loyalty, he applied to
ermany the shock tactics so effectively used on Britain and the
S. during World War II: he made his own opening to the East
d gradually shifted away from the kind of celebration of a "new
ermany" (heir to her greatness in her past but now willing to take
r place as France's aide in the new "European Europe"), so
aracteristic of his German visit in the fall of 1962. He now resorts
carefully worded reminders to the Germans of their past misdeeds,
the risk which their loyalty to the U.S. entails for their reunifica-
on, and of the interest France and the Eastern states (including
ussia) share in keeping Germany under permanent restrictions.
ad Germany been willing to follow France, he would have given
riority to the construction of a "half-Europe" that would there-
ter have been a magnet (as well as a guarantee of German harm-

[37] See Thomas Schelling's *Strategy of Conflict* (Cambridge, Mass., 1960).

lessness) to the East. Germany's refusal leads him to put the gradu
emergence of a "Europe from the Atlantic to the Urals" — inde
from the British Isles to the Urals[38] — if not ahead of at least on t
same plane as the development of the "European Europe" in t
West; for the containment of Germany, no longer assured in a d
united Western Europe of the Six, may still be obtained in a mu
larger framework. The implications are important. First, there is
considerable change in Germany's national situation. On the o
hand, its external component has been transformed. Whereas f
more than fifteen years both the U.S. and France carried out tacit
Robert Schuman's recommendation — "never leave Germany to he
self" — the Franco-American competition for German support, t
Gaullist refusal to tie Germany to France in a federal Europe so
speak for the knot's sake (that is, unless Germany follows France
America's disastrous emulation of the sorcerer's apprentice in tit
lating Germany's interest in nuclear strategy or weapons-sharing,
the belief, or under the pretext, of anticipating her appetite, all
these factors have contributed to loosen the bonds between Germa
and the West: to the European part of the West, because of t
slump in integration, and even to the U.S., because of America
failure to follow up after raising in Germany hopes that should n
have been raised, but which, once raised and frustrated, are unlike
to fade. On the other hand, and consequently, the domestic compone
of Germany's national situation has also been affected: Still cc
cerned with security as well as with reunification, but less and le
capable of believing that loyalty to their allies will deliver any good
the German leaders and élites may well come to feel less depende
and less constrained. Of course, objectively, the external constrain
remain compelling: a policy of self-assertion may not lead anywher
an attempt at bypassing the nuclear restrictions of the Paris agre
ments is not likely to make the East Europeans and the Soviets an
more willing to let East Germany go; and the price the Soviets ma
want to exact for reunification is not likely to increase Germa
security. But the fact that Germany's ties to Western powers a
weakening means at least potentially that the capacity to test tho
constraints by unilateral action may well be used. To be in a ce
with a chain around one's ankles and the hope of being liberated l
one's jailers in one kind of situation. To be in that cell without su

[38] See de Gaulle's reference to England in his press conference of Septemb
9, 1965.

chain and with such hopes gone is another situation, although the
ll has not changed.

In other words, although the impact of de Gaulle on Germany
far has not been a rebirth of German nationalism, it has been a
ansformation of the situation that gives to nationalism some chances
chances if not of external success, given the nature of the cell, then
being at least "tried." The temptation to use one's economic power
d potential military might in order to reach one's goals and the
ample of one's allies competing for accommodation with one's foe
e not resistible forever, especially if one's past is full of precedents.
) be sure, a nationalist Germany may well find itself as unable to
ake the walls or to escape through the bars as Gaullist France is
able to forge the "European Europe." But the paradox of a
visionist France, trying to change the international system to her
vantage despite her complete lack of "traditional" grievances
ost territories, military discrimination, and so forth), next to a
ermany full of such grievances, yet behaving in fact like a *status
to* power, may not last eternally. Of course, a less aggressively
ubitious France might not have prevented Germany from trying
follow her own path one day: the possibility of someone else's
litative *ubris* is no reason for one's own *effacement;* but precisely
cause the "essence and drama" of nationalism are the meeting
ith others, the risk of contagion — a risk that is part of de Gaulle's
amble — cannot be discarded.

Thus the nation-state survives, preserved by the formidable auton-
ny of politics, as manifested in the resilience of political systems,
e interaction between separate states and a single international
stem, the role of leaders who believe both in the primacy of "high
litics" over the kind of managerial politics susceptible to function-
ism, and in the primacy of the nation, struggling in the world of
day, over any new form, whose painful establishment might require
e's lasting withdrawal from the pressing and exalting daily
ntest.

V

This long balance sheet leaves us with two sets of questions: What
e the prospects in Western Europe? What generalizations can one
raw from the whole experience? As for the prospects, what precedes
ads perhaps too much like a post-mortem. Is there no chance for
e European Community? Is it condemned to be, at best, a success

in the economic realm but a fiasco in "high politics," something li
a hydra with one single body but a multitude of heads?

It would be presumptuous indeed to read hope out of court. One
the decisive elements in the movement's "spillback," de Gaull
nationalism, may not outlive him. His successors may have a l
sweeping vision and may make exactly the opposite gamble fro
his — that is, prefer the risks of the common enterprise, wh
rewards might be high if it works, to the dividends of national actio
they could indeed attempt to revive the Monnet concept of Europ
and even to overcome the deficiencies of functionalism by a leap in
more genuinely federal institutions. Moreover, whereas de Gau
has had the backing of a parliamentary majority hostile to supr
national integration and has exerted the kind of rule that part
and pressure groups do not affect much anyhow, his successors m
depend for domestic support and survival precisely on those part
and pressure groups which had started to weave a transnation
fabric. Should this be the case, the "Europe of the Six," instead
being as close as it now is to the traditional model of interstate rel
tions, might move again toward the other ideal-type, that of politic
community-building, so well described by Ernst Haas, who sees
it the wave of the future.[39]

Whereas in the case of a revival of German nationalism, t
prospect of failure may not be enough to deter an attempt, here
would maintain that an attempt would not be tantamount to succes
In the first place, while nothing (not even the Common Market)
irreversible, no important event leaves the world unmarked, and aft
the event one can never pick up the pieces as if nothing had ha
pened: this, which is true of the Common Market, is true also
General de Gaulle. It will not be easy to sweep under the rug t
curls of dust he has willfully placed in the sunlight; it will not
easy to ignore the kinds of questions he has asked, even if his answe
are rejected, precisely because they are the questions any Europea
enterprise would have faced sooner or later. Second, even the passin
of his nationalism might not transform the national situations of t
European nation-states so deeply that all the cleavages discussed he
would suddenly disappear. For, even if all the political leaders
Western Europe had once again the same non-nationalist approac
the differences in the national situations would still lead to diverger
definitions of the national interests. In particular, the problem

[39] See his essay "Technocracy, Pluralism and the New Europe," in Steph
R. Graubard (ed.), *op. cit.*, pp. 62-88.

clear weapons control and command in a grouping divided between
clear "have-nots" and nuclear "haves" may prove to be as in-
ictable, and to raise as much of an obstacle to community-formation
ong Western Europeans, as in the Atlantic alliance. The ideal
ditions not merely for the resumption but for the success of a
rward march would be a transformation of Germany's external
uation and of France's domestic one. If the search for a détente
ould lead the U.S. to put a rapprochement with the U.S.S.R. ahead
its bonds to West Germany, and if it became clear in West
rmany, as a result, both that security is neither the most urgent
oblem nor entirely provided any more by the U.S., and that
unification cannot be obtained from and through the U.S.; if, in
dition, such disappointment with the U.S. does not encourage West
rman leadership to follow a nationalist path, or if an attempt by
est Germany to obtain for itself from Moscow what its allies had
iled to provide for her should end in frustration, then — at last —
est Germany might be willing to accept a foreign policy close to
Gaulle's "European Europe" with its indifference to regimes
d ideologies, its repudiation of the cold war outlook, its opening
the East, and its cautious promise of eventual reunification at the
st of border limitations and arms restrictions. In other words, on
e German side, what would be required would be a "polycentric,"
t non-nationalist, reading of the external situation. This would be
kely to happen if at the same time France had given up her nation-
ist interpretation of "polycentrism," and become again more
mble, more willing to trust the Community organs, more in need
adopting European integration as a goal in itself. Such a possibil-
v would exist if, domestically, the impervious stability of de Gaulle's
gime were to be replaced not merely with a political system whose
xecutive would lean on an "integrationist" party majority, but
ith the kind of instability that both prevents political leaders from
ting on the world stage as if they were its managers and pressures
em into seeking a European solution, or alibi, for their difficulties.
urope as Germany's least frustrating framework, Europe as the
st compensation for France's domestic troubles, a Europe following
onnet's approach toward de Gaulle's objectives:[40] it may appear

---

[40] As Grosser points out in his book and the presidential election campaign of
65 confirmed, even the opposition to de Gaulle's foreign policy accepts his
tion of a "European Europe" and rejects American "hegemony" (with the
ception of a very few men like Reynaud or perhaps Lecanuet). There is dis-
reement about methods and style rather than on objectives.

like a dream; it cannot be dismissed. But whether it has a chan
depends essentially on *when* the General's nationalism will pass fr
the scene, on *what* degree of cooperation among the nations of We
ern Europe there will be at that time, on *whether* a new attempt
Britain to join the Community would introduce additional co
plications, on *what* the U.S. policy in Europe will be; the chan
depends on the timely convergence of too many variables to
counted on.

Against such a chance, there is too big a range of obstacles. Here
where the European experience is of general significance.

1. A first set of remarks deals with the conditions which t
national situations of the units engaged in an attempt to integra
must meet, lest the attempt be unsuccessful. Those situations oug
to be similar; but a generalization of this kind is almost worthles
what matters is the nature of the similarity.

a. Insofar as domestic circumstances are concerned, two conc
tions are essential. The first one is obvious at first sight, much l
so upon reflection: the units must be political communities, not
a substantive sense (common values and goals, *à la* Rousseau) b
in a formal one (the existence of intense communications and
common habits and rules across regional differences as well as acr
the borders of ethnic groups, tribes, or classes);[41] in other wor
transnational integration presupposes integration within the units

[41] I find Ernst B. Haas' definition of a political community in his *Uniting
Europe*, p. 5, (''a condition in which specific groups and individuals show m
loyalty to their central political institutions than to any other political
thority''), not very helpful in the case of states marked by severe domes
cleavages; there might be more loyalty to the center than to any other politi
authority merely because there is no other *political* authority, and yet one wo
still not be in the presence of anything like an integrated society.

[42] The distinctions I suggest are like marks on a continuum. 1. At one e
there are *cooperative arrangements* whose institutions have no autonomy fr
the various governments (O.E.C.D., the U.N. in most respects). Such arrang
ments in turn range from truly cooperative to hegemonial, that is, from rep
senting all the members to asserting the domination and extending the will
one of them. 2. Then there are *entities* which have *central institutions* endow
with some authority, in the sense of legal autonomy from the components a
legal power all over the territory of the entity, but which are *not* politi
communities in the formal sense, because of drastic discontinuities in commu
cations and transactions among the components, or because the cleavages wit
the entity deprive in fact the central institutions of autonomy or of much eff
tive power (that is, states such as the Congo or certain Latin American stat
supranational entities like the E.E.C., and, within the limits of effective milit
integration, N.A.T.O.). Such entities may be astonishingly resilient if they a
states, endowed with international personality and institutions that have

ese units need not be nation-states, in the sense of communities dowed with external sovereignty under international law; but nversely, if a newly independent state is merely a shell within ich there is no community yet, the cleavages that divide the pulation into separate communities will prove to be a decisive stacle to trans-state integration: domestic integration is a prequisite to the kinds of flows of transactions and of ideas which ans-state integration requires and will of necessity be the primary al of any leader who tries to be more than the representative of e dominant sect, class, tribe, or ethnic group. This explains why, r so many countries of Latin America, Latin American integration mains a chimera, and also why it has been so difficult in Africa d in Asia to move beyond the nation-state: in many cases, the state there, but not yet the nation.

The second condition concerns the structure of society and of the litical system in units that are political communities. The students integration have rightly stressed the importance of pluralistic cial structures and élite groups in the units that try to integrate. it success depends on more than a similarity of such structures: requires the simultaneous presence in the Executive of leaders o represent those sections of the élites that advocate union and ose power depends on the support of the integrationist élites and oups. To the extent to which many of the new states — those whose pacity to become viable nation-states is most dubious — are single-

---

rmal monopoly of force or at least a superiority of force over internal chalges; but if these entities are supranational (and especially when they are t merely a way of disguising the hegemony of one of the component members), y are likely to be highly unstable (see below) precisely because the entity's entral'' institutions are likely to be constantly challenged by the central institions of the component states, endowed with external sovereignty as well as th superior force. In other words, supranational entities will tend either to rogress toward stage 1 or to progress toward stage 3. 3. Next come entities ich are *political communities* in the *formal* but not in the substantive sense: at is, their central institutions have autonomy and power, there are common bits, and the rules that come from above are enforced across internal barriers, t the central institutions are not endowed with legitimacy all over the terory, and the habits and rules are not based on common values concerning the lity; this is the case of many nation-states, which have ''national consciousss'' but are not political communities in the last sense. 4. Here I refer to tion-states whose central institutions are altogether autonomous, effectively werful and legitimate, and whose society has shared values concerning the lity. These are political communities in the *substantive* sense. Needless to say, ey are not legion. The difference between stage 3 and stage 4 is largely a fference in the level and scope of consensus. I would reserve the term nation states in those two stages.

party states with so-called charismatic (or should one say autho tarian?) leaders, this internal condition for unification is missing.

b. Insofar as external conditions are concerned, what matters not that the units be in "objectively" similar situations at the tir when integration begins and while it proceeds. What matters "subjective" similarity — a similarity that is not the scholar's asse tion, but the policy-maker's conviction. The implication, which crucial, is that one must examine more than the relation of each ur to the international system at the moment. Even if this relation the same for all the units involved, one must go beyond: One mu also determine whether the units come to this moment and pla from similar origins and through similar itineraries, whether the are likely to proceed from this moment and place toward simil destinations. "Objective" similarity is disembodied — removed fro time and space. The similarity that matters is a similarity in t way in which different statesmen interpret a whole historical an geographical experience and outline the future in the light of th experience. Integration means a common choice of a common futur Success presupposes two sets of conditions, one about the past, o about the present.

As for the past, integration is likely to be more successful whe the voyagers' baggage is light. If the units' past international e perien̄ces have been long and heavy — long *or* heavy — if the sta apparatus has developed over decades and centuries, if the state ha quite simply, enjoyed an autonomous existence on the world scer for a long time, integration will not be easy. Is it an accident if th only successful example of voluntary unification in the modern wor is that of the U.S. — the fusion of units that had been colonies, n states, and in which neither the machinery of the state nor tradition of foreign policy had had the time to develop? In a sense, the she ding of overseas commitments by countries such as France an Britain should make their luggage lighter. But, as we have seen the case of France, the old burdens tend to be replaced by new tie the old *imperium* leaves lasting concerns, and the old responsibiliti do not disappear without leaving a sense of responsibility. Moreove even if the nations of Western Europe are less weighed down by th past than before, the present remains distracting enough.

The kind of similarity required in the present concerns the relatio of the units to the international system. A first question to be aske is the degree of *involvement*. When the similarity in the nation. situations is one of distance or insulation from the international sy

n, as was the case of the American states and to a large extent the
se of Switzerland after the Reformation, concentration on the dif-
ult job of unification becomes possible. A capital obstacle to
tegration anywhere in the world today is the loss of such distance,
e impossibility of such insulation, in the echo chamber of the
esent international system. This obstacle can, however, occasionally
cancelled. For there is a second question: the degree of *"compel-
gness"* of the international system; when the national situations
e similar because of an overwhelming external threat (as was
iginally the case with the Swiss cantons and the American ex-
lonies), unification for survival or security may become an impera-
ve. A compelling threat can make up for different pasts, and impose
common destination, when all divergencies about ultimate destinies
ve to be subordinated to the preservation of a chance for any
stiny at all. One can argue that this was Western Europe's condi-
on in the first ten years after the end of World War II. But the
untervailing force was the combination of the different pulls of
fferent pasts, with the different kinds of involvements in the
ternational system: All threatened from the East, the nations of
estern Europe nevertheless assessed differently the degree to which
is threat superseded every other aspect of international politics.
is not an accident if the nation that deemed the menace entirely
mpelling was Germany, divided and literally thrown face to face
th the threat at the exclusion of almost everything else. It is not
accident if France and Britain, entangled overseas and heirs to
urope's past, never let the threat from the East command their
tire foreign policy in the present[43] or assumed that it would in-
itably dominate their future. Moreover, Europe today is no longer
mpelled by the threat: Today's international system is a perverse
lucer to diversity. It inflates each national situation, while it
moves some of sovereignty's sting. In a way, the relative impotence
force, the postponement of the minute of truth, should reduce the
gnificance of all differences in national situations: The mighty
nnot use all the muscles they flex; the weakly can safely boast of
ore muscle strength than they have. But, in another way, since this
still a competitive system of fragmented states, Rousseau's iron
gic applies: Each state tries to exploit whatever margin of differ-
ce it has; each state, even when its objective position in the world
not so different from its neighbor's, stresses the marginal differ-

[43] Witness France's army strength in Algeria until 1962, and Britain's extra-
ropean troop commitments.

ences above the similarities; and, since it ultimately matters mu‹
less than before, the incentive to unification in order to "pull mo›
weight" is slim. The changes in the nature of usable power, in t]
relation between the uses and the achievements of power, give ev‹
to the weakest unit one asset in the contest — the power of its me
existence. The breakdown of the two polar camps, the kind of weigh
lessness with which restrictions on force endow the actors in the ne
international system, encourage the proliferation of different visio›
of the future or the tendency to live in the hazards and chances of
fascinatingly diverse present rather than planning too much for ‹
inscrutable future. The rational observer, outside the contest, c‹
preach that precisely because the stakes of the contest are mo›
symbolic than real — barring a holocaust that would equalize throu‹
annihilation — nation-states ought to be willing to unite even at t]
cost of transferring for a while their energy from the intoxicati›
but disappointing stage of world politics to the real job of comm
nity-building; for the outcome would be the appearance of a ne
actor whose power, by contrast with that of each old componer
could really be sufficient to make a difference. But the logic of cor
petition operates exactly the other way; it conforms to the Fren‹
proverb: one thing possessed is worth more than two things promise‹
In the immediate postwar system, European nations seemed oblig‹
to choose only between separate insecurity and the Atlantic shelte
The "halfway house" of Western Europe got started, but did n
progress far enough before the advent of the era in which the tem
tation of separateness started to smile again, and the reward f
separateness was a seat in the U.N.

It is the dialectic of fragmentation and unity (a single inte
national system, whose members may well be kicking and screami›
but have an interest in the avoidance of excess violence, that is,
behaving less asocially than before) which gives to the drama
Europe so much of its pathos. On the one hand, in a "finished world
dominated by giants, in a crowded world singularly resistant to t]
sweep of anyone's universal mission, there is something absurd ar
pathetic in the tenacious persistence of separate European nation›
wills. On the other hand, it is precisely because most of the differenc
between them have taken refuge in the realm of foreign affairs th
integration is so difficult, despite (or perhaps because of) the fa
that international politics today is more a stage on which one c‹
parade than a battlefield that seals one's fate.

2. A second set of remarks concerns the meaning of integration.
has become possible for scholars to argue both that' integration is
oceeding and that the nation-state is more than ever the basic unit,
thout contradicting each other, for recent definitions of integration
eyond the nation-state" point not toward the emergence of a new
id of political community, but merely toward an "obscur[ing of]
: boundaries between the system of international organizations and
: environment provided by member states."[44] There are two im-
rtant implications.

a. The first one is, not so paradoxically, a vindication of the
tion-state as the basic unit. So far, anything that is "beyond" is
ess": that is, there are cooperative arrangements with a varying
gree of autonomy, power, and legitimacy, but there has been no
ansfer of allegiance toward their institutions, and their authority
nains limited, conditional, dependent, and reversible. There is
re than a kernel of truth in the Federalist critique of functional
egration: functionalism tends to become, at best, like a spiral that
ls ad infinitum. So far, the "transferring [of] exclusive expecta-
ns of benefits from the nation-state to some larger entity"[45] leaves
: nation-state both as the main focus of expectations, and as the
tiator, pace-setter, supervisor, and often destroyer of the larger
tity: for in the international arena the state is still the highest
ssessor of power, and while not every state is a political com-
inity there is as yet no political community more inclusive than
: state.[46] To be sure, the military function of the nation-state is in
sis; but, insofar as the whole world is "permeable" to nuclear
apons, any new type of unit would face the same horror, and,
sofar as the prospect of such horror makes war more subdued and
nquest less likely, the decline of the state's capacity to defend its
izens is neither total nor sufficient to force the nation-state itself

4 Haas, *Beyond the Nation-State*, p. 29.
5 Ernst B. Haas and Philippe C. Schmitter, "Economics and Differential Pat-
ns of Political Integration," *International Organization*, Vol. XVIII, No. 4
utumn 1964), pp. 705-737, and p. 710.
6 One could argue that the entity of the Six, insofar as its functional scope
concerned (that is, the realm of welfare, which is certainly a significant part
politics) is a political community in the formal sense. My own analysis of
itical realities (by contrast with the law of the treaties that established the
ee communities) is more pessimistic; although I admit that because of the
mmission's role the entity of the Six came close to being a political comnity in the formal sense, recent events have underlined the precariousness of
Commission's autonomy and power.

into decline. The resistance of the nation-state is proven not on
by the frustrations of functionalism but also by both the promi
and the failure of Federalism. On the one hand, Federalism offe
a way of going "beyond the nation-state," but it consists in buil
ing a new and larger nation-state. The scale is new, not the stor
the gauge not the game. Indeed, the Federalist model applies
the "making of Europe" the Rousseauistic scheme for the creati
of a nation: it aims at establishing a unit marked by central pow
and based on the general will of a European people. The Federalis
are right in insisting that Western Europe's best chance of being ı
effective entity would be not to go "beyond the nation-state," b
to become a larger nation-state in the process of formation and
the business of world politics: that is, to become a sovereign politic
community in the formal sense at least. The success of Federalis
would be a tribute to the durability of the nation-state; its failu
so far is due to the irrelevance of the model. Not only is there ı
general will of a European people because there is as of now ı
European people, but the institutions that could gradually (aı
theoretically) shape the separate nations into one people are ı
the most likely to do so. For the domestic problems of Europe a
matters for technical decisions by civil servants and ministers ratḥ
than for general wills and assemblies (a general will to prosperity
not very operational). The external problems of Europe are matte
for executives and diplomats. As for the common organs set up by t
national governments, when they try to act as a European executi
and parliament, they are both condemned to operate in the fȯ
maintained around them by the governments and slapped down
they try to dispel the fog and reach the people themselves. In otḥ
words, Europe cannot be what some of nations have been: a peop
that creates its state; nor can it be what some of the oldest stat
are and many of the new ones aspire to be: a people created by t
state. It has to wait until the separate states decide that their peopl
are close enough to justify the setting up of a European state whȯ
task will be the welding of the many into one; and we have ju
examined why such a joint decision has been missing. The very ȯ
stacles which make the Federalist model irrelevant to nations t
diverse and divided also make all forms of union short of Federalis
precarious. Functionalism is too unstable for the task of comple
political unification. It may integrate economies, but either tḥ
nations will then proceed to a full political merger (which econom
integration does not guarantee) — in that case the federal moḍ

ll be vindicated at the end, the new unit will be a state forging its
n people by consent and through the abdication of the previous
arate states, but the conditions for success described above will
ve to be met — or else the national situations will remain too
ergent, and functionalism will be merely a way of tying together
e pre-existing nations in areas deemed of common interest. Between
e cooperation of existing nations and the breaking in of a new one
re is no stable middle ground. A federation that succeeds becomes
nation; one that fails leads to secession; half-way attempts like
pranational functionalism must either snowball or roll back.

b. But the nation-state, preserved as the basic unit, survives
nsformed. Among the men who see in "national sovereignty" the
mesis of mankind, those who put their hopes in the development
regional superstates are illogical, those who put their hopes in the
ablishment of a world state are utopian, those who put their hopes
the growth of functional political communities more inclusive than
e nation-state are too optimistic. What has to be understood and
died now — far more than has been done, and certainly far more
in this essay was able to do — is, rather than the creation of rival
nmunities, the transformation of "national sovereignty": it has
t been superseded, but to a large extent it has been emptied of its
mer sting; there is no supershrew, and yet the shrew has been
newhat tamed. The model of the nation-state derived from the
ernational law and relations of the past, when there was a limited
mber of players on a stage that was less crowded and in which
lence was less risky, applies only fitfully to the situation of today.
e basic unit, having proliferated, has also become much more
erogeneous; the stage has shrunk, and is occupied by players
ose very number forces each one to strut, but its combustibility
vertheless scares them from pushing their luck too hard. The nation-
te today is a new wine in old bottles, or in bottles that are some-
es only a mediocre imitation of the old; it is not the same old wine.
nat must be examined is not just the legal capacity of the sovereign
te, but the *de facto* capacity at its disposal: granted the scope of
authority, how much of it can be used, and with what results?
ere are many ways of going "beyond the nation-state," and some
dify the substance without altering the form or creating new
ms. To be sure, as long as the old form is there, as long as the
ion-state is the supreme authority, there is a danger for peace and
welfare; Gullivers tied by Lilliputians rather than crushed by
ans can wake up and break their ties. But Gullivers tied are not

the same as Gullivers untied. Wrestlers who slug it out with fists a
knives, prisoners in a chain gang, are all men; yet their freedom
action is not the same. An examination of the international impli
tions of "nation-statehood" today and yesterday is at least as imp
tant as the ritual attack on the nation-state.

3. A final remark concerns the future of integration. Prospects
genuine unification would improve if the international system creat
the conditions and incentives for moving "beyond the nation-state
In a world in which, on the one hand, many more units had succeec
in becoming genuine nations with pluralistic structures, in which,
the other hand, a return to multipolarity had resulted both in grea
autonomy for the subsystems and in a resurrection of interstate w
(in the form of limited conventional war or even geographica
limited nuclear conflicts), the conditions of unification would be n
at least in some parts of the world: a less universal and intense
volvement, a more compelling threat, greater internal harmony mi
allow the nation-state to supersede itself. But even so, the res
might simply be the agglomeration of many smaller nation-sta
into fewer, bigger ones; and there are more things in the heaven a
earth of possible international futures than in any philosophy
international relations.

Leon N. Lindberg

Integration as a Source of Stress
on the European Community System

.   .   .

In the pages that follow I offer an interpretation of the meaning
the recent crisis in the European Community and of its implica-
ns for theories and theorists of integration and for the future of
: Community. I do so painfully aware of the extreme difficulty of
king a fully reliable estimate without historical perspective and
th only a few of the relevant details to guide me. General de Gaulle
a master at leaving one in considerable doubt as to precisely what
is about and this has not made my task any easier. Two themes
ll be developed and explored below. First, de Gaulle's boycott of
: European Economic Community (EEC) machinery from mid-
65 into 1966 represents only one stage of a long-term struggle over
: institutions and operative rules of the European Community sys-
n among actors who accept that system and who employ features
that system to advance their respective strategies. Thus, instead of
king at the crisis as a contest between de Gaulle who seeks to
wart the inexorable march of the integration movement and those
o want to see that integration continues on to maturation, what-
er that may mean, I will suggest that it be viewed as a case of
at can be a source of persistent tension in all political systems,
d especially in incipient systems, i.e., the struggle over the form
d the content of the structures and procedures responsible for the
king of authoritative decisions. It would follow that the "com-
mise" solution or nonsolution reached at the end of January

Reprinted from *International Organization*, XX, No. 2 (Spring 1966), with the
mission of The World Peace Foundation and the author.

between France and its partners does not represent any final "⌐
nouement" to the crisis. Second, I will argue that the course of t
crisis and the strategies and responses of the major actors do n
contradict or invalidate theories of spillover or analyses of t
integration process but that they represent, in a perhaps perver
sense, striking demonstrations of the validity. The essence of t
European Community has been seen in the

> tendency for economic and social decisions to "spill over" into the realm
> the political, to arise from, and further influence the political aspirations
> the major groupings and parties in democratic societies.[1]

Integration has been seen as a process whereby important tasks a
delegated to central institutions, political actors restructure the
activities and expectations accordingly, and their loyalties begin
shift from national symbols, as earlier decisions

> spill over into new functional contexts, involve more and more people, ⌐
> for more and more inter-bureaucratic contact and consultation, there
> creating their own logic in favor of later decisions, meeting, in a p
> Community direction, the new problems which grow out of the earl
> compromises.[2]

The spillover process

> assumes the continued commitment of major participants to the process
> integration, it does not presume passionate enthusiasm and takes for gran
> opposition to specific items in the catalogue of integrative ventures. ⌐
> support for given steps rests on the convergence of expectations of the p
> ticipants; competing expectations and goals can be compromised on the ba
> of swapping concessions from a variety of sectors, all under the generaliz
> purview of supranational institutions and process. . . . The very penetrab
> ity of the national shell leaves the nation open to the lure of intersector
> bargains whereby one government is willing to take a loss in exchange ⌐
> a gain in another sector. . . . No statesman, even if he dislikes the proce
> can permanently isolate his nation from a commitment to unity which
> already partially implemented, unless he is willing to pay the price
> diminished welfare.[3]

While the crisis does not invalidate these analyses, it does make cle
once again the extent to which we have tended to treat reassertio
of purely political goals such as national grandeur or independer

---

[1] Ernst B. Haas, "Technocracy, Pluralism and the New Europe," in Step
R. Graubard (ed.), *A New Europe?* (Boston: Houghton Mifflin Company, 196
p. 65.

[2] Ernst B. Haas, "International Integration: The European and the U
versal Process," *International Organization,* Summer 1961 (Vol. 15, No.
p. 372.

[3] Haas, in Graubard, p. 73.

her as atavisms or at best as residual categories. *Grosspolitik* has
t lost its relevance, the nation-state has not begun to wither away,
d politics has not been emptied of its emotional, symbolic, and
amatic content. And yet the European Community *is* much more
an a classical type international organization, having given birth
institutions which play crucial roles in intra-Six bargaining, in the
ministration of the customs union, in the internal politics of the
ember states, and in the international system. The crisis adds to
r understanding of the dynamics of the system and of the various
nds of stress to which it is subject.

A System in Permanent Crisis

I wrote not long ago that the European Community was a crisis
stem, that the progress of integration implied not decreased conflict
tension but its continuation and probable intensification. Further-
ore, this would be the case even if the parties to the enterprise were
t deeply divided on basic foreign policy goals and did not manifest
ch strikingly different political styles.

e members of the Community do not confront each other only or chiefly
diplomatic gladiators; they encounter each other at almost every level of
ganized society through constant interaction in the joint policymaking
itexts of officials, parliamentarians, interest group leaders, businessmen,
rmers, and trade unionists. Conflicts of interest and purpose are inevitable.
ere is no paradox between the progress of economic integration in the
mmunity and sharpening political disagreement; indeed, the success of
nomic integration can be a cause of political disagreement. The member
ttes are engaged in the enterprise for widely different reasons, and their
tions have been supported or instigated by elites seeking their own par-
ular goals. Therefore, conflicts would seem endemic as the results of joint
tivity come to be felt and as the pro-integration consensus shifts.[4]

It is clear that as the Six move toward completion of the customs
ion and take the first steps in the direction of common policy
aking in such areas as agriculture, competition, and commercial
licy, the need will arise for common or coordinated approaches to
e whole gamut of classical economic policy. It will become increas-
gly difficult to deal with problems of economic growth and develop-
ent, maintenance of full employment, inflationary or deflationary
essures, or balance-of-payments difficulties through independent
autonomous action by the participant governments alone. Required

4 Leon N. Lindberg, ''Decision Making and Integration in the European
mmunity,'' *International Organization,* Winter 1965 (Vol. 19, No. 1), p. 80.

is the working out of common or coordinated approaches to regio
policy, social policy, labor mobility, the right of establishment, co
mercial policy, transportation, fiscal policy, countercyclical poli
and monetary policy, including domestic credit policies, exchan
rate harmonization, capital investment, etc.[5] If integration is
proceed, the member states will have to agree to strive toward su
policies through the Community institutional system and its ope
tional rules. Implied here is a process of negotiation and bargaini
that the parties accept as legitimate and essentially permanent.
view of the scope of policy making involved and the extent to whi
these engagements are likely to spill over into the foreign a
military policy fields, it is not surprising that the actors in
system would seek to shape the framework within which such negot
tion and bargaining take place, that is, the institutional system a
its operational rules. This is particularly to be expected when n
elites come to power who for one reason or another do not share
original integration élan which helped legitimize the institutions
their early years. The recent crisis in the Community is thus quali
tively different from the normal conditions of crisis because it cent
not upon disagreements over economic policy but rather upon
particular institutional system and operational rules that had evolv
since 1951, acceptance of which had been the *sine qua non* of
Community.[6] For this reason it seemed to raise for the first time
acute possibility that the system might not be able to respond to
stress and might founder, whether this took the form of a slow stag
tion or a spectacular crash.

According to David Easton, whose abstract model of the politi
system I have found most useful precisely because it takes as
central problem that of stress and the capacity of political syste
to respond to stress:

> To say that a system has failed may mean one of two things: that it
> changed but continues to exist in some form; or that it has disappea
> entirely. As the first meaning indicates, a system can be said to persist e

[5] For full discussions see Finn B. Jensen and Ingo Walter, *The Comm
Market: Economic Integration in Europe* (Philadelphia and New York: J.
Lippincott Co., 1965), and Bela Balassa, *The Theory of Economic Integrat*
(London: George Allen and Unwin Ltd., 1961).

[6] One can argue, and I think correctly, that the issue had only been ignor
but agreement to ignore does represent a kind of consensus too. Nor was
inevitable that the conflict would take the form that it did for we cannot der
general principles from the behavior of a de Gaulle. See Stanley Hoffma
"Europe's Identity Crisis: Between the Past and America," *Daedalus,*
1964 (Vol. 93, No. 4), pp. 1244-1297.

changes. At first glance this may seem rather paradoxical. . . . At the
least it helps us to understand what is meant by persistence if we inter-
its negative to mean, in its second sense, that a system has disappeared
pletely. For the given society authoritative allocations of values could no
ger be made.[7]

Thus, whether or not and to what extent the EEC is judged to be
danger of failure will depend largely upon the level of the system
h which we are concerned.

As Easton puts it:

t is the fact that persistence may include the idea of change that makes
vital and necessary to differentiate this concept from that of systems
intenance. . . . Maintenance is weighted with the notion of salvaging the
sting pattern of relationships and directs attention to their preservation.
sistence signalizes the importance of considering, not any particular
acture or pattern, but rather the very life processes of a system them-
ves. In this sense a system may persist even though everything else
ociated with it changes continuously and radically.[8]

though a full analysis of the European Community in systemic
ms will not be attempted here,[9] we should keep before us the above
tinction. In concrete terms we must distinguish between the
ropean Community system seen as a set of institutions and a
aracteristic operational code and the European Community con-
ved in terms of what, for want of a better term, we might call the
nfrastructure of integration.'' By this I mean the customs union,
new intra-Community trade patterns, the gradual interpenetra-
n of businesses, the network of contacts and consultations estab-
hed among businessmen, farmers, traders, laborers, civil servants,
., and the political impact of these patterns and commitments upon
policy-making processes of the participant governments. It is
tirely possible that the latter may persist through a structural
nsformation of the former[10] or that the existence of the latter
y actually constitute a source of stress on the former.[11]

David Easton, *A Framework for Political Analysis* (Englewood Cliffs, N.J.:
entice-Hall, Inc., 1965), p. 82. See also, David Easton, *A Systems Analysis
Political Life* (New York: John Wiley & Sons, 1965).
Easton, *A Framework for Political Analysis*, p. 88.
To be presented in a book now in preparation provisionally entitled *The
ropean Community as a Political System*.
Easton, *A Framework for Political Analysis*, p. 124.
In systemic terms this would be particularly paradoxical because it would
ply that a major stress-regulating mechanism of the system had become itself
ource of stress. See Easton, *A Systems Analysis of Political Life*, Parts IV
V.

AGRICULTURE AND THE FRENCH BOYCOTT

The surface origin of the crisis was the failure of the Six to ag
on the final details of the system for the financing of a common ag
cultural policy. This involved deciding how the costs of that pol
were to be allocated and how the benefits distributed. Since
amounts involved would be large (estimates range as high as $6
million to a billion dollars a year), the negotiations were slow a
arduous. Involved also were the demands of some of the members t
along with the transfer of authority to dispense sums of money
this order should go a transfer of a power of control to the Europ
Parliament and the proposal of the EEC Commission that it sho
be given its own sources of financial support from the proceeds
industrial tariffs and the agricultural levy system. Both propos
could be expected to limit the ability of any one government
manipulate the system. The formal deadline for decision on th
matters, agreed to in 1962, was July 1, 1965. Although the Six a
the Commission had not reached agreement on a number of import
matters by that date, the negotiation process had followed a famil
pattern and everyone (except the chief French negotiator) ant
pated that after a marathon session, perhaps a stopping of the cl
(both essential ingredients in the Community's rather cumberso
decision-making process), an acceptable formula would be achiev
Instead, on midnight of June 30, 1965, the French walked o
declaring that the others had proven unwilling to meet their obli
tions and that until they did France would boycott the Communit
institutions. In the week that followed it became evident that
French grievances went far beyond the matter of financing
agricultural policy, extending to a basic hostility toward the E
Commission, its strategy and "political pretensions," the federal
philosophy of integration, the voting system agreed to in the Tre
Establishing the European Economic Community (Treaty of Rom
and the "reluctance" of its partners to liberate themselves from
domination of the United States. The tenor of the French demar
was made clear in General de Gaulle's press conference of Septeml
9, 1965.

The three treaties setting up the ECSC, Euratom and the Common Mar
were concluded before the French recovery of 1958. This is why they t
account above all of the requests made by the others. . . . Furthermore,
three treaties set up an outline executive — a Commission independent
the States, even though they appointed . . . and paid . . . its members —

her with an outline legislature, a European assembly with members drawn
m the parliaments but none of them having been given anything but a
ional mandate by their electors.

his embryonic technocracy, in large part foreign, which was to trample
r French democracy and settle problems crucial to our existence, ob-
usly did not suit us when we decided to take our fate firmly in our own
ds.

his Community . . . [must be] fair and reasonable. . . . "Fair" means
t farm products must be incorporated . . . on terms specific to them. . . .
air" means that nothing which is important today in the organization, or
orrow in the operation of the Common Market, will be decided, let alone
e, by anybody but the authorities responsible in the six states, i.e. the
ernments controlled by the parliaments.[12]

)ne can interpret the French boycott and de Gaulle's speech as
ng so extreme and deliberately provocative that they had no mean-
except either as the first stage in a French withdrawal from the
mmunity or as moves intended to force the other member states
break it up rather than capitulate totally to French demands.[13]
is could have been accomplished gradually by disrupting the
mmunity system in such a way as to force other governments to
oke escape clauses and disengage from existing machinery. De
ulle might then blame the others for being insufficiently European
l thus minimize the political cost to himself of a collapse.

3ut such an interpretation never seemed entirely credible to me.
France withdrew or otherwise caused the total collapse of the
tem, France would forego its major lever for intervention in and
ssible disruption of its partners' internal affairs and its chief
rce of influence over its partners' policies toward the United
ites, the Soviet Union, and Eastern Europe. If the European
mmunity were to founder, West Germany, Italy, Benelux, as
leed the United Kingdom itself, would have no alternative to an
tlantic solution" and continued economic, military, and political
lbservience" to the United States. Furthermore, a "break" would
very costly to French industry and agriculture alike, as their
erest groups were at pains to make clear,[14] not to mention the

Le Monde, September 11, 1965. Only when the French finally returned to
Community bargaining table in January of 1966 did they issue a more
-ific set of demands. See the analysis below.

- Maurice Faure, "Le général de Gaulle a prononcé l'oraison funèbre du
ché commun," *Le Monde*, September 11, 1965. See also, Pierre Drouin,
-ûler le traité de Rome?," *Le Monde*, September 11, 1965.

- See, for example, the statements of the Conseil national du patronat français
[PF), *Le Monde*, July 2; and Fédération nationale des syndicats d'exploitants
coles (FNSEA), *Le Monde*, September 11; Centre national des jeunes

increased burdens on the French treasury for the support of ag
culture which might otherwise have been shared by the other E]
members. According to one French estimate,[15] its industrial expo
to the EEC had increased by 195 percent as compared with 40 p
cent to third countries while agricultural exports increased by ?
percent to the EEC as compared with 52 percent to third countr
Furthermore, French elites were certainly not unaware that Fra
had been, by and large, the most consistently successful of
member states in making its policy preferences prevail in the E
system. Many were also aware that these successes had been in la
part due to the formation of *ad hoc* alliances with the very C
mission that de Gaulle now seemed determined to emasculate.[16]

DE GAULLE'S STRATEGY:
EUROPE AS A TRAP FOR THE FIVE

It seems at least likely that de Gaulle has been *betting on*
permanency and irreversibility of integration, not challenging
Far from denying the effects of spillover and the political impl
tions of economic integration, he has based his strategy on th
while at the same time acting to limit their effects on himself.
has not intended to undo integration but to turn it to his c

---

agriculteurs (CNJA), *Le Monde*, October 16, 1965. The Fédération natioı
française des cooperatives agricoles de céréales estimated that French farn
would lose between 2,500-5,000 million new francs per year (*Agence Eur*
September 1, 1965).

[15] "Que perdrait l'économie française à la mort lente du Marché commun
Le Monde, September 19-20, 1965. Still another study indicated that Frɑ
along with Italy had gained the most in overall economic benefits from Euroɟ
integration.

VALUE OF EEC EXPORTS IN 1964 (1958 = 100)

	To EEC	To Rest of World	Differenc
France	305	137	168
West Germany	246	160	86
Italy	375	187	188
Belgium-Luxembourg	254	124	130
Netherlands	243	137	106
EEC Total	267	151	116

("Poker with Uncertain Stakes: The Economic Significance of the Com
Market and the Risks of the Present Crisis," *Common Market*, September 1
[Vol. 5], pp. 173-178.)

[16] For an analysis of major decision-making sequences in the early histor;
the Community, see my *The Political Dynamics of European Economic Inte*
tion (Stanford, Calif.: Stanford University Press, 1963), especially Chaɟ
VI-XIII.

poses. The other members of the Community are trapped by the
ic of spillover and by the web of relationships and commitments
ich have developed since 1950. They are also trapped by internal
itical weakness and indecision, anxieties about United States
icy in Asia, fear of United States economic penetration of Europe
l the competition of America's giant-size firms, United States
illation with regard to NATO, MLF, ANF,[17] and the apparent
nomic and political bankruptcy of the British. France is not
pped by integration, it is not "engaged" by the process, because
Gaulle is not as subject as his colleagues in the other member
ntries to internal political controls on his freedom of action and
ause, therefore, he is the only one willing to threaten to destroy
whole system if he does not get his way. As Michel Debré put it
cinctly: "France can succeed only by threatening to bolt the
mmon Market as a whole."[18]

The theory of integration and of the spillover process, which seems
be strikingly verified by de Gaulle's actions (if turned on its
d!), assumes the existence of a pluralistic political system gov-
ed by the traditions and assumptions of democracy and constitu-
nalism in which governing elites are obliged to constantly take
o account the values, interests, and preoccupations of the major
anized interests. But as Stanley Hoffmann has pointed out:

n in a pluralistic society, political power can come to be exerted by a
itical group that comprises a minority among *all* governing elites . . .
d] can rule without Parliament due to temporary dictatorship or direct
ular support. If this group either does not share the values of the elites
he other nations . . . the whole enterprise of integration may be jolted.
s is what has happened in France.[19]

With the December 1965 election returns before us it is clearly
oossible to argue that de Gaulle is able to act entirely without
ard for the internal repercussions of his actions. However, it is
ious that the French internal situation — the fragmentation of
opposition, the elimination of parliament as a meaningful institu-
i, the atrophy of the political parties, the degree to which de

The North Atlantic Treaty Organization, the proposed NATO multilateral
ear force, and the Atlantic nuclear force, respectively.
La Nation, September 15, 1965.
"Discord in Community: The North Atlantic Area as a Partial Interna-
al System," in *The Atlantic Community: Progress and Prospects*, eds.
icis O. Wilcox and H. Field Haviland, Jr. (New York: Frederick A.
ger, 1963), p. 11. See also, Lindberg, *The Political Dynamics of European
iomic Integration*, p. 293.

Gaulle was able to concentrate the reins of power in his own ha▮
— has given him a vast amount of discretion in dealing with Co▮
mon Market affairs. It is unlikely that his surprisingly poor show▮
in the December 5 balloting and the apparent pro-European prot▮
vote for Jean Lecanuet and to a lesser extent for François Mittera▮
will change this. De Gaulle still remains in full control of the sit▮
tion and there is still no truly credible alternative to de Gau▮
especially for the groups most committed to the Common Mark▮
i.e., industry, commerce, and agriculture. Most such groups w▮
reluctant throughout the crisis to take strong positions agai▮
de Gaulle for they are dependent upon him whether or not ▮
Common Market survives.[20]

This is not to say that French opinion has acquiesced in or gen▮
ally supported de Gaulle's actions. With the exception of Union ▮
the New Republic (UNR) spokesmen and long-time Gaullists the ▮
ternal reaction has been generally negative.[21] What was striking ▮
that with the exception of the farmers, criticism took the form ▮
expressions of "alarm," "grave concern," "extreme disquiet," "▮
prehension for the future," and the like, and very rarely[22] that ▮
direct attacks on the General himself.[23] The CNPF "regrette▮
de Gaulle's move and "feared serious repercussions for the Fre▮
economy," declaring that "the present uncertainty made for diffi▮
choices." The FNSEA (agricultural peak organization) ▮
"alarmed — the future is filled with uncertainty and risk." ▮
French Conseil économique et sociale (which groups representati▮
of all economic interests) in their debate on the government's rep▮
on the Fifth Economic Plan expressed their reservations and a▮
ieties because of the impact of "uncertainties about the future ▮
the EEC" and finally passed a resolution mildly critical of ▮
government.[24] Not surprisingly, farmers' organizations were ▮

[20] For a discussion of their predicament see F.-H. de Virieu, "Les organ▮
tions paysannes ne sont pas d'accord sur le sens à donner aux paroles du ▮
de l'État," *Le Monde*, September 11, 1965; and Pierre Viansson Ponté, "A▮
le conseil des ministres," *Le Monde*, September 17, 1965.

[21] For exceptions, see the statements by Count Coudenhove-Kalergi, *Age*
Europe, September 10, 1965, and André Philip, *Le Monde*, September 12 ▮
1965.

[22] Except for long-time Europeans (Jean Monnet, Maurice Faure, Pierre ▮
Etienne Hirsch, and Robert Lemaignen) or political opponents of the reg▮
(Gaston Defferre, Raymond Cartier, and René Blondelle).

[23] Our analysis is necessarily limited to published sources and hence we ca▮
say what kinds of pressuring and maneuvering went on behind the scene.

[24] See *Le Monde*, September 30, 1965, October 1, 2, 1965. The clause ab▮

st concerned for they stood to lose immediately from even a tem-
ary breakdown in the Community. At first they too were cautious
l limited themselves to expressions of support for European
egration as their only hope for a better life in the future, to
ials that there were reliable alternative outlets for French agri-
tural surpluses in Eastern Europe, the Soviet Union, or Com-
nist China, to declarations that they were ready to accept a
ertain amount'' of supranationality, and to urgings that France
urn to the bargaining table.[25] Finally, apparently in reaction to
continuing hard line taken by the government and especially to
October 20 speech of Foreign Minister Maurice Couve de Murville
the National Assembly, the FNSEA National Council voted a
ong antigovernment resolution which ended with an implicit
itation to farmers not to vote for the ''candidate of power'' in the
cember elections.[26] The behavior of the farm leaders and the
iency of the ''European issue'' in the subsequent election cam-
gn are certainly impressive evidence of the existence of strong
ernal support for the Community even though we do not know
v many farmers took their leaders' advice nor precisely how im-
tant the ''European issue'' was in accounting for the size of the
i-de Gaulle protest vote in both December elections.

)e Gaulle's behavior since the election would seem to indicate that
is anxious to restore his image as a pro-European while at the
ne time not reducing his freedom of action or his demands for a
ision of the EEC institutional system. France returned to the
C Council of Ministers and Couve de Murville abruptly changed
style of negotiation to one of extreme reasonableness and con-
ation but with an increased set of demands and always stressing
determination not to permit a situation in which France might
e decisions in important areas imposed on it by ''foreigners.''
the postelection cabinet reshuffle ''pro-European'' Minister of
riculture Edgar Pisani was shifted to a ''safer'' post, and Finance
nister Valery Giscard d'Estaing was eased out. Former Prime
nister Michel Debré, a long-time ''anti-European,'' returned to
government as a superminister in charge of economic and finan-

EEC and the dangers of interruption was adopted by a vote of 136 to 14,
h 34 abstentions.
[5] See the interview with Gérard de Caffarelli, President of the FNSEA, in
Monde, September 30, 1965, and the position of the young farmers' organiza-
, the CNJA, in *Le Monde*, October 16, 1965.
[6] See *Le Monde*, October 23, 1965, for a discussion and for the text of the
lution. For Couve de Murville's speech, see *Le Monde*, October 22, 1965.

cial affairs and with responsibility extending to industry, exter
trade, transport, and social affairs. These changes would seem to p
tend an effort to blunt what I have referred to elsewhere as
penetration of the Community system into national administrat
structures[27] while at the same time adopting a more liberal pol
toward domestic spending for social services and the like. Debré
also been a strong proponent of domestic economic modernization a
reform, especially in the field of agriculture. Since European integ
tion has been supported for "welfare reasons" and most vigorou
by reformist or modernizing elements among economic elites, th
moves seem designed to counter or compete with the attractions of
Community. Such a strategy makes good sense since it has been cl
that de Gaulle's nationalism has struck strong responsive cho
among the French[28] where pro-European opinion has been unifor
weaker than in the other countries of the Community,[29] notwithsta
ing the fact that the Community was born of French initiative a
imagination.

THE SUCCESSES OF INTEGRATION NEED NOT
STRENGTHEN THE INSTITUTIONS

Reactions on the part of governments, parties, and interest gro
in the other member states of the Community were anything
muted or reserved, especially after the September 9 press confere
De Gaulle was severely criticized and there was an impressive a
massive outpouring of support for the Commission and in favor o
continuation of the integration process as the only possible path
the future. Of special interest are the positions taken by inte
groups organized both at the national and the community le
These tend to support my earlier conclusions[30] that the integrat

[27] "Decision Making and Integration in the European Community," *Inte*
tional Organization, Vol. 19, No. 1, pp. 70-75.

[28] See, for example, a public opinion poll taken in July reporting on attit
toward de Gaulle's policies, "Ce que pensent les Français," *L'Express,* Au
2-8, 1965, pp. 6-7.

	Social	Economic	Foreign Policy	Education	Agricul
Satisfied	32	31	52	41	25
Unsatisfied	51	37	19	37	41
No opinion	17	32	29	22	34

[29] See "L'Opinion publique et l'Europe des Six," *Sondages,* 1963 (No.
pp. 46, 50-53.

[30] See Lindberg, *The Political Dynamics of European Economic Integra*

cess had been accepted, that it had been considered irreversible,
t economic groups had come to define their interests in terms of
and that any interruption of the enterprise would be considered a
astrophe. A few examples are in order to convey the tenor of these
ctions.

mmittee of EEC Farmers' Organizations (COPA):

continuation of present uncertainty is liable to have extremely serious
cts on farm economy and on the economy as a whole. . . . [We] urge the
to resume negotiation on the basis of the new Commission proposals.[31]

C Farm Cooperatives Committee (COGECA):

he halt in the development of farm policy is liable to create a radical
alance . . . and call past achievements into question.[32]

nference of EEC Agricultural Workers' Trade Unions:

he latest declaration by the President of the French Republic seriously
angers the foundations of integration. . . . [We] appeal to all the
ernments to maintain the supranational principles of the EEC and to
k a constructive solution.[33]

ecutive Committee of EEC Free Trade Unions (CISL):

eject with vigour the procedure contrary to the Treaty and democratic
es which consists to taking unilateral decisions concerning the existence
the Community through press conferences. Still look on the Paris and
ne Treaties as the solid and unshakeable basis of the endeavors to unify
rope politically and economically. Consider that the treaties are sacro-
ct. . . .
re resolved to take joint action against any attempt to bring back the
tem of bilateral or multilateral government relations, weakening the
mmunity institutions. . . .[34]

deration of EEC Industries (UNICE):

or a long time companies have based their programmes and choice of
nomic policy on the assumption that the Common Market will be achieved
full, and have done a great deal to further cooperation; any uncertainty
iable to jeopardize the structural transformations in hand. . . . The work
rted must be continued, deadlines observed, the Treaty observed in full.
. Industry would find it intolerable for this outlook to be compromised
ough political interference . . . realization of the economic union must
hand in hand with that of the customs union . . . common policies must

---

sim, and Lindberg, ''Decision Making and Integration in the European
mmunity,'' *International Organization,* Vol. 19, No. 1, pp. 56-80.
[1] *Agence Europe,* September 14, 1965.
[2] *Agence Europe,* October 4, 1965.
[3] *Agence Europe,* September 24, 1965.
[4] *Agence Europe,* October 4, 1965.

be instituted . . . and this cannot be accomplished without reciprocal c cessions and appropriate modifications of national policies.[35]

Permanent Conference of EEC Chambers of Commerce:

Fresh efforts must be made to preclude from being called into quest both past achievements and the possibilities for a transformation of ind trial and commercial structures and a better adaptation to industrial c petition.[36]

The "New Europe" has indeed created its own vested interes But the irony is that the success of integration can be, and in view were, used against the architects of that success — against "Europeans" in the Commission and in all the member countries would hypothesize that organizations like those quoted above a their constituent national units may well accept a Gaullist *structu adaptation* of the EEC system in order to maintain more or intact the almost completed customs union and the incipient econor union and so not to disturb new trading and investment patter etc.[37] In the terms introduced earlier in this article, groups co mitted primarily to the infrastructure of integration may not p ceive the institutional system and its operational rules as vital the persistence of that system. Such a position is especially attract to groups whose payoffs from the Community have derived from "negative" features of the process, i.e., tariff and quota disarr ment, and who are becoming more and more preoccupied with presumed dangers of United States economic penetration of Euro We must recall that integration has been supported not for identi reasons but for converging ones. Of the four types of pro-integrati aims I proposed in 1963,[38] integration as political unification, economic unification, as economic and political cooperation, and free trade, only the first necessarily implies defense of the Co munity institutional system and its operational code. Thus, it wou

[35] *Agence Europe*, October 7, 1965. National business reactions have been strong. See, for example, the statement of the Federation of Belg Industries (FIB):

The continued buildup and completion of this venture . . . is vital for economy. The fundamental decisions and the main options as to our co try's economic policy have and will hinge to a very large extent on outlook for European integration.

(*Agence Europe*, September 22, 1965.)

[36] *Agence Europe*, October 13, 15, 1965.

[37] Among economic groups only the trade unions make unambiguous strong statements about the institutional system.

[38] *The Political Dynamics of European Economic Integration*, pp. 108-1 289-290.

m, in the short run at least and as long as de Gaulle is in power,
t the successes of integration, which have been the work of the
titutional system and its code, have strengthened the hand of
most consistent opponent of that system and weakened that of
supporters!

The Timing of the Crisis

It seems likely that de Gaulle had understood the above situation
some time and that he had intended to make use of it to bring
out changes in the institutional system of the Community, certain
tures of which he has always strongly disliked.[39] We cannot be
e just when and how he became aware of the possibilities open to
1 or what combination of events made him confident of success.
me people place his decision as late as the final days of June 1965,
ers in April,[40] still others in 1963 or earlier.[41] Acceptance of the
t of these would help explain the French decision in 1963 to support
"Europeans' " call for a merger of the executives of the three
ganizations, the EEC, Euratom, and ECSC, to be followed by a
rger of the three Treaties themselves.[42] The "Europeans" saw
s not only as an administrative improvement but also as a symbolic
that would strengthen the prestige of the single new Commission.
Gaulle probably saw it as an opportunity to cause all the Treaties
be renegotiated in a setting of maximum advantage to himself.
cording to the original schedule, merger of the executives was to
accomplished as of January 1, 1966, and merger of the Treaties
o years later. At that time de Gaulle would have been in an excep-
nally strong position because the agricultural policy would have
n completed. France would have had most of what it wanted from

---

9 He has heaped scorn upon the Commission on many occasions: "These
ties have their technical value but have not, and cannot have, any political
hority or consequently be effective." And ". . . arbitrary outside tyrannies
the so-called supra-national institutions. . . ." See *France and the Euro-
n Community,* Occasional Paper No. 11 (London: Political and Economic
nning, January 30, 1961).

0 See "The Hour of Truth," *Common Market,* August 1965 (Vol. 5), p. 155.

1 See, for example, the articles by Robert Lemaignen, "La France manoeuvre
r vider le Marché commun de tout contenu politique," *Les Echos,* August
1965; and René Mayer, "Vingt ans après," *Le Monde,* September 17, 1965.

2 The Treaty Establishing the European Economic Community, the Treaty
ablishing the European Atomic Energy Community (Euratom), and the
aty Establishing the European Coal and Steel Community (ECSC),
pectively.

integration, and the others would have had very little with which
counter a Gaullist campaign.[43]

Perhaps the most striking evidence of de Gaulle's long-stand:
intention to "revise" the Community system is an incident repor
by René Mayer:

> As for me, I was not surprised either by the *incident* of the 30th of Ju
> nor by what we heard on the 9th of September. And here is why: The I
> time I had the chance to talk to the Chief of State about Europe was in
> autumn of 1963. . . . In the course of a reception . . . I had the occasion
> say that I had learned much those years in Luxembourg, when I presi‹
> over the high authority of the ECSC. I could go no further. The response
> General de Gaulle ended our conversation. . . . "Well, now you will have
> forget all that. I am going to *wipe* everything *away* and we will be‹
> again."[44]

While de Gaulle has had these things in mind for some time,
does seem likely that he had not originally intended to make
move before the common agriculture policy had been completed.
thus appears that the Commission, along with the Dutch, Italian, a
West German governments forced his hand. In the negotiations
the financial regulation they showed the greatest reluctance to gr:
French demands without getting in exchange some kind of supra
tional *"préalable"* in the form of an independent source of reve›
for the Commission and a commitment to increase the power a
the authority of the European Parliament. Furthermore, they sou‹
to limit the time period for which the regulation would apply and
fix maximum percentages for national contributions to the agric
tural fund. In addition the Germans argued that concurrent decisi‹
should be taken on tax harmonization, commercial policy, and
Kennedy Round of General Agreement on Tariffs and Trade (GAT
negotiations.

In spite of these problems most of the negotiators — apparen
including *most* of the French delegation — confidently expected t`
a compromise solution could have been reached after the us
marathon and final triumphant Commission intervention. Thou
precise details are not available it does seem that the French dele
tion did try to achieve a compromise, at least on economic pol
questions, and that de Gaulle's instructions to Couve de Murville

---

[43] This interpretation is strongly supported by the French insistence whe›
came back to the Council in January 1966 that the merger of the executives
carried out as rapidly as possible, hinting that if that were not done, it wc
resume the boycott.

[44] "Vingt ans après," *Le Monde*, September 17, 1965.

minate the negotiations came during the last few days as it became
arer that the Dutch and the Germans were not ready to back down
npletely.[45]

What seems to emerge is that de Gaulle decided to break off negoti-
ons if he couldn't get what he wanted without concessions to the
ers that might tie his hands in the future and without engaging
a Community-style marathon negotiation which would have added
the prestige of the Commission. Had they been willing to engage
a "marathon" it is clear that the French would have gained most
what they wanted of the finance regulation. The Commission's
ond set of proposals, which give in to the French on most points,
l the subsequent behavior of the Five demonstrate this. One might
culate that this "weakness" convinced de Gaulle that he could
voke the crisis, punish the Commission, change the rules, and still
what he wanted in agriculture. In the weeks following the break-
vn of negotiations and in the September 9 press conference de
ulle made it clear that as far as the French were concerned the
mmission was no longer an *"interlocuteur valable,"* that the crisis
s intended to demonstrate that only the governments could settle
portant issues, that *"l'Europe des patries"* was the *only reality,*
l that there was to be no nonsense about real powers for the Euro-
n Parliament or real authority and political initiative for the
mmission.[46]

THE TARGET: WHY THE FRONTAL ATTACK
ON THE COMMISSION?

As indicated before, de Gaulle has long disliked the Commission
l its pretensions to a political role in the process of integration.
t he had gone along with the system as long as the Commission's
ivities were consonant with French policy objectives, even permit-
g French negotiators to accept and indeed promote decisions that

---

⁵ Actually, for our interpretation it makes little difference whether de Gaulle
· intended the June negotiations to succeed or whether, as we have suggested,
made up his mind in the last few days to make his move at that time. One
 of reconciling all the diverse evidence is to suggest (and this is plausible to
 that de Gaulle was really carrying on a twin deception: vis-à-vis his partners
 he Community and vis-à-vis his own ministers, advisers, and civil servants,
 t of whom I am convinced were genuinely committed to the Community and
 ts operational rules. Support for this hypothesis comes from reports that
 ost all senior French delegates in Brussels were genuinely shocked at de
 lle's action.
³ See *Le Monde,* July 7, 8, 9-10, 1965.

helped expand the Commission's power and authority.[47] By
spring of 1965 the Commission had reached the apex of strength,
crucial role in the integration process was widely accepted, the co
mon agricultural policy seemed almost completed against heavy od
and Commission President Walter Hallstein was reported to ha
told United States journalists that he could be regarded as a kind
Prime Minister of Europe.[48] In March the Commission tabled
proposals for the financial regulations and their boldness surpris
even the most optimistic Europeans, for to the proposals on
financing of the agricultural policy, to which goal all had been co
mitted for some time, the Commission tied two proposals that w
clearly controversial and which the French had long since reject
namely, immediate independent financial resources for the Co
mission and new powers for the European Parliament. In exchar
for a very favorable arrangement on financing,[49] the French w
expected to accept the two ''political'' elements they had previou
rejected.

It appears that the Commission's boldness was a product of
own self-confidence and heavy pressure from some of the meml
states, especially from the Dutch. The proposal about granting
European Parliament real powers over the Community agricultu
budget was probably included because the Dutch Parliament h
made it a *sine qua non* for their acceptance of the whole system. T
proposal for independent financial resources was a pet project of
Commission for it would have enormously increased its power a
authority. Not only would the Commission receive as of 1967
proceeds from the agricultural levies collected at the Communit
frontiers, but it would also receive the proceeds from all *industr*
tariffs as well! What the Commission proposed then was an unc
ditional handing over of all tariff proceeds to itself. The amou
involved, possibly as high as $4 billion a year,[50] would have exceed
the actual Community budgetary outlay and would have given
Commission a new source of political leverage.

[47] See Lindberg, *The Political Dynamics of European Economic Integrati*
Chapters VII-XII.

[48] *Common Market,* September 1965 (Vol. 5), p. 190.

[49] According to one estimate of the agricultural budget, France would ha
paid 18 percent against West Germany's 39 percent. (*Le Monde,* April 14, 196
French farmers would furthermore have received at least 50 percent of the to
expenditures.

[50] A figure used by de Gaulle in his press conference.

Considering what was known of de Gaulle's goals[51] and sensitivities
d with the still fresh example of his veto of the British entry, one
y wonder if it was wise for the Commission to bring these dis-
eements so sharply and deliberately to the fore. Stress-reducing
havior in a precarious pluralist system, especially one like the
mmunity which is only incipient, frequently requires that im-
rtant issues upon which there is no consensus and much intense
aflict be resolved ambiguously, played down, or postponed entirely.
hether the stress-regulating mechanisms of the system were equal
such a task, whether de Gaulle himself would have behaved "ap-
opriately" had the Commission retained its prudence, is certainly
en to question.

This was apparently the last straw for de Gaulle and although
ne revision of the Community system had been long planned to
ing it more into line with his preferences, the severity and timing
the attack may well have been provoked by these proposals. De
ulle is reported unofficially and perhaps apocryphally to have
xploded" when the terms of the Commission's proposals were
plained to him and to have exclaimed, "Do they think they can
y off De Gaulle with such a piece of cheese?" and, "They have
pped being stateless — they are actually anti-state!" His Septem-
r 9 speech was full of anger and outrage at the Commission's
dacity:

The Commission suddenly abandoned its political reserve and formulated
ms . . . whereby it would have a budget of its own . . . the States having
de over into its hands the levies and customs receipts which would literally
ve made it a great independent financial power. And then those very
ites, having fed these enormous amounts to it at the expense of their tax-
yers, would have in no way supervised it. It is true that the authors of the
n alleged that the budget would be submitted to the Assembly for con-
eration.

1 To the French President EEC is no more than a special kind of international co-operation in technical-economic fields. As far as decisions to be
taken within EEC have any political implications, or concern vital interests
of internal or external policy, they can only be taken if there is agreement
between all six governments, for only in that case can the existence and the
functioning of EEC be reconciled with the retention of political sovereignty.
In other words, the French accept the supranational methods only in the
field of technical economics. In politics they reject every application of this
method of co-operation as being irreconcilable with national political sovereignty. Here there can only be room for the classic intergovernmental cooperation between countries.

ommon Market, September 1965 [Vol. 5], p. 183.)

But intervention by this Assembly, which is essentially an advisory bo‹ the members of which are in no way elected for this purpose, would mer‹ aggravate the usurpatory nature of what was being demanded.[52]

He also drew certain conclusions from the support the Commissi received from the other member states:

> Regardless of whether or not there was collusion between the Commissio supranational claims, the attitude adopted by certain delegations wh stated their readiness to approve them, support them, and finally the f‹ that certain of our partners at the last moment went back on what they h undertaken to do, we had no alternative . . . to break off the Brussels neg tiations. . . . However in the light of this event, we have been able to ass more clearly still what France might be exposed to in the future. . . . Fran could have had her hand forced in all economic contexts and as a result social and political contexts, and that even what seemed to be assured the agricultural field might, despite France, be again jeopardized at a moment.[53]

What is perhaps most striking in de Gaulle's speech is his decisi to do battle directly with the Commission. He would almost certain have preferred to ignore the Eurocrats as beneath his concern out the consideration that a direct confrontation could only close "t prestige gap."[54] Thus, the direct attack should probably be view as a left-handed sign of respect and as an indication that de Gau felt himself threatened by the Commission in some significant wa As a guide to what it is in the system and its rules that he fears, is instructive to examine the "ten proposals on the style of the Co mission" introduced by the French at the start of the January 19 negotiations.[55] *Le Monde* dubbed them "the ten capital sins that t Commission must no longer commit."[56] They included the followi demands: that the Commission should be required to "consult t governments" more extensively before making a proposal; that should never "unveil the tenor of its proposals to the Assembly or the public" before submitting them to the Council; that the Co mission should stop trying to assume executive powers or tasks volving "discretion or its own responsibility"; that the Commissi should stop trying to prescribe the "form, ways and means" where the states implement Council decisions; that the Commission show

[52] *Le Monde*, September 11, 1965.
[53] *Ibid.*
[54] See Stuart A. Scheingold, "De Gaulle v. Hallstein: Europe Picks Up Pieces," forthcoming in *The American Scholar*, Summer 1966.
[55] For the text of what came to be known as the "decalogue," see *Age Europe*, January 18, 1966.
[56] *Le Monde*, January 19, 1966.

op trying to act like a state in its relations with nonmember
untries or international organizations; that Commission members
should be required to observe a proper neutrality in their public
atements about the policies pursued by member governments'';
at the Commission should not have such an autonomous information
rvice; and that the Community's budget should be subject to more
fective supervision.

Aside from the predictable Gaullist sensitivities about protocol
nd the Commission's status ''pretensions,'' two things come most
rectly under attack here. On the one hand are the tactics of coali-
on building and risk escalation used by the Commission to put
ressure on the governments to accept Commission proposals by
tervening directly or indirectly in their internal politics.

In agriculture, Mansholt and the other Commissioners have tirelessly ex-
ained and actively espoused their proposals throughout the Community,
aling directly with politicians, high officials, and ministers, appearing be-
re interest group and party conventions, and participating in television
d radio debates. At the same time they have stressed the costs and risks
volved in a failure to act, seeking always to make use of or *create* dead-
es by linking various kinds of decisions together.[57]

n the other hand, de Gaulle is clearly uneasy about the Commis-
on's consistent efforts whenever it is called upon to make proposals
expand the role of the central institutions. While such proposals
equently involve only ''technical'' tasks, they are not without
olitical significance. Again agriculture has been an interesting
ortent of what might be expected in other areas as integration
roceeds.

With the adoption of the common agricultural policy the member states
ve delegated some important decision-making powers to the Commission,
d one can expect a continued expansion of its competence and authority
ring the third stage of the transitional period when majority voting be-
mes the rule in the Council. The Commission is responsible for the func-
oning of the marketing system; only it has information on what is going
throughout the Community and the expertise to handle problems in ways
ceptable to the member states. In the eyes of national administrations, the
thority and prestige of the Commission have grown with the implementa-
on of the common agricultural policy, much as they have with intra-Six
rgaining in the Council.[58]

rom de Gaulle's point of view it must certainly appear intolerable

---

[57] Lindberg, ''Decision Making and Integration in the European Community,''
ternational Organization, Vol. 19, No. 1, p. 65.
[58] *Ibid.*, p. 68.

that this "apatride, irresponsible word-machine" should prove successful at maximizing the spillover process, at appealing direct to groups and individuals in the several states, and at establishi: itself as a legitimate political power in Europe. His attack on would indicate that he takes these things quite seriously and th he fears the dynamism of a system that might outlive him and co tinue to "mislead" Europe and the French.

Thus, de Gaulle sees both opportunities and dangers in the ne situation created by the emergence and development of the Europe: Community. He has acted to frustrate institutional developmen that threaten to limit his freedom of action while at the same tin seeking to manipulate the system in his own interests by using it a bludgeon against his partners.

MINIMIZING RISKS

If our interpretation is correct and de Gaulle does not want bring down the EEC but to restructure it so as to maximize h leverage over the others, then he must have realized that he w: taking a calculated risk and that he was playing one of his last hig cards. If the others reacted by withdrawing from the system preferring its gradual demise to an acceptance of his demands, t} cost to France and to de Gaulle's own aspirations would have bee very substantial. Fred Iklé has written about the dangers of bargai: ing as de Gaulle so often seems to prefer, that is, by means "threats."[59]

Threats . . . are moves made by a party for the purpose of changing t} opponent's expectations and consequently influencing his choices . . . y(try to alter . . . expectations about *his* gains or losses that would result fro certain choices he can take. . . . In contrast to the warning, the threatener course of action that results in the opponent's loss is not, by itself, in t} threatener's interest. Indeed, this course of action may be costly for t} threatener — perhaps even more costly than the loss is for the opponent.

Consequently, de Gaulle has acted in at least four ways to minimi: the risk that the other countries would force him to fulfill his threa

[59] For discussions of de Gaulle's style, especially his dislike of a bargaining overt mutual exchanges and concessions, see Alfred Grosser, "Le Général et secret," *Le Monde,* September 14, 1965; Herbert Lüthy, "De Gaulle: Pose a: Policy," *Foreign Affairs,* July 1965 (Vol. 43, No. 4), pp. 561-573; and Stanl: Hoffmann, "De Gaulle, Europe, and the Atlantic Alliance," *International Organ zation,* Winter 1964 (Vol. 18, No. 1), pp. 1-28.

[60] Fred Charles Iklé, *How Nations Negotiate* (New York: Harper & Ro* 1964), pp. 62-63.

rst, he sought to reintroduce some ambiguity into the French posi-
n by "clarifying," "interpreting," and appearing to "soften"
e demands made in the September 9 press conference and through
pid changes in bargaining style. Second, he permitted certain
atures of the Community system to continue working, thus demon-
rating he had no intention to disrupt what had already been
hieved. Third, he pursued, with some fanfare, alternatives to the
EC. And fourth, he kept the pressure on the other members, either
rough selective internal boycotts of negotiations of special interest
one or another of them or through outside diplomatic maneuvers.

1) *La carotte et le bâton.* After a few days to let the full brunt of
Gaulle's attack in his September 9 press conference have its
ychological effect, a number of French officials, members of parlia-
ent, etc. — none of whom committed de Gaulle, of course — began
reassure all concerned about French intentions. Couve de Murville,
fore the French National Assembly on September 15, defended the
ommon Market against an attack by French Communist Party
ader Waldeck Rochet, stating that the French economy had bene-
ed substantially from the Common Market and that France had
ery intention of continuing with the enterprise.[61] Agricultural
inister Pisani declared that all France wanted was for its partners
stick to their obligations[62] and for the others to conclude a limited
ntleman's agreement whereby through an *interpretation* of the
reaty of Rome unanimous voting would extend to agricultural
atters in cases of serious distortions operating to the disadvantage
one or another partner.[63] Pierre Massé, head of the Commissariat
énéral du Plan de Modernisation et d'Equipement declared that
e government did not envision any hypothesis other than to pursue
e Common Market. "The government has not put the EEC to
eep and has not stopped saying that it is attached to the realization
the EEC. . . ."[64] Giscard d'Estaing on October 15, again before
e National Assembly, declared that the government felt that the
reaty of Rome should be complied with and that this meant customs
rriers between Common Market countries would be eliminated by
70 at the latest.[65]

Similarly, Maurice Schumann, President of the Foreign Affairs

[61] *Agence Europe*, Supplement, September 15, 1965.
[62] *Le Monde*, September 18, 1965.
[63] *Agence Europe*, September 21, 1965.
[64] *Le Monde*, September 30, 1965.
[65] *Agence Europe*, Supplement, October 15, 1965.

Committee of the French National Assembly and a long-time asso‹
ate of de Gaulle, in a debate with Paul-Henri Spaak in Brussels
September 27,[66] argued that de Gaulle's aim was not to tear ‹
the Treaty or empty it of its content or even demand a "lite›
revision." De Gaulle, he said, had no intention of setting the Co‹
mission aside, for it was an indispensable institution which

was to be congratulated for having played its role so well during 1963 a
1964, that of bringing about a rapprochement of government and Co‹
munity points of view.

But

by putting certain proposals to the public and the Assembly, knowing t›
they would not be accepted and could not be accepted in certain quart‹
. . . [it] put itself in a position that prevented it from acting on June 30.

Furthermore,

although a political authority will progressively and necessarily come i›
existence . . . the more the Commission wants to be that political author‹
itself, the more it will compromise its future.

On majority voting Schumann argued that "everybody agrees t›
the unanimity rule cannot be replaced with majority rule." Frar
did not want to abolish it, he said, but only suspend it so that ‹
could be returned to in the future when circumstances would perm›

The escalation of demands and hardened tone of Couve de M›
ville's October speech, while consistent with a strategy of keepi‹
the pressure on in a setting of uncertainty, may well have been ‹
initial French reaction to the surprising determination shown ‹
the Five to coordinate their resistance to the boycott by continuing ‹
meet in Brussels and to their efforts to pressure the French ‹
mobilizing public and elite opinion against de Gaulle's actions.

Under the pressure of the election campaign the French tone ›
came once again more conciliatory and their conditions for a ‹
sumption of the Community system more studiedly vague. Shor›
after the elections the French agreed to an extraordinary session ‹
the EEC Council of Ministers, to apply the 10 percent cut in int›
Community customs duties due January 1, 1966, and to extend ‹
four months the date when the 20 percent cut in the Communit›
external tariff, agreed to in 1962 in anticipation of the results ‹
the Kennedy Round, would have lapsed. When the French fina‹
returned to the Council in January, Couve de Murville was the mo‹

[66] *Agence Europe*, Supplement, September 28, 1965. For the full texts ‹
Agence Europe, Document Nos. 338, 339, 340, September 30, 1965.

sweet reasonableness while at the same time presenting a list of ɪximal demands.

2) Only a Partial Boycott. The French consistently made a dis-ɪction between those meetings and decision procedures which in-lved new undertakings and those which related only to keeping ɪe existing policies and machinery going. Thus, the French partici-ɪted in certain study groups, in meetings of the several management ɪmmittees for agriculture, in "technical" sessions of the special ɪmmittee for agriculture, etc. They also accepted "managerial" ɪd "technical" decisions taken by the other Five in the Council ɪd then submitted to the French for their approval by the Com-ɪunity's "written procedure." Of course, the French always chose ɪe occasion for their participation, thus keeping all in a state of ɪspense and making it clear that no dependable pattern could be ɪsumed. A case in point is the Community's 1966 budget, which the ɪench were widely expected to accept by written procedure in ɪecember 1965 because so many concessions had been made in ɪticipation of French sensitivities. In fact, however, the French ɪld back, including approval of the budget in their January pack-ɪe.

3) Other Alternatives. Much attention and fanfare were given to ɪe possibilities of new export markets, especially for agricultural ɪoducts, in Eastern Europe, the Soviet Union, and Communist ɪina. Pisani went to Eastern Europe on a "feasibility" study, a ɪw wheat sales contract was concluded with the Poles, and rumors ɪre floated about a French intention to open negotiations with the ɪnited States on a broad international agreement to terminate ɪtirely "artificial" support of farmers. Other stories were circulated ɪout French overtures to the British, and veiled allusions were made ɪ de Gaulle and others to the conditions under which the British ɪight take part in a system of "organized cooperation between ɪates." Some close observers considered that such offers to the ɪitish might well prove tempting and would really undercut the ɪsition of the Five and the United States.[67]

[67] The truth of the matter is that de Gaulle never wanted to keep Britain out of Europe: he wanted to prevent her (and succeeded) from taking part in the construction of a Europe he himself rejects, i.e., a Europe moving towards federal structures, which would be one of the pillars of the Atlantic Alliance. From the point of view of the Gaullist conception this is natural and reasonable, as clearly once Britain decided to join a "Community" and to accept integration, nothing would any more stand in the way of the fulfillment of this "dream" based on "false counsel." What General de

I would certainly not assume that de Gaulle was only bluffi
in these overtures. As Stanley Hoffmann has so aptly pointed out
de Gaulle always has tried to pursue several courses of action sim
taneously. It is not to be excluded that he would pull France out
the Community if the Five were to refuse totally to meet his d
mands. More likely would be a continuation or resumption of t
boycott of the institutions while selectively permitting benefic
aspects of the customs union to remain in force.

4) *Implied Blackmail.* Those countries dependent on extra-Co
munity trade came under especially severe pressure as de Gaulle
boycott of the Kennedy Round brought those negotiations to a virtu
halt. Without French agreement there could be little participation
bargaining and no Community acceptance of commercial agreemen
involving tariffs, quotas, agricultural protection, or the like. We
German and Dutch business circles were especially concerned wi
the possible repercussions of a failure of the Kennedy Round on the
future export markets. Among outside diplomatic maneuvers d
signed to heighten anxiety and increase the costs of resisting we
the much advertised French discussions with Poland and the Sovi
Union about the future of Germany.

RESPONSES OF THE OTHER ACTORS:
STRESS PERCEIVED AS UNIT-VETO BLACKMAIL

Your opponent may not heed your warning or not give in to your thre
for three reasons: he may expect that it will be less costly to absorb t
losses you predicted than to meet your demand; he may decide that the
losses will be less harmful than the damage done to his bargaining reput
tion by giving in . . . ; or, finally, he may not believe . . . that you w
carry out your threat.[69]

Calculations on all three of these dimensions are being made
each of the Community's other member states. How did they pe
ceive the crisis? How did they gauge the risks of accepting or r
jecting de Gaulle's demands? Did de Gaulle overestimate the i
terests, strength, and determination of those groups and elites who
primary commitment was to the system at the infrastructure lev

---

Gaulle wants, however, is a Britain playing her part in an alliance betwe
states. . . .

(*Agence Europe,* Comment, September 14, 1965.)

[68] See "De Gaulle, Europe, and the Atlantic Alliance," *International C
ganization,* Vol. 18, No. 1, pp. 1-28.

[69] Iklé, *How Nations Negotiate,* p. 63.

d underestimate the interests, strength, and determination of
ose whose primary commitment is to the present system with its
stitutions and its characteristic operational rules? Whereas a full
alysis of "who has what stake in which system" cannot be under-
ken here, a few suggestions will be made.

In my view, the crucial stress on the system did not come from the
ntent of de Gaulle's demands on majority voting or the powers of
e Commission. He is correct in asserting that few of the other
ember states have evinced great enthusiasm for majority voting,
itness the West German proposal in 1964 that such a procedure
t apply to future decisions on grain prices. All would have agreed
at it would not be used against the strong opposition of any state
at felt its vital interests were involved. As West German Foreign
inister Gerhard Schröder made clear on October 6:

> The rule could be applied on subtle lines. Practical considerations would
> ay the decisive role, since future cooperation between the Six would
> pend . . . on the unanimity of the partners. If this were so, it would be
> fficult to imagine one of the partners finding himself in a situation incom-
> atible with his vital interests.[70]

Thus, most of the governments of the Five probably feel that the
ystem could continue to function satisfactorily on the basis of
nanimity as it had done to date, that this was a necessary condition
f this kind of system, and that, indeed, it might be positively desir-
ble as long as major differences of opinion existed among the mem-
ers.[71]

The role of the Commission is more difficult. All governments and
ost of their civil servants and interest group leaders had come to
ccept its active role as the initiator, broker, and catalyst of the
ystem. But an active Commission is more important to some than to
thers as we have suggested earlier, and there is sufficient ambiguity
bout exactly what such a role demands. As the agreements reached
1 January 1966 reveal, some measure of "enforced prudence" was
cceptable without provoking a significant withdrawal of support
rom the system.[72] It was always possible to argue that it would be

[70] *Agence Europe,* October 6, 1965.

[71] The firmness with which the Five resisted the French demands in this
gard at the January 1966 Council sessions seems to me more attributable to
ars, fed by the way in which de Gaulle acted in the crisis, that the French
ould use the veto to block decisions of interest to others. Thus, they refused
accept any formal or informal provision that majority voting would not be
sorted to when a member's vital interests were involved.

[72] De Gaulle could have achieved this purpose much more economically, merely

impossible to keep a Commission with an independent role "only
the field of technical economics" from having a significant politic
potential as well, for given the nature of the Community enterpri:
the varied interests of the members, and the problems they wou
have to face, it seemed clear that some kind of political mediating rc
would always be required.

But what has stressed the system and may still cause political a:
other elites to withdraw their support is what Easton might call :
"anticipated output failure."[73] De Gaulle's acts, and especially h
style, undermine the very heart of the Community system, th
sense of "engagement," of being in the same boat, of being "co
demned to succeed," of being committed to solve mutual problems k
give-and-take in an institutionalized setting in which failures a
excluded and sensitivity is shown to each other's needs and pr
occupations. I wrote of decision making in the Council during t
first five years of the EEC that:

> The atmosphere is informal, for the Ministers know each other well k
> now, long, formal speeches are rare, laughter is easy, and there is a cle
> awareness of running a common project in which the problem is nev
> whether agreement is possible, but rather what level of compromise shou
> be sought. Participation has been in the spirit of joint problem-solvin
> instead of being limited to defending national points of view. . . . Bas
> confrontations of interest have occurred, but no firm pattern of blocs h
> been established, different members playing mediatory roles under differe
> conditions.[74]

It will be very difficult indeed and probably impossible to restore su(
an atmosphere as long as de Gaulle is in power. How the system w:
function without it and without an active Commission is impossib
to predict, and this uncertainty will certainty cause the decisi(
makers of the Five to question seriously the advisability of takii

by making a few strong statements with some veiled threats. He has not be
the only one to complain about those "technocrats in Brussels"; for examp
see Ludwig Erhard, "Was wird aus Europa," *Handelsblatt*, December 23-2
1960. It is interesting to this context to recall that the major reproach direct
to the Commission from the onset of the EEC has been that it was too co
sistently pro-French!

[73] Implicit in what I have already said about outputs is the idea that,
part, support for any of the political objects will, in the long run, depe:
upon the members being persuaded that outputs are in fact meeting the
demands or that they can be expected to do so within some reasonable tin
Output failure can be said to occur when members feel that outputs a
not likely to do so.

(Easton, *A Systems Analysis of Political Life*, p. 267.)

[74] Lindberg, *The Political Dynamics of European Economic Integration*, p. 7

ir countries into further economic and political integration with
ance under de Gaulle. De Gaulle has demonstrated by his style
d tactics in the current crisis what the others may look forward
or, at least, what they cannot risk *not anticipating*. Political deci-
n makers will not be able to avoid concluding that de Gaulle is
pable, whenever he pleases, of using integration as a tool of black-
il, as a bludgeon to force the others to accept French policy pref-
nces.

To understand the full impact of this we must recall the nature of
e enterprise, the potential inherent in the integration process for
tes to intervene or interfere continuously in the internal policy-
king processes of partner countries. As integration proceeds,
oblems will arise requiring common policies, mostly by unanimity,
., countercyclical policies, monetary policies, and the like. Veto
d boycott tactics cannot in themselves force the others to accept
ench terms, but they can prevent *any* decisions from being taken.
one or several of France's partners were to experience some kind
economic crisis, the solution of which required Community de-
ions because national capabilities for effective action had been
oded by the economic and customs union, who could exclude the
ssibility that a de Gaulle would make use of the opportunity to
thhold his participation in order to force a further adaptation to
s preferences in this or a totally different policy area? Surely
fferences of opinion between the French and the others in such
eas as East-West relations, the Atlantic Alliance, and the inter-
tional monetary system are important enough to make the risks
ry real indeed.

De Gaulle's maneuvers in the crisis indicate that this is exactly how
can be expected to proceed, witness his calling the entire Kennedy
ound into question through the boycott as a means of pressuring the
ermans, Dutch, and Belgians, who depend for their livelihood on
aintaining more or less intact their extra-Community trade pat-
rns, and his ominous exchanges with the Soviets and the Poles about
ermany's eastern borders and the future of reunification, tactics
signed to encourage the anxieties of those like Konrad Adenauer
ho fear an "encirclement" of Germany by France and the Soviet
nion. It would be much more difficult for the Five to reverse the
mpliment when France had need of a Community decision al-
ough the possibility cannot be excluded in a future that might see
weaker France and a more assertive Germany.

OPTIONS OF THE OTHER ACTORS

There were three main alternative lines of policy open to the oth
governments. They could have decided that it was too dangerous
proceed with integration at all, given the implications of the Fren
position. They might then have rejected any concessions on majori
voting or the powers of the Commission, as well as the pendi
agriculture financing issue, thus allowing the system to disintegra
and blaming it on the French. On the other hand, the Five could ha
resisted French demands while carrying on with integration and a
it implied ''with those who accept the Community arrangements la
down in the Rome Treaties, and to allow all other European states
come in as soon as they can adopt them.''[75]

If, by some ill chance, France were to decide of her own accord to wit
draw, to distort the machinery and the spirit, to discard the ideas she h
had since 1950, then the others would be forced to maintain and consolida
the arrangement which France has done so much to create.[76]

Finally, they could accept the new situation created by de Gaulle
demands on the premise that if they are to go on with the system i
institutional form and operational rules must be made minimal
acceptable to the major politically relevant actors. Within this opti
at least two kinds of strategies could be pursued, implying differe
goals, at least in the short run. The first would be to try to lim
involvement by cutting back on future integrative commitmen
and reducing the Community for the time being to a loose custor
union or even a free trade area. The second would be to go on wit
integration, calculating that French ''engagement'' was inevitab
with de Gaulle's passing and trusting that the old operational rul
might be restored or that some acceptable new balance would emerg

I know of no evidence to indicate that the first alternative, wit
drawal or acquiesced disintegration, was ever seriously considered b
any government. It would have meant virtual abandonment of
policy of twenty years standing, especially difficult to envisag
when it had seemed so close to fruition and when it had been accon
panied by such popular and tangible benefits. The importance of
personal and emotional commitment to a past policy cannot be unde
estimated as a factor inhibiting ''rational'' or decisive action, esp

---

[75] Jean-Charles Snoy as cited in *Agence Europe*, September 11, 1965.
[76] *Ibid*.

lly when the alternatives are so poorly defined. If no European
mmunity as a political framework, then what?

The second option, namely, a long-term *"solution à cinq,"* while
mbolically attractive and supported by many "Europeans" as the
ly way to save the Community, was fraught with difficulties. It
sumed that France would withdraw or could be forced out of the
mmunity and that the Five could withstand the internal and ex-
nal pressures that would have been involved. Most interest group
okesmen seem to have opposed it on the basis that its implications
re too unpredictable and would call all investment decisions, past
d future, into question. For politically weak governments like Italy
Belgium it would have been especially difficult. Similarly, a
ategically and militarily exposed West Germany would probably
ve found intolerable the risks of having bad relations with Eastern
d Western neighbors simultaneously. At any rate it soon became
ar that for most the *"solution à cinq"* was simply a short-term
ategy for putting pressure on de Gaulle in order to induce him to
derate his demands and return to the system.[77] It consisted of an
pressed determination by the Five to continue to abide by the EEC
eaty, to meet together in the Council, the Permanent Representa-
es, and working parties, to encourage the Commission to carry on
th its work as far as is possible, and to make clear to the French,
ecially to French public opinion, that they stood ready to resume
cussions on the agricultural finance regulation as soon as France
umed its place in the Council. As such it was an impressive effort
th considerable potential for the future and not unsuccessful, as
ll be discussed more fully in the concluding section. It also ap-
ars once again to illustrate the profound degree to which the Comnity's institutional system and operational rules had been accepted
a legitimate framework for decision making on matters of the
st fundamental political and economic importance.

Thus, the strategy pursued by the Five throughout the boycott
d the "terms" of the January 30 "agreement" implied an accept-
ce of some variant of the third option, and this would seem to
licate that de Gaulle reckoned correctly and has won the round.
hether this is necessarily the case and what its implications might
for the future of the Community will not be examined.

[7] It is interesting to note that the surprisingly strong opposition to de Gaulle
the December elections apparently further reduced the incentives to go it
ne without France.

DENOUEMENT AND PROSPECT

The crisis ended on January 30 of this year in the sense that "settlement" was reached on the issues raised by the French a they agreed to resume participation in the Council of Ministers a presumably in other Community institutions as well. But, for reaso to be elaborated below, it is very difficult at this stage to draw a balance sheet of gains and losses. Certainly the sense of engag ment in a common enterprise, the climate of trust upon which eff tive Community functioning has depended, has suffered serious But has anyone won? If the former atmosphere in the Commun was epitomized by then French Minister of Agriculture Pisan remark in 1961, at the end of a dreary Council session on agricultu that *"nous sommes condamnés à réussir,"* then the new situati may be represented by Dutch Foreign Minister J. M. A. Lu comment at the end of the crisis: "There are no victors and vanquished: we can therefore rejoice.''[78] Press comment was cu ously contradictory, lacking the Community euphoria that ordinar marks the end of a crisis. As the editor of *Agence Europe* noted:

Different views are to be found in a single country, not just between capital and another. Thus it is generally felt in Paris that as French reque were moderate and sensible, they have been accepted in substance. So reporters put this success into figures, by estimating that 75% of the Fre requests were accepted. This does not stop one Paris newspaper from talk about failure and humiliation. Some Dutch papers write about a "capitu tion" of the Five, others contend that the concessions were only appare One British newspaper asks why French claims collapsed like a house cards, while another of equal standing feels that the Commission has b put under tutelage and that France has kept her veto.[79]

Why there should be confusion is reasonably clear. First, what Gaulle was really after was always somewhat obscure and ambigu to the others. This was partly a style or tactic adopted by de Gau to reduce his risks, as we have argued above, but it is also a clas de Gaulle pose. As Herbert Lüthy has written:

Even the sphinx-like pose which he is fond of assuming is deliberate calculated; from his earliest writings, he has been consciously creating ideal portrait of *le grand chef,* who must, as he wrote in 1927, "poss something indefinable, mysterious . . . remain impenetrable to his subor nates, and in this way keep them in suspense." According to a more rec formulation of his, this mystery resides, too, in the political art of "

[78] *Agence Europe,* January 31, 1966.
[79] *Agence Europe,* February 1, 1966.

rstallizing in words that which the future is going to demonstrate, " of not
ining goals before being assured of their success, and then always appear-
; to have desired what comes to pass.[80]

cond, a close examination of the ''settlement'' reveals that very
tle was in fact settled and that the texts adopted are vague and
:ord little more than agreement to continue the struggle within the
•mmunity's institutional system. Most observers agreed that the
·ench could have achieved *that* without the crisis. What cannot be
·ar as yet is whether the French action will psychologically condi-
•n other actors in the system (including Commission and member
ıtes) to behave more cautiously and accept French-defined limits;
ıether a permanent anti-French coalition or a Franco-German split
s been created; whether in sum the system's capacity to perform
d thus assure a satisfactory flow of outputs has been significantly
mpromised. In fact, all that is clear is that the system goes on and
at its future content and form will continue to be determined by
e accumulation of decisions taken by a multitude of actors in a
riety of ''technical'' and ''political'' contexts.

The final bargain[81] consisted of: 1) statements on ''cooperation
tween the Council and the Commission'' and on majority voting
ɹith a French reservation); 2) agreements on a working program
r the Council, including approval of the pending EEC and Eur-
om budgets, and a simultaneous start of negotiations on financing
e common agricultural policy and on the Kennedy Round; and 3)
reement to start negotiations to choose the membership of a new
erged Commission.

If we compare the statement on cooperation between Council and
ɔmmission with the original French demands,[82] we find that the
•ints adopted, all toned down considerably,[83] concern not a ''code
 good conduct'' for the Commission but a series of ''practical
les'' *to be established by joint agreement* between the Council and
e Commission. On majority voting the settlement consisted of the
ve agreeing only that when very important interests were involved
e Council would ''try to arrive, within a reasonable time, at solu-
•ns that can be adopted by all the members,'' while the French
sisted that discussions should always continue until unanimous

30 *Foreign Affairs*, Vol. 43, No. 4, p. 561.
31 For details see *Agence Europe*, January 29, 31, and February 1, 1966.
32 See above, p. 250.
33 For example, it is ''desirable for the Commission to get into touch in an
propriate way'' with the governments before making a proposal, rather than
he Commission should consult. . . .''

agreement was reached, and all the Six agreed that these differenc
were "not such as to impede the resumption of Community work
Negotiations on agricultural financing and the Kennedy Rou
would be resumed with the *existing* Commission, and a new merg
Commission would be established only when its membership, Pre
dent, and Vice President had been agreed to by all the memb
states.[84] Thus, both the French and the Five held to their positio
with regard to the institutional system and majority voting, a
agricultural financing will still be tied into the Kennedy Rou
negotiations. The Commission has been subjected to a severe atta
which could limit somewhat its freewheeling practices, and t
French may still insist upon the "retirement" of some of its me
bers. But it is by no means assured that it has been rendered impote
or put under tutelage. What impact all of this will have on the i
stitutions depends on future pressures from the Council (not only t
French) on the Commission and on who will be the members of t
new merged Commission, and these will depend in turn on futu
bargaining between Commission and Council and on bargaini
within the Council between France and the Five. Furthermore, ev
if the institutions were subjected to a sort of national tutelage,
is not clear what the implications would be for integration or f
the system as a whole. Will the system necessarily collapse witho
an active and autonomous Commission? Is it to be excluded th
other institutions (the European Parliament or the Economic a
Social Committee) or actors (a Federator?) could provide altern
tive sources of initiative and impulsion? Has the Community n
proceeded to the point where if one institutional head is cut off,
will grow new ones because of the nature of the engagements of t
actors?

Although the crisis demonstrates once again that the integrati
process is discontinuous and subject to "intrusions" of *Grosspolit*
and that spillover depends as much on political choices as on econom
dynamics, the institutional system of the Community appears to ha
survived the crisis more or less intact. Only with the passage of ti

[84] It would make sense for a de Gaulle desirous of maintaining the system
settle for this, considering that he had made his point, that any Commissi
would be more cautious in the future, and that the frontal attack on the ins
tutions and the atmosphere of crisis were only forcing the Five into a doctri
defense, and trusting that the onslaught could be carried on in a more piecem
fashion in specific policy contexts. Furthermore, much might be eroded aw
during the three-year bargaining process over merging the three Treaties wh
would follow the merger of the executives.

ll it be possible to identify basic changes or to assess their significance. Yet the memory of the crisis and the threats posed to all ncerned can be expected to have other effects that may reveal emselves more immediately. Perhaps the most important of these the impact of the crisis on the environment of national goals within iich further integration will take place. How are governments likely behave in the new atmosphere of uncertainty?

The course of the crisis suggests three broad alternatives: to push ead with economic integration as spelled out in the Treaties and the context of the institutions; to limit future engagements to the inimum necessary to maintain the infrastructure; and to expand de Gaulle's example of maximizing the potential for unit-veto ackmail inherent in the system.

1) *"Business as Usual."* This is the official spirit of the January settlement and of governmental and interest group comment on e resumption of Community activity. I doubt that we can exclude at several, perhaps most, governments will try to restore the system 1958-1963 on the premise that de Gaulle represents a passing erration and that even he is now shown to be constrained by the istence of the Community. Integration still represents the wave of e future and its dynamics can be expected to continue to erode ay the obstructions. Besides, it represents an economic necessity if ll employment and prosperity are to be maintained and the United ates creeping economic imperium avoided. "Europeans" in and t of the Community and groups with a stake in welfare or planng programs of European scale, e.g., farmers or those in marginal sitions as in underdeveloped regions of the Community, can be pected to lend support to such a policy. Governments without eat-power pretensions or grievances against the political or military tus quo in Europe can be expected to pursue such a goal although e risks of subjecting themselves to unit-veto blackmail must weigh avily in the considerations of their policy makers.[85]

2) *Minimize Commitments.* Such a policy would recognize the rmanence and the indispensability of the infrastructure of integtion, but it would imply holding back on future integrative imitments and accepting or promoting a weakening of central titutions and processes, either as a short-term strategy or as a ıg-term goal. It could be especially attractive to economic groups ose benefits from integration accrue primarily from tariff and

[5] See the discussion below of alternative strategies for reducing the chances blackmail.

quota disarmament rather than common policies and to those w
oppose European integration at the price of dismantling NATO a
loosening the United States' European ties. It could also be attracti
to a de Gaulle who rejects the institutional implications of continui
integration or who fears eventual German domination of an in
grated European Community system. Is it to be excluded that he w
pursue such a tack once the common agricultural policy is secure
(It is perhaps paradoxical that a renewed interest in United Kin
dom membership by *all* the members of the Community could resu
from variants of this general policy option.) All governments purs
ing such a policy would have to simultaneously develop domes
alternatives to the welfare appeals of the Community; otherwise t
tension between the proponents of this option and those of "busin
as usual" would likely become too dangerous. De Gaulle's failure
do this during the crisis hurt him electorally, and he appears to ha
learned the lesson. The unanswered questions are: Can these gover
ments develop viable national alternatives? What degree of in
gration will be required to keep their economies stable? Isn't t
growing technological gap between the United States and Euro
especially in such industries as computers, nuclear power, and a
craft, likely to greatly increase the incentives for joint Europe
research and planning and hence for a more maximalist position
further integrative ventures?

3) Maximize Blackmail Potential. Such a policy of using the ne
opportunities made available by the system for influencing the b
havior of partner countries and thus controlling the outcomes of t
Community system or for forcing policy preferences on extra-Co
munity matters could be pursued with greater or lesser tact a
delicacy. Only France and Germany would seem to be in the positi
or to have the incentive to do so. But then some would describe mu
of the history of the Community to date as constituting a brilliant
successful French policy of using the system solely to advan
French interests while holding all other commitments to a minimu
Is it to be excluded that efforts to return to such a policy will be ma
by a more "diplomatic" future French leadership? Continued a
expanded *overt* pursuit by France of such a policy and *any* ove
effort by Germany could be expected to severely endanger the sy
tem. The course of the crisis *has* demonstrated that at present the
appear to be internally imposed limits upon the freedom of politi
actors to operate in this fashion, at least if they must threaten t
future of the system itself to carry it off. Is the trend toward t

velopment of more "diffuse support" for the Community system,
might be implied in the reputed "Europeanism" of French and
rman youth, or is it toward the emergence of new elites and new
ues (reunification) whose impact could have the opposite effect?
4) *Strategies for Reducing the Chances for Blackmail.* How can
vernments or groups pursuing some version of "business as usual"
"minimize your commitments" protect themselves against policies
unilateral exploitation or unit-veto blackmail?[86] The crisis offers
ne suggestive guides, and it appears to me that its ultimate effect
uld be to increase for many the incentives for strengthening the
stitutional system. Three kinds of behavior suggest themselves. A
st strategy might be to develop *structural means* to prevent ex-
oitation and blackmail. The strategy of the Five throughout the
isis, especially their determined defense of an autonomous Com-
ssion whose membership is not to be subject to unilateral purge or
telage, is an apt example. Their position on majority voting also
ems explicable in this context. The Five clearly sought to limit the
to to cases where well-recognized and clearly defined vital national
terests were involved and to exclude it from situations of primary
terest to other members of the Community. Whether such a distinc-
n is viable in practice remains to be seen. A second strategy might
volve overt threats of *economic reprisals* against the exploiting or
ackmailing government. Such a strategy might well be effective in
ase of blackmail involving exclusively economic policy bargaining,
t it did not appear to have been seriously considered in the
65-1966 crisis. Finally, further efforts might be made to reinforce
e development in elite and general opinion of a "diffuse support"
ich would inhibit recourse by any member to such a policy. Such
rms did exist in the Community but were clearly not observed by
Gaulle, though they may have operated ultimately to constrain
m. The Five and the Commission certainly sought to appeal to
em during the crisis.

The European Community has survived its most serious crisis
though the path of its future development is more obscured than
er. All of the governments would seem to have discovered that their
pendence on the system and the economic and political advantages
keeping it more or less intact outweighed the incentives they might
ve had for pursuing strategies that would have brought about its
llapse. Collapse or gradual decay is still possible, however, for the

[86] "Minimizing commitments" as such a strategy in itself has already been
cussed.

governments have also discovered the extent to which they are co strained and exposed in their internal and external policies by the involvement in the Community. There is a permanent tension in the system that overlays all the normal stresses one expects in multi tional systems, and that is the tension between those groups a individuals (businessmen, farmers, traders, planners, some po ticians) who are building up interests in the infrastructure of in gration and commitments to the institutions required by the infr structure and those whose ambitions, needs, or responsibilities f overall policy coordination and general foreign and military poli impel them to try to free their hands for independent action.

Lawrence Scheinman

Euratom:
Nuclear Integration in Europe

Originally conceived as a spearhead of the ''relance Européenne''
the mid 1950's, Euratom has reaped a bitter harvest. Expecta-
ns that it would be a successful venture in regional integration
rived from four fundamental premises, all or most of which ulti-
tely proved at least partially false: (1) that as it was a new field
ere would be few vested interests to overcome and little need for
e restructuring of impacted attitudes; (2) that the European
ergy deficit, so prominent at Euratom's outset, would continue
spiral upward making indigenous energy production from nuclear
rces a constant and vital need; (3) that the tremendous expense
volved in extensive nuclear research and development would induce
ntinued and increased nuclear pooling and the development of
mmon and joint ventures in a community framework; and, (4)
at as Euratom was a limited venture, more modest than either
e politically loaded and then defunct European Defence Comnity project or the idea of a general economic union, its prob-
ility for survival and expansion was high. In terms of functional
d neo-functional theory these were reasonably sound premises.
Although structured along the same lines as the EEC and, except
r its separate executive Commission sharing many of the EEC's
stitutions, Euratom has much less successfully weathered the
rms which have beleaguered both regional communities. Euratom

Reprinted from *International Conciliation*, No. 563 (May 1967), with the
rmission of the Carnegie Endowment for International Peace and the author.
wrence Scheinman has written the brief preface to his conclusions for this
ume.

was beset by a series of problems some of which stemmed from t
particularities of the subject matter and the organization itse
others of which would appear to be endemic to functionally spec
international organizations of the vertical-sector type. Shifts in t
nature and accessibility of energy sources very early in Euraton
life weakened one of the principal pillars on which the organizati
had been built. Efforts to create lateral arrangements with the Unit
States for reactor research and construction failed to adequat
invest the organization with new life. At the same time, the dispar
of national inputs and national interests in nuclear programs t
came more evident, and the sum of these disparities rendered co
munity coordination of national nuclear programs nigh impossit
These environmental factors were compounded by the full emerge
of organizational, political and economic-commercial nationali
which further corroded the brittle community organization. A la
of dynamic and resolute leadership on the part of the Eurat
Commission except for a very brief period rounded out the list
organizational impairments. Compared with the record of the Eu
pean Economic Community, Euratom made a very poor showi
Despite the many profound particularistic reasons for the failure
Euratom to live up to its expectations, it still may be asked whetl
it is only that community's fault for failure, or whether failure a
may be related to some of the theoretical premises upon whi
regional integration ventures are based. It is to that issue that we n
turn attention.

.   .   .

Euratom bears the indelible imprint of failure, and it is unde
able that the organization has not been able to cope with the pressu
and problems imposed on it by its constituents and its envir
mental conditions. Before proceeding further, however, it shou
be pointed out that Euratom has recorded a number of succes
and achieved some positive results. A critical question is whetl
the end product justifies the means, or whether the same resu
might not have been attained by other less ponderous means. V
may anticipate our conclusion at this point by stating that E
atom's modest achievements did not demand so vast an operati
measured in terms of administrative structure, money, and ma
power.

Euratom has unquestionably stimulated nuclear research in t
Community, and through the JNRC it has provided a focal po

common research efforts in a number of fields, principally on
ond-generation reactors such as ORGEL, the mainstay of Ispra.
e JNRC has also served as the locus for on-the-job training of
tallurgists, nuclear chemists, and physicists, and has been mainly
ponsible for data collection, automatic translation, and the largely
cessful program on the dissemination of basic nuclear informa-
n throughout the Community. The development of the Central
clear Measurements Bureau at Geel also ranks among successful
ratom ventures.

Despite the difficulties that have developed with the association
tracts and despite the failure of these contracts to coordinate and
vetail national research programs satisfactorily, especially in the
d of fast reactors but elsewhere as well,[1] it is clear that, at first,
association contracts were useful stimulants to broader Comnity research in the field of fast reactors, fusion, and nuclear
pulsion. Nevertheless, the fact remains that the level of achieve-
nt and the extent of common action might have been attained in
er less demanding organizational contexts, perhaps even within
framework of one of the other two supranational European com-
nities. The eventual merger of the three communities is very
ely to bring about just such an organizational pruning. Recent
cussions in the communities regarding general science policy
licate some feeling in the EEC Commission and the European
rliament that all science and technology policy, including the
clear sphere, should be integrated into the broader context of
nomic and industrial policy. Since the latter is under EEC
spices, the implication is that Euratom activities would be incorpo-
ed into a broader general framework entailing a trimming of the
clear organization.[2] Yet it does not follow that even the modest
ratom achievements could have been attained in as loose an
anizational context as the ENEA, which, while not suffering the
piriting and disruptive experience of Euratom, has settled for
ited goals.

Failures have resulted largely from the incapacity of the Commission to
ticipate fully either financially or in terms of personnel in the association
grams. Another example of noncoordination is found in the development of
terials-testing reactors. A Belgian reactor, the BR2, has been supported in
t by a Euratom contract and was intended to serve the entire Community.
pite its existence, France has constructed a comparable reactor, Osiris, thus
licating work and investment in the Community context.

For a discussion, see the statements of De Groote before the European
liament in *Agence Europe*, 24 Oct. 1966.

Up to this point we have been dealing with problems peculiar
Euratom: the specific economic and material environment of t
Community, the problem of national disparities, the development
nuclear nationalism, and the issue of executive leadership. There
another factor that concerns (but would not appear to be peculiar t
Euratom and may be endemic to any organization charged with c
cumscribed, functionally specific tasks — the question of the natu
and scope of the organizational bargaining context. Although Eu
atom lacks the depth of power found in the ECSC, such as t
capacity to give aid for various economic and social purposes,
levies, and borrow or lend funds, it is institutionally identical wi
the EEC, for the Community has a fairly autonomous scope of acti
in the field of external relations and certain proprietary rights wi
respect to basic nuclear materials. Institutionally then, Euratom
not particularly disadvantaged and in certain respects even favore
But if we compare the operational scope of Euratom and the EE
and their framework for constructive activity, the communities a
no longer comparable. While Euratom is confined to the single fie
of nuclear research and development, the EEC encompasses esse
tially all of the economic sectors not specifically subsumed either
Euratom or the ECSC. The only major exception is the energy sect
which is partially incorporated into all three communities.

The full meaning of this difference emerges from a considerati
of policy making. Even if we recognize that EEC tasks are p
marily regulatory and those of Euratom essentially promotion
both communities do seek to develop common policies in their resp
tive fields of activity. The main differences lie in the scope of activi
and the nature of the subject matter. With the benefit of hindsig
a number of interesting observations of theoretical relevance can
made. First, on the issue of scope, there are many reasons why t
EEC has scored impressively in the fields of tariff reduction, fact
movement, harmonization of law, and especially agriculture. In t
last sector, for example, the quality and dynamism of Commissior
Mansholt's leadership, the general agreement of the member sta
that a common policy was necessary, and the intense and unequivo
support for such a policy by a key member state, France (whi
tacitly made progress in agriculture a condition for advance el
where), are all extremely important factors.[3] But explanations ne
not and should not stop here; the bargaining context for EEC poli

---

[3] See Leon N. Linberg, ''Decision-Making and Integration in the Europe
Community,'' *International Organization*, No. 1 (Winter 1965), pp. 56-80.

velopment ought to be taken into account. EEC policies are rarely veloped as isolated sectors; policy decisions are consummated in ckage deals that incorporate national demands across a range of nomic activities. The first agricultural decisions in December 514 were linked to agreement on a community antitrust policy and passage from the first to the second stage of the transition period the establishment of the Common Market. The scope of comnity activity affords the EEC Commission the possibility of ding concessions across economic sectors, of balancing national nands, and of inducing states to accept short-term concessions in expectation of long-term over-all benefits. Even where policy isions are confined to a single sector, participants may bargain for toral concessions to obtain concessions in other sectors.[5]

Not so Euratom; adjustment of competing interests cannot be de by intersectoral bargaining because only a single sector falls hin the competence of the Atomic Community. Hypothetically, it not impossible to reach agreement that goes beyond the position of most reluctant participant in such a context, either as a result of jority voting procedures, or the delegation of increased authority d competence to the community institutions in order to overcome erwise unsolvable problems — a phenomenon that Ernst Haas termed "spill-over."[6] But to achieve this, a single sector requires eptional conditions — politically, economically, and in terms of ernal environment. These were the advantages of the ECSC, which its early years enjoyed favorable external conditions, sustained itical support, and economic conditions that dictated the utility functional sector integration. None of these conditions was ful-

The actual date was 14 Jan. 1962, but the device of "stopping the clock" midnight, 31 Dec. 1961, was introduced to accommodate the French demand the first agricultural decisions had to be agreed to before France would pt passage to the second stage of the transition period — a transition pro- d for in the EEC Treaty, Article 8. The fact that the EEC was able to ize "marathon-type" negotiations, racing against a deadline, provided psy- ogical advantages unavailable to Euratom.

A good argument can be made that Euratom might have gained some ngth from a phased and staged introduction of an atomic energy community. in other words, certain tasks had been specifically related to certain time ods and interrelated with progress or developments in a number of areas of ear energy, Euratom might have been in a stronger position to build coali- s of support and to activate national elites in the sense of developing a munity consensus sufficient to sustain the organization actively and per- ate its goals. However, many variables enter into the situation, and any ments on phasing and staging development must be read in context.

Ernst B. Haas, "International Integration: The European and the Universal cess," *International Organization*, No. 3 (Summer 1961), pp. 366-392.

filled with respect to nuclear energy. The very limitations th
functionalists and neo-functionalists assume to be beneficial
integration proved contributory to the disintegration of Euratom.

Intimately related to this is the nature of the subject matter.
the EEC, short-term concessions in well-established economic secto
might be made with the expectation that in the long run the cor
munity situation will improve and the conceding state will share
the profits of the new situation — states perceive that short-ter
concessions will trigger long-term gains and thus can be made wi
reasonable assuredness that the state has not contracted itself o
of the economic race. Euratom, however, is a new *technologi*
community, highly susceptible to rapid change. Today's resear
contract may be the key to tomorrow's market. Short-term conc
sions in these conditions may easily be perceived as long-run loss
Current low-capacity states like Italy or the smaller Euratom sta
perceive concessions to France or the Federal Republic simply as t
widening of an already unacceptable gap between themselves and t
high-capacity states. The latter, on the other hand, and especia
France, view concessions to low-capacity states as uneconomic allo
tions of limited resources that tend to compromise the nuclear futi
of Europe. This kind of thinking led to the broad coverage of t
fast reactor field by association contracts, even though many observ
felt that such relations with Belgium and the Netherlands were i
necessary and, with Italy, unprofitable. As noted earlier, states w
research contracts have a tendency to distribute material and supp
contracts largely to their national industry; consequently, techni
competence remains compartmentalized. Solution of such proble
by expanding the scope of central institutions, as postulated
integration theory (for example, by granting the Community s
veillance over the allocation of subcontracts), has not been c
templated or, when contemplated, usually rejected: such expans
would be politically unacceptable to France and economically rep
hensible to the Federal Republic's liberal-competitive approach.
has so often been the case, the convergence of French political
terests and the Federal Republic's commercial-economic inter
has had a disintegrative impact.

The problem of reconciling balanced industrial growth ame
participants with the efficient allocation of resources is an acute is
in the integration of underdeveloped areas.[7] In some respe

[7] See Ernst B. Haas and Phillipe C. Schmitter, ''Economics and Differer
Patterns of Political Integration,'' ibid., No. 4 (Autumn 1964), pp. 705-

ratom is less reminiscent of the EEC than it is of Latin American
l African economic communities. Although these communities
 multi-sector and Euratom single sector, like these non-European
ities, Euratom is a community in which there is a giant (in this
e France) among pygmies. Integration theory postulates certain
kground conditions necessary to the success of integration move-
nts, and one of these is the equivalence of size of participating
its.[8] Translated into terms of nuclear capacity, this condition is
ply not met in Euratom, and, judged by the impact of national
parities on general nuclear integration and on the ability of the
mmission to coordinate national nuclear policies, this condition is
extremely important one, especially where single sector integration
oncerned.

There is another dimension to the Euratom experience that raises
e questions about the comprehensiveness and adequacy of current
egration theory. In one of the most recent formulations of integra-
n theory, Ernst Haas and Phillipe Schmitter state:

gration can be conceived as involving the gradual politization of the
rs' purposes which were initially considered "technical" or "noncontro-
ial." Politization implies that the actors, in response to miscalculations
disappointment with respect to the initial purposes, agree to widen the
ctrum of means considered appropriate to attain them . . . that the actors
to resolve their problems so as to upgrade common interests and, in the
cess, delegate more authority to the center.[9]

ey further state that in the European context "our modal pattern
successful politization of economic unions, the element of auto-
ticity . . . is provided by the internal logic of industrialism,
ralism, and democracy."[10] These formulations prompt several
ervations.

t is evident from all that has been said before that in the case of
ratom, miscalculation, disappointment, or unfulfilled expectations
not result in an increased allocation of authority to central in-
utions. Politization of technical issues certainly took place, but
itization consisted in the hardening of national positions and
reased national determination to exercise ever closer control over
central institutions. Politization, in short, did not have an ex-
sive impact either with regard to the scope of activity or the
ns at the disposal of the central institutions. The Euratom trend
been toward intergovernmentalism, not toward supranationalism.

Ibid., p. 711.
Ibid., p. 707.
Ibid., p. 726.

This is perhaps best exemplified by the change of voting patt
between the first and second common research programs: in
former, research orientation not involving increased over-all exper
tures could be determined by qualified majority; in the lat
unanimity is required for any change. It required more than a y
to ''resolve'' the 1964 research program crisis, and central insti
tional authority or capacity was not advanced one whit. The pres
crisis remains unresolved, and the member states show increa
inclination to go their separate ways. In terms of the pattern
decision-making, there has been no upgrading of common intere
The 1964 crisis was broken only to prevent the total paralysis c
program that, in any event, would expire two years later. No st
wished to assume responsibility for outright destruction of the C
munity, the preference being apparently for phased asphyxiati
The important point is that crisis and politization have led to
integration, not integration.

It is difficult to answer the question *why* spillover has not wor
in the case of Euratom. Before turning to one of the more cru
factors from our point of view, several reasons might be advance(
partial explanations. First, if Euratom were to fail, it would
mean the end of regional integration in Europe, for there are still
EEC and the ECSC. Thus, states can afford to treat Euratom di
ently than they might if it were the sole regional integration vent
Second, no single state has a major stake in the success of the org
ization (unlike the situation in the EEC where France in one sec
and the Federal Republic in another made satisfaction of their
spective interests the *quid pro quo* for further over-all advance),
strong converging interests create the framework for bargain
power and institutional maneuverability. In the third place, si
1962 the Euratom Commission has been unwilling or unable or b
to take any important initiatives of its own, to seize the opportuni
inherent in crisis, or to further the cause of integration. When
the wake of the 1964 research crisis, the Commission did make
attempt to extricate the Community from its difficulties, it could
marshall the support or confidence of the member states, and
Commission remained peripheral to the final settlement. This
trasts sharply with the EEC Commission, which, if anything,
too hasty in taking initiatives (for example, during the crisis of J
1965).[11]

[11] See, for example, Leon N. Lindberg, ''Integration as a Source of Stres
the European Community System,'' ibid., No. 2 (Spring 1966), pp. 233-265

A fourth reason why Euratom did not follow a progressive inte-
tive pattern relates to the subject matter itself — atomic energy.
ree considerations come to mind in this regard: the problem of
tional security, political-economic interests, and the strategy of
egration. There is a French phrase that neatly sums up the first
nsideration — the problems of using atomic energy for sector inte-
ation in order to achieve political union as distinguished from
orporating the sector in a framework of an already agreed politi-
union: "*qui dit l'atome dit la bombe.*" It is quite reasonable to
derscore the relationship of nuclear power to military power and
tional security. Although in the case of Euratom not too much
ess should be placed on this factor, it is undeniable that the exist-
ce of a major military effort in one of the participant states
eserved and perhaps enlarged the gap of national nuclear inputs,
d that there is, because of the military importance, a symbolic and
ychological mystique attached to nuclear energy in general. Yet
 must bear in mind that nuclear integration never proceeded far
ough for the military issue to become important beyond the above
o points. Even granted the military problem, it may be argued
at there is enough separability between peaceful and military uses
 atomic energy and enough areas of purely peaceful development
or example, power, propulsion, desalination, and industrial and
ricultural research) to create a *champ de manoeuvre* for operation
 the spillover principle without encroaching on national security.
e barriers to integration were not fashioned in the defense
inistries.

The second and third considerations are interrelated. A technical
 economic community that aspires to serve as a vehicle of political
tegration — the *raison d'être* for the regional supranational ven-
res so far as the "Europeans" are concerned — cannot long re-
ain on the periphery of the political or go very far toward its goal
eled only by the *esprit européen* of technical experts in charge of
e organization. Some analysts allude to the distinction between
high" and "low" politics and argue that the pattern of integration
 more appropriate to the latter than it is to the former.[12] Euratom
stifies both to the tenuousness of the distinction between the polit-
al and the non-political and to the breadth of the "high" politics
tegory.

The issue of strategy raises the twofold question. If an attempt is

[12] See Stanley Hoffmann, "Discord in Community: The North Atlantic Area
a Partial International System," *ibid.*, No. 3 (Summer 1963), pp. 521-549.

made to achieve a *political* community through the integration
functionally specific sectors, is this a reasonable expectation, and a
all sectors equally suitable to the task? While the first question m
fall outside the scope of our inquiry, the second does not. T
nuclear subject is linked to a political objective and was at first cc
ceived as a relatively non-controversial stepping stone to that er
The assumption is one of a degree of separability from the mai
stream of political controversy — that the stepping stone, thou;
linked to, still remains, at least for a time, separable from the pl;
form to which it leads.

If coal and steel, as well as a significant number of other econom
sectors covered by the EEC, were selected for their partially pol
icized qualities, atomic energy has not provided such an advantage
Atomic development in any of its significant forms (outside of
limited number of areas that are not inherently expansive, includi
information dissemination, documentation, or the establishment
basic health norms) was never really outside the scope of "higl
politics or on the periphery of the political. Given its environment
context, atomic energy has not proven effective as a vehicle of fur
tional integration. What Euratom has lacked and what its leade
ship was never able to develop was an overarching, continuo
political commitment to achieve nuclear integration. In short, t]
controversial nature of the subject, heightened by the intensity
national divergencies, made the nuclear sector eminently unsa
isfactory as a stepping stone to political community.

The EEC and the ECSC have been able to survive the modulatio1
or even the total weakening of such commitment for different reason
the ECSC because of its functional autonomy as long as enviro:
mental conditions remain satisfactory; the EEC because of its va
scope of operation that ensures at least partial continuing commi
ment. As for Euratom, whether the issue is research, supply, •
industrial orientation and policy, it has always been essentially
political issue. The French demand for European nuclear indepen(
ence in the power reactor field, Italian demands for balanced tecl
nological and industrial growth in the Community, and the Feder.

[13] Where, as in CERN, nuclear energy has been the subject of cooperati
action, it has not contributed to integration or movement toward political cor
munity in any currently recognizable sense. In the case of CERN, activity
highly circumscribed, and politics is irrelevant to organizational tasks, b'
expectations are considerably lower than in the case of Euratom.

public's demand for commercial and industrial freedom are all
litical-level issues that come within the scope of "high" politics.
we consider the more clearly internal economic issues, such as the
anting of "common enterprise" status to various industrial enter-
ises in the Community or the allocation of research contracts, we
d that basic differences in needs, demands, and interests, reflected
the key factor of national disparities, have raised questions that
ve gone to the very core of Euratom and demand political, not
hnical, guidance. Yet, for reasons of politics and nuclear na-
nalism, conflict resolution has not been sought through the medium
increasing central authority.

The Euratom experience raises the question of the validity of the
nctionalist assumption that technical experts can achieve consensus
ere politicians fail. National technicians almost always have viewed
estions of common policies through nationally tinted glasses. To
e categories of organizational, political, and economic nationalism,
e might add the concept of technical nationalism in order to
commodate the problem of the limited horizons of technical experts.
ench experts, wedded to the virtues of natural uranium reactors,
ve been unable to come to terms with other national experts con-
nced of the virtues of enriched uranium reactors. For a number
years neither reactor held unassailable advantages over the other,
d technicians remained rooted in their national programmatic pref-
ences. More recently, the United States enriched uranium reactor
s achieved a breakthrough and proved to be more economical than
natural uranium rival. French technicians, however, are not pre-
red to shelve their huge investment and large-scale reactor program
d to convert to a system that would not only shift commercial
vantages to other Community countries but would also entail de-
ndence on foreign sources for fissile material; the latter creates the
ry dependence that French political doctrine shuns. We can do no
ore here than indicate that technical decisions may require political
tion to break technocratic deadlock.

Some of Euratom's problems might have been overcome in the
nse of positive spillover if certain conditions had prevailed: if
omic energy were part of a larger enterprise, that is, part of the
EC rather than of a single sector organization; or if external
ents had conspired to support the Euratom venture. We have
ready discussed the former condition; the latter exposes one of the
ortcomings of integration theory, the tendency to assume self-

contained inertia.[14] The first category of Euratom problems comes
mind here: the changed energy situation and the consequent (
emphasis of short-term needs. We need not belabor the point, f
we have already indicated how this change undercut one of the ba:
nonpolitical reationales for Euratom. However, the impact that su
a change might have on the integrative process must be stressed. \
can hypothesize with a certain degree of confidence that if the ener
situation had remained critical during the first several years
Euratom's existence, the member states would have been forced
increase the scope of activity of the central institutions and perha
also to have narrowed the disparities gap, thus facilitating the ta
of central coordination. In other words, spillover might have work
Once process and activity became internalized and routinized,
change in external circumstance might have been less disastrous f
the organization, although the experience of the ECSC in 1959
failing to acquire the necessary authority to deal with the coal gl
and the more recent difficulties in the coal and steel industries th
have nagged at the ECSC intrude somewhat on this hypothesis.
any event, Euratom would have been in a stronger position than
is today to sustain itself and to induce further national action in
common framework.

However, the other side of the coin should not be disregarded. T
includes the importance to the Community of United States suppo
demonstrated by refusals of Washington to renew bilateral agr
ments with Euratom states after their expiration, delivery of imp
tant quantities of fissile material through the Euratom supp
agency, the granting of special concessions on inspection and contr
(thus preserving to some extent the sovereign trappings of the me:
ber states), and the conclusion of large-scale research and react
agreements with the Community.[15] Each of these factors has be
significant to Euratom; all together they have furnished the Co
munity with resources it could not have acquired from its membe
In short, it has proved impossible to treat integration as a self-cc
tained process.

[14] For a discussion of some of these problems as applied to non-Europe
integrating contexts, see Joseph S. Nye, ''Patterns and Catalysts in Regio
Integration,'' *International Organization*, No. 4 (Autumn 1965), pp. 870-8

[15] At the time of this writing, it is not clear whether the proposed draft n
proliferation treaty will have an adverse impact on Euratom's safeguard a
control system. One of the possibilities is the transfer of these functions to ◆
IAEA and the application of uniform rules for all signatory states to ◆
prospective treaty.

EPILOGUE

We might take advantage of our theoretical discussion to close on a ore optimistic note. The European states are increasingly worried day about the "technological gap" developing between Europe and e United States in such crucial fields as space, electronics, and ta-processing. In the spring of 1965, France took the initiative of commending the development of a European scientific policy. Last ar, Italy postulated the development of a European technological mmunity that would expand to transatlantic dimensions. The EEC mmission recommended action in this field at the European Par- mentary Assembly in October 1966.[16] On 23 January 1967, Prime inister Wilson, in his strongest public statement on the United ingdom's intention to negotiate entry into the European Common arket, stressed the technological problem and his country's pre- redness to bring "all that British technology has to offer" to the uropean communities.[17]

The organizational context for such common actions has not yet en discussed, and the Gaullist preference for cooperative ventures ch as the Franco-British Concorde project or the European uncher Development Organization (a preference probably shared r the United Kingdom), as distinguished from supranationally rected common policies, raises many problems. Some Europeans, wever, have suggested linking a number of scientific and tech- logical sectors under Euratom auspices.[18] The acceptance of such linkage would allow Euratom to retain its institutional identity en after the merger of the three community executives, which is w expected to occur in late 1967. It is evident that some of the oblems discussed might be overcome in these new conditions; the ternal stimulus to continuous creative action still appears to be esent, and it is possible that the limited bargaining context prob- m will recede. These conditions might herald the rebirth of a styled scientific community that could serve as a new empirical sting ground for political and economic integration.

[16] *Agence Europe*, 19 Oct. 1966.
[17] *New York Times*, 24 Jan. 1967.
[18] See, for example, De Groote's statement in *Agence Europe*, 19 Oct. 1966.

SUGGESTIONS FOR FURTHER READING

Beloff, Max, *The United States and the Unity of Europe* (New York, 196:

Brzezinski, Zbigniew K., *Alternative to Partition* (New York, 1965).

Camps, Miriam, *European Unification in the Sixties* (New York, 1966).

Clark, W. Hartley, *The Politics of the Common Market* (Englewood Cli N.J., 1967).

Curtis, Michael, *Western European Integration* (New York, 1965).

Deutsch, Karl W., "Integration and Arms Control in the European Politi Environment," *American Political Science Review*, LX (June 196(pp. 354-65.

Deutsch, Karl W., Lewis J. Edinger, Roy C. Macridis, and Richard Merritt, *France, Germany and the Western Alliance* (New York, 196:

Diebold, William, *The Schuman Plan: A Study in Economic Cooperatic 1950-1959* (New York, 1959).

Duroselle, J. B., "General DeGaulle's Europe and Jean Monnet's Europ *The World Today*, 22 (January 1966), pp. 1-12.

Etzioni, Amitai, "European Unification and Perspectives on Sovereignt} *Daedalus*, 92 (Summer 1963), pp. 498-520.

Feld, Werner, *The Court of the European Communities: New Dimensions International Adjudication* (The Hague, 1964).

Graubard, Stephen R. (ed.), *A New Europe?* (Boston, 1964).

Haas, Ernst B., *The Uniting of Europe* (Stanford, Calif., 1958)

Hallstein, Walter, "Some of our faux problems in the EEC," *The Wor Today*, 21 (January 1965), pp. 10-23.

Hoffmann, Stanley, "Europe's Identity Crisis: Between the Past and Am(ica," *Daedalus*, 93 (Fall 1964), pp. 1244-97.

Inglehart, Ronald, "An End to European Integration?" *American Politi(Science Review*, LXI (March 1967), pp. 91-105.

Kitzinger, Uwe, *The Politics and Economics of European Integration* (N(York, 1963).

Krause, Lawrence B. (ed.), *The Common Market* (Englewood Cliffs, N.(1964).

Lindberg, Leon N., *The Political Dynamics of European Economic Integr tion* (Stanford, Calif., 1963).

——, "Decision Making and Integration in the European Community *International Organization*, XIX (Winter 1965), pp. 56-80.

Liska, George, *Europe Ascendent* (Baltimore, 1964).

Polach, Jaroslav, *Euratom: Its Background, Issues and Economic Implic tions* (Dobbs Ferry, N.Y., 1964).

Robertson, A. H., *The Council of Europe* (New York, 2nd ed., 1961).

Scheingold, Stuart A., *The Rule of Law in European Integration* (N(Haven, 1965).

Scheinman, Lawrence, "Some Preliminary Notes on Bureaucratic Relatio ships in the European Economic Community," *International Organiz tion*, XX (Autumn 1966), pp. 750-73.

Schmitt, Hans A., *The Path to European Union* (Baton Rouge, 1962).

Schopflin, George A., "EFTA: the Other Europe," *International Affai* 40 (October 1964), pp. 674-84.

tis, Jean, "ECE in the Emerging European System," *International Conciliation,* 561 (January 1967), pp. 5-70.

n der Beugel, Ernst H., *From Marshall Aid to Atlantic Partnership*
(Amsterdam, 1966).

n Bonsdorff, Goran, "Regional Cooperation of the Nordic Countries,"
Cooperation and Conflict, I (1965), pp. 32-38.

ndorf, Walter, "Monnet and the Action Committee: The Formative
Period of the European Communities," *International Organization,* XIX
(Autumn 1965), pp. 885-912.

rcher, Arnold, *The Struggle to Unite Europe* (New York, 1958).

PART FOUR

THE POLITICS OF ECONOMIC REGIONALISM IN LESS-DEVELOPED AREAS

Miguel S. Wionczek

Requisites for
Viable Economic Integration

The main body of what might be called the doctrine of regional
economic integration in Latin America was built, although not
systematically, on the writings of Dr. Raul Prebisch and certain
studies of the U.N. Economic Commission for Latin America (ECLA)
published during the course of the last fifteen years. Unfortunately,
little of this material is known outside the confines of the Latin
American economic profession. The integration doctrine elevates to
the multinational plane the thesis that economic development is
impossible without industrialization. According to this thesis, the
sustained growth of an underdeveloped economy depends on the
degree to which an active process of substitution of imports by
domestic production can be promoted, so as to extend the country's
capacity to import to cover the acquisition of an optimum volume of
capital goods and technology.

At the beginning of the 1950's, the process of import substitution
in the field of consumer manufactures in the larger countries of Latin
America had just about reached its limit, and the import capacity of
almost all the republics in the region ceased to grow at the rate
needed to finance the expanding cost of industrialization. This last
phenomenon is owing, among other causes, to the exceedingly rapid
technological progress made by the industrially advanced countries.
In addition, the development problem became complicated in the
region by the population explosion and the social tensions common

Reprinted with the permission of the author and publisher from Miguel
Wionczek (ed.), *Latin American Economic Integration* (New York, Frederick
A. Praeger, 1966). The author has revised and updated the essay for this volume.

to backward economies having an extremely inadequate distributi
of income[1] — tensions that have been brought to an even higher pit
because of the demonstration effect that the levels of welfare
world economic centers exert on the peripheral societies.

As an alternative to stagnation, it was logical that the idea
economic integration should arise. Its proponents maintain that t
creation of a regional market in response to the liberation of tra
currents among the nations in the area, the subsequent advanta
taken of economies of scale, and the coordination of national indu
trialization policies would enable a more rational mobilization
unemployed production factors and lead to an acceleration of Lat
America's economic growth. According to the same school of though
the principal obstacles that, in the recent past, have kept the
potentially available production factors from being incorporated in
the development process are the limitations of the national marke
and the imperfect functioning of international trade on a world-wi
basis.

As affirmed in one of the ECLA studies preceding the signing, i
1960, of the Montevideo Treaty and the General Treaty for Centr.
American Economic Integration, Latin America's basic problems

... can be solved only if the following fundamental fact is recognized: Lat
America, however great the external assistance it receives, however high t
rate at which its exports expand — and they cannot do so very rapidly -
will be unable to carry out its development plans, will be unable even
regain the rate of growth it achieved in the ten post-war years, unless
makes a sustained effort to establish within its own territory the capit:
goods industries of which it is in such urgent need today, and which it wi
require on a large scale during the next quarter of a century. ... In ord
to produce these capital goods and develop all the intermediate goods indu
tries required in order to launch these highly complex dynamic industri
... Latin America needs a common market.[2]

Several factors lie at the root of these economic arguments in favo
of integration: Latin America's reaction to the ever-widening di
ference between the levels of development and welfare in the worl
and the state of recurrent crises in which the region's economy find
itself; dissatisfaction — shared in increasing degree by other unde
developed regions — with international economic relations, based i

[1] Little is known about income distribution patterns in Latin Americ:
ECLA's *Estudios sobre las districubión del ingreso en América Latina*, release
in March 1967 (E/CN.12/770) represents a pioneering effort in this field.

[2] *The Latin American Common Market* (Mexico City: United Nations, 5
II. 1959; G.4), p. 1.

hat Gunnar Myrdal calls "a false principle of equality" among
ie unequal; and an awareness that, in the present world of political
id economic blocs, for bargaining power the weak countries of the
irious underdeveloped regions must depend on the possibility of
nifying their criteria and policies over against the industrial
nters of West and East.

In terms of historical experience, the aims pursued by the advo-
ites of Latin American economic integration and the policies they
ropose are hardly original. They are similar to the objectives sought
r the British colonies in North America when they obtained their
idependence from the metropolis at the end of the eighteenth cen-
iry. They also recall France's purposes in the face of Great Britain's
idustrial progress during the first quarter of the last century, and,
ot long thereafter, the establishment of the Zollverein in Germany
i the face of the economic hegemony of England and France. The
milarity between the present attempts at integrating national
:onomics of the underdeveloped regions into larger groupings and
ie development, up to the mid-nineteenth century, of national states
arting from small economic and political units should not come as a
irprise to those who are persuaded that "we are all aware of the
ict that we live in the most catastrophically revolutionary age that
en have ever faced."[3]

Nor is it surprising that attempts to establish a theoretical basis
ir the doctrine of Latin American integration, and of other integra-
on plans in the underdeveloped regions, should clash with the
eoclassic theory of international trade that originated in the indus-
ialized countries and was extended to the field of economic integra-
on in the comparatively recent past (the early 1950's). The same
iing happened at the close of the eighteenth century, when the
evelopment needs of what then were the peripheries of the Atlantic
orld encountered the classical theory of trade that had been worked
it in England. The current debates between the Marshall-Viner-
aberler and Nurkse-Myrdal-Prebisch schools, between the advocates
` free trade and the proponents of inward-directed development
vho transfer the "infant industry" concept from a country to a
gion) are not exclusively economic. Nor were economic arguments
ie sole basis for the no less violent controversy of a century and a
ilf ago between the economists of industrially advanced England

[3] Barbara Ward, *The Rich Nations and the Poor Nations* (New York: W. W.
orton, 1962), p. 13.

and the Alexander Hamilton and Friedrich List school,[4] whic
pleaded the case for the then underdeveloped United States ar
Germany.

The theoretical precepts on international trade advocated by tl
neoclassical school and its disciples cannot be applied to situatio
prevailing in today's world peripheries, for the simple reason tha
the representatives of the neoclassic school have limited interest i
the general problems of economic growth, nor do they take int
account the nature of the underdeveloped world and of its politic
social problems.[5] In consequence:

In contrast to the general richness and synthesized character of much
pure theory in its comparative statics, dynamic propositions in internation
trade are comparatively few and bear no trace of any uniform design, ea
having been developed in virtual isolation. Dynamic trade theory, where
exists, has grown up in an essentially *ad hoc* fashion and has witnessed no
of the interaction of analysis which usually accompanies the developme
of an area of knowledge and produces a common design, a unifying frame

All this would be relatively innocuous, albeit intellectually unsati
factory, if the matter at hand had only to do with speculative exe
cises indulged in by economically advanced countries. However, tl
problem becomes the basis of what J. K. Galbraith calls the "conve
tional wisdom,"[7] which, in turn, determines the doctrinal positio

---

[4] Sidney Dell, in his *Trade Blocs and Common Markets* (New York: Alfr
A. Knopf, 1963), pp. 207-208, quotes a very interesting statement by Alexand
Hamilton, which, with a few slight changes, could have originated today i
Latin America. Back in 1791, Hamilton wrote: "The United States cann
exchange with Europe on equal terms; and the want of reciprocity would rend
them the victim of a system which should induce them to confine themselves
agriculture, and refrain from manufactures. A constant and increasing necessit
on their part, for the commodities of Europe, and only a partial and occasion
demand for their own, in return, could not but expose them to a state of in
poverishment compared with the opulence to which their political and natur
advantages authorize them to aspire. . . . If Europe will not take from us tl
products of our soil, upon terms consistent with our interest, the natural remed
is to contract, as fast as possible, our wants of her."

[5] The proceedings of the international conference on trade theory, convoke
in the autumn of 1961 in Brissago, Switzerland, are meaningful in this co
nection. Sir Roy Harrod, one of the editors of these proceedings, pointed o
that the discussions had revealed "how radical a change in concepts is require
by the essential nature of growth theory, as contrasted with statics or com
parative statics." See International Economic Association, *International Tra
Theory in a Developing World* (New York: St. Martin's Press, 1963), p. xi

[6] J. Bhagwati, "The Pure Theory of International Trade," *The Econom
Journal*, LXXIV, No. 293 (March, 1964), 48.

[7] J. K. Galbraith, *The Affluent Society* (Boston: Houghton Mifflin, 1958)
chap. ii.

the industrial countries against the rest of the world and is
ansmitted through the imitation mechanism to the intellectual elite
the underdeveloped countries. When, in the name of these "con-
ntional truths," the underdeveloped regions are offered a series of
opositions concerning economic integration programs (which, for
at matter, are not longer followed very strictly, even in the coun-
ies in which they originated), there is a grave risk that the poor
gions, by accepting these precepts, would close one of the few roads
maining to them leading out of their situation of stagnation so
aught with social and political dangers.

Among the criteria that the advanced countries used to prescribe
til very recently for the underdeveloped world's integration pro-
ams, the following are particularly worthy of note:

1. Even admitting that regional integration in the underdeveloped
eas can increase the welfare of the participating countries — which,
cording to the neoclassic school, is by no means a certainty — the
sence of integration consists of the freeing of regional trade.

2. In order for a customs union in developing countries not to
ve harmful effects on such nations, as well as on the world economy,
degree of common protection for the participants should be pro-
ded for, no greater than the average existing formerly at the
tional level. The union should also establish a firm commitment
r the complete freedom of movement of all production factors.

3. Within the framework of a customs union, market forces should
left at liberty, so that they may determine the new allocation of
oduction factors on the basis of comparative advantage.

4. Since the objective of a customs union should be a more efficient
nctioning of competitive forces, any action tending to limit them
e.g., industrial-specialization agreements — would foster the emer-
nce of monopolistic situations, distort trade within the union itself,
d eventually lead to welfare losses.

5. Although it might be advisable for economic policies to be co-
dinated within the union to some extent, with the exception of a
mmon tariff this should not disturb the structure of existing
onomic relations with the rest of the world. It would be highly
dvisable, for example, to establish regional payments systems,
ce they would have a negative effect on free convertibility on a
rld-wide scale.

From a perusal of the literature published to date on the subject
economic integration in Latin America, it might be deduced that
position defined by these criteria has already been successfully

refuted. The fact is, however, that an analysis of the actual policie and concrete attitudes adopted within and without the region regard ing this matter does not support so optimistic a conclusion. In prac tice, the influence of the doctrines summarized above is felt at al times and in connection with integration problems of every type.

If the representatives of "conventional wisdom" were bette acquainted with the real world and realized that, instead of helpin solve today's problems in Latin America, their position creates other that are even more serious for the future, they would readily perceiv that their proposals have only an extremely tenuous bearing on th growth needs of underdeveloped areas. Hence, it is not a matter o abandoning a presumably optimum situation in favor of less advar tageous alternatives, but of seeking solutions that can prevent progressive worsening of the existing conditions.

The freeing of trade cannot be the sole objective of a customs unio in an underdeveloped area. In the first place, in the light of it present low levels, trade needs more to be promoted than freed Secondly, differences in the economic development levels within single region in these areas are much greater than those existin within the developed sector of the world economy.[8] Consequentl: unless the member countries all had comparable levels of unde development, a customs union in an underdeveloped environmen centering exclusively on the freeing of regional trade, would functio much after the fashion of trade between the industrial centers an the peripheries. The result would be an increase in the economi distance within this union in favor of those countries which ar better endowed with resources and whose acquired advantages ar superior. The history of two customs unions in Africa — the Eas African Common Market (Kenya, Uganda, and Tanzania) and th: of the recently dissolved Federation of Rhodesia and Nyasaland – demonstrates this truth conclusively.[9] Or reference might be mad

---

[8] The difference between the economic-development levels reached by Boliv and Paraguay, on the one hand, and Brazil and Argentina, on the other, is good deal greater than that separating any pair of developed countries in t Northern Hemisphere. The same phenomenon is even more accentuated in Afric

[9] The problems of tensions arising in East Africa from the free trade amor three "unequal partners" are treated in detail in Joseph S. Nye, Jr., *Pa Africanism and East African Integration* (Cambridge: Harvard Universi Press, 1965), Philip Ndegwa, *The Common Market and Development in Ea Africa* (Nairobi: East African Publishing House, 1965) and R. H. Green ar K. G. V. Krishna, *Economic Co-operation in Africa — Retrospect and Prospe* (Nairobi: London: Oxford University Press, 1966).

o an even more familiar case: the economic results of the unification f Italy one hundred years ago.

If the purpose of a customs union of poor countries is to promote conomic development, and if the latter is defined as diversification nduced in the production structure and in industrialization, a union night very well need more protection than that available to the par- icipants individually prior to the establishment of the union. This ituation would occur in the event that union-inspired economies of cale were to permit, under a certain margin of protection, an under- aking of productive activities that would be out of the question if onfined to the national framework of the member countries, e.g., vhen the size of the new market renders feasible the transition from he assembly stage to the production of certain durable and heavy nanufactures.[10] When considering a customs union for industrializa- ion purposes between two countries whose industrial sectors do not 'et exist, it is easy to refute *ad absurdum* the demand for a common xternal tariff equal to the average domestic duty rates in force.)bviously, a customs union in an underdeveloped area should not)e forced to maintain a common level of protection *no greater* than hat which each country has had previously. The common external ariff of a union will, in any case, be *less* than the national tariffs that vould be needed to permit each member the separate achievement of he level of development that the establishment of a union should nake possible.

As stated earlier, to leave the allocation of production factors ex- lusively to the free interplay of market forces would be equivalent o concentrating development on the more advanced countries among he union membership. Such a result would immediately run afoul f the prodevelopment pressures existing in the remaining union ssociates. Owing to the demonstration effect, the intensity of such pressures is perhaps greater in the extremely underdeveloped coun- ries than in those which have already traveled a certain distance oward the take-off stage. From an academic point of view, it might

[10] Sidney Dell is probably the only writer on customs unions who calls atten- ion to the following paradox: The present structure of the protection systems n effect in the majority of countries under development would permit them, in ase a union is established, to offer considerable concessions for competitive products from the area that they do not need, but allows scarcely any concession t all on goods that they do not produce and that are vital to development — imply because existing customs duties on these items are practically nil. See)ell's essay in this volume and his *Trade Blocs and Common Markets,* cited arlier in this essay.

be feasible to defend the proposition that, "A regional free-trad area [in an underdeveloped area] might increase inequality insid the region. . . . It should not, however, be assumed that an increas of inequality is necessarily bad, provided that the least favore become just a little better off; an increase of inequality may be just fied if it is the best way of getting quick progress in the region a a whole."[11] However, considering the political actualities of ou times, such an attitude is equivalent to asking for the impossible.

If, as appears to be the case, the integration program founde exclusively on the freeing of trade and on the *laissez faire* polic within the union cannot ensure reciprocity of union benefits for a participants, such a program is doomed to failure. Extremely unde developed countries have had such regrettable experiences in thei relations with the rest of the world, based on the false principle o equality, that it would be vain to try to induce them to enter int new agreements, this time regional ones, in which they would ru the risk that inequality within the area would become even mor pronounced. On the other hand, if they remain aloof from thes dangers, they may find themselves condemned to perpetual inferiorit and poverty. All this gives rise to the highly complicated problem c how to avoid intraregional conflicts and schisms that would under mine the objectives of economic regionalism and the intended con munity of interests of the underdeveloped sector of the worl economy.

Those who would entrust the fate of a customs union of countrie in process of development to the forces of free competition are en deavoring, quite superficially, to extend to the rest of the worl

[11] Sir Roy Harrod, in a review of Dell's book, cited above, published in *Th Economic Journal*, LXXIII, No. 292 (December, 1963), 708.

[12] Bolivia's postponement of joining LAFTA for six years, Ecuador's earl threats to withdraw from the association and the rebellion of Paraguay, Bolivi and Ecuador against the accelerated trade liberalization within LAFTA at th LAFTA Foreign Ministers meeting, held in Asunción, Paraguay in August, 1967 are cases in point. Moreover, the East African Common Market has almos broken up since its more underdeveloped members, Tanzania and Uganda, wer convinced that almost all the advantages of the customs union established mor than a quarter of a century ago have gone to Kenya. Although it cannot b demonstrated that Kenya has developed within the union at Tanzania an Uganda's expense, there is no doubt whatsoever that the benefits received b the latter two were a great deal more modest than those accruing to the forme Consequently, pressures by Tanzania and Uganda against the customs unio increased greatly after the decolonization of East Africa. The common marke was saved in mid-1967 only by considerable concessions offered by Kenya to he two less-developed neighbors under the new Treaty for East African Cooperatio which enters into force on December 1, 1967.

ctrines based on certain historical experience accumulated in very
nited fashion and under substantially different circumstances by
day's economically advanced countries. To reject all attempts
thin the scope of an underdeveloped economic union, rationally
d allowing for political exigencies, on the grounds that such an
deavor is harmful and conducive to monopolistic situations, would,
ce again, be indicative of a lack of knowledge of present-day
ality.[13]

The real choice of alternatives that an economic union in Latin
merica, Asia, or Africa must make, insofar as concerns the indus-
al activities representing the motive force behind development,
s between spontaneous monopolies and oligopolies, on the one
nd, and monopolies and oligopolies controlled by union authorities,
the other. Perfect competition is an extremely rare phenomenon
en in the advanced countries, and it should be recognized that it
a good deal scarcer in the rest of the world. The most effective
ay of controlling monopolistic tendencies that arise in the industrial
d service sectors in underdeveloped zones consists of promoting
e emergence of "countervailing powers," in the sense that Gal-
aith uses this expression.[14] Expansion of the domestic market to
fairly broad region or zone, social change stimulated by the process
rapid development, and the modernization of the state itself
nitially as underdeveloped as the economy and society) are the
e means of braking monopolistic tendencies, and that in varying
gree. Those who maintain that industrial specialization mechanisms
tablished by agreement are essential to the operation of an economic
ion of underdeveloped countries are not necessarily attempting to
omote monopolies. Their aim is, rather, to limit the waste of scarce
oduction factors, insofar as possible, and to create conditions
nducive to the progressive control of monopolistic situations and
e consequent attenuation of their negative aspects.

Given the fact that underdeveloped regions need regional devices
at are much more dynamic than those emerging in the already
veloped world, the establishment of a customs union in the under-
veloped sphere will bring with it the creation of a series of eco-
mic-policy mechanisms that, from the standpoint of traditional

---

[3] Such arguments were used by the United States against the Regime for
egration Industries, established in Central America in 1958 at the early stage
the Central American Common Market.

[4] See J. K. Galbraith, *American Capitalism: The Concept of Countervailing
wer* (Boston: Houghton Mifflin, 1956).

theory, appear to be heterodox. Such mechanisms must seek 1
eliminate the numerous obstacles that originate in the present syste
of world trade and are opposed to the expansion of intraregiona
economic relations, and should likewise assure members of a fa
share of the benefits derived from customs-union operations. Sin
association in an economic union involves partial abdication
national sovereignty, and since nationalism is one of the princip
forces of action in underdeveloped countries, integration movemen
face a very complex problem: How can the need for multinationa
cooperation be reconciled with the demands of each nation's intern
politics, motivated by the sometimes sound and sometimes perver
pressures of economic nationalism?

In the light of these considerations, and keeping in mind that r
economic and political theory on customs unions applicable to unde
developed regions has yet been formulated, it should be helpful 1
draft a brief outline of the conditions that an integration progra
should meet in order to avoid predestination to failure.

The foundation of the integration program must be a custon
union or a common market that, by definition and from the outse
entails the commitment to coordinate the trade policy of the ass
ciate countries vis-à-vis the rest of the world. In such a union,
would appear to be necessary to free the bulk of *traditional* intr
regional trade immediately and set up mechanisms for the progressi
liberalization of various new product groups, taking into accou
the relative significance of those production sectors in terms of t
common development of the area. The system of exceptions shou
be quite rigid, being limited to certain agricultural products f
domestic consumption and to such manufacturing activities as weig
heavily in the industrial product of the member countries at the tin
the union is established. If necessary, by means of special prior agre
ments in which diverse criteria should be taken into account — amor
them, possibly, reciprocity — certain of the excepted items cou
remain outside the liberalization program even after the custon
union is fully organized.

The decision to reach the customs-union stage in progressi
fashion should be accompanied by the immediate creation of
regional payments agency designed to: (1) promote transactions i
area currencies; (2) eliminate the need for financial dealings throug
intermediary countries located outside the zone; (3) provide cred
for the member countries (prudently limiting it to instances of tra
sitory disequilibrium in their over-all balance of payments); an

) serve as an instrument to enable the monetary authorities in the
ea to maintain periodical contact with each other.

In view of the differences existing at the time the union is created,
th respect to both development levels and the availability of pro-
iction factors, neither the freeing of trade nor the functioning of
payments mechanism can ensure equal benefits for all the member
untries. Thus, the problem of reciprocity appears to be the thorniest
d most difficult one of all, for it involves a concept that is political,
well as economic, and hence defies measurement. In the stages
at preceded the signing of the Montevideo Treaty, ECLA advo-
ted the introduction within the liberalization mechanisms of ele-
ents that would ensure the highest possible degree of trade
uilibrium within the zone. The treaty itself contains clauses that
able the acceleration or attenuation of the rate of liberalization in
e case of countries that suffer from chronic maladjustment of their
mmerce with the area. However, such attempts to relate reciprocity
clusively to total intraregional trade (in keeping with the original
ea) or to the new interchange promoted by the association (as
pulated in the Montevideo Treaty) do not appear to have given
tisfactory results, quite probably because they took into account
ly one aspect of the integration program. The concept of reci-
ocity has to be a broader one and might well comprise four essential
pects of integration: balance of payments; over-all growth; indus-
ialization; and the relative level of development.

In this way, a completely new definition of equitable participation
a customs union would be established. This definition would have
start with the assumption that, in order to operate efficiently, an
tegration program should be based on an aggregate of regional
d national policies that prevent the emergence of severe disequilib-
im in intraregional trade; guarantee comparable long-term rates of
velopment; and, at the same time, shorten the economic distance
thin the zone and assure that all members in the union will partici-
te in the industrialization process.

Assuming that it were feasible to reconcile these objectives without
ntralizing economic policy decisions in a supranational agency —
iich, in the light of present conditions in Latin America, could
arcely be considered a realistic premise — an integration program
sed on a customs union would have to be equipped with a series
specific instruments that go beyond the trade and payments fields.
ie fairly obvious initial need would be to establish instruments
coordinate investment and industrialization policies and to offer

additional support to the relatively less-developed member countri
It is doubtful that these tasks can be undertaken without recourse
regional-development planning. In this regard, it is very discouragi
that no one in Latin America — at the government level — is willi
to face up to this integration-program requirement. This is just a
other of the many examples of the sort of wishful thinking so
vogue among Latin American politicians and economists: If re
problems are not talked about, they will somehow disappear.

Coordination of investment and industrialization policies requi
further, the existence of a regional financial agency endowed wi
sufficient resources for the execution of infrastructure and producti
investment projects that are multinational in scope.[15] It implies, al
a joint policy of fiscal incentives for new productive activities carr
ing a high priority within the framework of regional developme
This policy also calls for a common code to govern the treatment
foreign private investment. Finally, to eliminate completely t
danger that the new productive activities will be concentrated in t
more advanced countries in the union, additional mechanisms a
essential that, by means of agreements, will enable equitable speci
ization in the industrial field and will compensate for the fiscal loss
that the relatively less-developed countries might incur during t
first stages of integration, until such time as the emergence
regional industries in those nations serves to offset such losses.[16]

In summary, to keep intraregional political tensions from detra
ing from its effectiveness, an integration program aimed at acceler
ing development will have to incorporate the following elements :
treaty for the gradual establishment of a customs union; a region
mechanism for settlements and monetary-policy coordination;
regional development bank; a system — also coordinated — to pr
vide incentives for regional and external private investment;
instrument that promotes the above indicated aims of "industri
specialization by agreement"; and a fund to compensate those cou

[15] Such an agency exists within the Central American Common Market in t
form of a Central American Bank for Economic Integration. The new Trea
for East African Cooperation encourages the establishment of a regional indu
trial development bank. In respect to the future Latin American common mark
a similar role could be played by the Inter-American Development Bank.

[16] It is true that the Conference of the Contracting Parties to the Montevid
Treaty has adopted many resolutions that define and broaden the special prefe
ential regime for the less-developed LAFTA members. Nonetheless, as h
occurred in the case of other Conference decisions, they have not been supp
mented as yet to a degree which would compensate the weakest LAFTA me
bers for their inability to produce goods for export to the region.

ies which are relatively less developed. In addition, the efficient
nctioning of all these elements presupposes that the developed
ctor of the world economy will coordinate its economic-aid policies
ward the customs-union territory.

Advocating a program of this nature — given Latin America's
esent circumstances — may appear to be too ambitious if not
diculously Utopian. Such, however, is not the case. The Central
merican economic integration program contains almost all the
echanisms enumerated above: the customs union, which was to
perfected before the end of 1966; the Payments Clearing House
d Monetary Council; the Central American Bank for Economic
tegration (CABEI); and the Agreement for the Equalization of
scal Incentives. Since the economic distance between the five
publics is relatively short and Central America does not appear
need a compensation fund for the weaker members, all that is
king to complete the integration mechanism is the smooth func-
ning of specialization by agreement and the equitable distribution
new industrial activities. It was hoped that the latter role would
filled by the Central American Integration Industries Regime, but
e life of this treaty, to date, has been very precarious, owing in
rge part to the negative attitude assumed by the United States, on
e basis of doctrinal considerations not applicable to underdeveloped
eas. In any event, the Central American Common Market authori-
s are cooperating in the field of industrial integration. They have
reed on the special treatment for productive activities, which estab-
hes a priori uniform tariffs of a protectionist nature for a series
new regional industries, and have decided to extend the regional
licy of industrialization, supported by CABEI financing, to con-
mer-goods industries, as well as to those supplying raw materials,
nifinished products, and capital goods.

How may one draw a comparison between the requirements of
cacious integration and the workings of the Latin American Free
ade Association, which was established in 1960? It should be recog-
zed that the mechanism in LAFTA's case, although it has undeni-
le possibilities, is a much weaker one than that operating in Central
merica. To illustrate: The Montevideo Treaty does not require that
e member countries establish a customs union, although it opens
e way for them to do so. LAFTA does not have as yet any meaning-
l mechanism for the clearing of payments and for monetary
rdination, although a cumbersome scheme for bilateral balancing
payments within the limits of bilateral swing credits, established

in 1966, may eventually lead to a multilateral clearing arrangemen
The LAFTA Secretariat and Permanent Executive Committee a
extremely weak and refer even the most trivial decisions to t
member governments.[17] It does not have a regional financial agenc
nor does it, for the immediate future, provide for any coordinatic
whatsoever of fiscal and investment policies. It is not equipped wi
a permanent mechanism that would stimulate industrial specializ
tion by agreement or serve as the basis for arriving at an understan
ing regarding procedures to be followed in favor of the less-develope
member countries. Almost all that LAFTA has done to date wi
regard to the foregoing has been to pass resolutions placing on reco
the intention to achieve the appropriate objectives. More importa
still, LAFTA, with very few exceptions, does not enjoy decisi
political support within and without the region — a fact borne o
by the four years preparations of a hemispheric summit meeting f
purposes of accelerating integration, a meeting which finally to
place at Punta del Este in April, 1967. Even at that summit meeti
the main emphasis was put on trade liberalization, a task that, a
though favorable to integration, is becoming more difficult from o
annual negotiation meeting to the next (because of the lack of t
other mechanisms mentioned). Trade liberalization, by itself, c
hardly be expected to accomplish Latin American integration, ev
if the next twenty-five years are spent in the attempt.[18]

Among most experts on Latin American integration there is
surprising degree of agreement, despite certain doctrinal and pr
cedural discrepancies, regarding what must be accomplished in ord
to make LAFTA an efficient integration instrument and to prepa
the way for a later American common market to be set up accordi
to the 1967 Punta del Este meeting's recommendations before 198
The majority concur in recognizing the urgent need to accelera
progress in the direction of a common market — i.e., to establish

[17] This observation does not mean to minimize the technical work perform
by the LAFTA Secretariat and Permanent Executive Committee and reflected
over 180 resolutions adopted up to the beginning of 1967 by the Conference
the Contracting Parties to the Treaty of Montevideo and in the documentati
prepared by various permanent advisory commissions established in 1963.

[18] It is true that during the first five years the Montevideo Treaty was
effect intrazonal trade increased from $361 million to $665 million, measured
terms of exports. However, the share of these intraregional transactions tak
up in new products, and especially manufactures, continues to be negligible.
the same rate of expansion continues, which is very doubtful, by 1970 int
LAFTA trade will amount to some $1.5 billion, or less than 20 per cent of t
global foreign trade estimated for the eleven member countries in that year.

mmon customs tariff applicable to the rest of the world; to revise
horoughly present negotiating procedures regarding reciprocal
istoms concessions and discontinue product-by-product bargaining
a favor of across-the-board reductions applicable to groups of
roducts; to institute a system of regional payments clearings and
ttlements that will stimulate regional-trade expansion and advance
uty-reduction goals and industrial agreements; to revise the bases
r industrial ''complementation'' agreements and convert them into
mechanism for specialization, allowing for the needs of the less-
eveloped countries; to persuade existing regional and extraregional
nancial agencies to lend economic aid to integration, for their par-
cipation in that activity to date has been extremely limited; and,
nally, to strengthen LAFTA agencies, following the example set by
he Central American Economic Council and the European Eco-
omic Community Commission.

In order to strengthen the Latin American integration program,
LAFTA countries must, however, not only make major political
ecisions but must also support them by action on many economic
ronts at the same time. The political decisions were apparently made
t the 1967 hemispheric summit meeting, but the general climate for
nplementary action is not propitious. Integration has the support
f the most dynamic elements in the Latin-American societies, but
heir combined weight is not impressive. Perhaps the most positive
henomenon is the ever-increasing interest shown by private sectors
n the region in opportunities offered them by LAFTA; because of
he saturation of domestic markets, they have been forced to seek
ew outlets for their industrial production. But the very fact of
narket saturation and of fear of competition makes the entrepreneurs
ehave superficially like ''integrationists.'' What motivates them in
eality — and, as yet, in insufficient measure — is the possible in-
rease in export trade, with little regard for any other aspects of
egional integration and cooperation.

At the same time, the active or passive enemies of Latin American
ntegration are legion. Heading this group are politicians and govern-
nent officials who use supernationalism as a demagogic weapon to
ivert social tensions that are building up in their respective coun-
ries, failing to realize that in this way they are only aggravating
he critical situation over the long run. The crux of the matter, the
rue nucleus of the arguments with regard to LAFTA's future, a
Iexican economic journal maintains, may be summed up in a single
uestion: ''At a time of burgeoning nationalism in Latin America,

how can supranational solutions be implemented at short term?'
A clear answer to this query is not possible, for other forces a
added to irresponsible and parochial nationalism. First, there is t
dead weight of bureaucracy, the scourge of government apparat
at all levels — apparatus that are not even in a position to opera
in accordance with a coordinated national concept (as witness t
wavering policies and contradictory and eventually self-defeati
actions that often characterize governments' behavior in matte
pertaining to LAFTA) and, hence, are even less able to respond
the requirements of a regional approach. Then, there is the pr
dominance, in public as well as private sectors, of positions inspir
by the traditional doctrines briefly outlined at the beginning of th
essay and originating in an imitation of ideas that have currency i
the already industrialized countries. Finally, there is opposition c
the part of vested interests of two types: medium-sized domest
industries that have enjoyed a situation of privilege under prote
tionist systems; and certain larger foreign industries whose oper
tions in Latin America are based on dividing the regional mark
among their branches. There is no indication whatsoever that th
odd coalition — made up of supernationalistic politicians, burea
crats, entrepreneurs, and industrialists of the old school, plus certai
foreign interests — plans to give up. Anyone acquainted with th
background of the annual LAFTA negotiations and of three consec
tive meetings of the LAFTA Foreign Ministers Council knows tha
interests opposed to integration have won a series of importar
battles. The fact that they also were defeated on not a few occasion
is attributable to the growing and effective support that the integra
tion program is receiving from a minority of politicians and techn
cians who have a more modern mentality, and thanks to whom th
idea is beginning to make an emotional appeal to Latin America
public opinion. Nevertheless, the battle is an unrelenting one, and it
results should become quite apparent at a very early date.

It is true that there are those who believe in the automatism o
economic integration. Such a line of reasoning, however, is much mor
applicable to economically advanced regions, where conditions favo
a long-term economic policy having relatively clear objectives, an
where the operation of efficient, democratic forces countervails th
vested political and economic interests. In Latin America's case

[19] See ''El creciente nacionalismo en América Latina permitirá la planeació
a nivel continental?'' *El Correo Economico* (Mexico City), I, No. 13 (May 3
1964), 1.

AFTA has only two alternatives: to pick up speed and move in
e direction of a sub-continental common market, agreed in prin-
ole at the Punta del Este summit meeting of Spring, 1967, or to
e ground and become just another of a series of rather ineffective
gional mechanisms. One will know the outcome before the present
cade runs its course.

Robert W. Gregg

The UN Regional Economic Commissions and Integration in the Underdeveloped Regions

It is the purpose of this article to examine the role which the thr
regional economic commissions of the United Nations serving t
developing world[1] play, whether consciously or unconsciously,
promoting integration within the regions which they serve. Tl
emphasis is upon economic integration, not because it is more impc
tant than political union or federation or because it is a necessar
antecedent to political integration. No attempt is made here to esta
lish the thesis that the relationship between economic and politic
integration is that of a continuum.[2] Any contribution which the U
regional economic commissions make to regional or subregional int
gration will almost certainly be in the economic area, given the
terms of reference, the nature of their work programs, and tl
environmental conditions in which they operate. Economic integr
tion resulting from ideas and initiatives originating in the region
commissions *may* contribute to the evolution of political union.

In this context integration may be defined as the transformatic
of an international subsystem in a direction in which more weight

Reprinted from *International Organization*, XX, No. 2 (Spring 1966), with t
permission of The World Peace Foundation and the author.

[1] The Economic Commission for Latin America (ECLA), the Economic Cox
mission for Asia and the Far East (ECAFE), and the Economic Commissi
for Africa (ECA).

[2] For a recent discussion of this relationship see Ernst B. Haas and Philip
C. Schmitter, ''Economics and Differential Patterns of Political Integratio
Projections About Unity in Latin America,'' *International Organizatio
Autumn 1964 (Vol. 18, No. 4), pp. 705-737.

corded to decisions and actions in the name of the aggregate of
tors. In other words, the nation-state ceases to be an autonomous
cision-making unit with respect to certain important policies; the
cus of economic problem solving is to some extent shifted from the
ate to an intergovernmental or supranational body.[3]

The role of the regional economic commission in this process is dif-
ult to assess. It is only one of several agents which may inspire
tegrative experiments; what it promotes could often more accu-
tely be described as cooperation, which is clearly a much more
odest relationship than integration. However, if the commission has
thrust which is regional in scope and emphasis and if it contributes
a way of thinking about economic problems which permits and
courages the delegation of more authority to some new and larger
nter, then the commission may be said to have an integrative
tput.

The UN Setting

Article 68 of the United Nations Charter provides for the creation
commissions under the aegis of the Economic and Social Council
COSOC) and suggests functional criteria for their establishment.
e legislative history of the Charter reveals little interest in spa-
lly as opposed to functionally defined institutions in the economic
ld.[4] However, it was not long after San Francisco that the UN
barked upon a policy of regionalization in the economic sphere,
step neither invited nor precluded by the Charter. The rationale
r the creation of the first commission, the Economic Commission
r Europe, was postwar reconstruction. In an early instance of UN
alition politics, however, the Asian and Latin American states
gaged in some effective logrolling which led to the creation of
mmissions for each of those regions over the opposition of Western

[3] This definition is adapted from that employed by Haas, which focuses on
itical integration. See, for example, Ernst B. Haas, "International Integra-
n: The European and the Universal Process," *International Organization*,
mmer 1961 (Vol. 15, No. 3), pp. 366-367. See also the related definition, also
ived from Haas, employed by Jean Siotis: *"Integration occurs when con-
sus formation tends to become the dominant characteristic of relations among
ors in a system."* (Jean Siotis, "The Secretariat of the United Nations
onomic Commission for Europe and European Economic Integration: The
st Ten Years," *International Organization*, Spring 1965 [Vol. 19, No. 2],
178.)

[4] The question is probed in a recent book by Robert W. Macdonald, *The
ague of Arab States* (Princeton, N.J.: Princeton University Press, 1965),
apter 1.

European and North American Members.[5] Thus, by March of 19
the UN had created three regional economic commissions,[6] had la
the foundation for honoring the claims of other regions,[7] and h
broadened the mission of these commissions from reconstruction
economic development.

In effect, the regional economic commissions, while subsidia
organs of a universal international organization, are in a very re
sense regional organizations with all that that fact implies wi
respect to relative environmental homogeneity. What is more, th
are not regional replicas of the parent organization. They are mo
limited in purpose, embracing the economic and social tasks of t
United Nations but not, in any direct fashion, its tasks in the fiel
of peace and security, self-determination, or human rights. Where
the UN itself has been characterized by several historic phases,[8]
manifestation of environmental instability which has militat
against integrative precedents, the regional commissions have be
buffeted much less directly and obviously by the shifting winds
cold-war and colonial conflict. Although the commissions have n
been guaranteed an integrative impact by their locations in t
sheltered coves of relatively greater environmental stability, t
absence of environmental phases, coupled with the exclusively ec
nomic and social content of their terms of reference, has facilitat
comparatively stable agreement within the commissions on the tas
which are to receive primary attention.

Furthermore, the commissions enjoy a considerable amount
institutional independence from the parent organization. It is tr
that in a formal sense they are very much an integral part of t
United Nations. Their budgets are a part of the UN budget; the

[5] For a description of debates and bargaining which led to the creation
ECE, ECAFE, and ECLA, see David Wightman, *Toward Economic Coope*
tion in Asia: The United Nations Economic Commission for Asia and the F
East (New Haven, Conn.: Yale University Press, 1963), Chapter 2.

[6] ECE was established under ECOSOC Resolution 36 (IV) of March 28, 194
ECAFE under ECOSOC Resolution 37 (IV) of March 28, 1947; and ECI
under ECOSOC Resolution 106 (VI) of February 25, 1948.

[7] The Economic Commission for Africa was established under ECOSOC Re
lution 671 A and B (XXV) of April 29, 1958. Establishment of a commissi
for the Middle East has been considered and would almost certainly have be
accomplished were it not for the enduring schism between the Arab states a
Israel.

[8] For a discussion of these historic phases see Ernst B. Haas, ''Dynam
Environment and Static System: Revolutionary Regimes in the United N
tions,'' in Morton Kaplan (ed.), *The Revolution in World Politics* (New Yor
John Wiley & Sons, 1962), pp. 267-309.

ffs are part of the staff of the UN's Department of Economic and
cial Affairs, subject to the same rules and regulations; their
ecutive Secretaries are selected by the Secretary-General. Their
ms of reference, which are quite modest in scope, specify that they
all act within the framework of UN policies and under the general
pervision of the Economic and Social Council.[9] But these limita-
ns are deceptive. In practice the commissions have more discretion
an their terms of reference suggest and consequently more capacity
taking initiatives, independently of New York, appropriate to
needs of the region. This independence should not be exaggerated.
t it is an important fact, one which makes it possible to speak of
commissions as agencies which may have an ideology and a thrust
their own, shaped to some extent by their UN connection but not
inhibited by it as to deny them a distinct influence upon the regions
y serve.

Although each commission has developed its own distinctive style
d carved out its own areas of emphasis, all have experienced an
pansion of tasks and a gradual strengthening of their positions
thin their respective regions. This shifting role was the theme of
ne remarks by Philippe de Seynes, Under Secretary for Economic
d Social Affairs, which are quite revealing of the gulf between the
nking of headquarters and that of the regional centers.

far as the regional commissions are concerned, we were more or less
ninated, over a long period, by a way of thinking which doubtless origi-
ed in a desire to simplify and clarify matters. According to that way of
nking, the regional economic commissions were organs which should de-
e themselves to research and study and which should be barred from what
termed operational activities.[10]

tergovernmental study groups, serviced by secretariats performing
earch and conference machinery functions, would almost certainly
t have been in a position to make much of an impact upon their
gions. But the commissions, in every case but to varying degrees,
ve exceeded this minimalist level of involvement in the affairs of
eir respective regions. There are several explanations for their
ength,[11] but in essence ECLA, ECAFE, and ECA have grown

Their terms of reference may be found in annexes to the annual reports of
commissions to ECOSOC. For recently amended versions, see Economic and
ial Council *Official Records* (37th session), Supplement No. 2, Annex III
CAFE); Supplement No. 4, Annex III (ECLA); Supplement No. 7, Annex
(ECE); and Supplement No. 10, Annex III (ECA).
0 UN Document E/CN.12/572, March 5, 1961, pp. 1-2.
1 One UN official, a long-time observer of the commissions, attributes it to

and assumed more importance both within the UN system and with their respective regions because they are a product of that syst and perform an essential function within it.

This phenomenon is attributable to the environmental chan; which have transformed the international system since the Kore War and the comparatively stark bipolarity of the UN's early yea The tacit agreement to encapsulate[12] the more destructive levels cold-war conflict; the pronounced increase in the number of in pendent underdeveloped states; the emergence of a crude UN pai system which is, to a very considerable extent, a multiregional s tem; the evolution to paramountcy of the economic tasks on ` UN's long agenda; the resultant increase in opportunities for b gaining among the UN's "parties" — all of these interrelated fact have contributed to the strengthening of the regional economic cc missions. The recent campaign to decentralize authority for some I economic and social programs from Headquarters to the region commissions may be viewed as a natural culmination of these chan; in the environment within which the UN system functions.[13] Region groups have quite naturally tended to upgrade in importance th UN structures which are most conspicuously their own, whose sec tariats have consciously been given a regional coloration, wh announced purposes correspond most closely with their own perce tions of the UN's most important tasks. The commissions have i only acquired a symbolic importance; they have also become vehic whereby the claims of developing states upon the UN could articulated with the assistance of a professional secretariat attur to the interests of the region. They are peculiarly agencies for acti of the region, by the region, and for the region.

---

the inclusive character of their membership within their respective regions; th tendency to act by agreement rather than by voting; a self-imposed discipl which induces them to behave in accordance with Charter principles and sembly and ECOSOC resolutions; and a marked degree of regional consciousr and solidarity. See W. R. Malinowski, ''Centralization and Decentralization the United Nations Economic and Social Activities,'' *International Organi tion,* Summer 1962 (Vol. 16, No. 3), pp. 523-524.

[12] The term is Amitai Etzioni's. See his article ''On Self-Encapsulating C flicts,'' *Journal of Conflict Resolution,* September 1964 (Vol. 8, No. 3), 242-255.

[13] For a more detailed discussion of decentralization, see the author's chap ''Program Decentralization and the Regional Economic Commissions'' ir forthcoming book under the general editorship of Gerard J. Mangone to published in 1966 by Columbia University Press.

The Regional Setting

What each of the regional economic commissions has sought to accomplish and what it has achieved have been conditioned in large measure by the regional context in which it has had to work. Is there a tradition of thinking about the region as a unit? Is the geographical scope of the region natural or artificial? What are the economic, social, and political conditions which prevail within the region? To what extent is it characterized by industrialization and economic diversification? How much functional similarity exists among units? What conditions prevail with respect to such variables as elite complementarity? All of these considerations enter into any assessment of the prospects for integration.[14]

The Economic Commission for Europe, for example, is distinguishable from the other commissions in that it serves a region which, for all the vicissitudes of European interstate relations, has traditionally been described as a community. As Jean Siotis has noted in a recent and perceptive essay on the role of ECE,[15] the central task for the commission has been to prevent the disintegration of Europe into two implacably hostile and self-contained regions. The main element in the organizational ideology of the first Executive Secretary, Gunnar Myrdal, was his belief that ECE should be used as a bridge of functional cooperation between East and West, and that it should strenuously resist all efforts to institutionalize within ECE the rift between the two blocs. The Secretariat's problem was to find specific tasks which could fan the flickering flame of "Europe." The other three regional commissions, which are the primary concern of this article, have had a somewhat different problem. Fragmentation has, of course, accompanied decolonization, especially in Africa; but a sense of community had not been a characteristic of these areas, and a principal task of the commissions has been to assist in the creation of such a sense of community, rather than to prevent the collapse of a previously existing one.

Moreover, these regions, quite aside from their lack of historical

---

[14] Conditions conducive to integration are discussed, *inter alia*, in Haas and Schmitter, *International Organization*, Vol. 18, No. 4, pp. 705-737; Haas, *International Organization*, Vol. 15, No. 3, pp. 366-392; and the recent book by Haas, *Beyond the Nation-State: Functionalism and International Organization* (Stanford, Calif.: Stanford University Press, 1964).

[15] Siotis, *International Organization*, Vol. 19, No. 2, pp. 177-202.

cohesiveness, are to varying degrees artificial in the geographic sens
Much the most arbitrary of the regions is Asia and the Far Eas
ECAFE's domain extends from Iran to Western Samoa and fro
Mongolia to New Zealand; Saudi Arabia and Israel have recent
requested membership. Surely this is a single region in name onl
appropriate perhaps for an administrative subdivision of the U
but not as a candidate for economic or political integration. Th
Economic Commission for Africa serves a region which looks mo
logical on the map but which is really an amalgamation of sever
regions, including the very dissimilar areas separated by the va
expanse of the Sahara. ECLA's domain, extending from the R
Grande and the Straits of Florida to Tierra del Fuego, is also ge
graphically arbitrary, a fact recognized by the division of the are
into two subregions, with a main office in Santiago and a subregion
office for Central America in Mexico City.

More significant than either the absence of a regional tradition a
the presence of unwieldy regional boundaries are the economi
social, and political conditions prevailing in each region. The e
vironmental conditions necessary for political integration are mo
exacting than those for economic union, but there would appear
be a relationship between successful economic integration and suc
factors, identified by Ernst Haas, as comparability of unit size ar
power and of pluralism plus elite complementarity and the rate a
transaction among units. If recent experiences with integration yiel
any lesson, it is that urban-industrial societies with a relatively hig
level of economic diversification are better candidates for more rapi
progress toward union than are underdeveloped, monocultur,
societies. Ironically, the integration movements in Europe, when
optimal environmental conditions exist, are probably an importan
factor in spurring experimentation with economic unions in area
which otherwise fail to meet some of the criteria for integration. I
spite of this incentive and that supplied by a shared state of unde
development and discouragingly slow progress toward overcoming i
the regions served by ECLA, ECAFE, and ECA do not present
profile conducive to economic union or even to very elaborately inst
tutionalized cooperation. Some subregional clusters of states ma
constitute more promising laboratories for integration, but all ar
defective on one or more important counts. Although any generaliza
tion is differentially applicable among the regions, it is safe to stat
that the great majority of states within all three regions tend to b

onomically dependent upon a very few primary commodities and
trade predominantly with states outside the region.[16]

THE REGIONAL ECONOMIC COMMISSIONS

The environmental setting in which each of the three regional
ommissions exists would appear to be unpromising for economic,
uch less political, integration. This does not mean, however, that
e commissions have not engaged in activities or promoted policies
hich may be described as integrative. It is the function of the
ollowing analysis to identify the integrative output of ECLA,
CAFE, and ECA.[17]

Integrative output of a regional commission is shaped, to a very
nsiderable extent, by the political and economic forces which operate
pon that commission. Governments bring to the regional commis-
ons different perceptions of national interest and different attitudes
ward institutionalized forms of regional cooperation. Although a
ommission may pursue policies at variance with the preferences of
me of its members, the integrative output of a commission is not
kely to be significantly greater than the receptivity to integration
f the commission's members. Integrative output is thus a product
f national policy inputs, adapted by the commission with the vital
ssistance of an international secretariat which can articulate nascent
terest in the idea of integration, synthesize diverse policies and
roposals with an integrative content, and otherwise supply creative
adership. The focus here is primarily upon what the commissions,
nd more particularly their secretariats, do rather than on the policy
puts of member governments.

Several questions may be asked in order to facilitate judgment of
e integrative output of the regional economic commissions.

) What has been the ideology of the leadership of the regional com-

[16] For statistical data on these and other indicators, see Bruce Russett and
hers, *World Handbook of Political and Social Indicators* (New Haven, Conn.:
ale University Press, 1964). For useful classification schemes, see Gabriel
lmond and James S. Coleman, *The Politics of the Developing Areas* (Prince-
n, N.J.: Princeton University Press, 1960). For data on trade, see, *inter alia*,
obert M. Stern, "Policies for Trade and Development," *International Con-
iation*, May 1964 (No. 548), and the sources cited therein.

[17] Many of the judgments made in the following sections are based upon
terviews with UN Secretariat personnel at Headquarters and in the regional
ficers of ECLA in Santiago and Mexico City, ECAFE in Bangkok, and ECA in
ddis Ababa.

mission? Has it been significantly oriented toward economic probl¢
solving at a level higher than that of the nation-state?

2) What has been the degree of initiative assumed by the commissi
secretariat for skewing the work program of the commission in
regional direction?

3) What has been the institutional legacy of the commission's acti
ties? Is there a residue of organizations or programs with regional
subregional outlook which are thriving?

4) What has been the flow of regionally minded commission sec⌐
tariat personnel into positions of influence within individual sta¶
and especially into government posts with planning responsibilitie

5) What has been the centripetal pull of the commission itself as
source of regional pride and purpose? Is there evidence of growth
respect for the commission secretariat as a kind of intellectual lo¢
stone for the region?

The terms of reference of none of the regional economic comm¤
sions speak specifically of integration of the whole or of portions
their regions as one of their purposes, much less their paramou¶
purpose. However, there is ample latitude for such an interpretati
in authorizations to study regional economic and technical problen
to initiate measures for facilitating regional economic and soc:
development, and to help formulate policies as a basis for practi¢
action in promoting country and regional development. The probl¢
is not whether the commission may or should be used as a fulcrum f'
transferring expectations for growth and development from the sta
to some larger unit; it is whether such an effort has been made
whether that has been the net result of activities undertaken by t
commission.

It is very difficult to identify that component of the work of
regional economic commission which has a regional as opposed to
country orientation. There is very little to be gained by an attem
to factor out of the work program those activities which are co¶
cerned with the region as a whole or with some subregional groupi¶
of states. Virtually all of the work carried on by a regional secretari
may be infused with the imperative of regionalization or, conversel
none of it. What matters is not the frequency of such phrases
"regional programs of cooperation" or "development on a su¶
regional or regional basis," phrases liberally sprinkled throu¶
descriptions of commission projects, but the extent to which t
appearance of an integrative mission is supported by the appropria

ix of project significance and timeliness, the commitment of the secretariat, mutual reinforcement of various elements of the commission program, and governmental receptivity (or at least absence of active hostility).

ECLA

Of the three regional economic commissions serving the developing world, the Economic Commission for Latin America has made the most sustained and conscious effort to achieve a manner of thinking about economic problems of individual countries which would result in a shift of emphasis from decision making by and for the state to decision making by a collectivity of states for the economic benefit of the whole as well as each of the parts.

In part this is surely the consequence of a combination of environmental factors which produce a net political input more receptive to integration. There is the frequently cited evidence of comparatively greater cultural homogeneity; there is the fact of a much longer postcolonial history; there is statistical proof of a higher mean gross national product (GNP) per capita;[18] there is the history of common concern for the economic and geopolitical reality of the hemispheric hegemony of the United States; there is the relative absence of intra-regional quarrels and of regional diversions from the task of economic growth and development. This does not mean that economic and political differences do not exist and are not reflected within ECLA. The United States has frequently been a dissenting member, taking exception to economic theories which have permeated Commission discussions and actions and occasionally placing a strain upon relationships among the Commission's Latin American members. The Cuban revolution has introduced a new ideological dimension into Commission debates.[19] There have been policy differences arising from different perceptions of advantage and disadvantage in specific ECLA program proposals. The case of Venezuelan reluctance to join the Latin American Free Trade Association (LAFTA) is a well-known example, one which conditioned ECLA's recommendations on the subject.[20]

[18] See Russett, especially Table 44, pp. 155-157, and Table B.2, pp. 294-298.

[19] Note that the Cuban application for membership in the Latin American Free Trade Association (LAFTA) was rejected. See Sidney Dell, *Trade Blocs and Common Markets* (New York: Alfred A. Knopf, 1963), p. 265.

[20] See the September 1960 statement of the Bank of Venezuela:
> Any common market or free trade area will leave us producing nothing but petroleum and iron ore, and importing everything else. Our textiles cannot

But it has been the Secretariat of ECLA which has attracted th most attention and made the most conspicuous contributions to int gration in Latin America. As Albert Hirschman remarks,

The arresting feature of ECLA is that it possesses attributes not frequentl encountered in large international organisations: a cohesive personalit which evokes loyalty from the staff, and a set of distinctive beliefs, pri ciples, and attitudes, in brief an ideology, which is highly influential amon Latin American intellectuals and policymakers.[21]

ECLA's long-time Executive Secretary, Dr. Raúl Prebisch, supplie the ideology which infused the Secretariat with a sense of purpos and gave the Commission its sense of direction. There are many wh will take issue with Dr. Prebisch's economics but none who will dis pute the contention that his views have had an impact in Lati America, and indeed beyond that region.

The essence of the Prebisch-ECLA position has been that th economic difficulties of the developing countries are attributable t the prolonged and continuing deterioration in their terms of trade To remedy this condition and overcome dependence of the peripher, (developing states) upon the center (developed states), industrializa tion via the mechanism of a preferential regional market is proposed To avoid a situation in which some states within Latin America woul benefit from such a market at the expense of others, ECLA has pro moted a doctrine of regionally balanced economic growth, wit formulas for reciprocity and complementarity "to assure that every body would be cut in on the deal, that nobody would gain dispropor tionately."[22]

The institutional embodiments of this philosophy and some of it subthemes are the Central American Economic Integration Program the Latin American Free Trade Association,[23] and, in a somewha

---

compete with Brazilian textiles, our coffee cannot compete with Colombia coffee and our meat cannot compete with Uraguayan meat. For us a fre trade area is utopian at the present time.
(Quoted in Dell, p. 274.)

[21] Albert O. Hirschman, "Ideologies of Economic Development in Lati America," in Albert O. Hirschman (ed.), *Latin American Issues: Essays an Comments* (New York: Twentieth Century Fund, 1961), p. 13.

[22] Haas and Schmitter, *International Organization*, Vol. 18, No. 4, p. 730. Fo a recent, definitive statement of the ECLA-Prebisch theses see *Towards Dynamic Development Policy for Latin America* (UN Document E/CN.12/680 Rev.1), December 1963.

[23] The Central American Agreements embrace Costa Rica, El Salvador, Guate mala, Honduras, and Nicaragua. LAFTA includes Argentina, Brazil, Chil Colombia, Ecuador, Mexico, Paraguay, Peru, and Uruguay. For a recent stud of LAFTA, including the role of ECLA in its creation, see Miguel S. Wionczek

ifferent sense, the United Nations Conference on Trade and Development (UNCTAD). ECLA-sponsored studies and negotiations, fed y ECLA research, led directly to the creation of the two subregional ssociations in Latin America. It is interesting to note that ECLA, one of the four regional commissions, has not established an elaborate substructure of committees and other standing subsidiary bodies or its various fields of work. The only two exceptions are a Central merican Economic Cooperation Committee and a Trade Committee, nd it is no accident that the former played a key role in the evolution of the General Treaty on Central American Economic Integration (and its predecessors, the Agreement on Central American ntegration Industries and the Multilateral Treaty on Central merican Free Trade and Economic Integration) and that the tter performed a similar function with respect to the Treaty of ontevideo creating LAFTA.

This is not the place to evaluate either the Central American conomic Integration Program or LAFTA. Either or both may agnate in the face of conditions which do not appear to be optimal or economic integration, much less politization. Haas argues that AFTA in particular must experience a "creative crisis" and be essed with the dynamic leadership of a reform-monger if this now eak and to a considerable extent untested economic union is to evelop in the direction of political union.[24] However, the important oint to be made in the context of this article is that while LAFTA d the Central American Agreements have now assumed the burden serving as vehicles for integration, it is ECLA which played the talytic role, launching both experiments. Moreover, it has the ntinuing task of supplying creative leadership, indirectly through e force of ideas or directly through ECLA-trained personnel, with hich to meet challenges requiring adaptation. The ECLA Secretariat has already displayed some aptitude for creative adaptation. s Hirschman notes, ECLA "has transferred the principal center its activity from one area to another as it ran into difficulty or creasing returns,"[25] but it has managed to do so without sacrifice identity of its personality. The Commission, for example, spent a mber of years urging upon Latin American governments the tailed programming of economic development; the shift to com-

Latin American Free Trade Association,'' *International Conciliation*, January 65 (No. 551).

[24] Haas and Schmitter, *International Organization*, Vol. 18, No. 4, pp. 732 ff.

[25] Hirschman, p. 20.

mon market studies reflected, in part, frustration with the limite
impact of its programming activity.

It may be that the Commission has been guilty on occasion of
utopian cast of mind or, conversely, that it has had more prosa
purposes than integration in mind, as Sidney Dell alleges with h
observation that LAFTA was in part the product of a desire
observe General Agreement on Tariffs and Trade (GATT) rules, n
to achieve economic integration.[26] In either case, ECLA has noneth
less contributed as has no other agency to a reexamination
economic, and hence political, relationships within and among Lat
American states. As one observer remarks, Prebisch has been
"creator of enthusiasms and a destroyer of illusions."[27] He has mac
ECLA a force to be reckoned with in the western hemispher
When policy decisions affecting economic development, industrializ
tion, and trade are pending within a state, the outcome is likely to I
affected by the Cassandra-like warnings of ECLA's annual report
by the recommendations of one of ECLA's economic developmen
advisory groups, or by the very existence of an ECLA-fostered fr
trade machinery. Moreover, such decisions may be influenced by tl
presence within the government of economists who have held pror
inent positions on the ECLA staff.[28] More than in any of the oth
regions there is a significant flow of senior officials between the Cor
mission Secretariat and the governments of member states.

Several years ago, one observer credited Prebisch with the feat
making ECLA into a kind of responsible political opposition in Lat
America.[29] It is submitted that ECLA even has one foot in tl
government in some states. However, as Haas points out, tl
técnicos have an uneven influence throughout Latin America; h
observation that they might be able to exert considerable influen
in a number of the more advanced countries of the region "*if* the
lines of rapport with major political groups were stable"[30] is illu
trated by the exile of one of ECLA's more prominent "exports,
Celso Furtado, from Brazil.

[26] Dell, p. 264.

[27] Roberto de Oliveira Campos, quoted in Hirschman, p. 27.

[28] Among the more prominent have been Victor L. Urquidi and Carlos Qui
tana in Mexico, Celso Furtado in Brazil, José A. Mayobre (now Executi
Secretary of ECLA) in Venezuela, Hugo Trivelli in Chile, and Regino Boti
Cuba. Similarly, upon Juan Perón's overthrow, the government of Argenti
requested Prebisch to make an economic survey of that country, his own.

[29] Andrew Shonfield, *The Attack on World Poverty* (New York: Rando
House, 1962), p. 49.

[30] Haas and Schmitter, *International Organization,* Vol. 18, No. 4, p. 731.

In spite of the recognized expertise in the ECLA Secretariat and the presence of the ex-ECLA personnel in many governments[31], several N officials have remarked that ECLA's impact is weakened by the reoccupation of its Secretariat with economic theory. Thus it has been alleged that ECLA underestimates the problems of negotiability; phrased another way, ECLA has been accused of a reluctance to get its hands dirty with operational complexities. As one UN official observed, the ECLA Secretariat is probably the only agency in atin America that could find the common denominators for implementing economic integration programs but does not possess the bent of mind necessary to do so.

In respects other than ideology, its translation into a work program with institutional results, and the interchange of senior economists, the Economic Commission for Latin America has not performed in a manner conspicuously different from that of ECAFE or ECA. What has distinguished ECLA's activities is that the integrationist ideology permeates the otherwise routine research and advisory services. For example, as a result of ECLA initiatives an Institute for Economic and Social Planning was established with UN Special Fund and Inter-American Development Bank (IDB) support in Santiago; Dr. Prebisch became the Institute's first Director General, and this prospectively influential training organ proceeded to assume responsibility for advisory groups which ECLA had pioneered, for the important economic development training program, and for research with respect to planning. The curriculum will not necessarily produce integrationists; but the close historical, physical, and personal links with ECLA suggest that the Institute may become an important training ground for regionally minded economists. Similar institutes have been created in Bangkok for Asia and the Far East and in Dakar for Africa, but while these bodies may relieve the regional economic commissions in those areas of in-service training responsibilities, the possibility is remote that they will in the near future serve as incubators for integrationists.

One final observation should be made concerning the political role of the Economic Commission for Latin America. The recurrent conflict between the UN and the Organization of American States (OAS) in the peaceful settlement and enforcement fields[31] has had an interesting corollary in the competition between ECLA and the Inter-American Economic and Social Council (IA-ECOSOC) of the

OAS. Although the Alliance for Progress has fostered formal stru̇c-
tures for bringing activities of the two organizations into harmoniou̇s
relationship,[32] the resultant coordination has been superficial an̤d
ECLA and IA-ECOSOC remain distinct and competing entities. ̣It
is not an exaggeration to state that the prestige within the regiȯn
enjoyed by ECLA, an organization in which the United States ha̤s
usually been a minor and dissenting participant, has been enhance̤d
by the fact that the OAS is widely viewed as a United States-dom̤-
inated institution. Regional pride in ECLA and a disposition ṭo
listen when ECLA prescribes for the region's ills may be inverselẏ
related to regional acceptance of the OAS machinery.

ECAFE

If the number of experiments in regional and subregional organiza̤-
tion is any yardstick, Asia promises least progress of any of the d̤e-
veloping regions toward economic, much less political, union. Reason̤s
for Asian separatism are not hard to find. The litany of obstacles ṭo
cooperation has been cited many times: the region's geographi̤c
dispersion; its religious, cultural, and linguistic diversity; its deȩp
political cleavages; the vast disparity in unit size. It is within thi̤s
milieu that ECAFE operates.

Functional similarity is conspicuously lacking in this sprawling
region. Two of ECAFE's territorial members (Australia and New
Zealand) are "high mass-consumption" societies with a GNP per
capita of more than $1,300; four (Afghanistan, Burma, Laos, and
Nepal) are "traditional primitive" societies with a GNP per capita
of less than $70; and only a handful, including only one major state,
Japan, have a GNP per capita of as much as $200.[33] Clusters of states
of roughly comparable size and power are divided by religious, ideological, and other deeply rooted animosities. If civil strife is divided
into personnel wars, authority wars, and structural wars,[34] in Latin
America such strife has usually been of the first two types, while in
Asia it has frequently been structural; thus it has had much wider

[32] An *Ad Hoc* Committee on Cooperation was established to guarantee coordination between the OAS, ECLA, and the Inter-American Development Bank
(IDB). ECLA is also linked to the Inter-American Committee on the Alliance
for Progress (CIAP), a committee of IA-ECOSOC, in an advisory capacity.

[33] Classification and data are from Russett, Table B-2, pp. 294-298.

[34] This typology is developed by James N. Rosenau, "Internal War as an
International Event," in James N. Rosenau (ed.), *International Aspects of
Civil Strife* (Princeton, N.J.: Princeton University Press, 1964), pp. 45-91.

epercussions and has made it more difficult for the Commission to
ive undivided attention to economic development problems.

Among other inputs which have inhibited ECAFE's deliberations
re the deep-seated suspicion of Japan's leadership, dating back to
he days of the Coprosperity Sphere; anxiety about and some re-
entment of India's claims to leadership within the region and the
Commission;[35] dissension introduced into the Asian scene by the
reation and continued existence of the Southeast Asia Treaty
Organization (SEATO); the presence within ECAFE, alone of the
hree commissions, of both the United States and the Soviet Union;
nd the fact that mainland China is within the geographic scope of
he Commission but that the Peking government, a brooding presence
n all Asian affairs, is not a participant. In such an atmosphere economic progress is difficult, and no better or more enduring example
an be found than Pakistan's lukewarm attitude toward the activities
of ECAFE, a function of India's leadership of and stake in the
Commission's affairs.

ECAFE has had no ideological thrust remotely comparable to that
of ECLA. To say this is not to disparage the leadership of ECAFE
but to record a fact. The impact of the Commission has simply been
quite negligible. ECAFE's early years were characterized by the
Commission's domination by non-Asian states. It was not until the
Lahore Agreement of 1951 that the Asian states succeeded in convert-
ng the Commission into a body which could do what its Asian members wanted it to do without interference, and indeed blocking votes,
rom outside powers.[36] In the words of David Wightman, the Agreement "affirmed that ECAFE existed primarily to serve the interests

[35] Figures supplied to the writer on a visit to ECAFE in 1964 revealed that as
of that time India had as many professional staff serving on the Commission's
Secretariat as Pakistan, Burma, Ceylon, Indonesia, and Iran combined.

[36] See Wightman, pp. 50-52. A memorandum presented by the Executive Sec-
etary, P. S. Lokanathan, at the 1951 session of the Commission catalyzed support for the following declaration by the Commission:

Member governments feel, however, that the time has come when clearer
recognition should be given to the principle that member countries belonging to the region should take their own decisions in the Commission on
their own economic problems. . . . In pursuance of this principle the member countries of the Commission not in the region would be willing, as a
general rule, to refrain from using their votes in opposition to economic
proposals predominantly concerning the region which had the support of a
majority of the countries of the region.

(See Economic and Social Council *Official Records* [13th session], Supplement
No. 7, paragraph 341.)

of its Asian members.''[37] This rudimentary triumph did not, o course, define those interests or guarantee that the Asian states an a secretariat consisting largely of their nationals would undertak a program with integrative purpose or potential.

Although it would be a mistake to underestimate the significanc for Asia of the ''Asianization'' of the only important regional bod in the entire continent, it must be noted that the subsequent per formance of ECAFE has not created apprehension and dissatisfactio outside of the Commission comparable to that generated by ECLA In other words, ECAFE is regarded as a relatively ''safe'' commis sion; the Lahore Agreement has not proved to be a Pandora's box There has been little friction between ECAFE and the UN, whic in this case means both the predominantly Western leadership withi the Department of Economic and Social Affairs and the influentia Western states on the Economic and Social Council and in the Secon (Economic and Financial) and Third (Social, Humanitarian, an Cultural) Committees of the General Assembly. ECAFE may fairl be characterized as the most UN-minded of the regional commissions The assessment implicit in this characterization, and one explicitl voiced by some UN staff members, is that the Secretariats in Nev York and in Bangkok are both cautious, slow to embrace new ideas generally satisfied to perform routine tasks efficiently. Furthermore a capacity for self-criticism, so necessary to continuing redefini tion of tasks and the growth of influence, has been conspicuousl lacking in ECAFE's leadership. ECAFE may do well those thing that it does, but such an organization is unlikely to contribute signifi cantly to the transformation of thinking either of economists o politicians within its member states.

Having stated that Asia is not Latin America and ECAFE no ECLA, it is necessary to scan the performance of the Commission fo islands of impact in an unpromising sea. The first Executive Secre tary, P. S. Lokanathan, had early indicated his determination not t preside over a mere study group.[38] Yet the Working Group of Ex perts on Regional Economic Cooperation for the ECAFE Region, ii an important report submitted to the third Executive Secretary U Nyun, in 1963, observed that

increased regional cooperation as envisaged in this report requires the estab lishment of decision-making machinery, in contrast to the largely consultativ machinery which ECAFE has provided for the past seventeen years.[39]

37 Wightman, p. 52.
38 *Ibid.*, p. 286.
39 UN Document E/CN.11/641, p. 69.

ıring ECAFE's long years as consultative machinery/study group, e ground was being laid for "joint efforts to secure the common or tegrated development of basic facilities of natural resources" and, pefully, for "those forms of co-operation which arise from the eatment of the region as a whole, or parts of it, as a single arket."[40] The habit of consultation had to be instilled first; the onomic map of the ECAFE region had to be charted. Both the map d the habit have been improved by ECAFE's existence and the list ECAFE-inspired projects of regional or subregional import is ginning to lengthen. The roster includes the Mekong River Project, e Asian Highway, the Asian Institute for Economic Development d Planning, Intraregional Trade Promotion Talks, the Conference Asian Planners, the Ministerial Conference on Asian Economic operation, and the Asian Development Bank.

These frequently cited evidences of ECAFE's salutary role in that nflict-ridden region fall into two categories. The Mekong Project, e Highway, and the Institute are similar in that discussions have en followed by action in each case and in that they do not involve y sacrifice of the right of member countries to determine their own velopment and commercial policies. The Institute, as noted earlier, comparable in form to one established through the initiative of CLA, but its integrative potential will probably depend upon the velopment of a curriculum with a self-consciously regional view-int. The Asian Highway will no more lift the eyes of planners be-nd the boundaries of nation-states than will the ECE-sponsored nvention for transport of goods by roads under customs seal in urope[41] although a comparison of the two projects underscores the dimentary nature of ECAFE's task. However, the Asian Highway symbolically important, "a modern revival of the ancient caravan utes along which traveled not only goods but peoples and ideas."[42] nlike most highway projects, it is not a response to traffic but a omoter of it. The Highway, in other words, *may* in time help to eate environmental conditions which are favorable to integration.

The other major project associated with ECAFE initiative is the velopment of the Mekong. Perhaps no other experiment in regional operation within the developing regions of the world has received ore attention. Much has been made of the fact that under ECAFE's

---

[40] *Ibid.*, pp. 53-54.
[41] See *Fifteen Years of Activity of the Economic Commission for Europe, 47-1962* (UN Document E/ECE/473/Rev.1), pp. 16, 81.
[42] Wightman, p. 221.

patient nurturing the Mekong Project has gone forward durin
periods of bitter political and even military conflict in the Southea
Asian subregion. By any standard ECAFE's performance has be
a creditable one.[43] The Coordination Committee, a brainchild of t
Commission's second Executive Secretary, C. V. Narasimhan, is
unique instrumentality in Asia, a body composed of representativ
of the four riparian countries with authority to raise funds ar
approve programs for implementation. It was not intended to be
supranational body and it has not evolved in that direction, b
under "the ECAFE umbrella"[44] the Committee has survived ar
registered tangible progress. Some of the most critical hurdles l
ahead, and the pattern of cooperation for decisions with respect
surveys and dam construction may not spill over into decision ma
ing with respect to costs, benefits, or modes of operation, not to me
tion other questions involving subregional development. Nevertheles
one is compelled to agree with Wightman that "the tinder of tl
ECAFE vision has been set alight."[45]

The second category of ECAFE initiatives includes those base
upon the assumption

that the purpose of any major measures of intraregional co-operation mu
be to give the trade and production structure of the ECAFE countries
more regional orientation.[46]

This theme is not new, dating back at least to Lokanathan's aid
mémoire to the heads of delegations at a Tokyo session of the Con
mission in 1955;[47] but the ECAFE Secretariat approached the ar
of regional planning circumspectly for many years. Wightman tak
the Secretariat to task for its failure to pursue the matter mo
vigorously, suggesting that "a touch of questing boldness on th
theme would not have been amiss"[48] as long ago as 1955 and offerin
in mitigation the Secretariat's new preoccupation with the Mekon
Modest steps in the direction of regional cooperation in the field
trade and development were taken with the inauguration of Intr
regional Trade Promotion Talks in 1959 and Conferences of Asia
Planners, the first of which was held in New Delhi in 1961. Bot

---

[43] See *ibid.*, pp. 183-202; and C. Hart Schaaf and Russell H. Fifield, *Tl
Lower Mekong: Challenge to Cooperation in Southeast Asia* (Princeton, N.J
D. Van Nostrand Co., 1963), especially Part II.

[44] The figure is Wightman's.

[45] Wightman, p. 197.

[46] UN Document E/CN.11/641, p. 57.

[47] See the discussion in Wightman, pp. 104-105, 292-294.

[48] *Ibid.*, p. 297.

ere instituted only after strong opposition had been overcome and
ily with the constructive if belated leadership of the Secretariat.
ut periodic discussion is no substitute for joint action, and of the
tter there has been very little to date. The discussions may be mov-
g in the direction of limited action, however. Two groups of
.perts have rendered reports, the first in 1961 and the second in
)63, which not only urge cooperative regional action but also stress
.e need to establish machinery for the purpose.[49] The Manila Min-
terial Conference on Asian Economic Cooperation used the second
' these two reports as its principal working paper and resolved
pursue most of its objectives.[50] But except for the important
:reement on establishment of an Asian Development Bank (which,
the recommendation of the Expert Group, would finance only
gional projects), the level of commitment has been low, with em-
1asis still upon further *ad hoc* meetings of representatives and
.pert groups. The institutional equivalent of LAFTA, not to men-
on the European Economic Community (EEC), is still over the
)rizon.

Unlike ECLA, ECAFE has had no appreciable impact upon its
ember states through the placement of regionally minded officials
om the Commission Secretariat in important government posts.
ot only has there been a less coherent gospel of regionalism to carry
ick to the service of individual governments, but there has also been
much lower turnover among senior officials. There is less enthusiasm
ir new blood in the ECAFE Secretariat than in any of the other
mmissions. The result has been the perpetuation of the tradition
caution and a failure to build useful bridges between the Secre-
riat and the ministries concerned with development questions. In
neral, the recommendations and activities of the ECAFE Secre-
riat seem to occupy no very prominent place in the discussion of
licy within governments.

ECA

The Economic Commission for Africa is still the least developed
1d hardest to categorize of the commissions, as one might expect
: an organization which is less than eight years old and more than

[49] Consultative Group of Experts on Regional Economic Cooperation in Asia
.961) and Working Group of Experts (1963). See UN Documents E/CN.11/
.5, February 13, 1963, and E/CN.11/641, Appendix V, Annex 2.
[50] The Ministerial Conference's resolution on Asian economic cooperation
)pears in UN Document E/CN.11/641, pp. 2-3.

half of whose members have been independent states no more th&
six years. Every effort has been made to give the Commission pari'
with ECLA and ECAFE, however, and in UN circles there are tho&
who insist that the real meaning of ECA is "every cent for Africa.
In its relatively brief life ECA has overtaken the other commissio&
in size of staff,[51] in the volume of UN regional technical assistan
projects,[52] and in the number of subregional offices.

In spite of all this activity, and some would say in part because &
it, ECA has not yet developed a distinctive style of operation or a
identifiable sense of direction. Most of its membership lived unt
recently as colonies either of France or of the United Kingdom, an
economically most ECA members still remain within the orbit of t&
former metropolitan power. The preferential treatment accorde
countries in the French Community by the EEC and countries of t&
British Commonwealth by the United Kingdom is "a disintegratin
factor in Africa, and tends to perpetuate the cleavage between t&
British and French areas of the continent."[53] Furthermore, the p&
litical boundaries make even less economic sense on this badly fra&
mented continent than they do in other areas. The number of stat&
involved in any regional or subregional negotiations looking to ec&
nomic union would necessarily be large if negotiations are to be ec&
nomically meaningful, and yet the larger the number of participan&
the more difficult the task of mutually satisfactory negotiation.

Nor are the fragmentation of Africa and the fact of distinctiv
areas of residual British and French influence the only significar
forces acting upon the Commission. The Pan-African leadershi
aspirations of some African states are viewed with suspicion b
others; there are latent problems in the relationship between t&
Arab members of ECA, especially the United Arab Republic, an
the sub-Saharan African states; there has been competition over t&

[51] Professional staff as of April 1 in each of several recent years:

	1960	1962	1964
ECAFE	78	75	87
ECLA	87	87	103
ECA	34	70	102

(Figures supplied by the Administrative Management Service of the UN Se&
retariat and by the individual commission secretariats.)

[52] In 1965 the UN was executing agency for regional projects in Africa unde
the Expanded Program of Technical Assistance (EPTA) and its own regula
program totaling approximately $1,520,000; most of the projects were decentra'
ized to ECA. This is to be compared with the figures for Asia ($1,010,000) an
Latin America ($1,000,000). (UN Document E/4075, June 14, 1965, p. 24.)

[53] Dell, p. 286.

cation of subregional offices. Of singular importance has been the
ntinuing struggle for self-determination of the indigenous African
ipulation in the southern quarter of the continent. This issue, which
iites African states as does no other, has also distracted ECA from
; economic tasks. Although ECOSOC "resolved" the problem in
'63 by expelling Portugal from membership in ECA[54] and suspend-
g South Africa until conditions for constructive cooperation had
en restored by a change in that country's racial policies,[55] in the
rger sense ECA functions at less than full effectiveness because
e primary preoccupation of many of its member governments re-
ains the colonial and racial issues.

Another issue which has preempted the attention of the Commission
the Africanization of the ECA Secretariat. ECA is the only one
' the three commissions serving the developing world the majority
' whose professional staff is not indigenous to the region. But the
.lent pool in Africa is still shallow, a stubborn fact which has made
difficult to Africanize the Commission's Secretariat. The effort to
） so continues, however, with the result that ECA's staff, in spite
 ˸ some areas of considerable skill, is not yet either particularly
fective or stable. Nor was there stable leadership at the top during
ie critical early years. The first Executive Secretary, Mekki Abbas,
\d only a brief tenure, and the second, Robert K. A. Gardiner, spent
\s first year in the post on assignment in the Congo (Leopoldville).
olitical considerations have dictated that there be a French-speaking
frican Deputy Executive Secretary, and the result seems to have
en to smuggle the continent's divisions into the Secretariat rather
\an to ameliorate the problem. As a result of uncertain leadership,
aff deficiencies, lack of experience, and the imperatives of Africani-
\tion, ECA has had to move with "deliberate speed."

Although ECA has been plagued by the existence of barriers not
'its making, it has been spared some other problems which could
ave complicated its efforts to establish itself as an effective force
ι Africa. In the first place, neither the United States nor the Soviet
'nion is a member although it was originally assumed that both
ould be; this has partially removed from ECA the propensity,
ften noticeable in ECAFE, to substitute ideological argument for
ιore pragmatic discussion of hard issues. In the second place, the
'rganization of African Unity (OAU) had not yet been launched
·hen ECA was created in 1958. Had the order been reversed, ECA

---

[54] ECOSOC Resolution 974 D III (XXXVI), July 24, 1963.
[55] ECOSOC Resolution 974 D IV (XXXVI), July 30, 1963.

might have failed, its role preempted by another organization, pr spectively stronger because its participants are foreign ministe rather than economic and finance ministers. On the other hand, t relatively late establishment of the Economic Commission for Afri meant that the conference habit, dating back to Bandung in 195 was built into ECA as it had not been in the case of ECAFE.

Like ECLA, ECA has had to compete with other regional organiz tions; and like ECLA, ECA has benefited in this competition from i "regional purity." ECA's principal strength, however, derives fro the simple fact that it has survived while other African organizatio have folded. The Organization of African Unity is, of course, vei much alive; but the OAU has come to depend upon the ECA Secr tariat to do its economic and social work, a relationship which tl Commission has encouraged and which is facilitated by the locatic of both organizations in Addis Ababa.

In the final analysis, there is probably not now in Africa a dispos tion to see economic problems as the most critical ones. This tak pressure off ECA, but it also deprives ECA of some of its prospectiv importance and suggests that African political leaders will probabl not for a time tolerate the emergence of strong leaders within tl ECA Secretariat. The prospect, therefore, is for a further develo] ment of Secretariat strength; continued leadership in such area as the development of statistical standards through the Conferen of African Statisticians; the gradual assumption of more operation responsibilities under the decentralization program; an expansion (advisory and training services through the African Institute fc Economic Development and Planning in Dakar; and the furthe elaboration of an economic profile for the continent. The impact the EEC, the example of LAFTA, and participation in planning fc UNCTAD are making the ECA Secretariat more integration con scious. It has prepared preliminary documentation on the subject c an African common market,[56] helped to launch an African Develop ment Bank, worked with a group of experts in the preparation of report on an African payments union,[57] organized industrial cc ordination missions to several subregions in Africa, and laid th groundwork for a standing Conference of African Planners. Thi list of activities could be expanded. There is obviously a great dea of ferment within ECA, but the fact remains that virtually every on of these programs is still on the drawing board. What is more, th

[56] See UN Document E/CN.14/261 and Corr.1.
[57] UN Document E/CN.14/262.

ans are still fuzzy and Commission discussions still deal in gen-
alities, as evidenced by the following excerpt from the summary of
scussions during a recent ECA session : ''The creation of an African
mmon market was a generally accepted goal. What remained to be
termined, was the best way of going about it.''[58]

It may be that the most significant impact of the Commission upon
tional political systems will be registered through the subregion-
ization of ECA's structure and work program. One UN official
ens the subregional aspects of ECA's activity to the submerged
rtion of an iceberg. Although the iceberg analogy may seem
matically out of place in a discussion of African affairs, it is true
at ECA has created subregional offices for West Africa in Niamey,
r East Africa in Lusaka, for North Africa in Tangier, and for
ntral Africa in Leopoldville; that it has curtailed the number of
rge meetings in favor of small, specialized subregional meetings in
ch fields as trade, energy, industry, and transport; that many of
e regional technical assistance projects proposed and implemented
 ECA are organized subregionally (such as the Regional Center
r Demographic Research and Training in Cairo, serving Algeria,
bya, Morocco, the Sudan, Tunisia, and the United Arab Republic,
d the subregional statistical training centers which serve different
ents from such points as Yaoundé, Accra, Rabat, and Addis
baba). This emphasis upon the subregion is made explicit in a
cent statement of the Executive Secretary of ECA, who noted that
there was to be economic progress in the foreseeable future,

ch country would have to determine its development strategy and each sub-
gion its machinery for cooperation. Groups of countries should decide on
teria for sharing out new industries, and conferences should be superseded
 closer negotiations between countries.[59]

y focusing its studies increasingly upon subregional groupings of
ates and giving its industrial coordination missions subregional
signments, the Secretariat has sought to translate this appeal into
ate policy. The talk of an African common market has a regionwide
vor, and the Secretariat is trying to develop an integrated African
lecommunications network with the help of the International Tele-
mmunications Union (ITU), to nationalize African air transport
 cooperation with the International Civil Aviation Organization
CAO), and to promote a trans-Sahara road link, all objectives

58 Economic and Social Council *Official Records* (37th session), Supplement
. 10, paragraph 234 (c).
59 *Ibid.*, paragraph 109.

which transcend any one subregion. However, the principal thrust
ECA is today subregional, suggesting that the Commission is comi
to terms with some of the geographical and linguistic realities
Africa.

RECAPITULATION AND
SOME TENTATIVE CONCLUSIONS

The foregoing paragraphs constitute a *tour d'horizon,* a necessari
brief and limited inquiry into the nature of the momentum, if an
imparted by ECLA, ECAFE, and ECA to the regions which th
serve. Hopefully they offer a few benchmarks for further study
the extent to which the commissions have assumed an integrati
function.

Earlier in the article five questions were raised relative to t
performance of the commissions. They concerned the ideologic
leadership of the Executive Secretary; the tangible initiatives tak
by the commission, as reflected in the work program; the institution
legacy of the commission at the regional or subregional level; t
flow of regionally minded personnel from commission secretariat
positions of influence within states; and the image of the commissi
within the region. Although it is difficult to measure leadership a
initiative or to pin down such an elusive commodity as image, a ve
rough scale of integrative output can be constructed, ranging fro
nil through marginal, low, modest, and substantial to high, for ea
of the five areas. A net evaluation should then be possible.

	ECLA	ECAFE	ECA
Ideological leadership	Substantial	Low	Marginal
Tangible initiatives	Substantial	Modest	Marginal
Institutional legacies	Modest	Low	Marginal
Personnel mobility	Modest	Marginal	Marginal
Regional image	Modest	Marginal	Low
Net evaluation of integrative output	Modest	Low	Marginal

ECLA has had the highest integrative output. Certainly the e
vironmental conditions in that region are more conducive to this ki
of thrust than those in Asia or Africa, but ECLA could easily ha
fallen into the rut of a more limited role. Instead, its leadership h
been characterized by an ideology which, while short of supranatio
alism, has nonetheless been instrumental in focusing attention
regional approaches to problems previously deemed domestic.
initiatives have given meaning to that ideology, putting it to wo

a program which has given to the region several modest but pioneering projects, some of which may yet acquire supranational traits. Alone of the commissions it has a record of senior staff mobility, a phenomenon which spreads ECLA's ideas and prestige and which reflects at least some willingness to entertain some of those ideas. The commission has a strong image although it is predictably controversial; at least it is paid the compliment of attention.

ECAFE, on the other hand, has been handicapped by the vastness and variety of its region, by the shadow of Communist China, by fear of domination by India and Japan, by a protracted quest for identity, and by an uncritical attitude toward its own performance. No organizational ideology or comprehensive program for regional growth and development has been put forward by the Commission's leadership. In this case, the *ad hoc* initiatives of the Commission have anticipated the development of an ideology, and one or two of these, e.g., the Mekong Project, are monuments to ECAFE's creativity and perseverance. Although the Commission has been called extravagantly an economic parliament for Asia, there is little evidence that this wish, if wish it is, will become father to the fact. ECAFE's integrative output has been low.

The third commission in the developing world, ECA, is even weaker than ECAFE in every respect except image. This is not surprising, given its relative newness and growing pains. That its image in Africa exceeds its accomplishments is due to a variety of factors, including the importance attached to international organization generally on that continent. Otherwise, it is too early to make a judgment about ECA, except to say that to date its integrative output is low, buoyed only by the growing consciousness of a common cause among all African peoples from which ECA benefits and to which it may in time contribute.

In all three cases the judgment as to integrative output is based upon the complete record. If one were to look only at the current situation, it is doubtful if ECLA would stand out so far above ECAFE. Some veteran observers at the UN think they detect signs of stagnation in Santiago, while ECAFE is coming to life. A flurry of excitement has attended the launching of the Asian Development Bank; on the other hand, the slow progress of LAFTA has eroded some of ECLA's enthusiasm, and continued uncertainty about the viability of the Alliance for Progress appears to have contributed to a state of suspended animation in ECLA. But these observations may only suggest that what distinguishes the regional commissions may be less important than what they have in common. If ECLA is in less creative phase, it may be that it has simply encountered some the boundaries imposed by environmental conditions, while ECAF may be discovering in the midst of regional conflict that it can (more, that the very urgency of the political situation may genera pressure for functional cooperation.

The performance of the commissions indicates that each of the like water seeking its level, will in time but at a differential rate pr duce some common institutions and policies. ECLA has frequent pioneered, although action by ECAFE and ECA has often had a independent genesis. Thus, the creation of an Asian Developmen Bank means that each region now has both a regional planning i stitute and a development bank. Neither is an instance of econom union, of course, but both reflect a capacity to cooperate in launchin institutions of continuing utility to the region as a whole. If neith promotes integration directly, they will at least afford an opportuni for nationals of several states from within the region to coopera in managing programs of regional scope, and they will hopeful contribute to a reshaping of national views about integration an national capacities to approach the subject seriously.

Similarly, recent measures of decentralization from UN Hea quarters to the commissions and attendant efforts to strengthen th latter's secretariats should provide more opportunities for the con missions to identify themselves with specific, concrete tasks (regional proportions. Although decentralization is primarily a mov ment to transfer UN decision making in the economic field from th hands of Europeans and North Americans to persons from the deve oping countries, not a movement to transfer decision making withi the region from the state to some subregional or regional organizatio it has the effect of focusing attention upon agencies of regional scop and upon projects of a regional rather than a country-by-countr nature inasmuch as it is regional projects which have been decentra ized.[60]

Another institutional development in which all three commission share and one which may have a profound impact upon their directio and function is the United Nations Conference on Trade and Deve opment. The Secretariats of ECLA, ECAFE, and ECA served a research staff for the several groups of developing countries whic joined forces to form the surprisingly cohesive and effective "77"

[60] For the most recent official statements on the status of decentralization se UN Documents A/6114, November 23, 1965, and E/4075, June 14, 1965.

Geneva. There is every reason to believe that they will continue to perform in the capacity of "secretariat for the poor," a role which the commissions have explicitly been invited to play. Dr. Prebisch has carried his economic doctrines from ECLA, where he made Santiago the most vital of the regional centers, to UNCTAD. Just as the commission secretariats helped to make the first Geneva Conference a success, so should the UNCTAD connection logically contribute to a broader, regional outlook within the commissions.

Although the subregional approach has been made most explicit in the case of ECA, all three commissions have been characterized by this kind of pragmatic response to the challenge of political and economic diversity within their regions. In spite of the concern of each commission for a whole region, many of the important instances of commission initiative, such as the Central American Agreements and the Mekong Project, have a subregional focus; the broader scope of LAFTA and the Asian Highway does not conceal the fact that both are primarily programs of a subregional nature, at least for the present. It would seem fairly safe to assert that the commissions will continue to explore the possibilities of subregional cooperation. If the commissions are less ambitious with respect to the geographic scope of their projects, they can perhaps afford to be more ambitious with respect to their integrative content.

All of this activity underscores the vitality of the commissions, but it does not mean that economic policy is about to be made at any level higher than that of the nation-state. Certainly the regional commissions themselves have no such mandate or the faintest prospect of acquiring one, and the evidence that ideas and initiatives emanating from the commissions will foster supranational decision making is fragmentary and on the whole disappointing. To date we have only LAFTA and the Central American Agreements as modest examples of economic union. Cooperation, not federation, has been the highwater mark reached by the commissions, and much of the cooperation is still in a rudimentary stage.

Integrative output of the commissions, we may conclude, is related closely to environmental conditions and resultant receptivity of member states to ideas and initiatives of the commissions and their secretariats. One of the principal functions of the commissions has been to increase the awareness of member states of the possibilities for cooperative economic behavior within the limits set by those conditions and to help devise schemes for mobilizing energies which will carry members to those limits. Hopefully, conditions and attitudes

will be modified in the process, thereby removing some of the limit
tions upon cooperative action within the region. In any event, wheth
the commissions will play a role of increasing consequence within the
respective regions depends upon their ability to increase their int
grative output by overcoming environmental impediments and
sustain their impact by creative adaptation in the face of inevitab
environmental changes.

J. S. Nye

Patterns and Catalysts in
Regional Integration

I

Is it possible to integrate states into larger unions without the use
f force? Should we think of a continuous "federalizing process"
n which economic integration is a first step?[1] Are there certain
onditions under which economic integration of a group of nations
utomatically triggers political unity?

Since in most historical instances of political union, political and
conomic integration developed more or less simultaneously, it is not
urprising that an apparent exception from recent history has at-
racted considerable attention. The European Economic Community
EEC) has had a strong impact both on statesmen from other areas
f the world and on theorists concerned with international organiza-
ion. Although a great number of questions remain unanswered about
he process of European integration, scholars have begun to ex-
lore the question of the extent to which theories developed primarily
pon the basis of the European experience can be generalized to
ther parts of the world.

As yet we have far too few cases to be able to make very sound
eneralizations about comparative regional integration. Some scholars
re not even sure whether the similarities between integration proc-

Reprinted from *International Organization*, XIX, No. 4 (Autumn 1965), with
he permission of The World Peace Foundation.

[1] See C. J. Friedrich, "International Federalism in Theory and Practice," in
lmer Plischke (ed.), *Systems of Integrating the International Community*
Princeton, N.J.: Van Nostrand, 1963), pp. 126-137.

esses in industrial and non-industrial contexts are sufficiently great
than the differences between the two contexts to justify a comparati
approach.[2]

A suggestion worthy of detailed critical attention as to how to
about comparative study of regional integration has been made
Ernst Haas and Philippe Schmitter.[3] These authors suggest a patte
of nine variables[4] whose interrelations may remain unknown b
which seem likely to intervene more or less consistently betwe
economic and political unions. By hypothesizing this pattern, Ha
and Schmitter lead us to seek possible functional equivalents f
variables which may be missing in particular cases.

The value of the Haas-Schmitter approach is limited, however,
difficulties concerning two of their underlying concepts and by
related ambiguity which results from their failure to spell out t
relationships between their variables. The questionable concepts a
the idea that "the relationship between economic and political unio
had best be treated as a continuum" and the characterization
integration as "gradual politization of the actors' purposes whi
were initially considered 'technical' or 'noncontroversial,' " resultii
in an outcome of "automatic politization" where

all other things being roughly equal, a "high" scorer in our categories
likely to be transformed into some species of political union even if some
the members are far from enthusiastic about this prospect when it is argue
in purely political terms.[5]

How accurate is it to conceive of an integration process in the ca
of developing areas as a continuum? And is the nature of the proce

[2] Ellen Frey-Wouters, "The Progress of European Integration," *Wor
Politics,* April 1965 (Vol. 17, No. 3), p. 461.

[3] See Ernst B. Haas and Philippe C. Schmitter, "Economics and Differenti
Patterns of Political Integration: Projections About Unity in Latin America,
International Organization, Autumn 1964 (Vol. 18, No. 4), pp. 705-737; a:
Philippe C. Schmitter and Ernst B. Haas, *Mexico and Latin American Econom
Integration* (Berkeley, Calif.: Institute of International Studies, 1964), pp. 1-3
The Haas-Schmitter scheme is concerned with that aspect of the spectrum
integration in which increasing interdependence is sufficient to support politic
institutions. This might also be called unification. To avoid confusion, my usa;
of "integration" in this article follows theirs. "Federation" refers to a pa
ticular institutional form of political union.

[4] *Background conditions:* 1) size of the units, 2) rate of transactions,
extent of pluralism, and 4) elite complementarity; *conditions at the time*
economic union: 5) governmental purposes, 6) powers of union; and *proce
conditions:* 7) decision-making style, 8) rate of transaction, and 9) adaptabili
of governments. See the table on p. 343.

[5] Haas and Schmitter, *International Organization,* Vol. 18, No. 4, pp. 707, 71

ally "politization"? The idea that there may be discontinuities in
the integration process — gaps which call for some extraneous *deus
machina* to overcome — has been suggested about the European
process. The distinction tends to be made not so much between economics and politics as such as between "high" and "low" politics.
"High" politics is symbol laden, emotive, and based on attitudes
characterized by greater intensity and duration than "low" politics
which is consequently more susceptible to the rational calculation of
benefits associated with economic problems. Whether the distinction
is phrased in terms of high and low politics, *gemeinschaft* versus
gesellschaft, or Edmund Burke's nation versus trading company, the
essential point seems to be that what is true about integration in the
one sphere may not be true in the other.[6]

We do not know yet whether the alleged discontinuity will prove
crucial in Europe. Intense and durable (*gemeinschaft*) loyalties tend
to follow and coexist with associational or instrumental (*gesellschaft*)
attitudes after some period of time. The crucial variables determining
whether the alleged discontinuity disrupts an integration process
would then be the length of the "period of vulnerability" before less
durable and intense instrumental loyalties are reinforced by more
durable and intense communal loyalties and whether the integration
process is confronted with a grave crisis that would cause actors to
reverse decisions on instrumental grounds during the "period of
vulnerability." It is conceivable that if the European Economic
Community is not threatened by a depression or similar grave crisis
before durable loyalties are established, the gradually rising price
of disruption may make the theoretical discontinuity between the
two types of politics irrelevant, as the Haas-Schmitter approach
suggests.[7]

In many underdeveloped areas (and probably among Communist
countries), however, much that in the European context would be
simple welfare politics becomes tinged with emotive and symbolic
content that is usually associated with national security politics.[8]

[6] See Stanley Hoffmann, "Discord in Community: The North Atlantic Area
as a Partial International System," *International Organization,* Summer 1963
(Vol. 17, No. 3), pp. 521-549; Karl Deutsch, "Supranational Organization in
1960's," *Journal of Common Market Studies* (Vol. 1, No. 3), pp. 212-218;
Edmund Burke quoted in Arnold Zurcher, "The European Community — An
Approach to Federal Integration," in Plischke, pp. 87-88.

[7] For evidence that this is occurring, see Leon N. Lindberg, "Decision Making
and Integration in the European Community," *International Organization,* Winter 1965 (Vol. 19, No. 1), pp. 56-80.

[8] The content of "high" politics may vary with the context. In some

One consequence of this is that there is less opportunity for auton
mous bureaucrats to go quietly about the business of integration
"noncontroversial" spheres.[9] The major problem then is not, as
Europe, whether some crisis will make the theoretical discontinui
between the two types of politics relevant. It is as though the integi
tion process had already reached the "high" politics area before t
benefits from the welfare politics of integration had become gre
enough to encourage the learning of new behavior. If the problem
most underdeveloped areas is one of premature "overpolitization
then it is not helpful for comparative study to conceive of the integi
tion process as "gradual politization." If we wish to continue to co
ceive of integration as politization, then we must add the concepts
"depolitization" (possibly a corollary of the growth of politic
pluralism which might accompany economic development) and eve
tual "repolitization." Since this would probably involve a tin
period of generations, we might prefer to alter the characterization
integration as politization to allow us to be more discerning in t
shorter run.

If everything tends to be "high" politics, then the image of
continuum and the theoretical discontinuity between two types
politics are not relevant to an integration process in this type of
underdeveloped context. Nonetheless, we might wish to speak
"institutional" discontinuities in such a context. In theory, we ca
conceive of a whole spectrum of possible institutional arrangemen
between economic and political union. But in some underdevelop
areas, parts of the theoretical institutional continuum may not
politically relevant. For instance, given a politics of strong person
control of state and party machinery, institutional arrangemen
which do not promise sufficient immediate centralization of power
attract key political leaders to the new center may be unviable. T
possibilities suggested by the concept of a continuum may not ex
in practice.[10]

The other major problem with the Haas-Schmitter approach

---

instances, economic problems like location of industry may show more of t
aspects of "high" politics than a subject like defense which is usually ass
ciated with "high" politics in Europe.

[9] The almost impossible problem of avoiding political entanglement is
scribed in detail by Albert Tevoedjre, former Secretary-General of the Uni
africaine et malgache (UAM), in *Pan-Africanism in Action* (Cambridge, Mas
1965).

[10] It is possible to conceive of bridges for this institutional gap, for instan
the allowing of key leaders to hold office in their territorial bases and at t
new central level simultaneously. However, this may be difficult in practice.

ir failure to be more specific about the relationships between their
ciables. Is their list of nine variables merely a handy checklist
e others which have been published,[11] or is it designed to tell us
re? For instance, are high scores (or functional equivalents) on
nine variables a sufficient condition for ''automatic politization''
en in an underdeveloped or Communist area where a small, con-
ry-minded elite is in complete control of the political machinery?
d are each of the variables (or functional equivalents) a necessary
dition for automatic politization? If one or more of the variables,
high elite complementarity in conditions of high transactions,
sufficient in the political context of an underdeveloped area, of
at value then is the rest of the scheme? When must we find func-
nal equivalents and when need we not bother? Finally, the term
unctional equivalence'' tends to imply the existence of system or
terdependence, yet it is precisely this aspect which is absent from
e Haas-Schmitter scheme.

The best way to illustrate both the value and the problems of the
aas-Schmitter scheme as an approach to integration in underde-
loped areas is to apply it to what once appeared to be one of the
st promising cases in the underdeveloped world, the attempts of
st Africans to form a federation on the basis of their economic
ion in 1963.

II

The states of former British East Africa (Kenya, Tanzania, and
ganda) constitute an area the size of Western Europe. However,
1963, they had a combined population of only 25 million and a
oss domestic product (GDP) the size of that of a European city
550 million). The East African states provide a particularly in-
resting example of the problems of creating political unions in
frica not only because their three leaders met in June 1963 and
edged that they would federate before the end of that year (a
edge not fulfilled) but because so many of the conditions for suc-
ssful federation between states existed in East Africa. Using K. C.

[11] See, for instance, the ten variables listed by Karl Deutsch and others,
*litical Community and the North Atlantic Area: International Organization
the Light of Historical Experience* (Princeton, N.J.: Princeton University
ess, 1957), pp. 123-154. For an example of their limited value in an African
ntext, see Chapter 11 of the excellent study by William Foltz, *From French
est Africa to the Mali Federation* (New Haven, Conn.: Yale University Press,
64). Haas is aware of this problem and helped to call it to the author's
tention.

Wheare's criteria, the East Africans enjoyed geographical neighb-
hood, prior political association, and roughly similar colonial politi-
institutions. They were motivated by desires to gain and mainta
their independence, to gain economically, and to have a stronger
fense through federation.[12]

Moreover, the East Africans had a considerable degree of soc
integration. Not only do the East Africans have a common el
language (English), but Swahili serves as an indigenous ling
franca in Tanzania, most of Kenya, and parts of Uganda. Nairobi, t
capital of Kenya, serves as a commercial center of East Africa, a
Kenyan newspapers are read in the other two countries. Many me
bers of the elites of the three countries, including 40 percent of t
cabinet ministers, attended Uganda's Makerere College and, at t
other end of the social spectrum, a number of Kenyan workers (a
a lesser number of Ugandans and Tanzanians) travel to the oth
countries for labor.

East Africa is connected by more than 4,000 miles of railway, t
capitals are within a long day's drive of each other over all-weath
roads, and East African Airways (EAA) schedules flights to near
all parts of the area. Though a large majority of the population
each country is rural and illiterate and communications cannot co
pare with those in Europe, the beginnings of impressive social int
gration — of the growth of transnational society — exist. Certainl
in transportation, language, education, telecommunications, and ne
media, the East Africans are more socially integrated among the
selves than they are with any other countries.

Colonial rule bequeathed an impressive degree of function
cooperation to the East African states. By 1927 the United Kingdo
had created an East African common market, and in the 1930's var
ous common services such as postal and telecommunications admini
tration, meteorology, locust control, air service, and higher educatic
were established. After the Second World War, a central bureaucrac
and legislature were established for the common services. This orga
ization, the East Africa High Commission, was only reluctantl
accepted at first, but, with the coming of independence to Tanganyik
in 1961, farsighted African leaders arranged for the maintenance

---

[12] See K. C. Wheare, *Federal Government* (3rd ed.; London: Oxford Unive
sity Press, 1953), p. 37. Although Kenya is involved in a territorial dispute wi
its northern neighbor, Somalia, Uganda has disproportionately large neighbo
to the north and west, and Tanzania harbors refugees from Portuguese Ea
Africa to its south, none of the East African states felt an absolutely compellir
need to federate for the sake of defense.

e organization in slightly altered form as the East African Com-
on Services Organization (EACSO).

EACSO consists of an "Authority" composed of the heads of
vernment which decides specified matters on a unanimous basis,
Central Legislative Assembly (CLA) indirectly elected by the
ree territorial legislatures and limited in jurisdiction areas of
ACSO competence, four ministerial committees including one
binet minister from each territory which meet four times a year to
ersee the administration of the various services, and a bureaucracy
aich includes a Secretary-General and some 300 senior civil ser-
nts with headquarters in Nairobi.[13] This executive is not as strong
the Commission of the European Economic Community, and there
neither a detailed treaty governing the common market nor a
risdiction to try infringements of the cooperative arrangements
there is in Europe.

EACSO plays a large role within the underdeveloped East African
onomy. It has nearly 21,000 full-time employees (including un-
illed labor) and accounts for nearly 8 percent of the GDP, but most
this is accounted for by its three most important services, the
lf-financing communications services (East African Railways
d Harbors [EAR&H], East African Posts and Telecommunications
EAP&T], and East African Airways). EACSO also administers
ut does not set the rates of) income and excise taxes, meteorology,
d civil aviation and runs eleven research institutes.

In their common market the East Africans enjoyed almost free
ovement of goods as well as labor and capital. Major exceptions
ere certain agricultural products. Transactions were made easier by
e existence of a common currency although this involved the
onetary rigidity of a currency board since there was no central
nk. Although interterritorial trade was about one-fifth of external
ports, trade between the East African territories grew more rap-
ly after World War II than did their trade with the outside world.
 particular, Kenya's exports of light manufactures to the rest of
ast Africa grew rapidly. When this caused loss of customs revenue
 the other partners, a distributable pool (based on 40 percent of
mpany income tax and 6 percent of customs and excise revenue)
as established to help compensate Uganda and Tanganyika.[14]

---

[13] Some services and research institutions have headquarters outside Nairobi.
[14] For a detailed description of EACSO, the East African common market,
d the frictions involved, see Joseph S. Nye, Jr., "East African Economic
tegration," *Journal of Modern African Studies*, December 1963 (Vol. 1,

Despite adjustments, it has not been so easy to separate hig
politics from technical economic cooperation in the context of ec
nomically underdeveloped countries whose political leaders are i
terested in using government power for rapid economic and soci
change. Frictions developed between the three countries in tl
coordination of foreign economic policies, in the coordination of d
velopment plans, in the tendency for new industries to cluster
Kenya, and in the reluctance of Ugandans to have Kenyans compe
in the Ugandan labor market given the general conditions of u
employment in East Africa. Disputes also arose over the distributic
of the benefits of various services. The rigid monetary policy caus
interterritorial problems, and there was no agreement over wh
powers should be given to a central bank.[15] Finally, in 1964, Ta
ganyika, long the strongest and most ideologically committed adv
cate of cooperation and federation, threatened to withdraw from tl
common market and from some of the common services and to esta
lish a separate currency. After hastily convened talks, an arrang
ment was reached which allows East African countries to prote
certain of their industries against each other's competition — tl
first major breach of the common market. In addition, the East Afr
cans agreed that of six new industries, three would locate in Ta
ganyika, two in Uganda, and one in Kenya. Even this agreement h
failed to remove the sources of friction.[16]

The East African experience suggests that in the political ar
economic setting of the new African states, a high degree of ec
nomic integration spills over into political integration or spills bac
To a considerable extent, Tanganyika accepted a number of cor
promises on functional cooperation as a first step to federation. I
June 1963, when the East African leaders announced their intentic
to federate, it seemed that this policy of sacrifice and restraint c
full exercise of sovereignty had borne fruit. After a few weeks
discussion, however, talks on federation bogged down and, by tl

---

No. 4), pp. 475-502. See also *East Africa: Report of the Economic and Fisc
Commission* (Cmd. 1279) (London: Her Majesty's Stationery Office, 1961); a
Benton Massell, *East African Economic Union* (Santa Monica, Calif.: RAN
Corporation, 1963), pp. 1-89.

[15] In 1963 Erwin Blumenthal of the Deutsche Bundesbank suggested a tw
tiered banking system in a report to the Tanganyikan government, but it h
not been implemented. See *The Present Monetary System and its Future* (D
es Salaam, Tanganyika: Government Printer, 1963).

[16] See *Kampala Agreement* (Dar es Salaam, Tanzania: United Republ
Information Service, 1964).

d of the year, Tanganyikan enthusiasm and patience had been
verely sapped. Many observers attributed this failure in the federal
gotiations to the dissimilarity of political institutions, in particular
the continued strength of the separatist Buganda area in Uganda.
ctually, this was only a minor factor. It was those Ugandans who
d previously been most committed to the idea of federation (and to
e ideology of Pan-Africanism) who became reluctant to surrender
eir control over the power to reshape their local society.

In part, personal fears contributed to Ugandan hesitation — it is
metimes said that no executive agrees to a merger if it means the
imination of his position. But the Ugandan concern was not some-
ing that could be solved simply by insuring that a few jobs went
the right people. The Ugandans balked at economic and institu-
onal issues which affected Ugandans' power over such matters as
onetary reserves, public debts, location of industry, and location
the capital. As representatives of the smallest and landlocked state,
gandans opposed those provisions of the draft constitution which
ovided for a powerful presidency, a weak upper house, and central
vernment power over Ugandan resources.

On the other hand, any compromise weakening the proposed con-
itution would have meant that the proposed federation would not
ave had sufficient power to redistribute industry and resources
om richest Kenya to poorer Tanganyika in order to satisfy the
tter state. In short, Tanganyika was dissatisfied with the status
o for economic and ideological reasons and strongly favored a
ntralized federal pattern. Uganda, for political reasons, preferred
e status quo to a centralized federal pattern. Kenya, which gained
ost from the status quo economically, was interested in any com-
omise which preserved its economic gains but leaned toward Tan-
nyika in political preferences. As the prospects of federation faded,
anganyika became less willing to compromise on functional inte-
ration.[17] In the aftermath Kenya has become somewhat disen-
anted with its concessions on industrial location, Uganda has an-
ounced plans for establishing its own central bank as well as its
tention of withdrawing Makerere from the University of East
frica, and Tanzania has promoted arrangements that will terminate
e common currency. Whether these indications of further spillback
ill prevail, as seems likely, or whether alternative positive indicators
ch as plans to establish a common shipping line and to extend

[17] For details on these problems, see Joseph S. Nye, Jr., *Pan-Africanism and
st African Integration* (Cambridge, Mass.: Harvard University Press, 1965).

functional cooperation to include Zambia will result in stability, t
prospects for spillover into political union have enormously weaken(
since 1963.

III

A minor difficulty in applying the Haas-Schmitter framework
East Africa (see the table on p. 343) is that East African econom
union began much earlier under British colonial rule. Nonetheles
given the commitment of the new elites, we can take 1961 as a seco)
starting point. Turning first to the background conditions, in 19(
the comparable size and power of the units judged in terms of t]
"specific functional context of the union"[18] was somewhat u
balanced in favor of Kenya which sold more than twice as much
its partners than it bought from them. The effects of this imbalan(
however, were not unfavorable to further politization and inde(
served as a positive stimulus for Tanganyika. Imbalance in size d
contribute to the failure of politization in 1963, but not imbalance
terms of the specific *functional* context of the union. Uganda w
willing to maintain the imbalanced status quo. It was its small
population (seven million compared with Tanganyika's ten ar
Kenya's eight and one-half) in the context of *political* union whi(
caused its elite to fear loss of control of the nation-building, resourc
allocating governmental machinery.

Parenthetically, there may be a limit beyond which increasin
disproportion of size in both functional and political contexts e'
hances the prospects of political union. It can be argued that t]
formation of Tanzania in 1964 depended in part on the fact tha
Tanganyika was 360 times the size of its tiny, defenseless, islar
neighbor, Zanzibar. We will return to this point below.

The rate of transactions in 1961 was high by African standar(
even though the proportion of intramarket trade to total trade wa
about half that of the EEC. In elite complementarity, the commc
educational and political background of most East African leade
— at Makerere College and through participation in the Pan-Africa
Freedom Movement of East and Central Africa (PAFMECA) -
should give East Africa approximately as high a score in this regar
as the postwar European leaders of the EEC.

The major background condition in which East Africa received
low score was on the existence of modern (functionally specific

[18] Haas and Schmitter, *International Organization*, Vol. 18, No. 4, p. 711.

COMPARISON OF ECONOMIC UNIONS[a]

	EEC	EACM[b]/- EACSO	LAFTA
BACKGROUND CONDITIONS			
1. Size of units	mixed	mixed—	mixed
2. Rate of transaction	high	mixed+	mixed
3. Pluralism (modern)	high	low	mixed
4. Elite complementarity	high	high—	mixed
Total Judgment	high	mixed	mixed
CONDITIONS AT TIME OF ECONOMIC UNION			
5. Governmental purposes	high	mixed+	low
6. Powers of union	high	mixed—	low
Total Judgment	high	mixed	low
PROCESS CONDITIONS			
7. Decision-making style	mixed	mixed	mixed
8. Rate of transaction	high	mixed+	mixed
9. Adaptability of governments	high	mixed	mixed
Total Judgment	high	mixed	mixed
CHANCES OF POLITICAL UNION	good	possible	possible-doubtful

[a] Adapted from Haas and Schmitter, *International Organization*, Vol. 18, No. 4, p. 720. I have used Haas' judgment of scores for the European Economic Community and the Latin American Free Trade Association (LAFTA) but have used new scores for East Africa and suggested the alternative outcome of "political union" rather than "automatic politization."

[b] East African common market.

roups. The underdeveloped economies did not generate the full range of economic interests, middle-level managers to articulate and organize them, or pluralist ideologies to protect them that industrialized European economies generate. In theory, traditional groups might serve as a functional equivalent. In certain cases, tribal ties cross borders facilitate political integration. However, a stronger case can be made for the proposition that strong traditional pluralism generally increases the insecurity of a modern African political elite and makes it more reluctant to enter political unions with countries whose leaders are more firmly in control. The strength of traditional groups in Uganda hampered the development of a single party system comparable to that in Tanganyika and thus contributed to the fear on the part of the Ugandan political elite that they would lose political power in a larger union.

We can find a more plausible functional equivalent in the broad

sense in which Haas and Schmitter saw the *"técnicos"* with their U
Economic Commission for Latin America (ECLA) ideology as pe
forming an analogous function with respect to initiation of LAFT
that modern groups converging in a pragmatic calculus of benefi
did for the EEC.[19] The small political elites with their ideology
African unity very nearly served as a functional equivalent in tl
heady period following the May 1963 Addis Ababa Summit Confe
ence of Independent African States (which established the Organiz
tion of African Unity [OAU]). But when the Ugandan elite later fe
threatened by its earlier commitment, the dominant position of tl
small elite proved a sufficient condition to prevent spillover and tl
ideology was sufficiently diffuse to allow of reinterpretations to fit th
new attitude of the elite.

Moreover, as Ernst Haas and Philippe Schmitter note about tl
Latin American Free Trade Association, such a functional equivale
may be adequate for creation of a union but inadequate for its mai
tenance. What is more, it may even hinder its maintenance. An Ea
African federation might have encountered the problems of the Ma
Federation in West Africa. Small political elites committed
African unity were a functional equivalent for the missing conve
gence of modern groups in the formation of the Mali Federation, b
the same ideology blinded the Sudanese leaders to the concessio
they would have to make to Senegal to maintain the Federation.[20]

On the conditions at the time of the African confirmation of tl
economic union in 1961, East Africa gets a "mixed-plus" ratin
(the only doubt concerned part of the Ugandan elite) for havin
converging economic aims with a strong political commitment
eventual political union. On the powers or strategy of the unio
East Africa received only a "mixed" score. Despite the existence
a supranational bureaucracy disposing of nearly 8 percent of th
GDP (or more than the governmental budgets of Tanganyika
Uganda), there was no firm timetable for the dismantling of obsta
cles, and voting formulas emphasized unanimity. Moreover, nor
partisan regional bureaucrats were in a poor situation to take ind
pendent action in the highly politicized atmosphere of East Afric

As for the process conditions, East Africa received a "low-mixed
mark on decision-making style. Some committees of uninstructe
experts worked well, particularly in the financial and communic

---

[19] Schmitter and Haas, *Mexico and Latin American Economic Integratio*
p. 33.
[20] Foltz, pp. 118-165.

ons fields. Others, particularly in the politically sensitive fields of
commerce and industry, were reduced to lowest common denominator
solutions.

The score was "mixed-plus" with regard to the rate of transactions
after union. On the one hand, East African trade compared with
trade with the outside world increased in importance for each of the
three countries, and infrastructure was improved. On the other hand,
mobility of labor and educational interchange tended to decrease.

As for learning or adaptability of the governmental actors and
their ability to use crises for redefinition of aims at a higher level of
consensus, East Africa receives a "mixed" score. Awareness on the
part of governmental actors of the serious problems in their economic union contributed to the abortive attempts to create a federation. When this failed, the Tanganyikans precipitated a crisis which
the East Africans used as a stimulus for working out a compromise
solution which involved some infringement of the market but fore-
stalled at least for a while its total disruption or the disruption of the
services. Something better than a low score is deserved for attempts
to use crises to redefine aims at the *highest level politically possible*
rather than allowing spillback to proceed unchecked — even if the
attempts prove futile in the long run.

IV

Although the Haas-Schmitter framework directs our attention to
many of the relevant variables, it does not always lead us to ask
the right questions about them. Moreover, since the relationships
between the variables are not spelled out, it treats them all equally,
whereas there is reason to believe that relations between the elites is
by far the most important variable. One of the basic problems with
the Haas-Schmitter framework as a starting point for the comparative study of regional integration is that this "revised functionalism" still places too little emphasis on conscious political action.[21]
The concept of "automatic politization" smacks too much of the
functionalist preference for "the administration of things" — at
least for application to developing areas like Africa. This is not
based upon supposed irrationality of Africans. Careful calculation
of welfare benefits and economic interests when making decisions
makes sense only when the political framework within which in-

---

[21] See Ernst B. Haas, *Beyond the Nation-State: Functionalism and International Organization* (Stanford, Calif.: Stanford University Press, 1964), Chapter 1.

terests interact can be taken for granted. Most African states are st[] involved in determining and changing the structure within whi[] interests work. In such conditions, the primacy of politics mak[] sense.

In East Africa a small political elite in each country is intent [] using the powers of the captured colonial state to create a nation[] community; the prevalent ideology, influenced by the need for unit[] in the struggle for independence is more centralist than pluralis[] and the underdeveloped economies do not generate the full range [] economic interests or the middle-level managerial skills to organi[] what specific interests do exist. The resulting dominance of th[] political elite can in certain conditions be sufficient for achievemer[] of political union; but it also means that the transition from ec[] nomic union to political union is more visible and correspondingl[] more easily disrupted. Functionalist theory seems to rely on a ce[] tain invisibility of integrating forces, due either to the complexity [] industrial society or to a fit of absentmindedness on the part [] political leaders. Neither condition is likely in the highly politic[] atmosphere of new African states.

It is true that the East Africans often tended to become caught u[] by the "either-or" aspects of their situation and failed to explor[] all the institutional possibilities.[22] But it would not be wise to attrib[] ute the East African failure to unique conditions. As we suggeste[] earlier, many developing countries have small elites whose im[] patience, insecurity, or concern with nation building leads them t[] allow their prestige to become involved in even technical matter[] This makes institutional compromise difficult and provides ground[] for our view that interim arrangements between economic and politi[] cal unions may fail to attract the critical political leaders to the ne[] center if too much power is left with the component states. Thi[] seems to have been a problem in the West Indies where the importan[] Jamaican politicians remained primarily concerned with Jamaica[] politics and were ready to sacrifice West Indian union for the sak[] of success in Jamaica.[23] Similarly the French West African Federa[]

[22] In November 1963, two political scientists attending a university conferenc[] on federation in Nairobi submitted a memorandum which brought to the atten[] tion of East African leaders the number of alternatives available. See A. H[] Birch and R. L. Watts, *Alternative Ways of Distributing Authority Withi[] Federation* (Nairobi, mimeographed, 1963).

[23] See Hugh W. Springer, *Reflections on the Failure of the First West India[] Federation* (Cambridge, Mass.: Harvard University, Center for Internationa[] Affairs, 1962).

on was not strong enough to attract the critical leaders to Dakar,
articularly after the changes of 1956.[24] Presumably, this difficulty
not limited to poor areas, and political involvement in technical
atters in centrally planned, Communist Party-controlled countries
akes it equally difficult to conceive of the integration of the Council
or Mutual Economic Assistance (COMECON) areas as a problem of
ncreasing politization.[25]

Another reason that the Haas-Schmitter scheme is not adequate
s a framework for the comparative study of regional integration is
at it diverts attention from extraneous factors which cannot be
tted within the nine variables. Yet a "catalyst" may be almost a
ecessary condition for integration in underdeveloped areas.

. . .

More attention must be paid to the external environment of world
olitics in which an integration process takes place. Even European
ntegration was helped by its initiation–in an environment in which
Europe had (as a result of war) undergone a drastic change from
utonomous actor to pawn in a bipolar power struggle. The impor-
ance of factors outside the economic integration process is suggested
y the comparative success of political unions formed in developing
reas while the colonial power was still present (or played a large
art) and the relative absence of successful political unions of under-
eveloped countries after independence.[26] Nearly all successful polit-
cal unions in Africa, for example, have either occurred before in-
ependence and/or involved United Nations actions (Ghana-British
ogoland, Somalia-British Somaliland, Cameroun-British Came-
oons).

One exception to the rule is the still uncertain union of Tanganyika
nd Zanzibar as Tanzania. If anything, the great disproportion in
he size and strength of the two partners suggests the partial rele-
ance of the Bismarck model which Haas and Schmitter exclude
rom their concern. Similar circumstances might arise between
Senegal and Gambia or some of the other West African enclaves.
But the model is Bismarckian with severe limitations. Because of the

[24] See Foltz, *From French West Africa to the Mali Federation,* and Ruth
chachter Morgenthau, *Political Parties in French-Speaking West Africa* (Ox-
ord: Clarendon Press, 1964), Chapter 8.

[25] See Andrzej Korbonski, "Comecon," *International Conciliation,* September
964 (No. 549), pp. 3-62; and Kazimierz Grzybowski, *The Socialist Common-
ealth of Nations* (New Haven, Conn.: Yale University Press, 1964).

[26] Of course I am not arguing that formation under colonial rule is a sufficient
ondition for success of a political union.

existence of international organizations which dampen open conflic
the disproportion must be so great that it allows a Goa-like *fait a
compli* if open force is used, or else there must be severe internal con
fusion if subversion is used. In other words there are great limits c
the use of military force as a catalyst in today's environment, bu
the possibility is not entirely excluded, particularly if military for
is held partly in abeyance and is used to limit the number of altern:
tives available to a small country.

Another possible catalyst in today's environment might be ec
nomic aid. Most African countries are highly dependent on outsi
aid and in principle this might allow donors to provide the extra con
ditions needed to supply the political will for bridging discontinuitie
which might arise in an integration process. In a world of compet
tive aid giving and with countries extremely sensitive to infring
ment of new sovereignty, it is uncertain how effective a catalyst th
can be, but it could be important if potential "federalizers" chos
to use their power for this purpose.

My concern here is not with the source of catalysts (if any) fo
African integration, but with the need for some concept like "cata
lyst" to supplement the conditions established in Haas' nine var:
ables. To state that a catalyst is a necessary condition for spillove
from economic to political union in an underdeveloped setting may b
too strong. We would need only a single case to disprove this. Thoug
this case does not yet exist, it seems reasonable to allow for its possi
bility by merely stating that in studying regional integration in a
underdeveloped setting, one should focus not only on the proces
variables but also look for possible *dei ex machina*.

This formulation leaves open the possibility of purely voluntar
regional integration in developing areas, while it also prevents scho
ars from allowing a preference for "peaceful" integration to diver
them from the full range of relevant factors. Moreover, even if :
catalyst is stated to be a necessary condition, whether this make
"peaceful" or "voluntary" integration impossible depends on th
definitions of those terms and the type of catalyst involved. Wha
degree of outside limitation on the range of choices available t
integrating elites is necessary before we call a process "involun
tary"? "Voluntary" is a relative term which can be applied in a
least a qualified sense so long as some alternatives remain. Similarly
if the catalyst is a qualified "Bismarckian" type such as we dis
cussed above, we might hesitate to call the process "peaceful.'
However, what if the catalyst is a consortium of aid donors?

To answer these questions we may wish to elaborate the concept
: catalyst although by its nature it will remain to some extent
nbiguous. We might, for instance, wish to distinguish passive en-
ronmental catalysts from active catalysts which we might term
federalizers'' or ''unifiers.''[27] We might distinguish between cata-
sts or unifiers which involve military force and those which do not;
ose indigenous to a region and those foreign. We might distinguish
etween catalysts which are effective only for the initiation of an
tegration process and those which can be effective at various stages
the process. With more empirical work we may be able to develop
eneralizations between types of catalyst, types of discontinuities,
d types of setting as described in the Haas-Schmitter pattern
ariables. My main concern in this article, however, has been to
tablish that the Haas-Schmitter scheme is not yet the framework
hich we need for a comparative study of regional integration both
ecause of problems with its underlying concepts and its ambiguity
out relations between the variables; and to suggest that any suit-
ole framework must provide for attention to outside environmental
ctors of world politics.

[27] C. J. Friedrich has suggested that ''integrating federalism'' may call for
''federalizer.'' See *New Tendencies in Federal Theory and Practice*, A Report
iven at the Sixth World Congress of the International Political Science Asso-
ation (Geneva, mimeographed, 1964).

E. Kanovsky

Arab Economic Unity

In an article published in January 1966, a *New York Times* co
respondent described the newly-formed Arab Common Market as a
organization without much prospect of surviving another year
This view parallels the skepticism with which Western observe
view the many attempts of the Arab League to foster greater unit
among its members. The most publicized aspects of Arab unity (an
disunity) have been in the political and military spheres. What v
propose to examine is the feasibility of the League's many proposa
to foster Arab economic unity, culminating with its ambitious plan
to establish an Arab Common Market.

Of the thirteen Arab League countries, only four decided to joi
the Arab Common Market, the UAR (Egypt), Syria, Iraq an
Jordan. The League of Arab States came into being in 1945 wit
seven member countries, and as others attained their independenc
they were admitted to the League, Algeria being the last to joi
in 1962. Regional economic development has always been accorde
a high priority in League plans, but real progress has been limited
In 1953 two economic conventions were signed, one designed t
facilitate the exchange of goods, and the other governing trans
trade. The trade agreement provided for custom exemptions o
almost all raw materials produced in the region, and a 25 per cer
reduction of customs duties for most industrial products, largel
processed agricultural products such as textiles, flour, vegetable oil

Reprinted from *The Middle East Journal*, XXI, No. 2 (Spring 1967), with tl
permission of the publisher and the author.

[1] *New York Times*, January 21, 1966, p. 74.

ıd canned foods. The agreements also provided for favored treat-
ent in the transfer of payments and capital transfers. However,
ıere were loopholes in these agreements. They exempted goods sub-
·ct to government monopoly and those commodities the importation
ſ which any country decided to ban completely.² In the context of
ıcreasing nationalizing of industry and of foreign trade in a number
ſ Arab countries (mainly Egypt, Iraq, Syria and Algeria); the
ıtablishment of many government monopolies in many Arab coun-
·ies; the strong protection provided to "infant" industries in most
ɔuntries and the chronic shortage of foreign exchange which plagues
ɪl but the countries with great oil income, these exemptions sharply
ɔduced the effectiveness of these economic agreements. Furthermore,
ıese conventions were not in any way binding upon the member
:ates. They were set up as sort of master blueprints suggesting bi-
ıteral trade agreements among the member countries, to be nego-
ated under the aegis of the Arab League.

Until 1960, the Arab League's Economic Council was tied to the
'ollective Security Pact of 1950, making its activities subservient to
ɔlitical and military considerations. After this provision was
emoved in 1960, Morocco and Libya joined the Economic Council.
Ɔecisions were subsequently taken to set up a number of joint Arab
ɪnterprises including the Arab Potash Company to aid Jordan in the
xploitation of the Dead Sea, the Arab Navigation Company, the
ɪrab Oil Tankers Company and, most important, the Arab Develop-
ıent Bank, which was decided upon in 1957. To date it seems that
ɪnly the first of these resolutions has been implemented.³

In 1958, the Arab League Economic Council approved, in prin-
ɪple, the organization of a Council of Economic Union. In 1962, the
greement was signed by five countries — Jordan, Kuwayt, Morocco,
yria and Egypt. Within the next year and a half, Yemen and Iraq
ecame signatories to this pact.⁴ The agreement finally led to the
ecision to establish the Arab Common Market, scheduled to come
ɪnto force on January 1, 1965. However, only four countries ratified
he Arab Common Market agreement, Egypt, Syria, Iraq and Jordan.
ʼemen's withdrawal is a reflection of the civil war in that country,
nd is, in any case, of little economic significance. The failure of the
Kuwayti parliament to ratify the agreement (after the Kuwayti

---

² Robert W. Macdonald, *The League of Arab States* (Princeton University
·ress, 1965), pp. 197-8.
³ *Ibid.*, pp. 202-7.
⁴ *Ibid.*, p. 215.

government representative had signed the Economic Unity Pact), the
refusal of Morocco to enter the Arab Common Market, and the non
participation of Saudi Arabia, Lebanon, the Sudan, Tunisia, Liby
and Algeria require explanation.

The Economic Unity Pact is ambitious and far-reaching in it
scope. It aims to emulate the European Economic Community (mor
commonly known as the European Common Market). It is not satis
fied with the more limited aim of the European Free Trade Asso
ciation (the United Kingdom, Norway, Sweden, Denmark, Austria
Switzerland and Portugal), namely the elimination of trade barrier
within the Association. The Arab Common Market envisages no
only the elimination of all tariffs (within five years for agricultura
products and ten years for industrial commodities), but the eventua
establishment of a unified and integrated economy encompassing al
member countries. The pact envisages a common external tariff unde
unified administration; uniform legislation and regulations relating
to import and export procedures; uniform transport and transi
laws ensuring freedom of transit and of access to harbors and air
ports; uniform policies relating to agriculture, industry, real estate
and commercial and monetary activities; coordination of labor law
and social security legislation; freedom of travel; unhampered
capital transfers; freedom of work, residence and economic activity
in any member country and unhampered rights of ownership and
inheritance.[5]

It would seem that these plans ignore both economic and politica
realities. While it is true that Lebanon, Syria and Jordan (and to a
lesser extent, Egypt and Iraq) carry on a sizeable inter-Arab trade
even in these countries economic interests would have to be far
stronger in order to overcome the political and non-economic centrif-
ugal forces which run counter to the goals of the Economic Unity
Pact.

Economic theory tells us that free or freer trade and the freedom
of movement of capital and labor should provide long-run economic
benefits to those who subscribe to these principles. However, the
implementation of these principles involves many dislocations in the
economic sectors of these countries. The prudent utilization of fiscal
and monetary policy, as well as other governmental actions, is necessary in order to facilitate and ensure the consequent reallocation of
labor and capital resources. Political and social, as well as economic,

[5] *Ibid.*

ealities in the Arab countries would tend to cast doubt on the ability f the authorities to execute such policies, even were they convinced hat it is in their true (economic and non-economic) interest so to do.

When the union of Syria and Egypt took place in 1958, the motives /ere clearly political. However, the result was a sharp increase in rade between the two regions of the United Arab Republic. Syrian mports from Egypt in 1961 were more than five times their level in 957 (prior to the union). Syrian exports to Egypt showed marked luctuations, partly a result of governmental policy (which was con-rolled by Egypt) and partly as a result of sharp fluctuations in yrian agricultural output. However, the sharp increase in trade etween Egypt and Syria was at the expense of Syria's traditional rading partner, Lebanon. Trade between the neighboring states was irtually stopped.[6] Economic factors were of considerable importance n bringing about the breakup of the union in the fall of 1961, hough they had been of minor importance in its inception. The conomic factors which were instrumental in the dissolution of the mion included the resistance of the Syrian commercial and landed nterests to the nationalization and socialization measures instituted y the Egyptian authorities in Syria, and the imposition of stringent 'oreign exchange regulations which inhibited the freedom of Syrian raders. The concurrence of the union with a period of extended lrought in Syria added to the strains.[7]

This experience (as well as the short-lived Iraqi-Jordanian Union n 1958, and the abolition of the Syrian-Lebanese Customs Union in 1950) illustrates some of the difficulties which lie in the path of Arab League attempts to bring about all-embracing economic unity. Ex-:luding political convulsions similar to those in 1958 (which led to :he United Arab Republic and the Jordanian-Iraqi Union as counter-poise), the basis for Arab economic unity must be a real and visible short-run mutuality of economic interests, which are not in serious :onflict with political and social realities. This implies not only com-plementarity of the economies of the member countries as they are today, but as they are planned for the future as well. As of now the only Arab country which has developed industry to a significant extent is Egypt. Only there has industrial development gone beyond the initial phase, which usually includes textiles and apparel, food processing and the like. Egypt produces steel, cars, trucks, tractors, motors, tires, durable consumer goods, paper and cardboard, glass,

[6] *Ibid.*, pp. 200-1.
[7] Charles Issawi, *Egypt in Revolution* (Oxford University Press, 1963), p. 61.

cement, pharmaceuticals, dyes, cosmetics and many other industrial products. But the Egyptians have had trouble in exporting their industrial wares. Quality has been unsatisfactory at times, and prices have been high.[8] It is for these reasons (and others, economic and political) that Egypt is the most potent force in the Arab League pressing for economic unity. However, while the other Arab countries have not reached this level of industrial development, their development plans lay great stress on increasing industrialization. Permitting Egypt to have free and unlimited access to their markets would preclude the protection of existing or potential infant industries in other Arab countries. The example of Rumania's refusal to acquiesce to the Soviet Union's plans for economic integration in the Soviet Bloc, when it was destined to be an agricultural sector within this Bloc, is instructive.

Things may well have turned out differently if the history of European conquest, occupation, administration and liberation of the Arab countries had been otherwise. The Ottoman Empire was indeed a large free-trade area, but the pressures of the European powers and their open-door policy to European goods effectively thwarted any attempts at industrialization.[9] The political boundaries of the Arab countries and the legacy of European colonial rule were often at odds with the economic (as well as non-economic) interests of the newly independent Arab states. However, having attained independence, each country set up its own governmental apparatus along with plans for economic autarky. Some countries, mainly Egypt, Iraq, Syria and Algeria, have moved towards "socialism" in varying degrees. All the Arab countries, with the possible exception of Lebanon, have exercised an increasing amount of government controls, planning and direction. The success of the European Common Market is based, in part, on the freedom of entrepreneurs (foreign, as well as those of the member countries) to invest and produce for a larger market. The success of the European Common Market was enhanced by the attraction of foreign, especially American, capital. The experience of the Central American Common Market (constituting underdeveloped countries and therefore more comparable to the Arab states) is quite similar. The relative failure of the Soviet Bloc's attempts to achieve economic integration and economic development in Eastern Europe, is, I believe, partly due to state controls and to the exclusion of foreign venture capital. There is some evidence

[8] *New York Times*, January 27, 1967, p. 54.
[9] Issawi, p. 19.

that recent events in the Eastern European countries point to a modification of these policies. Since the latter half of 1965 the pendulum seems to have swung in the direction of fewer state controls in Egypt, Iraq and Algeria, and for a short while, in Syria. The Egyptian government has announced the establishment of a "Free Zone" in Port Said and has invited foreign capital to invest in the Zone, on liberal terms. However, so long as these countries maintain rigid economic controls, it would seem that they will prove to be a deterrent to Arab economic unity plans. This would, I believe, be the case even if all the Arab countries were socialistic and rigidly state-controlled. The difficulties are compounded when some follow liberal and capitalistic policies and others do not.

An analysis of Arab economic unity efforts requires a detailed examination of the resources, trade patterns and economic development in each of the Arab countries. Within the context here only the pertinent highlights can be discussed.

The four North African Arab states, commonly referred to as the Maghrib — Morocco, Algeria, Tunisia and Libya — have been moving, albeit slowly, towards greater Maghribi economic cooperation. In 1964, a conference of the Maghrib decided to set up a permanent commission to study all possible areas of economic cooperation, their relationship with the European Common Market, and the improvement of regional transportation and communications.[10] In 1965, they decided to set up an industrial research center in Tripoli (Libya) and to coordinate policies relating to the export of olive oil, wine and citrus fruits, and the development of a steel industry. In June 1965, Tunisia signed a commercial agreement with Morocco removing duties on primary products and industrial goods. This agreement paralleled a similar agreement with Algeria.

At the end of 1966, the UN Economic Commission for Africa sent a mission to Tunisia to draw up an industrial chart for the Maghrib with a view to examining how best to coordinate the various economic development plans for the region.[11] However, lest these various steps taken in the direction of Maghribi economic cooperation be viewed over-optimistically, it should be pointed out that this UN Commission had already published a study made in January 1964 in which it proposed coordination and development of large scale industries

[10] *The Economist Intelligence Unit* — Algeria, Morocco, Tunisia, November, 1965, pp. 1, 2.

[11] Kingdom of Libya, Ministry of Economy and Trade, *External Trade Statistics*, 1965, pp. 1-4.

particularly in the fields of energy, mining, fertilizers, steel, metal working, engineering, chemicals, pulp and paper, glass, cement and textiles. They pointed out that many of these industries would no develop properly unless there was a greater degree of regional co ordination and accessibility to the Maghribi market as a whole.[1] To this date the steps taken to implement the UN Commission' proposals, as well as the various decisions of the Maghrib Permanen Consultative Committee, are minimal. In the words of the Moroccai Foreign Minister, "the economic integration of the Maghrib is being delayed by the selfish interests of technocrats, capitalists and various administrations."[13]

These four countries are closely tied to the economies of Western Europe. Algeria, Morocco and Tunisia, even after gaining politica independence from France, retain very strong ties with the ex colonial power. French culture and institutions are dominant; French economic aid is crucial for their development plans; their currencies are tied to the franc, and a significant or overwhelming part of their foreign trade is carried on with France. Since the middle of 1966 a European Common Market commission has been considering an application by these three Maghrib states for admission to the European Common Market. This commission has proposed to the Council of Ministers (of the European Common Market) that it negotiate association agreements with the three countries. During 1965, these states exported goods and services to the European Common Market worth $1,107 million and imported $928 million. Most of this trade was with France. The Maghrib states have appended to their application for admission four additional requests, namely, assistance in economic development, technical cooperation, financial cooperation and the free movement of manpower to Europe.[14] It is obvious that these trends towards Maghrib cooperation and economic association with the European Common Market must necessarily attenuate Arab League plans for pan-Arab economic unity.

In spite of the fact that Algeria has recently assumed the rôle of a major oil producing country, it is beset with very serious economic difficulties. Out of a population of 12 million, about three million are unemployed. The number of industrial jobs has not changed in the

---

[12] *Report of the Economic Commission for Africa,* United Nations, Industrial Coordination Mission to Algeria, Libya, Morocco and Tunisia, Feb. 5, 1964, p. 72.

[13] *Middle East Economic Digest, (MEED),* Nov. 25, 1966, p. 591.

[14] *MEED,* January 5, 1967, pp. 15-16.

st few years and, with 200,000 entering the labor force every year, ıe problem of the unemployed becomes more acute. In the growing rban sector it is estimated that one-half are unemployed.[15] In 1960 ıe urban sector encompassed about one-third of the population and nce the exodus of the French in 1962 there has been a strong migra- ɔry movement to the towns. Its rain-fed agriculture is subject to ery wide annual fluctuations. The problems of agriculture are enor- ıous; among them are erosion and the continued use of primitive ıethods. Manufacturing industry is little developed except for some ɔod processing, building materials, textiles and chemical industries nked to phosphate and other mineral deposits. In 1964 the produc- ion of most manufactures was well below the pre-1962 level. There re two vehicle and one tractor assembly plants working far below apacity.[16] In 1963, 50 per cent of its exports consisted of petroleum, wo-thirds of which went to France and almost all of the remainder ɔ other European countries. More recent oil discoveries indicate that s importance has grown since 1963. Other exports are wine, olive il and other foodstuffs, as well as iron ore and phosphates. Over 80 er cent of these products went to France, almost all of the remainder ɔ other European countries. The pattern of imports was similarly ne-sided. Eighty per cent were from France, another six per cent rom the US (mostly under the Food for Peace program), and al- ıost all of the remainder from other European countries.[17]

Morocco's economy is dependent upon agriculture and mining, and ıore recently, tourism. Phosphates constituted one-quarter of total xports in 1965 and the rest consisted of other minerals, citrus, anned fish, wine and other fruits and vegetables. Two-thirds of xports went to Europe in 1964 and about the same percentage of nports came from Europe and the US.[18] About three per cent of nports were from Arab countries, mostly from neighboring Algeria nd from Libya. Similarly two per cent of exports went to Arab tates, mainly Algeria. Morocco's population, 13.3 million in 1965, as one of the highest growth rates in the world. However, during ıe first half of this decade economic growth has been only about one- alf of the rate of population growth, so that *per capita* income has

[15] *New York Times*, Jan. 16, 1967, p. 12 and Jan. 20, 1964, p. 45.

[16] *Economist Intelligence Unit* — Algeria, Morocco, Tunisia — Annual, 1966, p. 2, 4, 7.

[17] *Etudes Economiques sur la Syrie et les Pays Arabes* (Damascus), July, 965, p. 144; *Data on the Economy of Algeria*, June, 1965, US Department of ʻommerce, p. 7.

[18] *Etudes Economiques*, August, 1965, p. 160.

been declining.[19] The pressures of unemployment in the growing urban sector, and hidden unemployment in its stagnant agriculture though not quite as severe as in Algeria, are nonetheless great. The brightest spot is the rapidly growing tourist trade which brought in $70 million in 1965 and is continuing to grow rapidly.

Tunisia's economy is, broadly speaking, similar to that of Morocco. It is dependent upon agriculture and mining, primarily, citrus, wine olive oil, phosphates and other minerals. In 1964 over one-half of exports went to France, but as a result of political difficulties with France and its cancellation of preferential treatment for Tunisian exports, France absorbed but 31 per cent of its exports in 1965. Most of the exports went to other European countries. The European countries (mainly France) and the US provided about three-fourths of imports. Five per cent of its imports were from Arab countries in 1964, about one-half consisting of oil imports from Saudi Arabia and Libya. However, new oil discoveries in Tunisia were expected to make it self-sufficient in oil in 1966 and even provide a small surplus for export in 1967. Nine per cent of its exports went to Arab countries, almost all to neighboring Algeria and Libya.[20] Tunisia, with a population of 4.5 million, about one-half engaged in agriculture, has been more successful in its development plans than Algeria and Morocco. Industrial production, mostly on a small scale, has been increasing by about six per cent per year. Its trade balance in 1965 was the worst in its history, with exports covering less than half of imports, but the rapid development of tourism and oil production irrigated agriculture and new industries are expected to improve matters.

Libya was one of the poorest countries in the world in the 1950's. Vast oil discoveries have revolutionized its economy. *Per capita* income, estimated at $40, shot up to almost $500 in 1966. Its exports (over 99 per cent crude oil) go to Western Europe. The small amounts of Libyan oil imported by the other North African countries have ceased as a result of oil discoveries in these countries. Large oil revenues have provided the fuel for ambitious development plans. However, Libya's small population (1.6 million) and its present though rising, low level of education makes it necessary to import labor, especially teachers and technicians. However, two sabotage incidents in 1965 perpetrated against American-owned oil installations have deepened the Libyan government's fears of subversion and

---

[19] *Middle East and African Economist* (New York), May, 1966, p. 76.
[20] Banque Centrale de Tunisie, *Rapport Annuelle*, 1964, p. 45.

einforced its previous decision to reduce its heavy dependence on
he Egyptians even for badly-needed teachers, engineers and other
echnicians.[21] It has contracted with Morocco and Sudan for the
mportation of labor, generally unskilled.[22] Libyan imports have
isen very sharply, almost all from the US and Western Europe.
Arab sales to Libya constituted two per cent of the total in 1963 and
hree per cent in 1965. This has come about largely as a result of the
lmost five-fold increase of Lebanese exports to Libya between 1963
nd 1965. The Lebanese provided 36 per cent of Arab sales to Libya
n 1965 and the Tunisians another 30 per cent.[23] Libya, with very
arge and growing foreign exchange earnings in convertible cur-
encies, has little economic incentive to provide special preferences
o goods of other Arab countries. It is using its large revenues to
nodernize its agriculture and diversify and expand its very small
ndustrial establishment. It sees no justification for providing a
narket for the higher priced and qualitatively inferior industrial
goods of Egypt and some other Arab countries.

The two remaining Arab countries in Africa, Egypt and the
Sudan, differ radically in their policies relating to Arab economic
nity. Unlike Egypt, which has a big stake in Arab unity plans for
oth political and economic reasons, the Sudan is a passive member
f the Arab League and its attitude towards Arab economic unity is
listinctly lukewarm. The Sudan is overwhelmingly an agricultural
ountry. Eighty-six per cent of its population of 13 million are en-
aged in agriculture, providing 55 per cent of gross domestic product,
vhile only five per cent were engaged in manufacturing which pro-
ided ten per cent of gross domestic product. However, development
lans call for an annual increase of 21 per cent in the manufacturing
ector, and, in fact, between 1953 and 1963, the growth rate of this
ector was 15 per cent annually.[24] Over one-half of total exports is
rovided by the cotton crop. Other than cotton, the main exports are
eanuts, gum arabic, sesame and other agricultural products. Geo-
raphically, its exports are widely dispersed. The major purchasers
vere the Western European countries, India, Japan and China (in
964). The only Arab customers of some significance were Saudi
Arabia and Egypt. About eight per cent of total exports went to

---

[21] *New York Times,* January 23, 1967, p. 16.

[22] *New York Times,* January 20, 1967, p. 85.

[23] Kingdom of Libya, *External Trade Statistics,* 1965, pp. 1-4.

[24] Robert F. Meagher, *Public International Development Financing in Sudan*
Columbia University, 1965), pp. 1, 4, 5.

Arab countries, almost all to these two countries. The major supplier
are the UK, West Germany, Japan, the US, India and Egypt. Th
Arab countries provided six per cent of Sudan's imports, almost al
from neighboring Egypt.[25] Egyptian exports to the Sudan wer
based, to a considerable extent, on the latter's decision to accep
Egyptian goods in payment for Egypt's debts to the Sudan. In th
words of one observer, "Khartoum is resigned to the prospect o
being repaid in kind, which is better than not being repaid."[2]
Egyptian exports to the Sudan increased sharply in 1964, and the
dropped below their 1963 level in 1965. On the other hand, Saud
Arabian purchases rose sharply in 1965.[27]

Egypt is the leading Arab country in political, cultural and mili
tary spheres, and with its population of 30 odd million (about 2
per cent of the total population in the Arab states) dominates th
Arab world. To the Egyptians rapid industrialization is not only th
key to economic development, but is of paramount importance i
attaining and maintaining "national self-respect." According t
government statistics, industrial production more than doubled be
tween 1952 and 1965,[28] raising its share of GNP from ten per cen
to 23 per cent. The largest growth rates were in petroleum refining
chemicals, pharmaceuticals, electronics and building materials. How
ever, in terms of both employment and exports, Egypt is still mucl
dependent on agriculture. Though the urban population is rapidly
increasing (and with it the problems of unemployment), about 6(
per cent were classified as rural in 1966. During the first five yea
Development Plan (1960-1965), the share of agriculture in employ
ment dropped from 54 per cent to 52 per cent and its share i
national income from 31 per cent to 27 per cent. The share of industry
rose from 11 per cent to 12 per cent in employment and from 21 t
23 per cent of national income.

In 1960, 68 per cent of Egypt's commodity exports consisted o
raw cotton. By 1965 these exports had increased only slightly and
constituted 56 per cent of the total. On the other hand exports o
cotton yarn and fabrics increased sharply from ten per cent of tota
exports in 1960 to 18 per cent in 1965. The special arms and ai
agreements with the Soviet Bloc have markedly altered Egypt'

[25] The Republic of the Sudan, *Economic Survey, 1964*, p. 63; *Foreign Trad
Statistics*, Annual, 1964, pp. 24-5.

[26] *Economist Intelligence Unit* —Egypt, Libya, Sudan — Annual, March, 1965
pp. 4-5.

[27] Bank of Sudan, *Bulletin*, April-June, 1966, pp. 36-7.

[28] *New York Times*, January 27, 1967, p. 65.

rading patterns. In 1965 the Bloc purchased almost one-half of Egypt's exports and provided almost one-fourth of its imports. Western Europe purchased one-fifth of its exports and provided one-third of its imports. The US provided one-fifth of imports (almost all US aid) and purchased three per cent of exports. This constituted a sharp drop from 1964 when it provided 30 per cent of Egypt's imports. Further curtailment of US aid will undoubtedly show up in the 1966 figures. Egypt's imports from Arab countries have fluctuated widely. After reaching a low point in 1961, they increased substantially in the following three years, mostly as a result of crude oil imports, and then fell slightly in 1965. They constituted about eight per cent of total imports in 1965. Exports to the Arab states have been much more stable. They also increased from their recent low in 1961, until 1964, and then fell somewhat in 1965, in spite of a general increase of 12 per cent in Egyptian exports in 1965. They constituted seven per cent of total exports. The main Arab customers were Lebanon, Sudan, Saudi Arabia, Jordan and Iraq. About two-thirds of Egypt's imports from the Arab states were from Saudi Arabia, Libya and Kuwayt, mainly crude oil. Recent oil discoveries in Egypt will probably further reduce these imports, as was the case in 1965. The other Arab suppliers provided mainly agricultural products.[29]

It is estimated that in the early 1960's GNP increased at an average annual rate of six to seven per cent (in real terms), and then dropped to about two to four per cent more recently, barely enough to keep up with the growth of population. Inflationary pressures have increased considerably to about 15 per cent per year. Unemployment figures are unavailable, but hidden unemployment is widespread in both the farm and urban sectors. In order to reduce the pressures of unemployment, officials compel the factories (mainly government-owned) to hire more labor than managers deem necessary. The same is true in the government bureaucracy. It is estimated that the factories are operating at 50 to 70 per cent of capacity, due, in part, to the acute lack of foreign exchange with which to purchase imported components and parts.[30] This, in turn, raises the costs of production and makes exporting much more difficult. Egypt's serious economic difficulties in the mid-1960's, highlighted by its very low level of foreign exchange reserves and mounting foreign debt, and the sale

[29] National Bank of Egypt, *Economic Bulletin*, Volume 19, no. 2, 1966, pp. 156-9; *MEED*, January 5, 1967, p. 20.

[30] *New York Times*, November 6, 1966, p. F1, Nov. 28, 1966, p. 14.

of one-third of its gold reserves in 1966 to ease the crippling shortage of foreign exchange,[31] have been caused by a number of factors. According to a US Department of Agriculture study, crop output between 1948 and 1963 showed an average annual increase of two per cent while the rate of growth in demand for food increased at a rate of four per cent.[32] Indications are that the gap has further widened since 1963. Food imports in 1964 were two and one-half times their level in 1960 and constituted about one-quarter of total imports. Until the Second World War, Egypt had usually been a net exporter of food. The US aid program filled most of the gap until 1964, when it reached $175 million. This aid was sharply curtailed in 1965 when it fell to $45 million, and was largely eliminated in 1966. The rapid pace of industrialization was often typified by poor planning and execution. Large-scale military expenditures, accentuated by the Yemen civil war, have further weakened the economy. A poor cotton crop in 1966 further weakened the shaky balance of payments. The deficit in the balance of trade increased from $96 million in 1960 to $327 million in 1965. In the first half of 1966 the deficit was $184 million as compared with $41 million in the first half of the previous year. Increasing revenues from the Suez Canal and tourism have not sufficed to close the trade gap.

What all this helps to explain, in my opinion, is that Egypt's abiding interest and pressure on behalf of Arab economic unity are based on economic, as well as political, considerations. With a larger Arab market, Egyptian industry would become more profitable, its balance of trade would improve, and it could provide more employment to its large and growing population. Egypt's balance of trade with the Arab states is negative, with exports covering about half of imports between 1963 and 1965. Arab economic unity plans would give Egypt greater accessibility to the oil revenues of Kuwayt and Libya, and would immeasurably strengthen its own currency. Freedom of movement of labor would provide greater access to labor-deficient areas, especially Kuwayt and Libya, increasing the flow of remittances from these countries.

Syria's economy is basically agricultural, accounting for 35-40 per cent of national income and about one-half of the labor force. The rapid growth in cotton production has made this the leading export, providing almost one-half of the commodity exports. In years

---

[31] *New York Times*, Jan. 27, 1967, p. 54.

[32] US Department of Agriculture, *Changes in Agriculture in 26 Developing Nations* — 1948-63, p. 19.

f plentiful harvests it also exports grain, and usually has an export-
ble surplus of fruits, vegetables and wool. Industry accounts for
bout 13 per cent of total employment and about the same share of
national income. The only industrial export of significance is textiles
which accounted for nine per cent of total exports. Industry has
hardly gone beyond the initial stage, which includes textiles, food
processing and some building materials. This sector had been growing at an annual rate of seven per cent between 1956 and 1964, but
wholesale nationalization in 1964 and 1965 brought about some stagnation.[33] However, the Development Plan calls for the expansion of
consumer durables, tractor assembly, paper production, and other
industrial products.

Syria's negative trade balance is mostly covered by oil transit payments (over two-thirds in 1964 and 90 per cent of the trade gap in
1965). The Soviet Bloc has provided economic as well as military aid
in recent years. The projected plan to dam the upper Euphrates, with
the Soviet Union providing financial and technical aid, as well as
loans from Bulgaria and Czechoslovakia, will further tie the Syrian
economy to this Bloc.[34] The Soviet Bloc and China purchased one-
fifth of Syrian exports in 1960 and over one-third in 1965. Western
European purchases show wide annual fluctuations. In 1965 one-fifth
of Syria's exports went to Europe. Sales to Arab countries have also
shown wide annual variations, responding to political as well as
economic factors. Between 1953 and 1958, from 35 to 40 per cent of
its exports were sold to other Arab states. The political union with
Egypt (in 1958) raised this to 46 per cent. Following the dissolution
of the union in 1961, sales to Arab countries declined to 28 per cent
of total exports in 1962, and 36 per cent in 1965. The greatest increase was in sales to Lebanon, which absorbed over one-half of
Syrian exports to Arab countries between 1962 and 1964 and over
60 per cent in 1965, re-establishing the trading patterns prevailing
prior to the political union with Egypt.

Syria's main suppliers were the Western European countries. As
the trade with the Soviet Bloc has increased sharply since the later
1950's, providing 16 per cent of commercial imports in 1965, so has
the proportion of Western Europe diminished from over one-half of
total imports in 1963 to 37 per cent in 1965. Imports from the US
have fluctuated widely in response to US aid programs, declining

---

33 *Economist Intelligence Unit* — Syria, Lebanon, Jordan — Annual, 1966, pp.
3, 4, 7.
34 *New York Times*, Jan. 16, 1967, p. 62.

from 15 per cent of total imports in 1961 to seven per cent in 1965.
The Arab countries provided 25 per cent of Syria's imports in 1960
and declined to 16 per cent in 1965. The bulk of Syrian imports from
the Arab countries was from its neighbors, Iraq (oil) and Lebanon
(agricultural produce).[35]

It is noteworthy that Syria, which is most vociferous in its espousal
of Arab nationalism and Arab unity, has taken measures to protect
its small industrial base which it plans to expand. It has restricted
the re-export by Lebanon of European and Arab goods to Syria, because this practice is regarded by some Syrian enterprises as harmful
to local industry. Certain products (mainly textiles), which were
permitted to enter Syria under the Arab League trade cooperation
agreement, are now banned unless they contain a specified percentage
of material of Lebanese origin.[36]

Lebanon's economy differs radically from that of all the other
Arab states. With the exception of Kuwayt and Libya, its *per capita*
income and living standards are the highest in the Arab world. It is
a stronghold of free enterprise against the trend of Arab socialism
espoused by Egypt and emulated by Syria, Iraq and Algeria. Since
exchange controls were abolished in 1948, it has become the Arab
world's major financial center. The institution of banking secrecy
in 1956 stimulated a large inflow of capital from Lebanese emigrants,
the Persian Gulf states, and capital fleeing socialization measures
and political and economic instability in other Arab states. Major
Western corporations and banks maintain regional offices in Beirut.

Although agriculture employs about one-half of the labor force
(many part-time) it contributes only one-sixth of the national income. The concentration is upon fruits, vegetables and livestock
products. Industry employed about 12 per cent of the labor force
and accounted for 15 per cent of the national income. It is generally
small-scale and concentrated in textiles, food processing and some
building materials. Lebanon has been dominated by merchant and
commercial classes and has not, heretofore, followed the policy,
typical for developing countries, of providing strong tariff protection
and subsidies to the industrial sector. Nevertheless, industry seems
to have developed quite rapidly. The number of employees tripled
between 1958 and 1965, and capital invested quadrupled. It would

---

[35] *Banque Centrale de Syrie*, 1966, no. 13, pp. 36-7; *MEED*, Jan. 5, 1967, pp.
23-4.

[36] *MEED*, April 22, 1966, p. 177.

eem that as industrialists grow in numbers and in power, and indus-
rial workers begin exercising their power through their unions,
ressure for tariff protection will increase. It was recently reported
hat the government is considering higher tariffs to encourage in-
ustry and especially to protect infant industries.[37] Urban unemploy-
nent, aggravated by the migration from the rural areas and the
ncreasingly adverse balance of trade, provides additional pressures
owards protection of industry. One can surmise that the recent bank-
uptcy of the largest bank in Lebanon has weakened the power of the
ommercial classes and thereby strengthened the growing power of
he industrial sector.

Between 1960 and 1963 commodity imports were four times ex-
orts; in 1964, five times exports; and in 1965 almost six times the
alue of exports. In 1964 the inflow from tourism, airlines, banking
nd other services as well as emigrant remittances were more than
ufficient to offset the large trade imbalance.[38] At the time of writing,
he 1965 figures are unavailable, other than the trade imbalance
hich showed a further increase of 58 per cent. The main suppliers
1964) were Western Europe, the US (14 per cent) and Syria (11
er cent). The only other Arab suppliers of some significance were
audi Arabia and Iraq (oil) and Egypt and Jordan. Imports from
ll the Arab states were one-fifth of total imports (in 1963 and 1964)
f which more than one-half were from Syria. However, Lebanese
xports go mostly to the other Arab countries, mainly Saudi Arabia,
yria, Jordan, Kuwayt and Iraq. Exports consisted largely of fruits
nd vegetables, and some textiles.

Lebanese attitudes towards Arab unity have always been tempered
y the almost equal division between Muslims and Christians. Many
ebanese view the Arab Economic Unity Pact as "Pan-Arab econ-
mism" to which they are opposed.[39] Bilateral trading agreements
ight interest Lebanon, relying on its shrewd and experienced
aders to exploit these to its advantage. This was, indeed, a factor
a the Syrian decision to abrogate the Syrian-Lebanese Customs
nion, in 1950. Lebanon has a near monopoly in the Arab world in
anking and commercial services, and this would be attenuated by
al freedom of movement of capital. The growing industrial sector
pposes freer trade. Government ownership and controls in the more

[37] *MEED*, May 6, 1966, p. 199.
[38] *Wall Street Journal*, October 21, 1966, p. 6.
[39] *Commerce de Levant* (Beirut), September 18, 1965, pp. 1-6.

"socialistic" Arab states hamper Lebanese entrepreneurship
Finally, its close association with the European Common Market
limits the scope of any regional economic association.

Jordan has recently enjoyed a very high rate of economic growth
— an average of nine to ten per cent between 1958 and 1964. How
ever, a poorer crop in 1965 and a drought in 1966 have curtailed thi
expansion. The main factors contributing to this growth rate wer
large doses of US aid, which helped in the development of agricul
ture, industry, mining and the improvement of transportation an
communications. Agriculture employs about three-fourths of th
labor force and accounts for a sixth to a fourth of national income
Since most agriculture is dependent on rain, there are wide annua
fluctuations. Industry has been developing rapidly and is encourage
by a highly protective tariff — or a complete ban on the importatio
of competing industrial products. It is small scale, concentrated i
food and textiles, as well as cement. The current Development Pla
calls for a considerable expansion of existing units as well as th
founding of new industries including ceramics, pharmaceuticals
glass, batteries, paper, bus assembly and so on.[40]

Jordan's balance of trade shows a very large deficit, with commod
ity imports more than seven times the value of exports in 1964 an
1965. The deficit is covered by US (and some UK) aid, oil transi
rights, tourism, UN support for Jordan's Palestinian refugees (abou
one-third of Jordan's population of two million), and remittance
of Jordanians working abroad. Phosphates constitute about one
fourth of total exports, with most of the remainder consisting of fres
fruits and vegetables. The bulk of the phosphates have been sent t
Yugoslavia and India, and the agricultural produce to the neighbor
ing Arab states. Over two-thirds of exports are sold to the Ara
countries, mainly, Lebanon, Kuwayt, Saudi Arabia, Syria and Iraq
Jordan's main suppliers are the US (aid program) and Wester
Europe. The Arab states supplied about 18 per cent of total import
in 1964 and 1965. Syria provided five per cent of total imports i
1965; Lebanon seven per cent (five per cent in 1964) ; Saudi Arabi
(oil) four per cent; and Egypt two per cent (three per cent in 1964)
Imports from other Arab countries were insignificant. Imports from
Egypt are based, in part, on a recent triangular trade agreemen
whereby Yugoslavia pays for prior phosphate imports from Jorda

---

[40] Central Bank of Jordan, *Quarterly Bulletin*, 1966, p. 27.

for which it was unable to pay in hard currency) by transferring he accumulated blocked balances to Egypt.

Unlike the three other members of the Arab Common Market Egypt, Syria and Iraq) Jordan has a private enterprise economy, vith fewer and less rigid controls. According to a *New York Times* orrespondent, Jordan's motives for adhering to this pact are mainly olitical, namely, the need to pacify her own Arab nationalists, inerited with the annexation of the West Bank of the Jordan in 1948. Iowever, it seems that its formal adherence to the Arab Common Iarket was effectively diluted by a long list of exceptions to free rade. The exceptions were almost all industrial products produced 1 Jordan as well as all categories of imports which yield substantial ustoms revenues. In fact, Jordan is not alone in taking these steps. 'he other Arab members have countered with their own lists of xemptions designed to protect their own industries and to maintain heir customs revenues. In all the Arab countries (other than the ichest oil states), as in most developing countries, indirect taxes, xcises and customs are the prime source of government revenue.

Iraq is the world's eighth largest oil producer, and the fifth in the Iiddle East (following Saudi Arabia, Kuwayt, Libya and Iran). hough the impact of oil revenues is felt throughout the economy, he direct employment of Iraqis in this industry is less than one er cent of the labor force. Over one-half of the labor force is engaged 1 agriculture, but (owing to the preponderance of oil) generates bout one-fifth of national income. Ten per cent of the labor force is ngaged in industry and accounts for about the same share of na-onal income. Industry is generally small scale, concentrated in xtiles, food processing and construction materials. In recent years here has been a good deal of diversification of industry with the evelopment of a metal industry, plastics, pharmaceuticals and me electrical appliances. Current industrial plans call for a hemical/petrochemical complex, a steel mill and others. It is note-orthy that the current Development Plan (1966-1970) allocates 28 er cent to industrial development as compared with 26 per cent to griculture.[41]

Oil exports accounted for about 94 per cent of total exports in the st few years, the bulk of which was sold to Western Europe. In the on-oil sector, agricultural exports predominate, especially dates,

[41] *Economist Intelligence Unit* — Iraq — Annual, 1966, pp. 12, 21, 22.

which usually account for about one-third of non-oil exports. In fac
Iraqi dates account for 90 per cent of international trade in thi
commodity. Cement is the only non-agricultural export of signif
cance. In view of the overwhelming importance of oil, the Ara
countries account for a very small share of Iraq's exports, four pe
cent in 1965. However, in the non-oil sector, they account for a
increasingly large share, varying with crop and political conditions
in 1964 their share was 40 per cent and 45 per cent in 1965. In 196
the main Arab customers were Lebanon, Egypt, Kuwayt, Saud
Arabia and Syria. Iraq's imports from the Arab states constitute
five per cent of the total in 1965, almost half of which was fror
Lebanon. Jordan, Egypt and Syria were the only other Arab sup
pliers of significance. About 40 per cent of Iraq's imports were fro
Western Europe in 1965; ten per cent from the US and Canad
(annual fluctuations are largely due to political relations wit
Washington and the extent of US aid) and over one-fourth from th
Sino-Soviet countries. Here, too, political conditions are crucia
Between 1962 and 1965 imports from these countries doubled, raisin
their share from one-sixth to one-fourth of the total.[42] The same
true of trade with the Arab states. In 1962 Iraqi exports to neighbo
ing Kuwayt were almost nil as a result of the economic boycott follov
ing Iraq's claim to sovereignty over Kuwayt. In 1965 Iraqi export
to Kuwayt were one-fifth of its (non-oil) exports to Arab countrie
The worsening of relations with Syria was partly responsible for
sharp curtailment of trade between these two countries in 1965. O
the other hand, Egypt's position in the Iraqi political scene is increas
ingly a dominant one and the very sharp increase in trade betwee
Iraq and Egypt in recent years reflects this fact.

Iraq is richly endowed with natural resources — oil, large areas o
arable land, water and minerals. Given political stability and with it
large oil revenues, it has the potential of developing its economy an
of executing its industrial development plans. The rapidly increasin
population, the movement to the urban centers (about one-fourth liv
in the capital city) and an unemployment rate of ten per cent (i
1963), create powerful pressures for the rapid expansion of urba
jobs. Government policy is to prohibit the importation of commod
ties which are locally produced. Though Iraq adheres to the Ara
Common Market, one can envision a conflict between its espousal
Arab economic unity and its own industrial development plans.

[42] Central Bank of Iraq, *Quarterly Bulletin*, no. 58, pp. 26, 27, 32, 33, 35.

Kuwayt's economy requires no elaborate description. Its oil
serves are the world's largest (one-fifth of the world's proved
serves) and follows the US, the Soviet Union, Venezuela and Saudi
rabia in oil production. With large oil revenues and a population
one-half million, *per capita* income approximates the US (though
s distribution is far more unequal). Agriculture is almost non-
istent, but new water distillation plants and an agreement with
aq for water supplies have recently stimulated an increase in
ultry and vegetable farms. The government is encouraging the
velopment of industry and has passed laws and allocated funds
r a major effort to diversify and protect local industry. Some light
nsumer goods industry has already been developed as well as some
ilding materials. A major petrochemical complex is being devel-
ed.

With oil revenues of $750 million in 1965 and additional expendi-
res by the oil companies, Kuwait is a major importer. The bulk of
s imports are from the UK and the US, plus West Germany, Japan
d Italy. Imports from the other Arab states accounted for six
r cent of the total (1961-64), mainly from Lebanon and, to a lesser
tent, from Syria, Jordan and Egypt. In the main, these imports
nsist of fresh agricultural produce. The only Kuwayti export of
y significance is oil, which is sold to Western Europe and Japan.
uwayt also derives some income as an entrepôt for the re-export of
ods to the neighboring states and principalities. Kuwayt's reasons
r refusal to ratify the Arab Economic Pact were reported to be:
e imposition of tariffs required by the agreement to restrict the
try of goods of non-member countries would raise the local cost of
ving: a fundamental incompatibility between the economic systems
d the interests of these countries; Kuwayt is not an industrialized
untry and needs no protection for its national products.[43] In view
the previous description of the Kuwayti economy and of the other
rab countries, one can note the following: Kuwayt has an abun-
nce of convertible currencies and can purchase in the most advan-
geous markets; Kuwayt has no problem in finding markets for its
ly product — petroleum; Kuwayt's plans to broaden and expand
s industrial base, with protection for local industry, would be
mpered by the free entry of industrial products from Egypt and
me of the other Arab states. The Arab Economic Unity Pact pro-
des for the free movement of labor and capital. The Kuwaytis are

---

[43] *Commerce de Levant*, July 3, 1965, p. 3.

nationally exclusive. They rarely grant citizenship to other Ara
(or other foreigners) who have settled there. They require both ent
visas and work permits for those wishing to come there to work. Tw
thirds of the labor force is foreign, consisting of skilled and unskill
workers. The political dangers inherent in an even greater expansi
of the foreign labor force are apparent. Licenses for business ventu
and social services are restricted to Kuwayti citizens (about one-h
of the population). It is noteworthy that at a meeting of the Ar
League's Economic Unity Council in 1966, Egypt, Jordan and Syr
agreed to abolish passport regulations on the movement of the
nationals. Kuwayt and Iraq refused.[44] Kuwayt feels that it is doi
enough for its poorer sister Arab states. It is a major source of forei
aid for these countries. The Kuwayt Fund for Arab Economic Dev
opment has an authorized capital of $200 million and by the end
1965 had lent $110 million to other Arab states. In addition, four
five times this amount has been lent by the Kuwayti treasury direct
to other Arab governments. Egypt has been a major beneficiary
this largesse — largely for political reasons. The Kuwaytis apparent
feel that they have shown sufficient evidence of their Arab loyal
without accepting the restrictions which an Arab Common Mark
would impose.

Saudi Arabia's economy and development are dependent on petr
leum. Well over half of GNP is derived from this source. Anothe
though far smaller source of foreign exchange is derived from Musli
pilgrims. Since population estimates vary from three and a half
seven million, *per capita* income cannot be calculated, but is o
viously far less than Kuwayt's with a somewhat lower oil income ar
a much smaller population. About 60 per cent of the population
rural; 20 per cent nomad and 20 per cent urban.[45] Agriculture
primitive but the government has allocated sizeable funds for moder
agricultural development with the aid of foreign experts. Irrigatic
projects and the discovery of large reserves of underground wate
should stimulate this development. Other than oil refining, the ma
industries are confined to a few consumer goods and handicraft
Until the end of the 1950's the country's large oil revenues wer
poorly utilized. The 1960's have seen rapid development of all ec
nomic sectors. Many building materials are produced. Plans call fo
the production of fertilizers, steel (from local ore deposits), tire
plastics, aluminum wares, flour and other commodities. The UN

[44] *MEED*, March 11, 1966, p. 110.
[45] *Middle East and African Economist*, May, 1966, p. 74.

ding in the establishment of an Industrial Research Institute. An
dustrial Credit Bank aids local industry, an American firm has
en engaged as a consultant in the development of a diversified
dustrial economy, and laws have been promulgated providing for
ecial concessions to local industry as well as tariff protection.

About one-third of Saudi exports (oil) were sold to Western
urope; Japan, 18 per cent; US, seven per cent, and 15 per cent to
e Arab states (1963-64). About 60 per cent of the latter are to
ighboring Bahrayn for re-export to other countries. The main
ppliers are the US (one-fifth), Western Europe (one-third) and
e Arab states (one-fifth). The latter supply mainly agricultural
oduce. Significantly, imports from Egypt were sharply curtailed
962-64), probably as a result of the deteriorating relations between
e two countries.[46]

Saudi Arabia's attitude towards Arab unity is undoubtedly af-
cted by the ideological and political conflict in the Arab League.
ing Fayṣal is the strongest opponent of the "revolutionary Pan-
rabism" of Nāṣir. "Arab socialism" is anathema to the Saudi
onarch. From an economic point of view, what has been said pre-
ously about Kuwayt would generally apply to Saudi Arabia.
urthermore, to the extent that it succeeds in developing a modern
riculture (and it has the land, water and capital) this would tend
reduce its heavy dependence on food imports (mainly from the
rab states). The modern urban economy has attracted many rural
wellers, resulting in unemployment in many parts of the country.[47]
he oil industry is capital intensive, so that other industries must be
veloped to increase employment opportunities.

Yemen is the least developed of the Arab states. Its current claim
fame is that it is the focus of a political and military struggle
tween Egypt and Saudi Arabia. At the same time it is the focus
Soviet-Chinese rivalry. The Yemenis have been very adept in
tilizing their position to acquire considerable economic aid from
e Russians, Chinese, Americans, Egyptians and Kuwaytis, as well
from West Germany, Hungary, Yugoslavia and others. Though
ere has been a marked improvement in the development of a
odern infrastructure, the military and political struggle hampers
onomic development. The fuller exploitation of its resources (favor-

[46] Saudi Arabian Monetary Agency, *Statistical Summary*, November, 1965,
. 32-5.

[47] US Department of Labor, *Labor Law and Practice in Saudi Arabia*, BLS
port no. 269, April, 1964, pp. 19-20.

able climate, adequate rainfall and arable land) must await t
return of peace. It is mostly a subsistence economy based on primiti
agriculture. Coffee, *qāt* (a mild narcotic leaf) and cotton are t
main exports. The main buyers are Aden, USSR, Yugoslavia, Egy
and China. The chief suppliers are Japan, West Germany, UK, Ira
the Soviet Union and Egypt. However, since Yemen's market eco
omy is so small, its foreign trade is insignificant even within t
context of the Arab League. Its foreign trade (imports plus export
was $25 million in 1964 as compared with Jordan's $165 million (wit
half of Yemen's population).[48] It may very well be that if pea
returns and a strong progressive and efficient government is estal
lished (not very likely in the near future), Yemen might find t
Arab League's economic unity plans desirable. The freedom of mov
ment of capital might attract Kuwayti and other Arab capital (f
other than political motives) and more Yemeni laborers mig
migrate to other countries (many are now working in Aden) an
thereby acquire modern skills, and increase remittances to Yeme

Muhammad Diab, of the Economic Research Institute at t
American University of Beirut, made a detailed study of inter-Ara
economic cooperation in the 1950's. Many of his findings are equall
applicable to the 1960's and the foreseeable future. He found th
the bilateral trade agreements brought about some increase in trac
flows, particularly in agricultural products. However, other facto
were also instrumental in this increased trade. The preferentic
treatment incorporated in these pacts with respect to agricultur
products had not been subject (prior to the agreements) to custon
duties, or had been subject to negligible tariffs. The trade pac
were almost always of short duration, usually one year, subject
renewal. Under these conditions long term planning and investmen
were hazardous. Non-tariff restrictions on trade (quotas, impo
licenses, foreign exchange allocations, et cetera) robbed inter-Ara
trade agreements of the greater part of what they had to offer fc
creating market situations which would be more conducive to th
efficient regional allocation of resources. The governments have bee
hesitant to grant more preferences to manufactured products becaus
each has shown a jealous interest in protecting existing industri
and in reserving a place for new ones. Finally, he emphasizes th
generally accepted fact that economies of scale (and the resultin

[48] Agency for International Development (unpublished data), April, 1966.

ecialization and efficiency) are much more applicable to the indus-
al sector than to the agricultural sector.[49]

Diab confines himself to an analysis of the Eastern Arab states,
gypt, Syria, Lebanon, Jordan, Iraq and Saudi Arabia. The inclu-
on of the other seven Arab League states and the socialization
easures of Egypt, Syria, Iraq and Algeria in the 1960's add further
mplexities to an analysis of Arab economic unity plans. Sum-
arizing the prospects for these plans I believe that the following
ould be pertinent: the agricultural sector as a whole would not
esent a serious obstacle, since the growth of population and in-
mes usually exceeds the present or prospective productive capacity
this sector. However, even in this sector there are potential areas
conflict, notably in cotton and fruit production. The main area of
nflict is the industrial sector. In the European Common Market
d the European Free Trade Association all the member countries
ere in advanced stages of industrial development at the time of the
reements. In the Arab countries, industrial development is in its
cipient stages, but one country, Egypt, far outranks the others in
s present level of development and its capacity for expansion, given
wider and protected (from Western competition) market. It might
argued that the range of industrial products is so wide that there
enough latitude for a regional division of labor and specialization.
reality, industrialization in many or most developing countries
kes a very similar form, namely, textiles, food processing, cigarettes,
usehold articles, consumer durables and some "prestige" projects
ch as steel and vehicle assembly. There are some differences, of
urse, especially where natural resources of a unique nature are
esent. But by and large, the lack of specialized skills, and the grow-
g pressures of population and unemployment dictate quite similar
dustrialization plans. A prime source of government revenue in all
t the richest oil states is customs duties. Direct taxation is subject
widespread evasion and requires a level of sophistication not
ually found in developing countries. Within the range of indirect
xes, tariffs are most easily enforceable.

Balance of payments difficulties which usually plague all but the
chest oil states dictate the imposition of non-tariff restrictions on
ade in the form of quotas, import licensing, exchange controls,
ultiple exchange rates and "sophisticated" barter arrangements.

[49] Muhammad A. Diab, *Inter-Arab Economic Cooperation, 1951-60* (Economic
esearch Institute, American University of Beirut, 1963), pp. 87-9.

These restrictions could conceivably be reduced or eliminated by "Arab Payments Union." A resolution to set up such an instituti was adopted by the Arab Economic Unity Council in mid-1966 Whether, and in what manner, this resolution will be implemente it is too early to say. The adherence of the wealthier states to th union would mean, in effect, their subsidization of those states su fering from balance of payments difficulties. Furthermore, some the countries (Algeria, Tunisia and Morocco) are tied to the "Fra Zone" and others (Jordan, Kuwait and Libya) are tied to t "Sterling Zone." In reality, Egypt has been in the forefront of the Arab countries engaging in the bilateral barter agreements wi other countries, Arab and non-Arab. In a candid, though unrealist statement an Egyptian minister declared, "A system has been esta lished whereby we can avoid future (foreign) debts." That syste is barter.[51] This runs counter to the avowed aims of Arab econom unity, i.e. a more efficient regional allocation of resources. Freed of movement of capital is restricted by government controls and/ ownership of industry. These controls usually mean that politic considerations dictate economic policies. Government monopolies foreign trade impose non-economic criteria on the determination trade policy. The success of other common markets has been enhanc by the attraction of foreign capital and know-how. The politic instability which afflicts many of the Arab states and their aversi to private capitalists, especially foreigners, hampers such a develo ment in the Arab Common Market. The Maghrib states have speci arrangements with the European Common Market and are seekin associate status there (similar to Greece and Turkey). This mu limit the scope of any Arab economic unity agreements to which th would be a party. Libya, Kuwait and Saudi Arabia with their larg and growing oil revenues are not concerned with the problem of see ing markets for their exports or capital for economic developmer Only non-economic considerations could impel them to adhere to th Arab Common Market. Even these countries seek to diversify the one-sided economic structures through industrialization and prote tion of their "infant industries." The Arab Economic Unity Pa calls for free movement of labor. Kuwait has a population which more than half non-Kuwayti, and a labor force, two-thirds foreig In order to minimize political dangers it has imposed strict entr

[50] *MEED*, July 1, 1966, p. 293.
[51] *Economist Intelligence Unit* — Egypt, Libya, Sudan, March, 1965, p. 8.

strictions. The only other labor-short Arab country is Libya, and has restricted the entry of Egyptians, again for political reasons. Finally, what were the incentives of the four countries which did in the Arab Common Market? Other than political gains, Egypt the chief beneficiary of this agreement. The pressure to seek wider arkets for its industry, to reduce unemployment, to ease the balance payments difficulties through an Arab Payments Union, to ease the :port of Egyptian labor and thereby increase remittances, are all ertinent. Furthermore, its trade balance with the other Arab states negative and provides it with leverage in its agreements with these untries.

Though Syria and Jordan carry on a large inter-regional trade, it ould seem that their motives for adherence to the Arab Common arket were more political than economic. The internal political ructure in these countries as well as in Iraq is very unstable, and rab nationalist pressures are most pronounced. Any overt refusal conform with Arab nationalist aspirations would jeopardize their gimes. Along with their formal adherence to the Arab Economic nity Pact, they have stipulated many exceptions. These exceptions, ostly in reference to locally produced industrial products, negate any or most of the stated purposes of the agreements. The large gional trade carried on by these countries is mainly in agricultural roducts, which are usually not competitive. Rigid controls in Syria, aq and to a lesser extent, in Jordan, facilitate non-tariff restrictions trade. At the time of writing only two years have elapsed since the rab Common Market came into force, and the available data and e brief time lapse are insufficient to enable a more thorough analysis its efficacy. However, in a recent lecture given by an official of the yrian Ministry of Economy, summarizing the first two years of the rab Common Market, the official stated that trade among its members had dropped. Commenting on this, the Syrian official blamed is on the "Arab reactionary states" and on (unstated) restrictions.[52]

In conclusion, it should be emphasized that this analysis of the rab economic unity agreements and of the Arab Common Market pes not imply that there are no areas of fruitful and feasible economic cooperation. But, these would necessarily have to be less ambitious and much more limited in scope. Such projects as the coastal

---

[52] *MEED*, January 5, 1967, p. 1.

highway connecting Libya with Tunisia and Egypt; the highwa
connecting Saudi Arabia and Jordan; the reconstruction of the Hija
railway from Syria, through Jordan to Saudi Arabia; and the in
provement of communications in the Maghrib would have a positiv
effect on regional trade. Multilateral (rather than the usual bilateral
trade agreements among some of the countries taking into accoun
present and projected development plans, might be another avenu
of approach. However, even without taking into account the seriou
political rifts in the Arab League, the all-embracing Arab econom
unity agreements, culminating with the Arab Common Market, ar
least likely to succeed in the foreseeable future.

J. S. Nye

Central American Regional
Integration

. . .

LEVELS OF INTEGRATION

Whether caused by the "instant friendship" of ill-prepared summit meetings, the search for panaceas, or the deliberate effort to divert attention from internal problems, the most prevalent form of regionalism in less developed areas is an ephemeral expression of the supra-state sense of community without any significant restructuring of interests. This might be called "token integration" at the international level. Efforts to create Maphilindo in Southeast Asia, several recent Arab summit conferences, and declarations of intention to federate as a means of covering up real conflicts such as that between Kenya and Somalia in Northeast Africa are examples of this lowest expression of regionalism.

A higher level of integration is a "security community" in which regional institutions and symbols are sufficiently accepted to create a sense of illegitimacy of violent conflict among members even though they may be too weak to achieve economic benefits.[1] The Organization of African Unity, for example, had some initial success in attempting to create a security community. Another form of regional integration, involving a somewhat greater degree of interdependence, is "limited functional cooperation": the sharing of

Reprinted from *International Conciliation*, No. 562 (March 1967), with the permission of The Carnegie Endowment for International Peace.

[1] The term is developed in Karl W. Deutsch, *Political Community and the North Atlantic Area* (Princeton: Princeton Univ. Press, 1957), pp. 5-7.

costs of limited services, such as a regional airline, or monetar
cooperation among several former French African states, or th
establishment of regional development banks in Asia and Africa.[2]

International economic integration — a more complex level o
interdependence — includes a number of means of expanding marke
size by abolishing discrimination between economic factors belongin
to different national states. These are generally ranked in theor
from the lesser interdependence of a free trade area (abolition o
internal tariffs among members) to customs union (the addition o
a common external tariff) to common market (the addition of fre
movement of labor and capital) to economic union (the addition o
coordination of monetary and fiscal policy) to the greatest inter
dependence of *total* economic integration (the unification of eco
nomic policies). It is argued that this last stage would imply com
mon political control.[3] In practice these stages become somewha
blurred and the usage of the terms rather loose. For instance th
EEC involves considerable movement of labor and capital but stil
has not completed the abolition of internal tariffs or creation of th
external tariff. In Central America, the integration treaties in effec
create a stage between a free trade area and a customs union and cal
it a common market.[4]

Examples of significant economic integration are still rare. Th
Arab Common Market is stagnant, the Latin American Free Trad
Association (LAFTA) has bogged down, and several African effort
were stillborn. The highest level of economic integration among
sovereign states in the less developed world — the East African Com
mon Market inherited by Kenya, Uganda, and Tanzania from Britis

[2] See, for example, Albert Tevoedjre, *Pan-Africanism in Action: An Accoun
of the UAM* (Cambridge: Harvard Univ. Center for International Affairs
1965). Classifications of forms along a scale of interdependence are bound to b
somewhat arbitrary. Shared services in crucial areas can involve higher inter
dependence than the enlarged markets of economic integration imply. Similarly
shared services generally depend on, and can help reinforce, a security com
munity. Services of regional commissions of the United Nations are exceptiona
cases because of their external base of support.

[3] Bela A. Balassa, *The Theory of Economic Integration* (Homewood, Ill.
Richard D. Irwin, 1961), p. 2.

[4] Throughout this article, where it refers to Central America, common marke
is used in this sense. The term customs union is reserved, in Central America
for the free movement within the region of imported goods with some provision
for the distribution of the import duties on such goods. See Mauricio Bac
Muñoz, ''La Política y La Administración Fiscal: Anexo, Definiciones,'
Revista Conservadora del Pensamiento Centroamericano, No. 48 (Sept. 1964)
p. 33.

olonial rule — has declined since 1963, leaving the Central American
Common Market as the most prosperous example.

The fifth level of regional integration, direct political unification
(generally without prolonged preparation) has been tried by several
independent states (United Arab Republic, Mali Federation), but
success has been limited to absorption of small territories (Goa,
Zanzibar) by larger neighbors.

NATIONALISM

One reason frequently given to explain the problems and failures
of integration is "nationalism" — a word that explains little because it has been used to cover too much. In the sense of a widespread consciousness of belonging to a community associated with
a particular state, nationalism is stronger in Europe than in many
less developed countries, yet this has not prevented a considerable
degree of European economic integration.[5] In Central America, at
least among the nearly two-fifths of the population that is urban,
nationalism in the sense of a popularly felt right to exclude neighboring peoples from equal enjoyment of the resources of one's state
coexists with a considerable degree of economic integration.

Perhaps the problem in many less developed countries is less the
"profound feeling of nationalism" than the contrary. In situations
where nationalism in the sense of national consciousness is not
profound, political elites might be particularly tempted to choose a
highly nationalistic ideology and use the machinery of the state in a
highly nationalistic way in an effort to increase national consciousness
as a basis for their shaky authority — a process frequently called
"nation-building." Even with this distinction, however, nationalism
does not completely explain the problem since it is not clear why
some political elites in countries with weak national consciousness
opt for ultranationalistic ideologies and policies while others do not.

In short, nationalism is not sufficient to explain the complexity of
the problems of regional integration among less developed countries.
To take the most important problem of economic integration, why
should it not be possible for leaders of small underdeveloped states
to have the best of both worlds: separate national identity and pooled
markets? Why is it not possible to start with a minimal degree of

[5] See Stanley Hoffmann, "Obstinate or Obsolete? The Fate of the Nation
State and the Case of Western Europe," *Daedalus*, No. 3 (Summer 1966), pp.
862-915.

integration and gradually increase it as the benefits begin to be felt? People realize that they need more rather than less interdependence to preserve the benefits already gained; governments develop a certain adaptability in their behavior regarding limitation of sovereignty; and a sense of pride in common achievements begins to grow. In other words, why should the political theory of functional integration not work in less developed countries?

THE FUNCTIONALIST STRATEGY

The basic argument of "functionalism" as a theory of international organization is for a minimal frontal attack on state sovereignty, which is gradually made irrelevant by a reordering of the world along technical-functional lines.[6] The weakness of this "pure" functionalism is the absence of a strong link between technical and political matters, which makes political irrelevance likely. As revised and applied to Europe by neo-functionalist practitioners like Jean Monnet and theorists like Ernst Haas, functionalism avoids the legalistic frontal attack on sovereignty that federalists advocate. Instead it seeks out semi-technical tasks with a high degree of political relevance (for example, coal and steel in postwar Europe) and establishes supranational bureaucracies to deal with the tasks. Functionalism relies on the natural linkages of economic and social sectors and the prodding of the technocrats to persuade the governments to allow one common task to "spill over" into another.[7] Ultimate ends are deliberately left ambiguous, but it is generally assumed that the gradual addition of new sectors will lead to wide-ranging central institutions, which will gradually achieve a value of their own and act as a new focus for loyalties and expectations beyond the nation-state.

Thus functionalism places heavy emphasis on administrative capacity; on short run separability of economic questions from the mainstream of political debate allowing some important tasks to take on a sufficiently noncontroversial, technical aura to be left to technocrats; and on pluralism, permitting interest groups and individuals freedom to take advantage of new opportunities and to gradually

[6] See David Mitrany, *A Working Peace System* (London: Royal Institute of International Affairs, 1943); and ibid., "The Functional Approach to World Organization," *International Affairs* (July 1948), pp. 350-363.

[7] See Ernst Haas, *The Uniting of Europe* (Stanford: Stanford Univ. Press, 1958).

refocus their expectations and loyalties on the developing new center. In a sense, functionalism is a strategy for attacking the castle of national sovereignty by stealth, with interest groups as mercenaries and technocrats as agents within the walls to quietly open the gates.

POLITICS OF INTEGRATION

This gives a clue to the problems of regional integration in less developed areas. A quiet attack is difficult. In Africa, many leaders are still seeking "first the political kingdom"; in "Southeast Asia, matters that relate to the economy are subjects of high governmental priority," and "experience in Latin America shows that a regional grouping quickly comes up against all kinds of problems calling for solutions at the highest political level."[8]

Why is it so hard to separate economic tasks from the mainstream of political debate? Some economists argue that since markets are small (the LAFTA market is 25 per cent and the Central American market less than 2 per cent of EEC's market), entrepreneurs scarce, and infrastructure weak, reduction of tariffs and reliance on competitive market forces must be supplemented by bureaucratic measures that involve greater infringement of state sovereignty.[9] Moreover, pure market forces tend toward imbalance in the location of industry, and in less developed countries, industry is valued not only for its welfare effects but also for symbolic prestige effects. One would also expect that, where incomes are so low, welfare issues would be more controversial and less easy to bargain over than in more developed countries.

Many of the general characteristics of politics in less developed countries are difficult to reconcile with quiet functionalism. Leadership tends to be personalistic; heroes have trouble cooperating. The gap between the literate elite and the illiterate masses, the scarcity of organized interest groups, and the cultural cleavage between city and countryside, which might seem to free the hands of the elites for

---

[8] Joseph S. Nye, Jr., *Pan-African ism and East African Integration* (Cambridge: Harvard Univ. Press, 1965), p. 25; Bernard K. Gordon, *The Dimensions of Conflict in Southeast Asia* (Englewood Cliffs, N.J.: Prentice Hall, 1966), p. 142; and Sidney Dell, "Regional Integration and the Industrialization of Less Developed Countries," *Development Digest*, No. 3 (Oct. 1965), p. 45, respectively.

[9] Miguel S. Wionczek, "Introduction: Requisites for Viable Integration," in *Latin American Economic Integration*, ed. Miguel S. Wionczek (New York: Frederick Praeger, 1966), pp. 3-18.

international integration, have more often resulted in insecurity isolation, and diversion of attention to internal integration. Scarcity of middle level administrative manpower results in weak govern mental and political institutions, which are susceptible to disruption by the few relatively organized institutions such as the army. The adaptability of governments under these conditions tends to be low.

INTEGRATION IN CENTRAL AMERICA

Given the problems confronting regional economic integration among less developed countries, it is difficult to explain the relative success of integration in Central America, an area with an illiteracy rate of more than 50 per cent, an annual per capita income of less than $300, and an extremely high population growth rate of 3.5 per cent per year. Roughly equivalent in size to California, the 170,000 square miles of Central America are split into five small states, which in a century and a half of independence were frequently subject to outside intervention and served as prototypes for the name "banana republic." Coffee and cotton are in fact more significant exports than bananas, but the three crops account for roughly three-fourths of exports in what are still basically agricultural exporting economies.

In 1950, trade among the Central American states was only 3

TABLE 1
CENTRAL AMERICA[10]

Country	Area (Square Miles)	Population (Millions)	Population Density (Square Miles)	Per Cent Literate (10 Years & Older)	Per Cent Urban	GNP (Dollars Millions)	Per Capita Income (Dollars)
Guatemala	42,000	4.3	97	39	34	1,220	283
El Salvador	8,200	2.8	332	51	39	768	272
Honduras	43,000	2.1	47	47	23	453	207
Nicaragua	57,000	1.6	27	51	41	458	290
Costa Rica	19,700	1.5	68	86	35	528	365

SOURCES: SIECA, *Centroamérica y Su Mercado Común,* Vol. 3 (1965), and *Quarto Compendio Estadístico Centroamericano,* Vol. II (1965).

[10] Central American statistics are of very uneven quality and should be used to indicate orders of magnitude rather than for precise comparisons.

per cent of the area's total exports. By 1965, regional trade was 19 per cent of total exports, having quadrupled in value (from $32.7 to $136 million) since the signing of the General Treaty of Central American Economic Integration in 1960. Four-fifths of this trade was cleared in local currencies through the Central American Clearing House. In the past six years, new regional institutions in such fields as development banking, monetary coordination, air navigation, and tourism have been established, and the budgets and tasks assigned to a number of older institutions have been increased. In addition, a number of new private regional groups have been founded.

There is bound to be a certain degree of arbitrariness in the singling out of a few from among the many causes of a complex social process like the growth of regional integration in Central America. For instance, common language and religion undoubtedly play some small part, but in terms of comparative theory this is not a very interesting cause, for it is a characteristic shared with other countries (for example, Panama) that have not participated, and differences in language or religion have not prevented success in other common markets (for example, the EEC). Four major reasons, none individually sufficient to explain the Central American exception to the general experience of less developed countries, but each providing a part of the explanation, should be considered: the ideal of Central American political union, certain peculiarities in Central American political culture, the low costs in the early stages of the process, and favorable external factors.

The Ideal of
Central American Union

Central Americans frequently attribute at least part of their recent success to the historical fact that they once were united and have not forgotten it. Skeptics can point out, however, that Central America was never closely integrated, and that during the first century and a quarter of the region's division into separate national entities, the ideal of union was not sufficient to prevent the failure of some twenty-five formal efforts at reintegration — a remarkable average of one failure every five years.[11] As an explanation of success therefore, the ideal of union requires considerable qualification.

HISTORICAL PRECEDENTS

Central America first came into modern political existence as part of the Spanish empire in the middle of the sixteenth century. A measure of the impact of three centuries of colonial rule on regional identities is the peripheral position of Panama, which, although it is part of the same isthmus, was ruled from South America until 1903.[12] But the extent of colonial integration should not be overestimated. The theoretical centralization of the Spanish empire was diminished by conflicting boundaries of local authority and in any case was less important than the inadequacies of communication in the mountainous isthmus. Even as late as the 1930s, no all-weather roads connected the Central American capitals.[13] "Viewed outwardly this 'kingdom' was very logically a political unit, comprising the entire Central American highland. . . . But internally, the unity was not so apparent." The various groups of settlement were separated by wide spaces, and "by the end of the colonial period, the outlines of the five nations of today were quite discernible, each . . . conscious of its own identity, and much more conscious of its own problems and ambitions than of any sentiment of Central American solidarity."[14]

The absence of any real struggle for independence from Spain in 1821 or from Mexico, which the Central Americans joined until 1823, deprived them of a sense of shared suffering that might have helped to overcome the local jealousies and ideological rivalries that plagued the loosely federated "United Provinces of Central America." A weak presidency, strong states' rights, and paucity of economic and administrative resources made the federation in practice

[11] Thomas L. Karnes, *The Failure of Union: Central America, 1824-1960* (Chapel Hill, N.C.: Univ. of North Carolina Press, 1961), p. 243.

[12] Panama declined to join the Organization of Central American States in 1955 on the ground that "Panama belongs to South America." *Hispanic American Report*, No. 8 (Sept. 1955). It might be more accurate to describe the position as isolationism.

[13] Robert Bradbury, "Trade and Transportation: Dynamic Factors in Central American Development," in *The Caribbean: The Central American Area*, ed. A. Curtis Wilgus (Gainesville, Fla.: Univ. of Florida Press, 1961), p. 158.

[14] Francis M. Stanger, "National Origins in Central America," *Hispanic American Historical Review*, No. 1 (Feb. 1932), pp. 21 and 25.

"a league of towns, suspicious of each other and linked only by a common concern for protection." Racked by civil war, the union did not even create a "security community" in the terms we have used above. Some 7,000 persons (of a population of a little over a million) perished in more than a hundred battles and skirmishes between 1824-42.[15]

What federation did create was a political ideal of Central American union that led to the twenty-five attempted unifications mentioned above and plays a subtle part in economic integration today. Within twenty-five years of the collapse of the United Provinces in 1838, delegates (primarily from Liberal regimes in the three central states) met formally eight times in efforts to reestablish unity. During the last quarter of the nineteenth century, the success of German and Italian unification in Europe inspired Justo Rufino Barrios of Guatemala to try reintegration of the region by force.[16] Early in the twentieth century, under the new influences of the Hague peace machinery and active United States participation and after two short wars, Central American delegates met in Washington in 1907 to establish a Court of Justice composed of one judge appointed by each of the five legislatures, and a Central American Bureau. Within two years jealous governments had curtailed the activities of the Bureau. In 1917 Nicaragua (with the acquiescence of the United States, which had intervened in Nicaragua since 1912) ignored an adverse ruling — in effect terminating the juridical path to union.

After a coup d'etat in Guatemala destroyed attempts to recreate a federation made during the centennial anniversary of independence, the United States held a second conference in Washington, which established a second weaker court. This court, however, passed unnoticed from the scene in 1934. The depression and war years of the 1930s and early 1940s were marked by the rise of strong dictators who followed isolationist policies in regard to other Central American states. After the toppling of the dictators Hernández Martínez and Ubico in 1944, El Salvador and Guatemala attempted union in 1945 and 1946, but this beginning vanished in the turmoil of internal struggles for power.[17]

---

[15] Karnes, op. cit., pp. 92 and 94. See also Rodrigo Facio, *Trayectoria y Crisis de la Federación Centroamericana* (San José, Costa Rica: Imprenta Nacional, 1949), pp. 59-74.

[16] Mario Rodriguez, *Central America* (Englewood Cliffs, N.J.: Prentice-Hall, 1965), p. 101.

[17] Alberto Herrarte, *La Unión de Centroamérica: Tragedia y Esperanza* (2nd ed.; Guatemala: Ministerio de Educación Pública, 1964), pp. 204-211.

POSTWAR DEVELOPMENTS

In 1951, two parallel approaches were started — one by the ministers of economy and one by the foreign ministers — and the contrast between their subsequent paths is instructive. The Central American delegations to the fourth sessions of the United Nations Economic Commission for Latin America (ECLA) in Mexico in June included three ministers who had been trained abroad, considered themselves economists more than politicians, and were concerned about the dependence of their economies on world commodity prices and the problems that the small size of their national markets posed for the establishment of industry. Both at the June ECLA session, where a resolution was adopted favoring the integration of the Central American economies, and during a visit from Raul Prebisch and other ECLA officials in August, the ministers worked closely with the international civil servants, with whom they felt they had a great deal in common.[18] In October in San Salvador, the economic ministers collectively resisted efforts by the foreign ministers to incorporate them in a subordinate position into the new organization being founded by the foreign ministers. Instead the five economic ministers constituted themselves as the autonomous Committee for Economic Cooperation of the Central American Isthmus (CCE) with ECLA as their secretariat and held their first meeting in Tegucigalpa, Honduras, in August 1952.

In October 1951, the foreign ministers established the Organization of Central American States (ODECA). Influenced by the postwar interest in international organization, the foreign ministers believed that they could avoid the failure of "previous methods" at reconstituting the "separate parts of one and the same nation" because "modern international law offers adequate formulas to this end through the establishment of regional organizations."[19] The lawyers of the foreign offices were mistaken, however, in believing that their new organization was a significant departure from the past. The first meeting was marked by a Nicaraguan appeal for the traditional

[18] Interview with former ministers of economy: Jorge Sol (El Salvador), 15 Aug. 1966; Enrique Delgado (Nicaragua), 18 Oct. 1966; and Manuel Noriega Morales (Guatemala), 28 Oct. 1966.

[19] Eugenio A. Hernandez, S.J., "The Organization of Central American States in Historical Perspective," Ph.D. Thesis (Harvard Univ., 1963), p. 125; and James L. Busey, "Central American Union: The Latest Attempt," *Western Political Quarterly*, No. 1 (Mar. 1961), pp. 51-52, respectively.

"instant union," much to the embarrassment of the Costa Rican Foreign Minister. The second meeting was delayed when El Salvador's Foreign Minister, Roberto Canessa, closely supervised by President Oscar Osorio, proposed an anti-communist resolution, which led the leftist Guatemalan government (originally an initiator of the organization) first to postpone the meeting, and then, in April 1953, to withdraw from ODECA. It is interesting to note that ideological differences did not prevent Guatemalan economic ministers from actively participating in the more technically oriented CCE meetings in August 1952 and October 1953.

The return of conservative government to Guatemala in 1954 meant the return of Guatemala to ODECA, but not the end of the political problems that plagued the organization. At ODECA's first regular meeting in 1955, the President of Guatemala, Castillo Armas, emphasized that Central America had "the same race, language, religion, customs, traditions, economic resources, and even the same dangers," but the organization was nearly destroyed by the rivalry preceding the choice of J. Guillermo Trabanino, the Salvadorian Foreign Minister, as the first Secretary General. In 1959, ODECA nearly collapsed again over the choice of his successor. In the opinion of Marco Tulio Zeledón, a former official in the Costa Rican Foreign Office who eventually became the second Secretary General, the organization was largely ignored by the governments, which did not even bother to revise or discuss the memoranda on the year's activities in spite of earlier "promises and proclamations of lyric unionism."[20] Although the organization held two formal and four extraordinary meetings in the 1950s, both Secretaries devoted much energy to attempting to settle political disputes in the area. Although there has been a marked decline in interstate incidents in the 1960s, it is difficult to attribute the growth of a security community to the activities of ODECA. The major factors in settling inter-state violence in the 1950s were the United States and the Organization of American States (OAS), which intervened between Nicaragua and its neighbors in 1955, 1957, and 1959. In the case of the 1955 dispute, it has been alleged that one of the statesmen involved felt that ODECA was used as a tool by his opponents. The current administration feels that the political efforts of the past are not a good precedent for the organization in the 1960s.

[20] *Hispanic American Report*, op. cit.; Marco Tulio Zeledón, *La Odeca* (San José, Costa Rica: Colegio de Abogados, 1966), pp. 98 and 87; and Zeledón, interview, 12 Aug. 1966, respectively.

THE ECONOMIC APPROACH

Despite the political turmoil of the 1950s, the economic ministers were able to meet every year, albeit quietly and unofficially in 1954 and 1955, when general political tension and a possible dispute on economic policy between El Salvador and Nicaragua might have jeopardized progress. Their accomplishments (with the assistance of ECLA) were considerable: the liberalization of trade through a network of bilateral treaties; the establishment in 1954 and 1956 of the Central American School of Public Administration (ESAPAC) and the Central American Institute of Research and Industrial Technology (ICAITI); the signing of agreements on uniform road codes and customs nomenclature in 1956; provision for limited (about 20 per cent of items) multilateral free trade and allocation of new large scale industry in 1958 through the signing of the Multilateral Treaty on Central American Free Trade and the Agreement on the Regime of Central American Integrated Industries; the beginning (about 10 per cent) of equalization of external tariffs in 1959; and finally, in 1960, the establishment of the Central American Bank for Economic Integration (CABEI) and the signing of the General Treaty of Central American Economic Integration, which freed more than 90 per cent of the categories in Central American trade (74 per cent by value).[21] Along with these institutional achievements of the decade went a quadrupling of regional trade, with increases in every year except 1954-55. Subsequently, as we have seen, regional trade has quadrupled again, and new institutions have been added.

THE ROLE OF THE IDEAL

The contrast between the records of the two regional organizations is striking; it was CCE, less directly connected with the political ideal of Central American union, that flourished while ODECA stagnated. But it does not follow that the ideal has contributed nothing to economic integration. Its first role was the creation of a protective climate of ideas that has sheltered the movement from some of the vagaries of national political winds. Governmental power changed hands twice by force in 1963 (in Guatemala and Honduras)

---

[21] Secretaria Permanente de Integración Económica Centroamericana (SIECA), *Carta Informativa*, No. 17 (Mar. 1963). Costa Rica did not decide to sign the General Treaty until after a change of government in 1962. It officially joined in Sept. 1963.

and twice by free elections in 1966 (in Costa Rica and Guatemala) without affecting economic integration. Existing symbols and myths predispose politicians against directly attacking integration. Flags and emblems are variations of the old federal symbols; several constitutions have provisions referring to the restoration of Central America; and the shared holiday of independence is an occasion for Central American rhetoric. It is both fashionable and profitable in terms of reputation for politicians to support rather than oppose economic integration, and this contributes to a myth of irreversibility. Interest groups that are not sure whether they have been hurt or not, for example, some Honduran trade unions, nonetheless give the benefit of the doubt to the Common Market because they favor Central American unity.[22] Others, such as some Honduran importers, who feel that they have been hurt, are discouraged from mounting a frontal attack by the myth of irreversibility.

Second, the ideal of union provides, in the words of a leading technocrat, "a vocation for the minority who staff the integration organizations" and who could in many cases find more lucrative employment elsewhere.[23] Editorials in the organ of the Secretariat of the Common Market (SIECA) refer to final goals of "one Republic" and "reconstruction of our nationality." One observer reported in 1965 that a score of Common Market officials interviewed ultimately hoped for political union, and the overwhelming majority of some several dozen officials concerned with integration interviewed by the author responded similarly.[24] It is important to note, however, that although some form of political union is regarded as a long-range ideal (and even this to a lesser extent in Costa Rica), most of the men immediately concerned with economic integration consider it postponable in the short run. "Our common political past partly explains our success; we want political union some day, but economics has the priority now," says one technocrat.[25] In the words of one of the founders: "Political union is an ultimate ideal, but most Central American economists shun it now because we see from history that when we lack common interests, any egotist can split off a part. Until we have a full network of interests in all fields — trade, mone-

[22] Céleo Gonzalez, Secretary General, Federación Sindical de Trabajadores Porteños de Honduras, interview, 11 Oct. 1966.

[23] Pedro Abelardo Delgado, former Secretary of SIECA, interview, 28 Sept. 1966.

[24] SIECA, *Carta Informativa*, No. 14 (Dec. 1962), and No. 48 (Oct. 1965); and *Latin American Times* (New York), 22 July 1965, respectively.

[25] Raul Sierra Franco, Deputy Secretary, SIECA, interview, 13 Sept. 1966.

tary, fiscal, educational, legal — we cannot run the risk of allowing some colonel to bring it all down.''[26]

Third, the ideal of Central American union has, in the opinion of some participants, occasionally helped a number of governments if not to make sacrifices, then at least to interpret their interest in long-run terms instead of insisting on immediate benefits. Hard bargaining is more common than appeals to ''the widest spirit of Centralamericanism'' during meetings. Some observers, however, feel that the latter may have helped the government of Honduras to save face in reversing a decision giving one firm special import privileges that threatened to disrupt free trade in 1964,[27] or that it may have speeded the signing of a difficult protocol on grains in 1966.

In short, the past history of political union and its current residue both of lessons learned from previous mistakes and as a political ideal, provides part of the explanation of the success of Central American economic integration. But a century and a half of history including the comparative experience of ODECA and the CCE during the 1950s, demonstrates that the ideal of political union is a dangerous medicine healthful only in small doses.

Central American
Political Culture

Although the type of political process likely to be found in less developed countries makes regional economic integration difficult there are, of course, important differences among less developed countries. From the point of view of functionalist theory, ''if government is in the hands of some oligarchy that rules a tranquil and unmobilized people, in which mass emotions play no part and in which there is no general political participation, spontaneous or manipulated, the logic of the proposition may well apply.''[28] But this does not explain the Central American exception, for while the area's politics were once like this, they no longer fit the description

[26] Jorge Sol, interview, 15 Aug. 1966.
[27] SIECA, *Carta Informativa*, No. 37 (Nov. 1964).
[28] Ernst Haas, *Beyond the Nation-State* (Stanford: Univ. Press, 1964), p. 50

However, if this examination is broadened to include the concept of "political culture" (the set of attitudes, beliefs, and sentiments that govern behavior in the political system), and if it is argued that it may change more slowly than the rest of the political process, we have an important clue to the success of regional integration in Central America.[29]

POLITICAL SYSTEMS

Before plunging into Central American politics, it is important to note that Costa Rica differs considerably from its neighbors, and that this difference has frequently hindered the region's political union. In an area with little Indian labor, Spanish settlement resulted in an ethnically and economically more homogeneous society, which was fortunate in its relative isolation from the nineteenth century religious-ideological conflicts of Guatemala, and which today enjoys a high degree of literacy and nearly twenty years of democratically elected government.[30] Nonetheless, Costa Rica's characteristics represent differences of degree, not kind, from the rest of Central America. Costa Rica has had dictators, revolutions (as recently as 1948), and new constitutions, but fewer than the rest of Central America. It is most important for the purposes of this study, however, that in the aspects of political culture that help explain the success thus far of Central American integration, Costa Rica is not markedly different. Even in the most democratic system in Central America, an important decision like nonparticipation in the General Treaty in 1960 was made largely by the then conservative minister of economics.

In the four northern states (less so in Honduras), there are small wealthy oligarchies and impoverished rural masses, whose annual per capita income of $138 is one fourth of the urban average.[31] Moreover, the military, which in these countries receives from 10 to 16 per cent of national budgets, plays an important indirect, and sometimes direct, role in politics.[32] But characterization of the political systems as "praetorian states" or simple "oligarchies" would fail to

[29] Lucian W. Pye, *Aspects of Political Development* (Boston: Little, Brown & Co., 1966), p. 104.

[30] See James L. Busey, "Foundations of Political Contrast: Costa Rica and Nicaragua," *Western Political Quarterly*, No. 3 (Sept. 1958), pp. 627-659; and Frederick B. Pike, "The Catholic Church in Central America," *The Review of Politics*, No. 1 (Jan. 1959), p. 85.

[31] AID, Regional Office for Central America and Panama Affairs (ROCAP), *Country Assistance Program, Fiscal Year 1967* (declassified, 1965), pp. 1-7.

[32] *The Vision Letter* (New York), 21 Apr. 1965.

take into account those people who have been mobilized into national life, largely through moving to cities. During the 1950s, the urban population grew from one quarter to one third of the total. New "middle sectors" of the population enjoying more than six years of education, more than minimal living income, and access to modern communications media (including such occupations as skilled labor, junior officers, teachers, clerks, bureaucrats, and small businessmen) are estimated by one study to comprise some small businessmen) are estimated by one study to comprise some 25-35 per cent of the population in Costa Rica, 15-20 per cent in El Salvador, and perhaps 15 per cent in the other three countries.[33] Although these groups are not necessarily cohesive, they have a similar effect on the political process since their ability to manipulate abstractions and modern organizations makes nationalist appeals and political parties their natural instruments in bargaining for political power.[34] Although the victory of a political party in elections is not a guarantee of gaining or keeping power (witness the period of bargaining between the victorious *Partido Revolucionario* and the military while announcement of final election results was delayed in Guatemala in March 1966), party politics and appeals to broader participation complicate simple oligarchical descriptions of Central American politics The military is an ultimate base of power in most of the northern countries, but the political party is also an important instrument of government. Moreover, inexpensive transistor radios have begun to nullify illiteracy as a factor permitting complete oligarchical domination of parties. In the words of a Nicaraguan party official: "Every thing is changed from ten years ago. Now when we go to a village they are all up to date on what is happening in the capital."[35]

Guatemala, with its large unassimilated Indian population, probably has the lowest percentage of political participation; but whereas twenty-five years ago it may have been accurate to say that "Guatemala was run by and largely for a small group of large landowners allied with the officer corps of the army and backed by representatives of foreign corporations and the hierarchy of the Catholic church," subsequently the country went through a social revolution "of a type rare in Latin America."[36] In the early 1950s, one of

[33] United Nations Doc. E/CN.12/CCE/176/Rev.2, 18 Oct. 1960, p. 6.

[34] Charles Anderson, "Central American Political Parties: A Functional Approach," *Western Political Quarterly*, No. 1 (Mar. 1962), pp. 125-139.

[35] Alberto Chamorro B., Treasurer, Conservative Party, interview, 21 Oct 1966.

[36] Ronald M. Schneider, *Communism in Guatemala, 1944-1954* (New York

every four adult males was in a labor or agricultural union, and the majority of the adult population went to the polls. While the return to power of conservative elements in 1954 crushed the unions, it could not completely turn the clock back.[37]

Although Central American political systems are not now simple oligarchies allied with outside influences ruling unmobilized peoples, to a considerable extent they once were. This past has influenced two aspects of their political cultures that have been important in economic integration: political attitudes toward economic change, and the type of nationalism.

ATTITUDES TOWARD ECONOMIC CHANGE

Those holding political power in Central America traditionally were preoccupied with matters other than economic change. They viewed governmental power less as a means of economic transformation than as a means of ensuring a share of economic resources for themselves and their clique. The area was marked by frequent political changes that seldom involved great socio-economic change. On the contrary, one of the functions of the civilian or military politician allied with the economic elite (and enjoying access to its resources) was to prevent widespread socio-economic transformation. The role of the military in politics was "not the nationalistic militarism of the Near East, with its demagogic will to transform," but "power for power's sake."[38]

The political elite's lack of interest in economic change is, of course, a relative matter. For instance, the leaders of the East African Common Market countries, as heads of unstable states, were preoccupied with maintaining their political power. However, given the recent political history of the area (recent emergence from colonial rule and the effects of cold war tensions), their plans for economic transformation played a greater part in their ability to maintain that power. In contrast, when President Mendez Montenegro appeared on television in Guatemala and gave a speech

---

Frederick Praeger, 1959), p. 2; and Richard N. Adams, "Social Change in Guatemala and U.S. Policy," in Richard N. Adams et al., *Social Change in Latin America Today* (New York: Harper Bros., 1960), p. 234, respectively.

[37] Schneider, op. cit., p. 40.

[38] Victor Alba, "The Stages of Militarism in Latin America," in *The Role of the Military in Underdeveloped Countries*, ed. John Johnson (Princeton: Princeton Univ. Press, 1962), p. 165.

detailing his economic development program, a leading newspaper referred to his "total omission of political questions." In the mid-1950s both a democratically elected president like José Figueres of Costa Rica and a military-supported president like General Anastasio Somoza of Nicaragua were concerned with economic development of their countries, but they were *more* preoccupied with removing each other from power.[39] The concern of President Jacobo Arbenz of Guatemala with that country's rapid transformation in the early 1950s is an exception; had it continued and disrupted the integration movement (a fair probability), however, it might have been an exception that proves the following rule.

The importance of this political characteristic for the early success of economic integration was in providing the degree of separability of economic matters from the mainstream of political debate — the element of noncontroversiality — that functionalist theory suggests is necessary to allow technocrats to operate. The Central American "political culture" allowed a new generation of marginal members of the elite to use their economic and technical training (in many cases acquired abroad) to bring about change quietly. These "technocrats" combined the prestige of fairly technical training, usually in economics, with a broader than technical interest. In other words, a technocrat was less a pure technician than a new kind of politician whose style was that of the expert, and whose limited power arena was the bargaining room rather than the public square or military barracks.[40]

The position of being part, but apart, from the political mainstream meant that the technocrats were able to get political support when necessary but also were able to avoid political disruption. Thus the economic ministers were powerful enough to stave off the efforts of the foreign ministers to incorporate them in ODECA in 1951 — an incorporation that might have exposed them to the political turmoil of the 1950s. Instead, in 1955, when Nicaragua and Costa Rica were on the point of war, as a result of the counter-plotting of political exiles and the personal animosities of their two heads of states, their economic ministers met quietly and agreed that, while their governments were acting a bit foolishly, they would stick to eco-

[39] *El Imparcial* (Guatemala City), 30 Sept. 1966; José Figueres, interview, 9 Aug. 1966; and Enrique Delgado, interview, 18 Oct. 1966, respectively.

[40] Their power was based on their technical reputation. The new and more plentiful second generation of technocrats now staffing many organizations is less easily able to translate technical proficiency into power.

nomic business.[41] More recently, Costa Rica's refusal to recognize the military governments that came to power in Guatemala and Honduras in 1963 did not affect its participation in the various economic integration meetings.

The atmosphere of relations among the ministers of economy has generally been one of first names and shirtsleeves rather than the protocol of foreign ministers' meetings. In 1961, at a joint meeting of economic and foreign ministers to coordinate policy before the Punta del Este Conference, the division was not by nations, but by foreign ministers who spoke mainly of anti-communism, and economic ministers who insisted on meeting separately to work out more specific proposals.[42]

The ministers received presidential support, according to a former Costa Rican president, because "the Central American and integration ideas were fashionable; we did not think it would amount to much; and it was important to keep the economists happy. If I trusted the man I would sign his declaration." Former technocrats report that the elder General Somoza, who carefully supervised such ministries as Interior, allowed technocrats free rein in what he regarded as the technical field of economics, including their "playing at integration." Former President Villeda Morales of Honduras gave his economists political backing for integration when they asked for it, but did not regard the signing of the Multilateral Treaty in his capital in 1958 to be of sufficient political importance to require his presence.[43]

The ministers of economy remain the key link between the political and integration processes, constituting all or part of five committees and boards of organizations, but the degree of separation that they bridge has narrowed with time and has differed by country. Among other things, population pressures in El Salvador, and the greater economic sophistication and high degree of participation of the second generation of the Somoza family in the economy of Nicaragua, have brought more presidential attention to integration in these two countries. With the inclusion of new sectors and the growth of institutions, integration has become more difficult for politicians to ignore. For example, a Nicaraguan appeal over ministerial heads

[41] Jorge Rossi, former Costa Rican Minister of Economy, interview, 13 Aug. 1966; and Enrique Delgado, interview, 18 Oct. 1966.

[42] Jorge Sol, interview, 15 Aug. 1966; and Zeledón, op. cit., pp. 101-102.

[43] Interviews: José Figueres, 9 Aug. 1966; Enrique Delgado, 18 Oct. 1966; Jorge Montealegre, Corporación Nicaraguense de Inversiones, 18 Oct. 1966; and Ramón Villeda Morales, 15 Oct. 1966, respectively.

to several presidents ensured that a Nicaraguan would continue in the presidency of CABEI. (In contrast, the new Secretary General of SIECA was chosen by the economic ministers, and the nationality changed.) In Honduras, the government and opposition newspapers trade criticism over the initial terms and subsequent handling of Central American Common Market matters.[44] Some observers feel that Nicaragua's request for preferential treatment in 1966 (backed up with large banners in the main street of Managua) and the vehemence of the Salvadorian response may have owed something to the imminence of elections in the two countries, although the Common Market has not figured as a partisan issue.

The diminishing distance from political debate is viewed with equanimity by some who feel that the political conditions for further progress will, as the process becomes more complex, differ from those that were optimal for its creation. The former Secretary General of SIECA feels that many of the new tasks of integration "can only be viable if the presidents support them."[45] In 1959, when economists in the three northern states were distressed with the slow speed at which new items were being added to the *inclusive* list of freely traded goods established by the 1958 Multilateral Treaty, they solicited and received presidential support for the tactic of a tripartite agreement establishing virtually complete free trade except for a small list of *exclusions*. The three presidents met at El Poy in January 1960 and officially asked the ministers to prepare the "Tripartite Treaty" (Treaty of Economic Association), which was signed in February. Although the tactic failed to have an immediate effect on Costa Rica, it did bring Nicaragua (with personal attention from President Luis Somoza) to sign the General Treaty, which incorporated the new and more radical exclusive list approach, in December 1960. Within three years, Costa Rica also acceded to the Treaty.

CENTRAL AMERICAN NATIONALISM

The second and related characteristic of Central American political culture that permitted the economist-technocrats to initiate their changes quietly was the nature of Central American nationalism, particularly the nature of the nationalist ideologies. It is not ac-

---

[44] See, for example, *El Pueblo* (Tegucigalpa), 11 Oct. 1966; and *El Nacional* (Tegucigalpa), 13 Oct. 1966.

[45] Pedro Abelardo Delgado, as quoted in SIECA, *Carta Informativa*, No. 55 (12 May 1966).

curate to depict Central American states as devoid of national consciousness. Although about one half of the Guatemalan population lives as traditional or semi-traditional Indians outside the national frame of reference, there is, among the urban 35 per cent of the population at least, a sufficient national consciousness to allow politicians to rally support over: the recurrent dispute with Britain about Belice (British Honduras); Mexicans fishing in Guatemalan waters; and illegal Salvadorian immigration or allegedly unequal division of the waters of a lake shared with El Salvador. A border dispute between Nicaragua and Honduras aroused nationalist sentiments until it was settled by a decision of the International Court of Justice in 1960.

In terms affecting the integration movement, many Nicaraguans feel that they have been slighted in the allocation of institutions, and Honduran sensitivity about getting a fair share of the benefits of integration has interfered with the holding of several meetings. None of the countries has made important sacrifices of national interest. It should be noted that the sense of national consciousness has not been intensified by ideology to the point of excluding other senses of community, particularly the secondary, yet important, sense of "Central Americanism." A young Nicaraguan economist has said: "I feel as much Central American as Nicaraguan unless there is a crisis and then I feel more Nicaraguan." Similarly split attitudes were reported of a 1965 meeting of the Chamber of Commerce of Cortes in San Pedro Sula, Honduras. One half of the meeting was spent discussing the Common Market in a spirit of cooperation and the other half discussing the need for a refinery in Honduras for which the guiding argument was national prestige.[46]

In short, a considerable degree of national consciousness exists in most Central American states, but it has not been intensified to a high degree of exclusiveness by an elite nationalist ideology. In the past this was both because of the low levels of urbanization and the cosmopolitan, Europe oriented nature of the elites. Cosmopolitan social elites with a low sense of national identity still exist, but their share of political power has declined.[47] Among the nationalist elite

[46] Meldon E. Levine, *The Private Sector and the Common Market* (Princeton: Woodrow Wilson School of Public and International Affairs, 1965), p. 21, mimeographed.

[47] Adams, op. cit., p. 243. This is interpreted somewhat differently by Aaron Segal, "Integration and Developing Countries: Some Thoughts on East Africa and Central America" (unpublished manuscript, 1966). The author is grateful for the opportunity to read the manuscript.

today, the reasons for not developing a more intense and exclusive nationalist ideology are attributable partly to the past, but more to the distance from direct colonial experience and to appraisal of the limited political benefits available because of the geographical location. Many nationalists who wish to decrease their dependence on the United States and on world market conditions also accept that Central American states will (even after integration) always be small states within the sphere of influence of a giant neighbor. These nationalists, who make up the majority of the elite and are typical of the pragmatic reformers who staff the integration organizations, believe that their countries will profit most from a cautious (at times even suspicious) cooperation with the United Sates rather than bitter confrontation. According to a Latin American official of an international organization who worked in Central America: "Their nationalism is very sensitive and defensive, not grandiose or aggressive." A smaller group of nationalists agree that Central America has been in a United States sphere of influence, which they characterize as "neo-colonial," but reject the inevitability of this influence and build a more intense nationalist ideology in response to it.[48] That this group has not yet gained — or in the case of Guatemala in the early 1950s, held onto — political power is one of the political characteristics that has allowed Central Americans to make use of external aid to integration.

The Costs of
Economic Integration

It would be tempting to explain the Central American success in regional integration as a case in which the alternatives were so limited that the political and economic costs of integration did not matter. Certainly the size of each Central American state — comparable to that of Massachusetts, Tennessee, or Illinois — predisposes it more favorably to integration than does size in the case of Brazil, which is larger than the continental United States. But

---

48 See, for example, Juan José Arévalo, *The Shark and the Sardines* (New York: Lyle Stuart, 1961), p. 154. "Our lot is like that of the Belgian Congo, Nigeria or Madagascar."

even smaller states follow independent paths in other parts of the world.

Nor is simple economic determinism a sufficient explanation of success. There was still room for considerable short-run industrialization through import substitution in national markets,[49] and although the signing of the treaties from 1958 to 1960 coincided with a drop in the rate of growth of national product because of a fall in world coffee prices, the initiation of the integration movement in the early 1950s coincided with a period of rapid growth and high coffee prices. A partial exception was the farsighted concern that population growth created among the elite in El Salvador, where population density is nearly five times greater than the regional average.

A more relevant explanation may be that the economic and political costs in the early stages of the process have not been high, and that, in particular, no politically important interests have been hurt by integration. The fact that import substitution in small nation markets had not proceeded very far (in most countries, industry in the early 1950s consisted of textiles, sugar, cigarettes, matches, beer, and soft drinks) relieved the Central Americans of the problems faced by LAFTA in freeing trade of inefficient industries constructed behind high national tariff walls. During the early 1950s, many commercial and industrial interests were wary of free trade, which was supported almost exclusively by the technocrats. After 1958 (somewhat later in Nicaragua and Costa Rica), however, tangible benefits began to bring industrial support. This "conversion" was eased by the existence of excess capacity, estimated at about 30 per cent in 1962, which made initial tentative commitment possible without requiring new investment.[50]

POLITICAL COSTS OF INTEGRATION

Economic integration has not involved high political costs. Those it has caused, especially the opportunity costs of alternatives foregone, have not always been apparent readily because of the nature of the political culture we have discussed. Since coffee, sugar, and wheat (the latter affecting only small producers in Guatemala) are still among the few items excluded from free trade, the traditionally

[49] Pan American Union, *Economic Survey of Latin America, 1962* (Baltimore: Johns Hopkins Press, 1964), p. 253.

[50] SIECA, *Carta Informativa,* No. 55 (May 1966); and Alberto Fuentes Mohr, ''El Mercado Comun Centroamericano ante una Disyuntiva,'' *El Imparcial* (Guatemala City), 4 Dec. 1964, respectively.

powerful agricultural interest groups in these countries have paid little attention to the Common Market despite the fact that they may be paying slightly more for some of the Central American products they use. The fact that total imports have continued to rise and that many traditional importers are developing links with industry has allowed most commercial interests to offset any losses suffered from import substitutions engendered by the Common Market.

It seems that integration has not yet threatened any traditional power interests, aside from altering the importance of various ministers in national cabinets. The military has been little affected in any obvious way. Joint maneuvers, cooperation on security information, and the establishment of the Central American Defense Council and its Permanent Commission may have been helped by the climate created by the Common Market; but defense cooperation antedates the Common Market, involves no loss of sovereignty, and owes more to fear of subversion than to the technocrats.[51] It has been observed that "especially in the initial stages, tolerance of the reformer in the political arena is always tentative" and may be withdrawn when "it appears that the threat posed by the reformer is greater than the costs of excluding him from political participation."[52] Thus far, however, the reformers in the integration movement have not represented a threat.

Nor have the costs to the governments been high. One potentially serious cost is the loss of governmental revenue from imports of goods now being produced within the Common Market, a particular problem in developing countries, which lack the political and administrative capacity to impose effective income taxes. In Central America, income tax accounts for between 9.4 per cent of total tax receipts in Nicaragua and 18.5 per cent in Costa Rica while import taxes range from a third of receipts in El Salvador and Guatemala to nearly half (46 per cent) in Costa Rica. The problem has not yet become a major governmental concern in Central America because total imports into the area have continued to rise (and have been financed by growth in traditional exports and import of capital), and in some cases because consumption taxes have helped to provide revenues.[53]

---

[51] See Comisión Permanente, *Consejo de Defensa Centroamericana*, Año (Guatemala, Apr. 1966).

[52] Charles Anderson, " 'Reform-Mongering' and the Uses of Political Power," *Inter-American Economic Affairs*, No. 2 (Autumn 1965), p. 39.

[53] William S. Barnes, "Los Impuestos en el Mercado Común de la América Central" (San José, Costa Rica: INCAE, 1966), pp. 1-4, mimeographed; John

TABLE 2

MAJOR PUBLIC REGIONAL INSTITUTIONS

	Year	Pro-fes-sional Staff	Budg-et (Dol-lars)	From Central Amer-ican Govts.	From USAID	From Other Sources
SIECA (Guatemala)	1966	35	550,000	410,000	120,000	20,000
ODECA (San Salvador)	1965	10	305,000	125,000	180,000	—
ICAITI (Guatemala)	1965	40	730,000	260,000	—	470,000
ESAPAC (San Jose, C.R.)	1965	12	389,000	98,000	118,000	164,000
JOPLAN (Guatemala)	1965	18	500,000	—	—	500,000
CSUCA (San Jose, C.R.)	1965	3	107,500	22,500	—	85,000
COCESNA (Tegucigalpa)	1966	19	270,000	—	100,000	170,000
CABEI (Tegucigalpa)	1965	60	920,000	—	—	920,000
Monetary Council (San Salvador)	1966	5	75,000	75,000	—	—
TOTAL		202	3,771,500	915,500	518,000	2,329,000

SOURCE: ROCAP, *Country Assistance Program, Fiscal Year 1967*, July 1965, pp. 1-47; and interviews during 1966.

NOTE: SITCA (Managua) included under ODECA: Clearing House (Tegucigalpa) under Monetary Council. JOPLAN is to be merged into SIECA in 1967. Of $2.3 million from "other" sources, approximately $1.1 million is from sale of services (i.e., "self-financed"), the rest from United Nations, foundations, etc. The figures are accurate in magnitude but not always in detail. In addition, they do not reflect free facilities and rentals from governments of countries in which they are located.

In terms of direct financial cost, the price of running the integration institutions has been quite low: equivalent to roughly 1 per cent of the five government budgets or one-tenth of 1 per cent of the regional gross domestic product. Furthermore, the governments pay only a quarter of these costs directly, the largest part being met from earnings on services and foreign assistance. (See Table 2.) It might be argued that, in societies with as serious shortages of trained

Parke Young, *Central American Monetary Union* (Guatemala: ROCAP, 1965), p. 162; and Mauricio Baca Muñoz, interview, 6 Oct. 1966, respectively.

manpower as Central America, the two-hundred or so professiona
people working for integration institutions represent a more seriou
cost to the governments than does integration financing; but thi
cost is not strongly felt by the governments, four of which have n
career civil services and all of which have shown only a minor interes
in manpower planning.[54]

In terms of limiting their sovereignty — curtailing their freedom
of action — the governments have restricted themselves (within thei
treaty obligations) in such matters as signing independent trad
agreements with third parties, using tariff mechanisms to solve thei
recurrent balance of payments problems, or granting special treat
ment to certain industries (especially after the Convention on Fisca
Incentives is finally ratified by Honduras). On the other hand, whil
integration may have slightly curtailed the ability of the Centra
American states to obtain international financing for infrastructur
projects duplicating others in the region, it has not thus far seriousl
altered their decisions concerning national projects.[55] The regiona
road policy has not been very restrictive of national choices. In th
development of ports, the governments of Guatemala and Hondura
advocate the improvement of their Pacific ports of San José an
Amapala even though they duplicate nearby ports in El Sálvado
and Nicaragua. The Secretary of the Superior Council of Economi
Planning of Honduras has observed, ''We are still in the early stage
of integration and must think of our relative development insid
Central America. We cannot afford to depend totally on rival coun
tries,'' or, in the words of the President of the Central Bank o
Nicaragua, ''National development is basic for the success of regiona
development. . . .''[56] There has been no free trade in petroleum prod
ucts, since each of the governments has attempted to develop it
own refining industry. Nor has it been possible to reach agreement o
a regional quota for production of coffee, which still is the most vita
export of the area. Projects for linkage of the electric systems o
El Salvador and Honduras and supranational aspects of a new tele

---

[54] ESAPAC, *Diagnóstico y Macro Análisis Administrativos del Sector Públic
del Istmo Centroamericano* (San José, Costa Rica, Oct. 1965), pp. 26-30.

[55] See Eduardo Lizano, *La Crisis del Proceso de Integración de Centroaméric
(San José, Costa Rica: Univ. of Costa Rica, 1965), p. 17.

[56] Miguel Angel Rivera, Secretary, Consejo Superior de Planificación Eco
nomica, interview, 15 Oct. 1966; and Francisco Laínez M., *Discursos Pronun
ciados en el Acto Inaugural del Primer Seminario Nacional Sobre la Integració
Económica Centroamericana* (Managua, Nicaragua: Banco Central, 1965), p. 17
respectively.

ommunications system have been turned down for nationalistic
easons.

In the field of monetary policy, the success of the Central American
Clearing House, which was formed in 1961 and is basically an ac-
ounting arrangement that involves mutual extension of limited
redits in clearing some 80 per cent of visible regional trade in local
urrencies, has not been matched by the more ambitious Monetary
Council, established by the Central Banks in 1964.[57] According to
participants, the Executive Secretariat of the Council has remained
understaffed, the committees of the Council have barely functioned,
and the obligation of the banks to consult before introducing impor-
ant changes of policy has not been observed. While there has been
ome flow of Central American capital across borders, it is limited
by the absence of a regional capital market, and, in at least one
ountry, informal government pressure is used to discourage capital
movement.

Reaching agreement on the free mobility of persons has been more
difficult than ''opening the frontiers for the passage of potatoes and
ows.''[58] Various schemes for a freer labor market at the professional
or at lower levels have not been successful. Of two major cases of
ransnational labor in Central America, some 20,000 Nicaraguans in
plantation regions of Costa Rica have caused no problem, but the
xistence of from 125,000 to 300,000 Salvadorians in Honduras has
been a point of considerable friction.[59]

On the legal side, the Central American states have given little
power to the integration institutions; decision-making is still carried
ut by traditional diplomatic instruments, treaties and protocols to
reaties, which must be submitted to a slow cumbersome legislative
atification in each state. It has taken several years to achieve ratifica-
ion of some important protocols; at best the process takes many
months.

To assist in regional planning, the Central Americans have received
he Joint Planning Mission (JOPLAN), which they requested from
CCLA, the OAS, and the Inter-American Development Bank (IDB)

[57] Young, op. cit., pp. 28-30; and Salvador Gomez A., Chief of Operations, inter-
iew, 14 Oct. 1966. Technically the Clearing House has become a subsidiary organ
f the Monetary Council.

[58] Zeledón, op. cit., p. 96.

[59] Raul Hess, President, Central Bank of Costa Rica, interview, 22 Oct. 1966;
Hispanic American Report, No. 7 (1964). For the opposition of the Federation
f Honduran University Students to Salvadorian Immigration, see *La Prensa*
(San Pedro Sula, Honduras), 10 Oct. 1966.

and expect to incorporate soon into SIECA. Thus far the major activity of JOPLAN has been the strengthening of national planning offices and the centralization and classification of economic information. This, along with meetings of directors of national planning offices, has had some slight impact on national plans, but any serious coordination to avoid duplication, and especially any regional allocation of scarce resources, has yet to come. Since ambitious planning at the national level tends to have a disruptive impact on regional integration,[60] the weakness of national plans has mitigated the effect of the absence of a Central American plan. Nonetheless, in the area of industrial policy, the lack of a clear regional policy has been of some importance.

DISTRIBUTION OF INDUSTRY

The expansion of trade in industrial goods, which rose by 53 per cent during 1960-65, has been the most spectacular achievement of the Common Market. In the structure of production, however, traditional industries — mainly food products, shoes, clothing, beverages, and textiles — still represented some 73 per cent of the total industrial production in 1964.[61] Although the production of intermediate goods (for example, chemicals) has expanded, agreement on how to attract large-scale industries dependent on the total market has been plagued by disputes concerning location and "balanced development," which the less developed countries interpret to mean "balanced *industrial* development."

The Agreement on the Regime for Central American Integration Industries, which was signed in 1958 and became effective in 1963, was intended to ensure an adequate market for industries requiring access to all of Central America, and to ensure the allocation of such large industries among the countries. In return for special tax and import privileges and for the gradual decreasing of internal tariff protection against possible competitors (in effect, no free trade for competitors for ten years), large-scale ventures in new fields are to submit to detailed ownership, market, price, and quality controls by the integration institutions. Specific projects must be approved by

[60] For example, the case of Tanzanian planning in the context of the East African Common Market.

[61] Andrew B. Wardlaw, "The Operations of the Central American Common Market" (Guatemala: ROCAP, 1966), p. 18, mimeographed; and CABEI, *Investment Opportunities in the Central American Common Market* (Tegucigalpa, Honduras, 1965), p. 9, respectively.

protocols requiring national legislative ratification, a process that has taken several years when it has been applied, for example, to the production of tires in Guatemala, caustic soda and insecticides in Nicaragua, and plans for plate glass production in Honduras.

Undoubtedly one of the most important reasons for the scant use of the Regime has been the opposition of the United States government, which feels that the temporary monopolies created are less efficient than other means to the same ends, and which refuses to allow the use of United States funds for such projects. This scheme has also failed to command continued support from all Central American governments because of the delays, red tape, and problems of quality control involved. In 1963 the governments reinterpreted the allocative aspects of the scheme and adopted a supplementary Salvadorian proposal of a Special System for the Promotion of Production, which grants high tariff protection to plants in new fields once production is capable of supplying at least half the Central American market. It has been applied by a ratified protocol to light bulbs, bottles, and machetes, and in a yet unratified protocol to sulphuric acid, aluminum sheets, cylinders for gas, and toilet paper.[62]

The Special System, which relies on competition and ultimate sanction of tariff reduction by the Executive Council of the Common Market to protect consumers in regard to price and quality, has the advantage of being less cumbersome, but the disadvantage of doing little for (and perhaps even aggravating) the problem of allocation of industries to less favored areas.

Honduras and Nicaragua, whose share of purchases in Central American trade has gone up while their share (but not absolute value) of sales under the Common Market has gone down (see Table 3), have demanded special preferential treatment.[63] For four years

---

[62] See James D. Cochrane, "Central American Economic Integration: The Integrated Industries' Scheme," *Inter-American Economic Affairs*, No. 2 (Autumn 1965), pp. 63-74; Miguel S. Wionczek, "Economic Integration and Regional Distribution of Industrial Activities: A Comparative Study. Part I: Central America," *East African Economic Review*, New Series No. 1 (June 1966), pp. 55-68; and J. Alan Brewster, "The Central American Program for Integrated Industrial Development," *Public and International Affairs*, No. 1 (Spring 1966), pp. 5-35.

[63] For their arguments, see Manuel Acosta Bonilla, "Exposición sobre la participación de Honduras en el proceso de Integración Económica Centroamericana," *Foro Hondureña* (Tegucigalpa), Nos. 3-4 (Jan.-June 1966), pp. 1-18; and Ministerio de Economía, *Efectos del Mercado Comun Centroamericano sobre la Economía Nicaraguense* (Managua, Nicaragua, 1966), pp. 2-25, mimeographed.

TABLE 3

DISTRIBUTION OF REGIONAL TRADE:
PER CENT SHARE OF SALES AND
(PER CENT SHARE OF PURCHASES)

	1960	1963	1965
Guatemala	22.2(23.2)	28.8(27.3)	28.6(23.2)
El Salvador	38.7(41.3)	39.8(38.7)	33.9(31.2)
Honduras	22.7(16.2)	19.4(18.4)	16.3(19.4)
Nicaragua	10.5(8.5)	5.8(10.2)	7.4(15.5)
Costa Rica	5.7(10.8)	6.2(5.3)	13.8(10.8)

SOURCE: Andrew B. Wardlaw, *The Operations of the Central American Common Market* (Guatemala: ROCAP, 1966), p. 31, mimeographed.

Honduras refused to ratify the 1962 Protocol on Uniform Fiscal Incentives, which is designed to introduce order into at least part of the chaotic and wasteful granting of privileges by separate governments in their competition to attract industry. The major committees of the Common Market were unable to meet for nearly five months preceding September 1966, when a compromise was finally reached granting Honduras the right to allow 20 per cent greater exemption on import taxes for five years in order to attract industry, and preferential treatment before CABEI and international institutions to improve its less developed infrastructure.[64] The Nicaraguan case, regarded as less persuasive, was given to ECLA for study. However, this merely provided a solution for the immediate crisis; the problems of location of large-scale industry by no means have been solved.

INDICES OF INTEGRATION

This description of the unsolved problems of integration provides us with only part of the information we need to judge the level of political and economic costs and benefits: the glass is partly empty but it is at the same time partly full. By a number of indices, integration has made important progress.

Trade. In June 1966 the Common Market completed its five-year

[64] Because of CABEI's concern with balanced development, Honduras already ranked first in loans approved ($19 million of a total $78 million) by June 1966 but inefficiency of execution of projects in Honduras meant that it ranked third in actual disbursements. Wardlaw, op. cit., p. 86; and CABEI, *Préstamos Aprobados y Recursos Disponibles* (Tegucigalpa, 1966), mimeographed.

initial stage with 94 per cent of the items (95 per cent by value of 1964 trade) on the tariff schedule free from duties or restrictions. The expansion in regional trade has been impressive not only in absolute terms and as a percentage of total imports (see Table 4), but also in composition, which has changed between 1960, when agricultural and forestry products were more than 50 per cent, and 1965, when industrial products accounted for 72 per cent. Despite the problem of imbalances in participation mentioned above, over the five-year period, economic integration has helped bring the two southern countries (Nicaragua and Costa Rica) into the regional economy; their share of regional sales increased from 14 per cent in 1950 to 21 per cent in 1965.[65]

Communications. An important part of Central American integration plans is a program to improve communications, which now includes: an agreement to give priority to construction of thirteen roads (980 miles) of regional importance; a Central American Air

TABLE 4

GROWTH OF REGIONAL TRADE

Period of Bilateral Treaties			*Period of Multilateral Treaties*		
Year	*Dollars Millions*	*Per Cent Increase Over Previous Year*	*Year*	*Dollars Millions*	*Per Cent Increase Over Previous Year*
1950	8.6	—	1958	21.1	25
1951	10.2	13.6	1959	28.7	36
1952	10.8	6.3	1960	32.7	14
1953	11.9	10	1961	36.8	13
1954	14.0	18	1962	50.8	38
1955	13.1	—6	1963	72.1	42
1956	13.7	5	1964	106.4	48
1957	16.9	23	1965	136.0	28

SOURCE: SIECA, *Carta Informativa,* No. 58, 12 Aug. 1966.

[65] SIECA, *Carta Informativa,* No. 58 (Aug. 1966); and Wardlaw, op. cit., p. 19. Some economists believe that considering the number of items in regional trade that have had only a small part of their value added in Central America, it might be economically accurate to discount regional trade figures by one-third — still an impressive increase.

Navigation Services Corporation (COCESNA); and plans for an improved, albeit not supranationally organized, telecommunications system. The major role of this program can be judged from the fact that Central America has only 125 miles of highway per 1,000 square miles (the United States figure is 1,131 miles), and only 1,500 miles of public railways (and roughly the same amount in private service) of unstandardized narrow gauges connecting only two countries, Guatemala and El Salvador. Between 1953, when the United Nations Technical Assistance Administration and ECLA made the first detailed survey of Central American roads, and 1963, the mileage of paved and all-weather roads increased by two and one half times, from 6,100 to 14,900 miles, and the number of registered vehicles more than tripled. More recently, from 1959 to 1963, regional passenger traffic on Central American airlines increased by 76 per cent from 29,000 to 51,000, and regional airfreight rose by 139 per cent.[66]

In other communications areas, particularly more significant personal contacts, the weaving together of a transnational fabric of Central American society is still very rudimentary. Maps of movement of persons show that national borders are important barriers. National newspapers and radio tend toward parochial reporting, and — despite efforts to found one — there is no popular Central American periodical. Political parties and trade unions have few significant regional contacts, despite the existence of an Institute of Central American Trade Union Studies in Honduras (IESC) and efforts in 1965 to found an inter-union council. As for higher education, at best only a few per cent of Central American students study in other Central American countries, while some 14 per cent study in the United States.[67]

New sectors. The integration process has shown important, if modest, progress in the expansion of new sectors. Soon after the inauguration of the market in June 1961, the Central Banks agreed to the establishment of the Clearing House, which has facilitated regional trade and economized the use of scarce foreign exchange. Problems caused by the creation of exchange controls in Guatemala and El Salvador were overcome; a Central American bank check was

[66] Bradbury, op. cit., p. 157; and CABEI, *Central American Transportation Study* (Washington: Transportation Consultants Consortium, 1965), pp. 215 an 492.

[67] INCAE, *Problems and Opportunities: A Summary of the Demand Stud* (Cambridge, Mass.: Dober, Walquist, and Harris, 1965), pp. 5:27 and 28 Edgardo Sevilla I., Secretary, CSUCA, interview, 21 Oct. 1966.

created; and the portion of visible regional trade cleared rose to more than 80 per cent. On the other hand, as has been pointed out earlier, further steps toward monetary union, inaugurated in 1964, have been faltering.

The creation of a Council of Labor and Social Welfare at the ministerial level, with subsidiary technical commissions on labor and social security and within the framework of ODECA, has not yet had a major impact but is of potential significance. The technical commissions have held useful regional meetings on topics such as labor inspection and wage policies, and their existence has begun to stimulate efforts toward regional contacts among the labor movements. The Central American Tourism Secretariat was also established with in the formal rubric of ODECA but was located in Nicaragua. It has held two regional conferences on tourism and has recently persuaded the governments to make its part-time secretary and staff permanent. In addition, the directors of planning organizations (since 1964) and the ministers of agriculture (since 1965) have met to discuss common problems created in their fields by the Common Market.

As much an index of success as the addition of new sectors is the rejuvenation of existing ones. In addition to the functionalist "spillover" in the sense of expansion of a task to protect an uncompleted initial task, there is also a "domonstration effect spillover," in which less active institutions are stimulated to greater activity by the success of more active institutions — for example, the success of SIECA in persuading the Central American governments to increase its budget, staff, and tasks. Thus, since 1964, the Secretary of ODECA has been trying to increase the activities of the organization in more functionalist fields, such as labor, social security, and legal services, and to persuade the governments to increase its resources. Until 1961, the Central American School of Public Administration (ESAPAC) was small and somewhat oriented toward Costa Rica, the one country with a civil service. Since the formation of the Common Market and partly from its stimulus, ESAPAC has expanded its program, increased the proportion of other Central American students (the number of Costa Ricans declined from a quarter to a sixth of the student body), and has begun to orient its activities more toward integration problems. In 1965 the Superior University Council of Central America (CSUCA), which is composed of the rectors of the national universities and had not been notably dynamic since its foundation in 1948, agreed to meet more frequently, in order "to increase the dynamism in this field."[68]

Growth of key institutions. One of the most important indices of success is the growth of the key institutions of the Common Market: the Economic Council, consisting of the five ministers of economy; the Executive Council, generally composed of the five vice-ministers of economy; and SIECA, the Permanent Secretariat. At its third ordinary meeting at the end of 1964, the Economic Council, impressed with the growing burdens of problems to be solved, decided that it should hold its regular three- to five-day meetings four times a year and that the Executive Council should meet monthly.[69] The latter body now normally meets for approximately a week each month. Since it bears the brunt of preliminary decisions, there have been suggestions that it become a body in permanent session.

The growth of SIECA is reflected in governmental contributions to its budget, which have doubled over the first six years of the market; in the doubling of its staff; and in the addition in 1965 of new departments on taxes and trade policy to those already existing on infrastructure, agriculture, market, industry, statistics, law, publications, and administration. Tasks have not increased only on paper, but in practice, there has been a tendency for each ministerial meeting to add requests for new studies of solutions to thorny problems. These studies, such as the autumn 1966 recommendation that Guatemala reopen its borders to salt from El Salvador and that El Salvador tax Guatemalan cigarettes of a certain quality at a rate equivalent to that on local cigarettes, are generally accepted. Since the first Secretary General made it a point to channel longer range studies toward United Nations institutions and to keep for SIECA those with immediate policy implications, the Secretariat has developed certain *de facto* executive powers. A minor clause in the compromise agreement on special treatment for Honduras provides the beginnings of a legal basis for these powers. In addition, the Secretary General plays an important role in conciliation, arranging compromises and understandings to smooth the way for the meetings of the Councils.

[68] Albino Román y Vega, Secretary, ODECA, interview, 17 Aug. 1966; and Wilburg Jiménez, Director, ESAPAC, interview, 5 Aug. 1966. Sevilla is less convinced that the stimulus to increased activity of CSUCA came from outside the organization. See also SIECA, *Carta Informativa*, No. 50 (Dec. 1965).

[69] SIECA, *Carta Informativa*, No. 38 (Dec. 1964).

The institutions have been able to grow in "generational" as well as chronological age. Ministers of economy have changed frequently; the founders of the process are generally in peripheral positions; and new men have moved into the top technocratic jobs. Part of the success of the process has been the creation of what one former technocrat jokingly referred to as an "integration mafia" of some several hundred persons, half on "active duty" in the institutions and half working in the governments or private sectors of the countries.[70] On the other hand, the institutions have not yet done very much to broaden their "constituencies." The staff of CABEI has not developed business support that might counteract the close control of the governments. Few business or labor leaders have much knowledge of SIECA. As a result, many businessmen who do feel the need for more rapid decisions are nonetheless reluctant to press for increasing the power of SIECA because they fear that it would be like the red tape and delay of the national governmental bureaucracies with which they are already familiar.[71]

Private sector organizations and attitudes. The integration process has stimulated the foundation of a number of private regional organizations. Most important among these have been the Federation of Chambers of Commerce and Industry of Central America and the Central American Institute of Business Administration (INCAE). The Federation, founded in 1958, was relatively weak and unable to achieve significant coordination of business positions during its early years, but its criticisms, suggestions, and plans for establishing a permanent staff are beginning to increase its influence. INCAE, founded in 1963 by Central American businessmen with technical assistance from Harvard University, has graduated some 200 executives from four annual six-week courses and hopes to open its permanent school in Managua, Nicaragua, within another year. Of other private organizations, the IESC labor training institute in Honduras has done useful work, although its impact on integration has been small. The Association of Textile Industries and Federation of Chambers of Commerce, on the other hand, have been relatively inactive. In addition to these organizations, bankers, journalists, lawyers, economists, and accountants, among others, have established seminars and meetings on integration at the regional level.

---

[70] The term was coined by Daniel Tapia, formerly of CABEI, in an interview with Christopher Mitchell, 10 Sept. 1965; the estimate of size was made by Pedro Abelardo Delgado, 28 Sept. 1966.

[71] See *El Imparcial* (Guatemala City), 26 Aug. 1966.

In the absence of reliable opinion polls, statements about changes of attitudes must be impressionistic. Economic integration receives considerable favorable coverage on national radio and newspapers, but the orientation of the coverage is generally parochial, and there is little evidence that it has aroused any significant interest among unskilled urban workers or the rural majority. A number of observers report that in Costa Rica, however, the Common Market has had a considerable impact in broadening previously parochial attitudes in the relatively short period of four years. A poll of thirty Central Americans chosen on the basis of their present or potential influence to attend the INCAE courses in 1966 offers fragmentary evidence on attitudes. This poll indicated that, as a result of the Common Market, ten of the executives felt they worked longer hours; twenty said they invested more; more than ten had joined a business association; twenty-five said they used new techniques; and twenty-five felt their opportunities had improved. In accord with the low-cost thesis discussed earlier in this study, only three said they had lost profits, compared with fifteen of those polled who believed they received loans more easily. Seventeen expected the Common Market to lead to political union, while the rest expected new economic but not new political tasks. Ten claimed to be willing to have their country renounce all of its sovereignty for integration; about twenty were willing to have their country give up part of its sovereignty; and only two opposed the limitation of sovereignty. Interestingly, in this small sample, the Costa Ricans were no more nationalistic than their colleagues.[72]

Governmental behavior. Changes in governmental behavior as a result of integration have been minor but not insignificant. Many participants report that as the body of resolved problems has grown, arbitrariness in governmental behavior has diminished. Cases such as that of corrupt sanitary inspectors removing export goods of other countries from store shelves or of customs harassment at borders still come up, but with less frequency. Several businessmen have reported more serious and competent governmental attention to their problems attributable to Common Market pressures.

Although ministers of economy have changed frequently and the size of meetings is large (some thirty to fifty persons, including observers), the style of the Economic Council has been businesslike

---

[72] Carried out by the author in Aug. 1966. The sample included only one Honduran, but subsequent interviews indicate that this bias was not very important in determining the results.

and little given to oratory. The Executive Council meetings are smaller (usually twenty to thirty persons), and there tends to be considerable continuity among the second-level governmental officials who accompany the vice-ministers. These officials frequently form working groups at Council meetings, and there has been notable emphasis on common Central American interests rather than complete fixation on governmental positions. Majority votes, which mean a temporary decision subject to Economic Council action, tend to be much more rare than unanimity.

In general, governments have shown willingness to make compromises. A major exception was the crisis that arose early in 1966 over the demands of the least industrialized countries, Honduras and Nicaragua, for compensatory special treatment. For the first time meetings were disrupted and overt threats (as opposed to press "leaked" rumors) of withdrawal were issued. Although this seems to be evidence of retrogressive governmental behavior, it is worth noting that at the end of the crisis in September, it was the governmental representatives who overruled business opposition to arrange the compromise.

Geographical extension. The interest of a regional integration movement in the inclusion of neighbors is not a safe index of progress. It may mean that there has been sufficient success to create confidence in the ability to cope with new partners, but it can also indicate the opposite internal failures or stagnation disguised in geographical dilution. A compliment paid by a neighboring country's interest in the process may be a more useful crude index of success. Panama, which throughout the 1950s emphasized its historical separation from Central America, has since 1963 shown an increased interest in the possibility of participation in Central American integration. It has joined CSUCA and some subsidiary organizations of ODECA, and in 1966 commissioned two reports, which took a favorable view toward some gradual form of membership in the Common Market.

Other neighbors have also shown increased interest. Early in 1966, President Díaz Ordaz of Mexico made a rare presidential trip to Central America to offer increased cooperation; President-elect Carlos Lleras of Colombia met with Central American ministers and technocrats; and Venezuela offered financial cooperation to aid Central American leverage in borrowing in foreign capital markets. Rumors circulated of interest in eventual extension of the market to Caribbean states, among them the Dominican Republic.[73]

[73] See *Vision* (Mexico), 16 Sept. 1966.

External Factors

An integration process does not take place in an international vacuum. The type of international environment in which it is conceived and exists has a great deal to do with whether it succeeds or not. Some of the external factors that affect an integration process are of such a broad and general nature that whether they exist or not is a matter of historical fortune. Others are more the result of deliberate external action. Central America has profited from favorable external factors of both kinds.

PASSIVE FACTORS

Of the "passive" external factors that establish the climate of integration, the most important have been the geographical position of Central America in relation to the United States; the conditions of the international economy; and postwar trends in international organization.[74] The first of these, Central America's location in an area of traditional North American domination, has had several important effects. The region's location has kept it away from the center of cold war politics, which have exacerbated the problems of reconciling national policies in Africa and the Middle East. It is partly responsible for the existence of a climate that is favorable to both domestic and foreign private business, which has been a powerful motor of the Common Market. It affects the magnitude of United States aid and the willingness of moderate nationalists to make use of this aid. Finally, it helps to account for the establishment in the area of a "security community."

The condition of the international economy also has been important to integration. The depression of the 1930s shook Central American faith in world markets. The subsequent erratic performance of commodity prices (particularly as viewed through the lenses

---

[74] A possible fourth factor, fear of direct or indirect subversion from the Castro government of Cuba, has played a role in enhancing cooperation in defense matters and in stimulating the United States and, at times, Central American governments, but it has not been nearly as important to the Common Market as the other three factors.

of economic theory polished it by ECLA) provided a basis for mistrust that made the initiation of the integration process possible during a period of relatively high prices in 1951-52. Later, the signing of the major treaties coincided with — though it was not necessarily determined by — a period of depressed coffee prices.

Equally important among the passive external factors was the development of international organization after World War II. According to one participant in this process: "It is impossible to think of Central American integration without the United Nations, not just for its direct role, but for the climate that it created."[75] At a later period, the EEC was of some importance to Central America, both as an example of mature states pooling sovereignty and as a detailed paradigm for study by SIECA. Central American integrationists have a long history of sensitivity to larger international trends. In addition, some of the founders and key participants in the integration process have worked for international organizations and derived from them an intellectual focus, a source of political strength, and at times a sanctuary.

ACTIVE FACTORS

External factors of the "active" variety, involving deliberate decisions by those outside the region to help or hinder integration, include, among others: governments, international organizations, private foundations, and private investors. The degree and effect of their participation have varied over time, but by far the most important of these external factors have been ECLA and the United States government — a slightly ironic juxtaposition in view of their frequent differences in the past. ECLA with its greater power of intellectual appeal was an extremely important external factor in the initiation and early stages of Central American integration. The United States government, a latecomer with vast wealth, has been the more important external factor in upgrading and maintaining the process. Central Americans are not unanimous about the relative importance of the two factors, but the majority believe that ECLA's participation was a necessary condition, and that the United States, if not absolutely necessary, was, in a phrase frequently heard in Central America, "an important catalyst" without which the process would have proceeded more slowly.

[75] Pedro Abelardo Delgado, interview, 28 Sept. 1966.

ECLA, however, was not the sole originator of the idea of Central American economic integration. A number of young economists trained abroad had discussed the need to diversify their economies through industrialization and puzzled over the barriers presented by their restricted national markets. They were seeking a way to escape from what they considered "colonial economies" overly dependent on world commodity prices and the United States. Thus ECLA (which came into existence in 1948 despite United States reluctance) found fertile ground for its slogan "grow from within." Nonetheless, the elaboration of ideas, the promise and subsequent fulfillment of technical and financial support, the preparation of studies and reports by the Mexico office, and the goading and stimulating of committees and subcommittees by technocrats who stood above the conflicts of national interest, all made ECLA a crucial external factor in the 1950s.

After 1960, ECLA's direct role was diminished by the growing autonomy of the Central American technocrats, particularly by the establishment of SIECA in June 1961, and by the new interest of the United States and its ability to provide the larger financial resources needed at the more advanced stage of the process. By 1963, the United States, although a late starter, had already spent twice as much ($20 million) as the United Nations ($10 million) in support of Central American integration.[76]

The United States was at best indifferent toward Central American integration in the early 1950s. During this early stage, when ideas were more important than resources, the generally unsympathetic attitude of the United States government toward Latin American economic problems may have helped to stimulate the technocrats in their efforts to establish a new system. The first signs of a more positive United States attitude occurred in 1958, a year in which discontent with the results of United States economic policies toward Latin America led to the beginnings of a general reappraisal. However, Milton Eisenhower's favorable remarks about Central American integration during a visit to Central America in July 1958 were given more economic significance by Central Americans than they were intended to convey.[77]

[76] Carlos Castillo, "Growth and Integration in Central America" (Ph.D. thesis, Univ. of Wisconsin, 1965), p. 126.

[77] *Hispanic American Report*, No. 7 (July 1958); Joseph Pincus, *El Mercado Común Centroamericano* (Mexico: ROCAP, 1963), p. 51; R. Harrison Wagner, "Latin America and the Foreign Economic Policies of the United States" (Ph.D. thesis, Harvard Univ., 1966), pp. 256-293. On this point, the author is

The following spring, however, in the course of informal talks about the slow progress of integration with Salvadorian officials accompanying President Lemus to Washington, a high Department of State official indicated that the United States was "willing to help in any way we can," in the creation of "a real Common Market."[78] Subsequently, after two Department of State specialists were sent to Central America to study the means by which the United States could help, the three northern states used the brinksmanship tactics of the Tripartite Treaty (see p. 29), an important decision that led to eventual signing of the General Treaty. While some participants feel that the Central Americans might have gone ahead with this tactic without United States support, others felt that "U.S. support was necessary for this political tactic to work, both for the financial promises and to help us against pressure from ECLA when we broke their five country integration program." The former director of the ECLA office in Mexico feels that of greater importance than brinksmanship in the success of the tactic was the promise of outside financial help. In the words of an official from Nicaragua, which had been reluctant to accelerate the process and thus was the victim of the maneuver:

It was the possibility of special financial aid for Central American integration, which we were allowed to glimpse among very general declarations and which we interpreted with much optimism, that precipitated the signing of the multilateral treaty of 1960, despite the fact that from previous efforts we were not able to say that we had obtained a satisfactory experience justifying the acceleration of the process.[79]

Thus a strong case can be made that United States support was a vital condition for the important decisions that speeded up the integration process in 1960.

Subsequent United States support has been useful in the maintenance of the process. In August 1962, the Agency for International Development established a Regional Office for Central America and Panama Affairs (ROCAP) in Guatemala City. The staff has grown from five to more than fifty, and has a budget of $4.25 million for the fiscal year 1967 to support its program of administering aid that is

---

grateful for the opportunity to consult James D. Cochrane, "Central American Economic Integration: An Approach to Development" (unpublished manuscript).

[78] ROCAP, "A Report on Central America's Common Market and its Economic Integration Movement" (Guatemala: 1966), Section III, p. 1, mimeo.

[79] Castillo, op. cit., p. 90; and Francisco Laínez M., *Discursos Pronunciados* . . . , op. cit., p. 13, author's trans., respectively.

regional in scope to governments, regional institutions, and private organizations. United States funds provide only 12 per cent of the expenses of all regional organizations but more than half the budget of ODECA, a quarter of the budget of SIECA, and half the loanable funds available to CABEI. By early 1966, the United States had funded more than $83 million in support of Central American integration, including a $35 million commitment to a regional infrastructure fund promised by President Kennedy in his meeting with the Central American presidents in San José, Costa Rica, in 1963. In contrast, the United States committed roughly $300 million in bilateral aid to the five countries from 1961-65.[80]

This aid has played several positive roles. It has already been suggested that the lure of access to United States funds in CABEI (available only to countries that had ratified the General Treaty) was important. In general, Central Americans view integration as a reason for more aid rather than less. Economic issues tend to become easier to resolve when a larger slice of pie may be gained from taking a long-run view of one's interests, and United States aid has contributed to the expectation that the pie will grow. In addition, United States aid has stimulated investment in the Common Market through funds loaned to CABEI and private development banks and as a symbolic commitment that inspires confidence in Central American and foreign businessmen. In the view of some businessmen, this role of the United States is very important, since a common market without investment "would be merely on the books."[81] Finally, United States aid has breathed life into institutions such as ODECA and helped to keep the costs of integration to the governments low and thus more acceptable.

On the other hand, even when it is given with more farsighted than short-term political motives, United States aid presents Central Americans with some hidden costs that limit its effectiveness. Although the United States is a major supporter of the regional integration organizations, its bilateral relationships with the separate sovereign states have sometimes come into conflict with regional integration programs. In 1963, for example, the United States imposed brief but embarrassing limits on CABEI's business loans in

[80] ROCAP, ''A Report . . . ,'' op. cit., Section III, p. 4. AID, *Special Report Prepared for the House Foreign Affairs Committee. U.S. Overseas Loans and Grants and Assistance from International Organizations* (Washington: GPO, 1965).

[81] For example, Gabriel Mejía and Antonio Mata, interviews, San Pedro Sula, 11 Oct. 1966.

Honduras after General Lopez overthrew the elected Villeda government. Despite considerable discretion by ROCAP officials, United States aid reflects United States views of priorities, which do not always coincide with Central American views, and there are dangers that United States aid to peripheral institutions may sometimes diminish rather than enhance the financial commitment of Central American governments to the institution. In addition, political strings tied to short-run United States interest sometimes make its aid embarrassing to integration officials already wary to defend themselves against left-wing criticism of United States influence. For instance, CSUCA has felt some irritation with United States fears that aid funds might go to communists, and there is good reason to believe that the United States refusal to allow CABEI to use United States funds to finance projects under the integration industries scheme was heavily influenced by domestic United States political considerations.[82]

Other international institutions have also had a favorable impact on Central American integration, but it would be difficult to argue that their aid has been a major factor in the success. The OAS provides a forum in which five votes are a quarter of the total, and thus there is an incentive to coordinate foreign policy. The OAS, together with ECLA and IDB, supported JOPLAN. The Inter-American Committee for the Alliance for Progress issues reviews of Central American plans that take a regional viewpoint. The International Monetary Fund not only reinforces those who advocate policies of monetary stability (which tends to facilitate integration), but has also loaned personnel to the Monetary Council. The IDB has taken a considerable interest in the integration program, in organizing promotional seminars, and in providing a fifth of the loanable funds of CABEI. More recently, the International Bank for Reconstruction and Development (IBRD) has begun to view Central America as a region and has sent a large study mission to the area. Officials of both banks express an interest in identifying bottlenecks to integration and in providing resources to help overcome them.[83]

There are limits, however, on the degree to which international institutions can contribute to regional integration. The prospect of IBRD financing was not sufficient to obtain governmental approval for the supranational aspects of the telecommunications scheme. Nor

---

[82] See Raymond F. Mikesell, ''External Financing and Regional Integration,'' in ed. Wionczek, op. cit., pp. 206-211.

[83] Interviews with IBRD and IDB officials, Washington, 1-2 Aug. 1966.

was the prospect of IDB financing sufficient to persuade Honduras to agree to the connection of its electric system with El Salvador. ECLA's ideas — emanating from Santiago, Chile, and incarnated in the United Nations Conference on Trade and Development — remain popular and important among technocrats, but controls from ECLA's Mexico office (such as reluctance to give up certain committees) are not popular. The fact that there are several international organizations concerned with Central American integration helps to preserve the autonomy of the Central Americans for better and for worse. Competition with IDB helped stimulate a regional approach to Central America in the IBRD, but officials of both banks admit that the competition has also been part of the cause of the laxness of integration criteria in their loans.

Foundations have played important roles in the maintenance of CSUCA and the Institute of Nutrition of Central America and Panama (INCAP), but neither of these institutions has been of major importance in the integration movement. Private investors outside Central America provided an average of $22 million annually from 1957 to 1962 — a figure that Central Americans hope will double. In addition, the foreign entrepreneurs "introduced an important demonstration effect within the rank of Central American entrepreneurs."[84] Finally, the indication of growing interest on the part of Central America's neighbors has had a certain unifying effect. Among themselves Central Americans frequently say that to join LAFTA or "to speak to Mexico, we must be one."

A case can be made that favorable external factors were a necessary condition for the early success of Central American economic integration. But arguing that they were a necessary condition is far from saying that they were sufficient. Without Central American initiative and for the other reasons discussed, external factors would have been of no importance at all.

[84] Wionczek, "Economic Integration and Regional Distribution . . . ," op. cit., p. 66.

Conclusions

Projection of future success on the basis of the performance of the past five years is unlikely to be reliable in Central America for several reasons. Leaving aside such unpredictables as the rise in one of the countries of a strong leader with a nationalist ideology, there are good grounds for believing that the political non-controversiality and low level of costs of the past may diminish in the future. For instance, if inefficient assembly industries (adding little value to product) are established behind national grants of privilege in Central America, a set of possibly stagnating vested interests may be created. If national actors — central bankers wrestling with balance-of-payments problems or security officers attempting to control influences across borders — feel hindered by restrictions created by integration, it is reasonable to assume that the politics of the process will become more heated and make compromise more difficult.

If Honduras continues to lag in its rate of industrial growth because of poor infrastructure, the conflicts associated with the vague but emotionally important concept of ''balanced development'' may cause stagnation. Should political regimes intent on using the machinery of state planning to attempt drastic social change emerge in any of the countries, the impact on the ''political culture'' would almost certainly be nationalistic, which would make integration difficult to maintain, and it might also include intense anti-United States elements, which would inhibit both United States aid and private investment. On the other hand, in the absence of an indigenous regional capital market, foreign investment might come to play a large and conspicuous role, thus diminishing Central American faith in the market and creating a political climate in which a national mobilization regime could arise.[85]

Finally, simple projection of past successes into the future is inadequate since so much of the stimulus to change in Central America still comes from outside. The economies of Central American countries are still heavily reliant on world prices for three commodities and thus very vulnerable to depression induced from outside. Thus

[85] See Castillo, op. cit., p. 179.

far the Common Market has existed in a reasonably prosperous international economy. The growth of traditional exports and the attraction of foreign capital have financed the expansion of imports that accompanies the early stages of import substitution engendered by the Common Market. Should these conditions change, political pressures for national solutions to problems of government revenue or balance-of-payments difficulties could have a severe disruptive influence on the Common Market.

It is unlikely, on the other hand, that the ''active'' external factors will change much in the next few years. Neither is the political ideal of union likely to change drastically; if it varies at all, it will probably intensify rather than diminish (witness the apparent broadening of attitudes in Costa Rica). But it remains questionable whether or not these two factors will be sufficient to compensate for possible increases in political controversiality, awareness of rising costs, or changes in the passive external factors.

Unfortunately, functionalist theory is not very specific about how to determine when an integration process has come to an end or is in equilibrium. One approach is to view the growing politization of integration matters as a sign of progress on the path to final political union.[86] However, if a larger sense of political community, of common loyalties, does not grow at a rate commensurate with the politization of integration, the result may be stagnation or (if functionalists are correct about the linkage between sectors) a cumulative retrogression or ''spillback'' until the institutions and tasks of integration are at a level that the prevailing sense of community, expectations, and interests can support.[87] Such was the case with the Common Market in East Africa where the sense of regional community or loyalty was not sufficient to support the high level of economic integration that had been achieved under colonial rule.

In the case of Central America, it is probably true that the process is ''irreversible,'' as some technocrats describe it, in the sense that total collapse is unlikely, if only because of the interests that have been vested in the process and the existing sense of Central Americanism. On the other hand, it can be argued that with the exception of perfecting the customs union and some minor projects, the Central

---

[86] Ernst Haas and Philippe Schmitter, ''Economics and Differential Patterns of Political Integration: Projections about Unity in Latin America,'' *International Organization*, No. 4 (Autumn 1964), pp. 705-737.

[87] See Amitai Etzioni, *Political Unification* (New York: Holt, Rinehart and Winston, 1965), pp. 60-62.

American process will soon be in a state of equilibrium, with attitudes sufficient to support existing institutions but not much more. There would be sufficient integration to satisfy the popular sense of Central Americanism, to obtain the benefits of a larger yet protected market for industrialists, and to secure the benefits of special attention and bloc-voting power without sacrifice of much sovereignty for the politicians.[88] But further integration would involve higher costs, and from particular points of view, uncertain benefits. Opposed to this view is the functionalist one that, to protect integrated tasks from which they already benefit, interest groups will have to press for or at least acquiesce in the increase of further tasks linked to integration. In addition to this "technical spillover," there will be the activities of technocrats deliberately creating linkages and package deals regardless of whether there is a close technical connection, and the demonstration effects of activity in one organization stimulating new and existing organizations in the public and private sectors.

It is difficult at this point to be certain which of these alternative views of the future growth and interaction of regional institutions and attitudes will be closer to the truth. But we can abstract from theory and from the Central American experience certain conditions that seem important, perhaps necessary, for functional integration to be successful either in Central America in the future or in other less developed areas.

Regional ideology or identity. Some similarity of values and beliefs and some sense of regional identity are alone insufficient to bring about more than token integration, but the fact that they are insufficient does not mean they are unimportant. It has already been shown how the ideal of Central American union provides a sense of vocation for technocrats, sheltering them from ultranationalists; predisposes politicians and some interest groups away from frontal attack; and sometimes smooths the way for compromise in accord with long-term rather than short-term interests. This factor is likely to remain a positive influence.

Supranational technocrats and institutions. The existence of persons who can combine the prestige of training that is relatively technical with a larger than technical concern and a greater than national focus, along with institutions sufficiently free from direct national control to shelter them, is a crucial condition in mediating

---

[88] One occasionally hears other Latin Americans complain that the Central Americans are getting more attention than they deserve because of their integration movement.

governmental positions and upgrading common interests. While the Central American institutions have lacked supranational powers in law, they have enjoyed a sufficient degree of independence in practice to allow limited initiative. Although trained bureaucrats are one of the scarce resources of Central America, the weakness of the governments gives even the limited number of regional technocrats the power that goes with information. With the increasing complexity of integration, one of the determinants of future success will be the ability of the institutions to obtain new powers and staff.[89]

Expansive tasks. If institutions are limited to technically specific tasks that are easily confined within restricted spheres, or, conversely, given such amorphous tasks that they cover too much before capacities are developed, they will lack a precise point of leverage to move governments. INCAP is an example of specific functional cooperation with little expansive impact, whereas ODECA is an example of an organization given tasks so broad as to lack leverage. In contrast, SIECA was charged with specific tasks that continually involved other tasks with which the governments were concerned. It is interesting that government contributions to SIECA's budget have doubled in six years, while their contributions to ODECA's budget remained constant over fifteen years.

Political and economic separability. While it is important for technocrats to have expansive tasks that provide leverage on governments, there must also be a sufficient initial separation of the tasks from the mainstream of political debate to allow the technocrats to arrange the compromises that begin to restructure interests. With increasing complexity of integration and increased leverage, such separability is bound to diminish, yet, to a certain degree, successful integration will remain a matter of power though information — of tedious detailed studies more than flag-raisings. Central America was favored by this separability, and unless the political culture changes radically there is a good probability that a diminished degree of separability will persist.

Increasing communications and transactions. It is sometimes said that a high previous rate of transactions is necessary for successful integration and that this condition is rare among less developed countries. Given the Central American experience of minimal regional trade, poor communications, and relative isolation in 1950, this previous rate seems less important than the fact that transactions

[89] See United Nations Doc. E/CN.12/CCE/327/Rev.1, 4 Jan. 1966, pp. 145-155.

increase and communications improve during integration. An increase in communications is not sufficient for better understanding and the development of a sense of community, but it is generally necessary. The development of regional infrastructure and the contacts that go with increasing trade will continue to play an important part in Central America, although regional trade may increase at a less dramatic rate.

Capacity to respond. One reason that increased communications are important is that they improve the capacity of governments to respond to the problems of their partners — an essential capacity if the compromises necessary for continued integration are to be arranged. But a capacity to respond is determined not only by improved communications, but by sufficient security and stability in each country to permit the relevant sectors of the government to hear and respond to the messages of others. This is where too radical internal change can conflict with the needs of regional integration. In Central America, there has been instability, but the economists, because of their ability to separate themselves from it, have been able to hear above the "noise" and to respond, as for example in the conciliation of Honduras in 1966.[90]

Internal capacity to adapt. Unless internal political and social conditions exist that allow a country to take advantage of the opportunities provided by the reduction of tariff barriers, the opportunities offered by integration will be of little importance. The ability to grasp these opportunities is affected by the existence of and climate for entrepreneurship, the adaptability of governmental bureaucracies, and the internal political conditions. In addition, it is affected by the degree of modern pluralism: the existence of well organized groups pursuing their specific interests and thus providing organization, information, and frequently innovation. "In the absence of such forms of pluralistic association, the capabilities of the Western state are markedly reduced."[91] While modern pluralism has been limited in Central America, it has been somewhat more in evidence there than, for example, in Africa. Similarly, while entrepreneurship has been of a mixed quality, some has been very good, and the climate for it has been favorable. Certain of these factors can be increased by

---

[90] The image of internal noise interfering with interstate communications is developed by Karl W. Deutsch, "Communication Theory and Political Integration," *The Integration of Political Communities*, eds., Philip E. Jacob and James V. Toscano (Philadelphia: Lippincott, 1964), pp. 46-74.

[91] Anderson, " 'Reform-Mongering' . . . ," op. cit., p. 36.

external factors of aid and private foreign investment in the future, as well as by new private institutions such as INCAE.

Expanding domestic coalitions. Technocrats may be able to initiate an integration process. From the point of view of the political leaders, it seems inexpensive in terms of power to accede to their whims, but if the technocrats remain isolated and do not form coalitions with other groups, political leaders soon find that it is more expensive to continue to please them than it is to antagonize them. As integration progresses, decisions frequently become more difficult (as LAFTA found in its tariff cutting sessions), and increased political support becomes necessary.[92] An important means of securing additional backing is to ensure that benefits are felt by politically significant sectors before the burdens on them become too great. In Central America, integration was a matter for technocrats until 1958; then, with tangible benefits beginning to appear, business interests joined in support. As the process increasingly affects small farmers and as matters like mobility of labor or differences in wage policies affect workers, it will be necessary to increase the coalition in support of integration. The technocrats are becoming increasingly aware of this. Legislators have been invited to Economic Council sessions as observers; ministers of economy have held joint meetings with ministers of finance and of agriculture. Special seminars and visits have been used to interest students in integration, and SIECA assists chambers of commerce in holding seminars on integration. The strengthening of this coalition will be a crucial factor in future success.

Favorable international setting. The past and future importance of favorable passive and active external factors in explaining the success of Central American integration has already been emphasized. It is instructive to contrast the experience of Central America with that of the East African Common Market, which was more involved in cold war and anti-colonial politics.[93] This made it virtually impossible for foreign governments to openly support East African integration for fear of jeopardizing it. In addition, international organizations like the United Nations Economic Commission for Africa and the African Development Bank were new, under-

[92] See Ernst Haas and Philippe Schmitter, ''The Politics of Economics in Latin American Regionalism: The Latin American Free Trade Association after Four Years of Operation,'' Monograph Series (Denver: Univ. of Denver, 1965).
[93] See Joseph S. Nye, Jr., *Pan-Africanism and East African Integration,* op. cit.

staffed, and inexperienced in comparison with their Latin American counterparts.

An evaluation of these conditions of integration, suggested in part by theory and in part by the Central American experience of the past fifteen years, leads to guardedly optimistic conclusions about the future of functional integration in Central America. It is more difficult to be optimistic about the possibility of reproducing these conditions or of duplicating the Central American experience in other less developed areas. But our cases are few and our theory still young. We do not know if all of these conditions are necessary, though we might expect that if they were all present they would be sufficient for successful economic integration. The conditions that we consider necessary need only a single case for disproof, and it may be possible that in other less developed areas, equivalent rather than identical conditions may make functional integration possible.[94] Given the complexity and unpredictability of human society, useful theory must march a little, but not too far, in advance of past experience.

Regional integration is no panacea for the many social and economic problems (illiteracy, poor education, poverty, maldistribution of income, and high birth rates, among others) that afflict less developed areas, but it can make some difference. Central American economic growth rates in the 1960s have been among the highest in Latin America and are at least in part attributable to integration. Equally important has been integration's psychological impact. In the late 1950s, an observer came to the dreary conclusion that ''the tide of Central American politics is sweeping toward desolation if not complete destruction.'' In 1965, another observer reported that he had encountered a new mystique and, for the first time in years, ''optimism and enthusiasm.''[95] There is no doubt that the number of internal coups as well as petty conflicts of sovereign states has declined in Central America in the mid-1960s. How much, if any, of this has been caused by integration is difficult to say. Certainly a number of Central Americans believe that the obligations, institutions, and greater openness to outside influence (including that of more democratic Costa Rica) that go along with integration have decreased the arbitrariness of several Central American governments.

---

[94] See Haas and Schmitter, ''Economics . . . ,'' op. cit.

[95] John D. Martz, *Central America: The Crisis and the Challenge* (Chapel Hill, N.C.: Univ. of North Carolina Press, 1959), p. 26; and *Latin American Times* (New York), 22 July 1966, respectively.

Central American regional integration has been successful so far, but the easiest phase is over, and it is still too early to judge the total importance of the process in relation to the major social problems of the area. It is also too early to predict where it will lead to political union on the institutional side. In any case, this will not be the only standard in its evaluation. Many Central Americans will judge regional integration by whether it reinforces their security community, permits more efficient economic and industrial development, and facilitates democratic political changes. Many outsiders will judge it by its capacity to significantly limit sovereignty and provide evidence that small less developed countries can escape the restrictive confines of the classical nation-state pattern.

SUGGESTIONS FOR FURTHER READING

Castillo, Carlos M., *Growth and Integration in Central America* (New York, 1966).

Cochrane, James D., "Central American Economic Integration: The 'Integrated Industries' Scheme," *Inter-American Economic Affairs,* 2 (Autumn 1965), pp. 63-74.

Corkran, Herbert, Jr., *From Formal to Informal International Cooperation in the Caribbean* (Dallas, Southern Methodist University, Arnold Monograph Series. 1966).

Dell, Sidney, *Trade Blocs and Common Markets* (New York, 1963).

———, *A Latin American Common Market?* (New York, 1966).

Diab, Muhammad, "The Arab Common Market," *Journal of Common Market Studies,* IV (May 1966), pp. 238-50.

Gordon, Lincoln, "Economic Regionalism Reconsidered," *World Politics,* XIV (January 1961), pp. 231-53.

Green, R. G., and K. G. V. Krishna, *Economic Cooperation in Africa: Retrospect and Prospect* (Nairobi, 1967).

Haas, Ernst B., and Philippe C. Schmitter, "Economics and Differential Patterns of Political Integration: Projections about Unity in Latin America," *International Organization,* XVIII (Autumn 1964), pp. 705-37.

———, and ———, *The Politics of Economics in Latin American Regionalism: The Latin American Free Trade Association after Four Years of Operation* (Denver, University of Denver Monograph, 1965).

Herrera, Felipe, "The Inter-American Development Bank and the Latin American Integration Movement," *Journal of Common Market Studies,* V (December 1966), pp. 172-80.

Islam, Nurul, "Regional Cooperation for Development: Pakistan, Iran and Turkey," *Journal of Common Market Studies,* V (March 1967), pp. 283-301.

Mitchell, Christopher, "The Role of Technocrats in Latin American Integration," *Inter-American Economic Affairs,* 21 (Summer 1967), pp. 3-29.

Nye, Joseph S., Jr., *Pan-Africanism and East African Integration* (Cambridge, Mass., 1965).

Schaaf, C. Hart, and Russell Fifield, *The Lower Mekong: Challenge to Co-operation in Asia* (Princeton, 1963).

Segal, Aaron, "The Integration of Developing Countries: Some Thoughts on East Africa and Central America," *Journal of Common Market Studies*, V (March 1967), pp. 252-82.

Sewell, W. R. Derrick, and Gilbert F. White, "The Lower Mekong," *International Conciliation*, 558 (May 1966), pp. 5-63.

Springer, Hugh W., *Reflections on the Failure of the First West Indian Federation* (Cambridge, Mass.: Harvard University Center for International Affairs Occasional Paper, 1962).

Welch, Claude E., Jr., *Dream of Unity: Pan-Africanism and Political Unification in West Africa* (Ithaca, N.Y., 1966).

Wightman, David, *Toward Economic Cooperation in Asia: The United Nations Economic Commission for Asia and the Far East* (New Haven, 1963).

Wionczek, Miguel S., "Latin American Free Trade Association," *International Conciliation*, 551 (January 1961), pp. 3-79.

——— (ed.), Latin American Economic Integration (New York, 1966).

Publications Written under the Auspices
of the Center for International Affairs
Harvard University

BOOKS

The Soviet Bloc, by Zbigniew K. Brzezinski (jointly with the Russian Research Center), 1960. Harvard University Press. Revised edition, 1967.

The Necessity for Choice, by Henry A. Kissinger, 1961. Harper & Bros.

Strategy and Arms Control, by Thomas C. Schelling and Morton H. Halperin, 1961. Twentieth Century Fund.

Rift and Revolt in Hungary, by Ferenc A. Váli, 1961. Harvard University Press.

United States Manufacturing Investment in Brazil, by Lincoln Gordon and Engelbert L. Grommers, 1962. Harvard Business School.

The Economy of Cyprus, by A. J. Meyer, with Simos Vassiliou (jointly with the Center for Middle Eastern Studies), 1962. Harvard University Press.

Entrepreneurs of Lebanon, by Yusif A. Sayigh (jointly with the Center for Middle Eastern Studies), 1962. Harvard University Press.

Communist China 1955-1959: Policy Documents with Analysis, with a Foreword by Robert R. Bowie and John K. Fairbank (jointly with the East Asian Research Center), 1962. Harvard University Press.

In Search of France, by Stanley Hoffmann, Charles P. Kindleberger, Laurence Wylie, Jesse R. Pitts, Jean-Baptiste Duroselle, and François Goguel, 1963. Harvard University Press.

Somali Nationalism, by Saadia Touval, 1963. Harvard University Press.

The Dilemma of Mexico's Development, by Raymond Vernon, 1963. Harvard University Press.

Limited War in the Nuclear Age, by Morton H. Halperin, 1963. Wiley.

The Arms Debate, by Robert A. Levine, 1963. Harvard University Press.

Africans on the Land, by Montague Yudelman, 1964. Harvard University Press.

Counterinsurgency Warfare, by David Galula, 1964. Praeger.

People and Policy in the Middle East, by Max Weston Thornburg, 1964. Norton.

Shaping the Future, by Robert R. Bowie, 1964. Columbia University Press.

Foreign Aid and Foreign Policy, by Edward S. Mason (jointly with the Council on Foreign Relations), 1964. Harper & Row.

Public Policy and Private Enterprise in Mexico, by M. S. Wionczek, D. H. Shelton, C. P. Blair, and R. Izquierdo, ed. Raymond Vernon, 1964. Harvard University Press.

How Nations Negotiate, by Fred C. Iklé, 1964. Harper & Row.

China and the Bomb, by Morton H. Halperin (jointly with the East Asian Research Center), 1965. Praeger.

Democracy in Germany, by Fritz Erler (Jodidi Lectures), 1965. Harvard University Press.

The Troubled Partnership, by Henry A. Kissinger (jointly with the Council on Foreign Relations), 1965. McGraw-Hill.

The Rise of Nationalism in Central Africa, by Robert I. Rotberg, 1965. Harvard University Press.

Pan-Africanism and East African Integration, by Joseph S. Nye, Jr., 1965. Harvard University Press.

Communist China and Arms Control, by Morton H. Halperin and Dwight H. Perkins (jointly with the East Asian Research Center), 1965. Praeger.

Problems of National Strategy, ed. Henry Kissinger, 1965. Praeger.

Deterrence before Hiroshima: The Airpower Background of Modern Strategy, by George H. Quester, 1966. Wiley.

Containing the Arms Race, by Jeremy J. Stone, 1966. M.I.T. Press.

Germany and the Atlantic Alliance: The Interaction of Strategy and Politics, by James L. Richardson, 1966. Harvard University Press.

Arms and Influence, by Thomas C. Schelling, 1966. Yale University Press.

Political Change in a West African State, by Martin L. Kilson, 1966. Harvard University Press.

Planning without Facts: Lessons in Resource Allocation from Nigeria's Development, by Wolfgang F. Stolper, 1966. Harvard University Press.

Export Instability and Economic Development, by Alasdair I. MacBean, 1966. Harvard University Press.

Foreign Policy and Democratic Politics, by Kenneth N. Waltz (jointly with the Institute of War and Peace Studies, Columbia University), 1967. Little, Brown.

Contemporary Military Strategy, by Morton H. Halperin, 1967. Little, Brown.

Sino-Soviet Relations and Arms Control, ed. Morton H. Halperin (jointly with the East Asian Research Center), 1967. M.I.T. Press.

Africa and United States Policy, by Rupert Emerson, 1967. Prentice-Hall.

Europe's Postwar Growth, by Charles P. Kindleberger, 1967. Harvard University Press.

The Rise and Decline of the Cold War, by Paul Seabury, 1967. Basic Books.

Student Politics, ed. S. M. Lipset, 1967. Basic Books.

Pakistan's Development: Social Goals and Private Incentives, by Gustav F. Papanek, 1967. Harvard University Press.

Strike a Blow and Die: A Narrative of Race Relations in Colonial Africa, by George Simeon Mwase, ed. Robert I. Rotberg, 1967. Harvard University Press.

Aid, Influence, and Foreign Policy, by Joan M. Nelson, 1968. Macmillan.

International Regionalism, by Joseph S. Nye, 1968. Little, Brown.

OCCASIONAL PAPERS PUBLISHED BY
THE CENTER FOR INTERNATIONAL AFFAIRS

1. *A Plan for Planning: The Need for a Better Method of Assisting Underdeveloped Countries on Their Economic Policies,* by Gustav F. Papanek, 1961. Out of print.

2. *The Flow of Resources from Rich to Poor,* by Alan D. Neale, 1961.
3. *Limited War: An Essay on the Development of the Theory and an Annotated Bibliography,* by Morton H. Halperin, 1962. Out of print.
4. *Reflections on the Failure of the First West Indian Federation,* by Hugh W. Springer, 1962. Out of print.
5. *On the Interaction of Opposing Forces under Possible Arms Agreements,* by Glenn A. Kent, 1963.
6. *Europe's Northern Cap and the Soviet Union,* by Nils Örvik, 1963.
7. *Civil Administration in the Punjab: An Analysis of a State Government in India,* by E. N. Mangat Rai, 1963.
8. *On the Appropriate Size of a Development Program,* by Edward S. Mason, 1964.
9. *Self-Determination Revisited in the Era of Decolonization,* by Rupert Emerson, 1964.
10. *The Planning and Execution of Economic Development in Southeast Asia,* by Clair Wilcox, 1965.
11. *Pan-Africanism in Action,* by Albert Tevoedjre, 1965.
12. *Is China Turning In?* by Morton H. Halperin, 1965.
13. *Economic Development in India and Pakistan,* by Edward S. Mason, 1966.
14. *The Role of the Military in Recent Turkish Politics,* by Ergun Özbudun, 1966.
15. *Economic Development and Individual Change: A Social-Psychological Study of the Comilla Experiment in Pakistan,* by Howard Schuman, 1967.
16. *A Select Bibliography on Students, Politics, and Higher Education,* by Philip Altbach, 1967.
17. *Europe's Political Puzzle: A Study of the Fouchet Negotiations and the 1963 Veto,* by Alessandro Silj, 1967.